The Real History
OF THE
VIETNAM WAR

A NEW LOOK AT THE PAST

Alan Axelrod

STERLING
New York

STERLING
New York

An Imprint of Sterling Publishing
387 Park Avenue South
New York, NY 10016

ISBN 978-1-4027-9025-6

Library of Congress Cataloging-in-Publication Data

Axelrod, Alan, 1952-
  The real history of the Vietnam War / Alan Axelrod.
    p. cm.
  Includes bibliographical references and filmography.
  Summary: "Examines the history of Vietnam leading up to the war, investigates
the reasons for the conflict, looks at the war's escalation and progression (or
lack thereof), and explores its repercussions then and now"--Provided by publisher.
  ISBN 978-1-4027-9025-6
  1. Vietnam War, 1961-1975. I. Title.
  DS557.7.A95 2013
  959.704'3--dc23

                                            2012035507

Distributed in Canada by Sterling Publishing
c/o Canadian Manda Group, 165 Dufferin Street
Toronto, Ontario, Canada M6K 3H6
Distributed in the United Kingdom by GMC Distribution Services
Castle Place, 166 High Street, Lewes, East Sussex, England BN7 1XU
Distributed in Australia by Capricorn Link (Australia) Pty. Ltd.
P.O. Box 704, Windsor, NSW 2756, Australia

For information about custom editions, special sales, and premium and corporate purchases,
please contact Sterling Special Sales at 800-805-5489 or specialsales@sterlingpublishing.com.

Printed in Hong Kong

2 4 6 8 10 9 7 5 3 1

www.sterlingpublishing.com

For Anita and Ian

"Some ask if this is a war for unlimited objectives. . . . The answer is 'no.' Our purpose in Vietnam is to prevent the success of aggression. It is not conquest; it is not empire; it is not foreign bases; it is not domination. It is . . . just to prevent the forceful conquest of South Vietnam by North Vietnam."

★★★

—Lyndon B. Johnson, from his "Remarks on Receiving the National Freedom Award," February 23, 1966

"Everything depends on the Americans. If they want to make war for twenty years, then we shall make war for twenty years. If they want to make peace, we shall make peace and invite them to tea afterwards."

★★★

— Ho Chi Minh, December 1966

CONTENTS

THE REAL HISTORY OF THE VIETNAM WAR

PART ONE

EMPIRE, IDEOLOGY, HUMANITY

PART TWO

INSURGENCY

PART THREE

JOHNSON'S WAR

DRAMATIS PERSONAE

Abrams, Creighton Williams, Jr. (1914–74) U.S. general who commanded operations in Vietnam from 1968 to 1972.

Agnew, Spiro T. (1918–96) U.S. vice president (1969–73) under President Nixon; the "hatchet man" Nixon assigned to counter the antiwar movement; resigned in disgrace after indictment for tax evasion and bribery.

Ball, George W. (1909–94) As undersecretary of state (1961–66), opposed deepening U.S. involvement in the Vietnam War during both the Kennedy and Johnson administrations.

Bao Dai (1913–97) Emperor of Vietnam during French colonial rule (1926–45); later, French puppet "chief of state" (1949–55).

Brezhnev, Leonid (1906–82) General secretary of the Communist Party of the Soviet Union (1964–82).

Brown, Jerry (1938–) Liberal political activist and California governor (1975–83; 2011–).

Bundy, McGeorge (1919–96) National security advisor to John F. Kennedy and Lyndon B. Johnson (1961–66); one of the chief architects of U.S. escalation of the Vietnam War.

Bunker, Ellsworth (1894–1984) Served as U.S. ambassador to South Vietnam (1967–73).

Calley, William L. (1943–) U.S. Army second lieutenant convicted of murder for his role in the My Lai Massacre (March 16, 1968).

Carter, Jimmy (1924–) As thirty-ninth president of the United States (1977–81), made human rights a cornerstone of U.S. foreign policy.

Chiang Kai-shek (1887–1975) Chinese Nationalist (anti-Communist) military and political leader; briefly and reluctantly occupied southern Vietnam at the end of World War II.

Clifford, Clark (1906–98) Succeeded Robert McNamara as secretary of defense (1968–69) under President Lyndon Johnson.

de Gaulle, Charles (1890–1970) French president (1959–69) who proposed neutralizing and unifying Vietnam to end the cross-border and civil war.

Dulles, John Foster (1888–1959) Secretary of state (1953–59) under President Eisenhower; instrumental in establishing an uncompromisingly anti-Communist U.S. foreign policy.

Eisenhower, Dwight D. (1890–1969) As thirty-fourth president of the United States (1953–61), used the so-called domino theory to justify U.S. military aid to France in Vietnam.

Ellsberg, Daniel (1931–) In 1971, leaked the Pentagon Papers (which he had helped to write), thereby revealing the lies and errors behind U.S. involvement in the Vietnam War.

Ford, Gerald R., Jr. (1913–2006) Appointed to replace Spiro T. Agnew as U.S. vice president on December 6, 1973, became the thirty-eighth president of the United States upon the resignation of Richard Nixon on August 9, 1974 (served to January 20, 1977); the Vietnam War ended during his term.

Goldwater, Barry M. (1909–98) A "hawk" on Vietnam, this conservative Republican candidate for president in 1964 was defeated by putative "peace candidate" Lyndon B. Johnson.

Gruening, Ernest (1887–1974) U.S. senator from Alaska (1959–69); Gruening was an early Senate voice against U.S. involvement in Vietnam; with Wayne Morse, one of two senators to vote against the Gulf of Tonkin Resolution.

Harriman, W. Averell (1891–1986) A principal U.S. Cold War diplomat, Harriman supported covert support of the coup that overthrew South Vietnamese president Ngo Dinh Diem in November 1963.

Ho Chi Minh (a.k.a. Nguyen Tat Than, Nguyen Ai Quoc) (1890–1969) Founder and revolutionary leader of the Democratic Republic of Vietnam, serving as chairman of the Workers' Party of Vietnam (1951–69), first secretary of the Workers' Party of Vietnam (1956–1960), president of the Democratic Republic of Vietnam (1945–69), and prime minister of the Democratic Republic of Vietnam (1945–55).

Hoffman, Abbot Howard "Abbie" (1936–89) Radical U.S. political and antiwar activist who cofounded the Youth International Party (Yippies).

Humphrey, Hubert H. (1911–78) As vice president under Lyndon B. Johnson (1965–69), opposed the escalation of the Vietnam War, but as unsuccessful Democratic candidate for president in 1968, advocated "seeing the war through."

Johnson, Lyndon B. (1908–73) Vice president under John F. Kennedy, Johnson became the nation's thirty-sixth president when JFK was assassinated on November 22, 1963; reelected, he served until January 20, 1969. Johnson escalated U.S. involvement in the Vietnam War to a high of more than a half-million troops.

Kennedy, John F. (1917–63) The thirty-fifth president of the United States (1961–63), Kennedy commenced direct U.S. combat involvement in the Vietnam War. His future intentions in Vietnam were unclear at the time of his assassination on November 22, 1963.

Kennedy, Robert F. (1925–68) Attorney general in the cabinet of his brother, John F. Kennedy, RFK ran in the 1968 Democratic primaries as an antiwar candidate and had just won the California primary when he was assassinated on June 6, 1968.

Kerry, John (1943–) An early leader of Vietnam Veterans Against the War, Kerry rose to prominence in the antiwar movement. He went on to a political career as Democratic senator from Massachusetts (1985–) and candidate for president (2004).

Khrushchev, Nikita (1894–1971) First secretary of the Communist Party of the Soviet Union (1953–64) and chairman of the Council of Ministers (1958–64), Khrushchev was the Soviet leader during the early phase of the Vietnam War; a moderate influence, he was displaced by Soviet Cold War hard-liners just as Vietnam entered a phase of escalation.

King, Martin Luther, Jr. (1929–68) Paramount leader of the Civil Rights Movement, King had also become a powerful voice in the antiwar movement by the time of his assassination on April 4, 1968.

Kissinger, Henry (1923–) National security advisor (1969–1975) and secretary of state (1973–77) under Presidents Nixon and Ford, Kissinger was an architect of Nixon's strategy in Vietnam and the chief U.S. negotiator at the Paris Peace Talks.

Laird, Melvin R. (1922–) As secretary of defense under President Nixon (1969–73), Laird oversaw the withdrawal of U.S. ground forces from Vietnam and the end of the military draft.

Lansdale, Edward G. (1908–87) A USAF general, Lansdale was also an officer in the Office of Strategic Services (OSS) and the CIA; he was a U.S. adviser to the French against the Viet Minh and during 1954–57 supervised training of the Vietnamese National Army (precursor of the ARVN); he unsuccessfully attempted to dissuade Ngo Dinh Diem from rigging the 1955 referendum that created South Vietnam as a republic with Diem as president.

Lattre de Tassigny, Jean de (1889–1952) Commanded French troops in the First Indochina War (1946–1954) until illness forced his resignation in 1951.

Le Duan (1907–86) As top policy maker in Hanoi beginning in 1958, Le Duan drove the Vietnam War to a victorious conclusion despite horrific losses; led a unified Vietnam from 1975 until his death in 1986.

Le Duc Tho (1911–90) As chief North Vietnamese negotiator at the Paris Peace Talks, concluded with Henry Kissinger the Paris Peace Accords of 1973. Awarded (with Kissinger) the 1973 Nobel Peace Prize, although he declined it.

Lodge, Henry Cabot, Jr. (1902–85) A U.S. senator and diplomat, Lodge served as U.S. ambassador to South Vietnam during 1963–64 under Kennedy and Johnson; advocated making the nation a U.S. protectorate to prevent its collapse during the chaos that followed the ouster and assassination of Nguyen Dinh Diem.

Lon Nol (1913–85) After leading a coup against Cambodia's Prince Norodom Sihanouk, proclaimed himself president of the Khmer Republic (1972–75).

Madame Nhu (a.k.a. Tran Le Xuan) (1924–2011) Wife of Ngo Dinh Nhu and sister-in-law of Nguyen Dinh Diem, she became infamous as the "Dragon Lady," a beautiful, sinister, and enormously unpopular power behind the throne who was apparently indifferent to the welfare of the Vietnamese masses.

Martin, Graham A. (1912–90) Succeeded Ellsworth Bunker as U.S. ambassador to South Vietnam and presided over the evacuation of the U.S. embassy in Saigon in April 1975.

McCarthy, Eugene (1916–2005) Minnesota senator and antiwar Democratic presidential primary candidate in 1968 (also ran unsuccessfully in the 1972 and 1976 primaries).

McNamara, Robert S. (1916–2009) As secretary of defense under John F. Kennedy and Lyndon B. Johnson (1961–68), McNamara presided over the escalation of U.S. involvement in the Vietnam War, only to turn against his own policies by 1967; he resigned (probably under presidential pressure) early in 1968 to become president of the World Bank (1968–81).

Mendès France, Pierre (1907–82) Prime minister of France (1954–55); presided over the French withdrawal from Vietnam and the rest of "French Indochina."

Morse, Wayne (1900–1974) U.S. senator from Oregon (1945–69); an early congressional voice against U.S. involvement in the Vietnam War and (with Ernest Gruening), one of two senators who opposed the Gulf of Tonkin Resolution in 1964.

Navarre, Henri (1898–1983) French general who led his forces to defeat at Dien Bien Phu in 1954, precipitating the humiliating end of French colonial rule in Vietnam.

Ngo Dinh Diem (1901–63) U.S.-supported president of the Republic of Vietnam (South Vietnam) from October 26, 1955, until his overthrow and assassination (November 2, 1963).

Ngo Dinh Nhu (1910–63) The corrupt brother of Ngo Dinh Diem; a power behind Diem, he was captured and assassinated (November 2, 1963) along with him. His wife was the infamous "Dragon Lady," known as Madame Nhu.

Nguyen Cao Ky (1930–2011) Instrumental in the coup d'état that deposed Ngo Dinh Diem, Nguyen Cao Ky was prime minister of the Republic of Vietnam from 1965 to 1967; his ruthless and brutal tactics ended the cycle of coups that had characterized the government, but they increasingly alienated the South Vietnamese from that government.

Nguyen Khanh (1927–) An ARVN general, Nguyen Khanh was involved in many coups, including that against Ngo Dinh Diem in 1963; served as South Vietnamese prime minister and head of state in 1964; since 2005, he has been "chief of state" of the Government of Free Vietnam, an anti-Communist organization headquartered in Garden Grove, California, and Missouri City, Texas, and dedicated to the overthrow of the Communist government of Vietnam.

Nguyen Ngoc Loan (1930–98) Chief of police of the Republic of Vietnam, he was made famous (or infamous) by a widely published (February 1, 1968) Eddie Adams AP photograph showing him executing a VC prisoner at pointblank range in a Saigon intersection.

Nguyen Van Thieu (1923–2001) President of South Vietnam from 1965 to 1975, he denounced what he considered U.S. abandonment of his government and nation during the collapse of South Vietnam in 1975.

Nixon, Richard M. (1913–94) The thirty-seventh president of the United States (1969–74), Nixon expanded the Vietnam War into Cambodia and Laos and intensified the air war, even as he withdrew U.S. ground forces and pushed negotiations at the Paris Peace Talks. His involvement in the Watergate Affair forced his resignation as president on August 9, 1974.

Phan Boi Chau (1867–1940) Early leader of the Vietnamese independence movement and founder of the Vietnamese Restoration League.

Phan Chu Trinh (1872–1926) An early comrade of Ho Chi Minh and other Vietnamese activists who sought independence from France.

Pol Pot (a.k.a. Saloth Sar) (1925–98) Cambodian Maoist leader of the Khmer Rouge, who, as prime minister of "Democratic Kampuchea," perpetrated genocide throughout Cambodia. His rise to power was facilitated by the U.S. withdrawal from Vietnam.

Reagan, Ronald (1911–2004) The fortieth president of the United States (1981–89), Reagan is widely credited with psychologically rehabilitating the nation from what he called the "Vietnam syndrome."

Roosevelt, Franklin D. (1882–1945) The thirty-second president of the United States (1933–45), FDR advocated an end to French colonial rule in Vietnam, not through immediate independence but via a temporary international trusteeship; he died before this could be implemented.

Rostow, Walt Whitman (1916–2003) Deputy national security advisor under John F. Kennedy (1961) and national security advisor under Lyndon Johnson (1966–69), Rostow played a prominent role in shaping U.S. Vietnam policy.

Rubin, Jerry (1938–94) With Abbie Hoffman, cofounded the Youth International Party (Yippies) and was a leader of the radical wing of the U.S. antiwar movement; he later became wealthy as an early investor in Apple Computer.

Sainteny, Jean (1907–78) The French government dispatched him to Vietnam in 1946 to negotiate with Ho Chi Minh the reincorporation of Vietnam into French Indochina.

Shultz, George P. (1920–) Secretary of state under President Reagan (1982–89); opposed Secretary of Defense Caspar Weinberger's cautious post-Vietnam approach to war (the "Weinberger Doctrine").

Sihanouk, Prince Norodom (1922–) Served variously as king and prime minister of Cambodia, treading a razor-thin line between tolerance of the U.S. and Communist interests.

Stalin, Joseph (1878–1953) Soviet leader whose hard-line, anti-Western policies crystallized the major enmities of the Cold War and created the climate in which U.S. involvement in the Vietnam War came to seem (to many) a necessity.

Taylor, Maxwell (1901–87) U.S. general who served as President Kennedy's military adviser (1961–62) and chairman of the Joint Chiefs of Staff (1962–64); succeeded Henry Cabot Lodge Jr. as U.S. ambassador to South Vietnam (1964–65).

Thich Quang Duc (1897–1963) Vietnamese Mahayana Buddhist monk whose public self-immolation on a Saigon street (June 11, 1963) drew international condemnation of the pro-Catholic Ngo Dinh Diem government's persecution of Buddhists.

Truman, Harry S. (1884–1972) Thirty-third president of the United States (1945–53), source of the "Truman Doctrine" mandating the "containment" of the aggressive spread of Communism, and initiator of U.S. military involvement in Vietnam pursuant to that doctrine.

Vo Nguyen Giap (1911–) North Vietnamese general most responsible for shaping military doctrine and strategy in the Vietnam War; widely credited as the military leader who won the Vietnam War.

Weinberger, Caspar (1917–2006) As secretary of defense in the cabinet of Ronald Reagan (1981–87), Weinberger formulated the so-called Weinberger Doctrine, a post-Vietnam approach to deciding which wars to fight and which to avoid.

Westmoreland, William (1914–2005) U.S. general who commanded U.S. military operations in Vietnam from 1964–68.

AUTHOR'S NOTE

"**A**MERICANS WANT 'REAL' WARS LIKE WORLD WAR II and the [first] Gulf War, not limited wars like Korea and Vietnam," Michael Lind wrote in his 1999 book *Vietnam: The Necessary War.* "They want American soldiers to be sent into battle, if at all, to take territory, not to prop up weak and tyrannical regimes threatened by civil war, in order to signal American resolve in great-power showdowns." Maybe that's why it is so hard to write what I have attempted to write here: a single-volume, comprehensive, "real history" of the Vietnam War—a war with objectives that were not only limited but also highly questionable, often morally repugnant, and finally tragic; a war that never seemed "real" (unlike World War II) yet was real enough to kill 58,272 Americans and at least two million Vietnamese; a war that Americans really did not want, not even those Americans who sincerely, faithfully, desperately, or just plain stubbornly supported it, not even, finally, those Americans who commanded it and who fought it.

Yes, it is hard to write about something so painful, so elusive, so fraught with gallantry, noble intent, earnest error, blind stupidity, and base brutality. It is hard to write about national deceit and delusion. It is often hard to write about war, which routinely kills young soldiers, but it is far harder to write about a war that just as routinely killed children, mothers, grandmothers, and grandfathers. It is perhaps hardest of all to write about a war that offered an abundance of lessons, warnings, and cautionary tales—so many that "No more Vietnams" became a mantra of American politics and foreign policy— but nevertheless failed to stay the all-too-eager hands of twenty-first-century ideologues, demagogues, and an ill-prepared chief executive from taking the nation into new military adventures even less comprehensible than the often incomprehensible misadventure of Vietnam.

A minority among historians and political leaders believe that, while many errors were committed in prosecuting it, the Vietnam War was a "necessary war" (a proposition we will consider carefully). The majority, however, believe the entire American phase of the war, from covert start to naked finish, was a mistake. Yet both groups agree on one thing. Necessity or mistake, the Vietnam War was by no means an aberration in the American experience. Quite the contrary. As a generation of historians, novelists, and filmmakers discovered, the Vietnam experience is heavily freighted with the American character, psyche, and soul. Its events reflect backward on the nation's history and look forward to its future. To ponder it is to ponder the best and the worst about being an American, and that is what makes the effort of writing about it so poignant, painful, and difficult. It is also, of course, precisely what makes the study of the Vietnam War and its context so necessary, rewarding, and enthralling.

And so touchy. Even today, opinions about the war—its wrongness, its rightness, its absolute necessity, its absolute futility—are closely held and hotly argued. It is very easy to begin trying to write history and end up declaiming a rant or barely suppressing a cry. My aim has been to be objective but without pretending to be neutral. No American male who was of draft age in the late 1960s (as I was) can be genuinely neutral about the Vietnam War. I have nevertheless set out to portray all the major points of view, prevailing and evolving, on the American street, in Washington, in the military, in the media, in Saigon, in Hanoi, in the rural hamlets of South and North Vietnam, in Cambodia, in Laos, and in other parts of the world. I have tried always to empathize with each point of view, since to empathize is to understand without necessarily agreeing or forgiving. Doubtless, some readers will find me too objective while others will find me too partial, opinionated, or partisan. I ask only that you take from this book whatever you find useful. Objective, opinionated, and insufficiently or overly selective, it is nevertheless an honest narrative of an intensely painful and vastly revelatory swath of history through which I, like others who share my time and place, lived. I ask of you what I gave to my subject: empathy. The Vietnam War is very hard to write about.

As always, I owe a great debt to my editors Barbara Berger and Joe Rhatigan, to photo editors Sasha Tropp and Melissa McCoy, to production editor Scott Amerman, to interior designer Rachel Maloney, to cover director Elizabeth Mihaltse, to copyeditor Kalista Johnston, to Michael Fragnito, Sterling's editorial director, and to my agent, Ed Claflin.

—*Alan Axelrod*
Atlanta, Georgia

PART ONE

EMPIRE, IDEOLOGY, HUMANITY

CHAPTER I

PEOPLE OF THE GREAT VIET

Short Version of a Long History

ASK AN AMERICAN OF MIDDLE AGE OR OLDER to "comment on Vietnam," and you'll get a range of responses: Vietnam was a pawn in a Cold War "proxy war" between the United States on the one side and the Soviet Union and China on the other (or even a proxy war *among* the Americans, the Soviets, and the Chinese). Vietnam was a "domino" the United States wanted to keep from falling to the Communists and knocking over the other "dominoes" in Southeast Asia. Vietnam was a *local* civil war the United States turned into—or mistook for—a *global* ideological war between democracy and communism. Vietnam was a war of Western "imperialism" against "indigenous nationalism." Vietnam was a war against a national hero, Ho Chi Minh. Vietnam was a war against a communist tyrant, Ho Chi Minh. Vietnam was a totally unnecessary war, a mistake and a tragedy. Vietnam was a very necessary war to preserve American military and political credibility as the guardian of the free world. Vietnam was lost because Washington politicians wouldn't let the American military win it. Vietnam was lost because the American military, geared to fight a strategic war, a thermonuclear war, didn't know how to fight a guerrilla war. Vietnam wasn't lost at all. The war was simply unwinnable.

The one response you won't likely hear, at least not from Americans older than forty-five or fifty, is that Vietnam is a country—a place.

So deep are the scars the Vietnam *War* made on the American identity that it is easy to forget that, before it was a war, Vietnam was a *place*. Artifacts from the late Neolithic and early Bronze Age periods unearthed in Vinh Phuc Province testify to the fact that it had been a highly civilized place since at least two thousand years before the birth of Christ. Other archaeological finds suggest half a million years of human habitation.

INSIDERS AND OUTSIDERS

BRONZE AGE ARTICLES DATING from around 1200 BCE are prominent among archaeological finds in the Ma River and Red River plains, including ornate drums and an array of tools and weapons. This evidence suggests a high level of a chiefly rural civilization archaeologists call the Dong Son culture. In addition to farming, copper mining was a major occupation, and the people adapted to their low-lying, flood-prone environment by building stilt dwellings.

Some time prior to 257 BCE—and perhaps as early as 2879 BCE—the first of the Vietnamese dynasties was forged with the emergence of the Hong Bang, a dynasty of the semi-historical, semi-legendary Hung kings. They created what is generally considered the first identifiable Vietnamese state, called Van Lang. In 257 BCE, the Hong Bang Dynasty gave way to the Thuc Dynasty when Thuc Phan, probably a prince of the Chinese Shu state (although some Vietnamese claim for him an indigenous origin), defeated in battle Hung Vuong, the last of the Hung kings. As a result, Thuc Phan brought together the Lac Viet tribes (the Dong Son people) with his own Au Viet tribes to create a new state he called Au Lac, over which he proclaimed himself ruler with the title of An Duong Vuong.

This bronze dagger, from the Dong Son culture of Vietnam, may date from as far back as 500 BCE, making it one of the earliest artifacts of warfare ever discovered.

DETAILS, DETAILS
Combat by Proxy

Proxy war is a phrase that became familiar during the Cold War period (from the end of World War II until the fall of the Soviet Union early in the 1990s) to describe a war in which the principal combatants use third-party stand-ins to fight one another. Historians of the Cold War generally view both the Korean War (1950–53) and the Vietnam War as proxy conflicts between the United States on the one hand and the Soviet Union and/or China on the other. Fighting a limited proxy war was seen as an alternative to direct confrontation, which would all too likely result in a civilization-destroying thermonuclear World War III.

PREVIOUS PAGES:
Ancient-looking statues decorate the concrete tomb of Khai Dinh (1885–1925), who was emperor of Vietnam from 1916 to 1925 and a much-hated collaborator with France. The tomb, financed with onerous taxes levied against the Vietnamese peasantry, took eleven years to build, from 1920 to 1931.

If semi-legendary history is accurate, An Duong Vuong reigned for an impressive period of half a century, until he was defeated in battle in 207 BCE by a Chinese general, Zhao Tuo, who then consolidated all of Au Lac into a new state, Nanyue, also known as Nam Viet. Zhao Tuo, called Trieu Da in the Vietnamese language, founded a new Vietnamese dynasty, the Nha Trieu, which endured for more than ninety years under a succession of five kings.

DOMINATION AND REBELLION

ALTHOUGH CONSIDERED VIETNAMESE, the Nha Trieu (the Trieu Dynasty) was heavily dominated by familial and cultural connections with China. The death of the second Trieu king, Trieu Van Vuong, in 124 BCE brought his son, Trieu Minh Vuong, to the throne. He, however, had lived most of his life in China, not Vietnam, and had fathered a son by a Chinese woman named Cu Thi (who may well have been a daughter of the Han emperor Wu). Trieu Minh Vuong drew Nam Viet increasingly under Han domination. His death in 112 BCE brought his Chinese-born son, Trieu Hung, to the throne with the temple or throne name of Trieu Ai Vuong. Because the boy was no more than six years old at the time, his Chinese mother, Cu Thi, ruled as Empress Dowager. In effect, Nam Viet was now under the rule of a dowager and child king who were both ethnic Chinese.

Shortly after the ascension of Trieu Ai Vuong and his mother, Han emperor Wu summoned the pair to his court. Wu declared that the young emperor required his "protection," which apparently included the beheading of his mother. With the boy effectively a prisoner and the dowager empress dead, Emperor Wu dispatched in 112 BCE a 5,000-man Han army under Generals Lo Bac Duc and Duong Boc to invade Nam Viet.

Under orders of Nam Viet's prime minister, Quan Thai-pho, an army marched to the border to defend against the invasion, but the effort was undermined by fear that Trieu Ai Vuong, in the hands of Emperor Wu, would come to harm if the invasion were resisted. Quan Thai-pho therefore recruited another son of Trieu Minh Vuong, born of the late king's concubine, to assume the throne. His name was Trieu Kien Duc, and, taking the throne name Trieu Duong Vuong, he led reinforcements to the border. Patriotic and brave, he was nevertheless utterly inexperienced in political and military matters. The Han forces easily defeated the Nam Viet army, killing both Prime Minister Quan

Thai-pho and the Trieu king, Trieu Duong Vuong. Nam Viet was now proclaimed Giao Chi, a prefecture of the Han Empire.

For the next millennium, beginning in 111 BCE, what we know today as Vietnam was essentially a province of China. The relationship between the ethnic Vietnamese and their Chinese overlords was not simply one of conquered to conqueror. In many respects, the Vietnamese voluntarily embraced Chinese culture, including in matters of religion, art, architecture, music, and language, as well as in technology. Chinese forms of government were also not so much imposed as readily adopted. Divided into nine districts, the Gaio Chi prefecture was administered according to ancient Confucian traditions of philosophy and ethics as well as hierarchical rule.

Yet there was always something in the collective Vietnamese psyche that bristled at Chinese domination. Over the thousand years of Chinese rule, there erupted a good many revolts. During the first three-quarters of the twentieth century, when Vietnam variously rebelled against French, Japanese, and American domination, these uprisings figured in popular belief much as the story of David and Goliath figures in the Western Judeo-Christian tradition: as a mythology of justified rebellion, of right versus might, and, in the case of Vietnam, of a resolute nationalist spirit capable of overcoming whatever imperial giant sought to extinguish it.

The Sisters Trung

The most famous of the various Vietnamese rebellions against Chinese domination was that of the Trung sisters, Trung Trac and Trung Nhi, which began in 39 CE. They had been born into a military family in the Vietnamese countryside while their father was serving as prefect of the Me Linh district. The girls were apparently trained in the martial arts as if they had been boys. They took avidly to their military studies and may well have nurtured dreams of rebellion from early childhood, for their father's administrative position gave them a window onto a Chinese overlordship that had become particularly cruel and corrupt.

The rigidly bureaucratic Han steadily undermined the feudal society of the Vietnamese, installing venal and inefficient provincial administrations that drained the resources of Vietnamese nobles by routinely extorting bribes and imposing unjust taxes. When the Han Dynasty was disrupted in China by the short-lived and chaotic

An anonymous folk woodcut painter from Dong Ho village in Bac Ninh Province depicted the Trung sisters, early champions of Vietnamese independence, riding elephants into battle.

REALITY CHECK
The Naked Truth?

It is impossible to separate legend from history in the story of the Trung Rebellion. Legend has it that the Chinese dealt the Trung forces its final defeat not merely by attacking with vastly superior numbers, but also by attacking naked, knowing that this would have a powerful effect on the Trung army, which included many female warriors. It is said that the sight of the naked army so shamed the women that many ran from the field of battle—with at least one notable exception. Phung Thi Chinh, a noblewoman and warrior captain, was very pregnant. She delivered her infant in the midst of battle, took the baby in one arm, and used her other to wield her sword.

Xin Dynasty of Wang Mang, who reigned from 9 to 23 CE, the Trung sisters were increasingly drawn into an aristocratic Vietnamese independence movement. In the meantime, a prefect from a neighboring district paid a call on the Trung sisters' father, known to history only as General Lac. With the prefect came his young son, Thi Sach, who quickly fell in love with Trung Trac. The two were soon married.

By this time, in the year 24, Liu Xiu, a warrior leader of the imperial clan who was also known as Guang Wudi, seized control from the Xin, secured internal order in China, and reestablished Han authority over most of the border regions. This restoration intensified the severity of Chinese rule over the Vietnamese, and, about the year 39, Thi Sach was judicially murdered by a Chinese official on charges of having conspired with other Vietnamese nobles to oust the Han. This was sufficient to propel Trung Trac and her sister into the forefront of the independence movement.

As Liu Xiu advanced against what is now northern Vietnam to quell the growing rebellion, the Trung sisters began rallying troops, and on February 6, 40, Trung Trac appeared at the head of some 30,000 rebel soldiers mustered at the Hat estuary. Clad in full armor, she inspired them to a vigorous military campaign that, within less than a year, had succeeded in wresting control of sixty-five citadels from the Han, including one at Luy Lau, which was the scene of a battle that inflicted severe casualties on the Chinese.

Following the victory at Luy Lau, the Trung sisters proclaimed themselves co-queens of Nam Viet. Over the next two years they dispatched expeditions that drove the Chinese military out of the country. Despite these stunning successes, the Trungs remained insularly committed to their own kind, the old Vietnamese aristocracy, and therefore failed to build lasting support among the peasantry. Sensing vulnerability in disunity, Liu Xiu sent his general Ma Yuan into Vietnam in 43. An outstanding cavalry commander, Ma Yuan quickly overran Tonkin. The Trungs' large but poorly trained army was soon dispirited and overwhelmed. After suffering a crushing defeat near what is today Hanoi, the sisters withdrew to Hat Mon (Son Tay). Ma Yuan's pursuit was relentless, however, and he presided over the final decisive defeat of their army. Rather than surrender, the Trung sisters drowned themselves in the Hat River. Their suicide was sufficient to secure their enduring identity as martyrs to the cause of Vietnamese independence.

From Autonomy to Independence

After destroying the Trungs, General Ma Yuan went on to conquer Annam, the central portion of modern Vietnam. The Chinese dynasty he restored, the Han, endured and ruled over Vietnam until 220. It was followed by the Three Kingdoms (220–65), the Western Jin (265–317), the Eastern Jin (317–420), the Southern and Northern Dynasties (420–589), the Sui (589–618), and the Tang (618–907). It was only with the disintegration of the Tang Dynasty during the tenth century that Vietnamese independence, a movement that resurfaced periodically only to be crushed repeatedly, approached something like an enduring reality.

"Trung Trac, Trung Nha . . . established a nation and proclaimed their rule as easily as their turning over their hands. It awakened all of us that we can be independent. Unfortunately, between the fall of the Trieu Dynasty and the rise of the Ngo Dynasty . . . men of this land only bowed their heads and accepted the fate of servitude to the people from the North (that is, the Chinese)."

★★★

—Le Van Huu (1230–1322), in his *Dai Viet su ky*
(*Annals of Dai Viet*, 1272)

The late Tang Dynasty was even more corrupt and inefficient than the Han. Its administrators proved simply incapable of controlling a colonial empire. Early in the tenth century, therefore, Vietnam enjoyed, by default, a high degree of autonomy under the rule of the Khuc family. From this position of relative strength, in 938, a Vietnamese lord, Ngo Quyen, led an army against Chinese forces at the Bach Dang River. He scored a stunning ambush victory near what is today Haiphong, and thereby transformed autonomy into quasi-independence.

LINK

A Second First Morning

Five hundred fifty years after the Lam Son Uprising began, Tet—the familiar short form of Tet Nguyen Dan ("Feast for the First Morning"), the Vietnamese Lunar New Year—would be the day chosen for a massive Communist offensive against U.S. and South Vietnamese forces in the Vietnam War. Launched on January 30, 1968, the "Tet Offensive" may have involved as many as 595,000 North Vietnamese Army and Viet Cong troops. Although it was a tactical failure (Communist forces suffered a reported 111,179 military casualties, having inflicted somewhat more than 45,000 on U.S. and South Vietnamese forces), the Tet Offensive decisively undermined U.S. popular support for the war and was therefore a strategic triumph for the North. (See Chapter 10.)

GREAT VIET

THE CHINESE PROVINCE WAS GRANDLY RENAMED Dai Viet—"Great Viet"— and grew increasingly independent from China until, in 1009, with the ascension of the Ly Dynasty in Vietnam, it entered what some have called a golden era. These halcyon days continued through 1225, when the Ly gave way to the Tran Dynasty, which, in turn, endured until 1400. During the Tran epoch, Dai Viet successfully defended against Mongol invasions and kept the Chinese at bay through a combination of deft military operations and even more adept diplomatic maneuvering— supplemented by liberal payments of tribute to the Chinese court. This era also saw the growth of Buddhism in the region and its establishment as the state religion.

From 1400 to 1407, the Ho Dynasty was a weak successor to the Tran, and, with the rise of China's Ming Dynasty, that empire again came to dominate Vietnam, from 1407 to 1427. In 1418, the young Vietnamese nobleman Le Loi successfully led the Lam Son Uprising, beginning on the day after Tet, the lunar New Year holiday, in February 1418. By 1427, Le Loi achieved an overwhelming victory against the Ming overlords, drove them out, and the following year founded the Le Dynasty as Emperor Le Thai To.

The Le Dynasty took Vietnam to a new height, especially under Le Thanh Tong (1460–97), who transformed Great Viet into a growing empire through a series of wars against its southern neighbors, the Cham and Khmer kingdoms. Through this southerly expansion (called *nam tien*), Great Viet became greater still, annexing what are today the southernmost parts of Vietnam. By the start of the eighteenth century, Vietnam formed a kind of thick letter S on the map of Southeast Asia, creating a coast of about eight hundred miles from its top at the border of China to its bottom on the Gulf of Thailand.

A HERITAGE OF STRIFE

AFTER A MILLENNIUM IN THE SHADOW OF CHINA, Great Viet became a formidable power in Southeast Asia; yet as it overcame outside threats and absorbed next-door neighbors, it began to pull apart from within. The larger the country became, the weaker was the cohesion among its own provinces. Nowhere was this truer than along the kingdom's north-south axis. By the sixteenth century, even in the midst of continued expansion, Hanoi-based rulers found it increasingly difficult

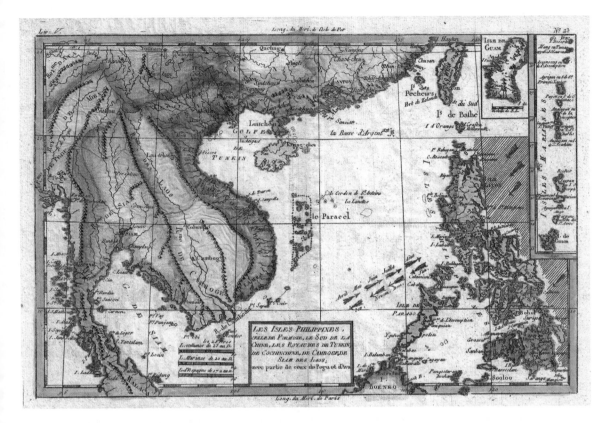

to project their power over any considerable distance—especially if that distance was south of Hanoi.

The cultural differences between North and South had always been significant, but after the region defeated its common enemy China, the North tended to remain entrenched in a tradition-bound feudalism whereas the South, which enjoyed greater availability of arable land, higher crop yields, and generally an easier way of life than the North, became more forward looking. Its people were more individualist in orientation—what we would call today more entrepreneurial in spirit.

The split between North and South would never be mended and, most immediately, led to a civil war in 1613 that more or less formally divided Vietnam between the South, ruled by the Nguyen lords, and the North, governed by the Trinh. Armed conflict continued sporadically well into the 1670s, when an uneasy truce was finally concluded. By this time, the Nguyen had pushed southern Vietnam well into the Mekong Delta.

This 1780 map of "Les Isles Philippines" was created by eighteenth-century French mapmaker Rigobert Bonne for an atlas by the historian and man of letters Guillaume Thomas François Raynal. It shows Vietnam ("Tunkin" and "Cochinchine"), Southeast Asia, and the South China Sea.

The Tay Son Rebellion

For a hundred years after 1670, "truce" hardly meant peace but, rather, sustained, albeit diminished, armed conflict. Then, in the 1770s, three Nguyen brothers, Nguyen Hue, Nguyen Nhac, and Nguyen Lu, began agitating for reforms in bold defiance of their own family. They led a rebellion in their home village of Tay Son in 1772, attacking and defeating Nguyen government troops at the nearby town of Qui Nhon in 1773. Word of this victory quickly spread the rebellion in the South. Word also reached the Trinh in the North, who exploited the instability of the Nguyen by invading the South and capturing the Nguyen capital city of Hue. They then reached out to the three brothers, whom they assisted in capturing Saigon (today Ho Chi Minh City).

The brothers were more than willing to take advantage of Trinh aid. They understood, however, that they were dancing with the devil and, in 1775, abruptly turned against their erstwhile ally, driving the Trinh out of Hue. Two years later, forces led by the Tay Son Nguyen brothers ravaged Saigon. They killed most of the ruling Nguyens—except for the teenage Prince Nguyen Anh, who fled and was joined in flight by a French missionary, Pierre Pigneau de Béhaine.

The Tay Son Nguyen brothers came to control all of central and southern Vietnam, but, in 1782, followers of Prince Nguyen Anh rebelled against the rebels and seized control of Saigon. The following year, the brothers reclaimed the city, forcing Nguyen Anh once again into flight. He holed up in Siam (Thailand), from where he recruited aid in resisting the Nguyen brothers. In this recruiting effort, Nguyen Anh was ably assisted by Pigneau de Béhaine, who appealed to the French government for aid. Hurtling toward revolution, the court of Louis XVI promised aid but failed to deliver it, whereupon Pigneau de Béhaine personally recruited an army and navy of French soldiers of fortune.

In the meantime, the Tay Son brothers took advantage of the growing anarchy throughout the North to seize control of Hanoi. After overthrowing both the Later Le Dynasty and the Trinh family, the brothers reunified Vietnam, each of them taking governing responsibility for a region. In Siam, however, Nguyen Anh managed to muster an army, which he led in an amphibious landing in the Mekong Delta region. He marched on Saigon, which fell to him in September 1788.

FORGOTTEN FACES
Father Pigneau de Béhaine

Pierre Joseph Georges Pigneau (1741–99), also known as Pigneau de Béhaine and, in Vietnam, as Ba Da Loc, was born in Origny-en-Thierache (modern Aisne), France.

Trained as a Catholic missionary, he sailed for southern Vietnam under the aegis of the Paris Foreign Missions Society in December 1765. He did not arrive at his destination, Ha Tien in Cochinchina (southern Vietnam), until March 1767. There he headed the Seminary of the Holy Angels, which had been established earlier by the Paris Foreign Missions Society. The following year, Pigneau de Béhaine was jailed on unfounded charges of having harbored at the school a fugitive Siamese prince. Confined for some three months in a *cangue*, a heavy iron pillory fastened around his neck, the missionary endured, was released, and returned to the school. Barely surviving an attack by pirates in 1769, he was forced to move the school to India.

While he taught in India, Pigneau de Béhaine also mastered both Chinese and Vietnamese, writing a Vietnamese-Latin dictionary in 1773. In February 1774, he was appointed Bishop of Adran (modern Orhaneli, Turkey) and Apostolic Vicar of Cochinchina. He then set off for Macau to recruit mission staff for his return to Ha Tien. Before leaving Macau, he published a catechism in the Vietnamese language.

In March 1775, he was back in Ha Tien and, two years later, in 1777, gave refuge to fifteen-year-old Nguyen Anh, who had fled during the Tay Son Rebellion. Pigneau de Béhaine allied himself with Nguyen Anh in his effort to reestablish his family's dynasty. In 1780, Pigneau de Béhaine was instrumental in obtaining Portuguese weapons to arm Cochinchinese troops and also procured three Portuguese men o' war for Nguyen Anh.

Early in 1782, Nguyen Anh suffered a series of reverses against the resurgent forces of the Tay Son brothers, but, by the fall of the year, Nguyen Anh and the bishop were back in Saigon. Their return was brief. Defeated and pursued again, they fled to Siam. Pigneau de Béhaine now mustered Siamese support for Nguyen Anh, but, in January 1785, a Siamese fleet was disastrously defeated on the Mekong River, and both Nguyen Anh and Pigneau de Béhaine retreated to the Siamese court. The bishop appealed to his native France for support. Failing to garner interest, he sailed to Pondicherry, India, from where he negotiated an alliance between Nguyen Anh and Portugal, which was signed in Bangkok on December 18, 1786.

In 1787, Pigneau de Béhaine returned to France to plead Nguyen Anh's case at the court of Louis XVI. In tow was the young Prince Canh of Cochinchina, who created a sensation at court and facilitated the conclusion of a treaty on November 21, 1787, between France and Cochinchina in the name of Nguyen Anh. Naval and ground support was promised, but the approaching French Revolution prevented fulfillment. Proclaiming his intention to "make the revolution in Cochinchina alone," Pigneau de Béhaine set about enlisting French soldiers of fortune and cobbling together a navy. He was remarkably successful, and, beginning in 1794, he personally participated in all of the military campaigns against the Tay Son army. After a successful campaign to capture the fortress city of Qui Nhon in central Vietnam, Pigneau de Béhaine succumbed to dysentery on October 9, 1799. Accorded the equivalent of state funeral with full military honors, the bishop was honored by Nguyen Anh with a funeral oration that called him "the most illustrious foreigner ever to appear at the court of Cochinchina."

Assisted by Pigneau de Béhaine's French volunteer forces—the first time in history that a Western military formation participated in a Vietnamese war—Nguyen Anh held Saigon. With the aid of his volunteers, beginning in 1789, he began to win back territory from the Tay Son rebels. His crowning triumph came in 1792, when he and his allies destroyed the entire Tay Son fleet. Although the three brothers continued to fight, the loss of their fleet was irreparable. By 1793, all three had died; their sons quickly proved themselves incapable of continuing the war effectively; and by the start of the nineteenth century, in 1801, Nguyen Anh recaptured Hue.

Nguyen Anh used his victory as a platform from which to proclaim himself Emperor Gia Long of what was again called Nam Viet— "Southern Viet." Having re-established the Nguyen Dynasty, Gia Long sought and secured recognition from China in 1804.

> **"[We] rallied together and outshone each other in the accomplishment of duty, looking for ways to take advantage of opportunities to launch operations. . . . Every day intervening constantly, many times he marvelously saved the situation with extraordinary plans."**
>
> ★★★
>
> —Nguyen Anh (Gia Long), funeral oration for Bishop Pigneau de Béhaine, December 8, 1799

AN EMPIRE TAKES ROOT

AS GIA LONG, NGUYEN ANH SUCCEEDED in once again establishing an independent Vietnamese kingdom, although he had not untied all the strings to other empires. While China acknowledged the independence of its former province, Gia Long imposed on the country a Confucian form of administration that was even more classically Chinese than what generally prevailed in China. Of even greater consequence was the fact that Gia Long had created his kingdom with the help of a Frenchman, Pigneau de Béhaine, whose troops continued to assist him until 1802.

The Jesuit Mission

Although Pigneau de Béhaine had failed to deliver official French military intervention in Vietnam in 1787, Frenchmen had been operating in the region since the Jesuits established a mission in Hanoi in 1615. Father Alexandre de Rhodes arrived in 1620 and began to proselytize extensively, alarming one of Vietnam's ruling lords, Trinh Trang, who ordered his expulsion in 1630. Father Rhodes returned a decade later, provoking the ruler of Vietnam's southern provinces, Nguyen Phuc Lan, to hand down a death sentence, which he subsequently commuted to permanent exile. In Rome, Rhodes agitated for the building of more missions in Vietnam, which resulted in the creation of the Paris Foreign Missions Society in 1659. In the meantime, he wrote an important early history of the "Kingdom of Tonkin."

The Imperial Mission

Rhodes clearly failed to convert Vietnam to the Catholic faith, but he did enjoy success in converting France—albeit gradually—to awareness of and

This crude map of Tonkin ("Tunkin" on the map) is one of the earliest Western maps detailing northern and central Vietnam. It was drawn for Father Alexandre de Rhodes's Histoire du royaume de Tunquin, *which was published in Rome in 1650. The image reproduced here is from the French edition of 1651.*

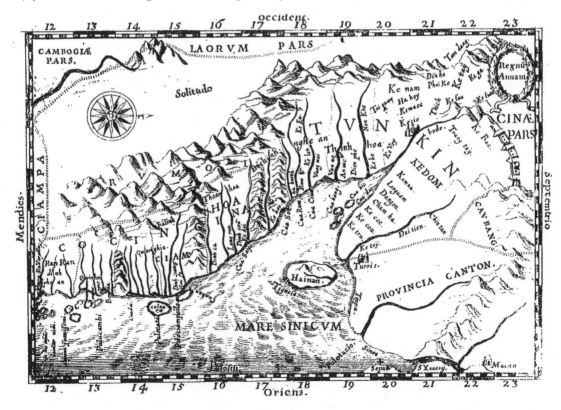

interest in Vietnam. Through the eighteenth century, contact between the region and Europe, especially France, increased. Trading relations were established and grew. In the case of Franco-Vietnamese relations, missionary work played an increasingly significant role as well.

By the mid-nineteenth century, the French government, under Napoleon III, suddenly awoke to the significance of the foothold the Paris Foreign Missions Society had established in "Indochina," especially when that foothold was threatened by Vietnamese resistance.

The rulers of the reestablished Nguyen Dynasty resented the Catholic presence in their kingdom and grew determined to resist. In part, the resistance was a matter of defending sovereignty against outsiders. In part, it was an effort to protect the state religion, Buddhism, from encroachment by a foreign faith. And in no small part, the resistance was driven by a key class in Vietnamese society, the courtesans, who saw their place in the order of life put under grave threat by a religion that insisted on absolute monogamy.

In 1856, Louis Charles de Montigny, France's envoy to the royal court of Thailand, successfully concluded a treaty with Bangkok allowing French warships to access the port and guaranteeing religious freedom in the kingdom. The following year he journeyed to Vietnam, confident that he could repeat his success there. He made four demands: that France be permitted to establish a consulate in Hue, that trade be made totally free, that religious "persecution" end, and that French missionaries be allowed to preach without interference. When the court of Emperor Tu Duc categorically rejected all of these demands, Napoleon III dispatched Admiral Charles Rigault de Genouilly, veteran of an expedition against Algiers, of the Crimean War, and of the Second Opium War (against China), to Vietnam. The emperor framed the expedition as a mission to protect French interests in Vietnam, including the right to spread the gospel, and as a punitive response to the execution of a pair of Spanish missionaries on orders of Tu Duc. Commanding a coalition of 2,500 French troops augmented by Filipino forces supplied by Spain, Rigault de Genouilly landed at Da Nang on August 31, 1858.

French Indochina War

The Frenchman expected a cakewalk to victory. Instead, he was confronted by resistance that was both determined and tenacious. The citadel at Da Nang fell to the admiral on September 12, after nearly two weeks of hard fighting. The French and Filipino forces occupied it and were almost immediately counterattacked by Viet forces, which laid the garrison under a yearlong siege. By the time it ended, some nine hundred Frenchmen had been killed in battle or had succumbed to tropical disease, and in March 1860, the garrison was withdrawn.

In the meantime, on February 16, 1859, Rigault de Genouilly landed a fresh contingent of French regulars and Algerian and Senegalese colonial troops in an assault on Saigon (today Ho Chi Minh City). His troops took the city, but it was again besieged by Viet forces. The admiral dispatched a 700-man relief force, which attacked some 10,000 poorly armed Viets on April 23, 1859, scattering them.

Rigault de Genouilly now returned to Da Nang and, on May 8, 1859, personally led a counterassault on the Vietnamese siege lines. He made headway but failed to completely break the siege. As for Saigon, the Viets mounted a new blockade. Falling under severe criticism for his inability to bring the war to a swift conclusion, Rigault de Genouilly was sent home and replaced by Admiral François Page, who led an initial amphibious assault of twenty-seven warships and 3,500 infantrymen. Finally, on February 24, 1861, 8,000 French troops attacked what were now about 32,000 Viets at Chi Hoa, at last shattering the blockade of Saigon and prompting Emperor Tu Duc to cede to France ports in Annam (today central Vietnam) and Tonkin (the northernmost part of present-day Vietnam) and considerable control of Cochinchina (the southern third of Vietnam). France promised to seek no further territorial gains but did demand the right to enforce protection of the Catholic faith and to engage freely in trade. Along with the initial territorial concessions, these provisions ensured a French presence in Vietnam.

THE PATTERN

THE HISTORY OF VIETNAM from its origins through the nineteenth century reveals a strikingly repetitious pattern of strife between the imperial ambitions of outsiders and the aspirations for independence among the indigenous peoples—aspirations attacked both from without and within (for Vietnam was long torn by internal conflict) yet never definitively crushed.

The French incursions both followed and intensified the ancient pattern. The nineteenth-century French emperor Napoleon III, seeking

ABOVE: An anonymous depiction of the French capture of Da Nang in 1858.

RIGHT: These French soldiers in tropical uniform were photographed in Tonkin about 1890. The image first appeared in Aventuriers du Monde *by Corneille Tumelet-Faber.*

to compete against other European imperial powers, seized on defense of the Catholic faith as a pretext for building an empire in Indochina. The French Indochina War of 1858–63 laid the foundation of empire and, putatively, set limits to it. True to the pattern, however, those limits proved very short lived. In 1864, Cochinchina was formally declared a French territory, and in 1867 the provinces of Chau Doc, Ha Tien, and Vinh Long came under French control.

An additional component of the historical pattern working against Vietnamese sovereignty was the tendency of outsiders, whether Chinese, French, or—later—American, to look upon Vietnam as merely part of a greater region. For the United States in the mid-twentieth century, Vietnam was the strategic keystone of "Southeast Asia."

In the nineteenth century, for France, it was the principal prize of what would be "French Indochina."

Napoleon III eagerly acceded to the request of Cambodia's King Norodom in 1863 to establish a protectorate over his country, and in 1867, Siam (Thailand) agreed to relinquish its long-held suzerainty over Cambodia and recognize the French protectorate in return for control of the provinces of Battambang and Siem Reap, which Siam subsequently annexed. With Cambodia safely in the French fold, France next fought China in the Sino-French War of 1884–85 to settle the question of control over Tonkin (northern Vietnam). The French victory was both lopsided and decisive. For the loss of some twenty-one hundred killed or wounded (more succumbed to disease), French forces killed or wounded more than 10,000 Chinese and Vietnamese troops, securing by the 1885 Treaty of Tientsin a protectorate over Tonkin as well as Annam (northern and central Vietnam). Added to Cochinchina (southernmost Vietnam), this gave France dominion over the entire country. Along with Cambodia, the three regions were officially brought together in October 1887 as French Indochina. French victory in the Franco-Siamese War of 1893 ended in an "Entente Cordiale," by which Laos was added as well.

The Vietnam "pattern" was completed by one final feature. France did not call its Southeast Asian colonial holdings an *empire*. Instead, it designated French Indochina as a "federation" of "protectorates," each under its own monarch. Each of these men, however, was a mere figurehead, entirely pliable to French administration. The downside for France was that it was obligated to prop up its pasteboard monarchs, regardless of their popularity or (far more often) their lack thereof.

French Indochina would endure until 1954. That was a long time to sustain what was essentially a fiction, a political and diplomatic charade. An empire so hollow, no matter how grand its name, is bound sooner or later to implode and thereby slip from even the tightest grasp.

TAKEAWAY

A Country in Contention

Throughout its long history, Vietnam was coveted by outsiders—dominated by China for a thousand years, by France for nearly a hundred, and pulled at by the Soviet Union, the People's Republic of China, and the United States—as well as torn by internal political, cultural, and economic strife. A small country, it was long perceived to be the keystone of Southeast Asia, a strategic prize to be fought over by competing empires. As for the indigenous people, the Vietnamese, their aspirations and needs were either manipulated from the outside or ignored completely. The result was at least two millennia of bloody conflict *before* what the United States calls the Vietnam War.

CHAPTER 2

TOWARD THE TWILIGHT OF EMPIRE

The Slow Rise of Nationalism

AMERICANS, AT LEAST THE GENERATION WHO LIVED through the Vietnam War, are accustomed to thinking of that conflict in narrow terms of ideology: Communism versus democracy, imperialism versus nationalism. They also see the war through the prism of American self-identity as a mighty military power devoted to the defense of the "free world" yet not at the cost of igniting a thermonuclear *third* world war. Those same Americans tend to assume that France thought of French Indochina in roughly analogous terms. Empire in this part of Southeast Asia was an opportunity to spread and defend Catholicism, the equivalent of the French state religion. It was an opportunity for Napoleon III to endow both his reign and his nation with some semblance of the imperial glory that had prevailed during the reign of his uncle, the first Napoleon. And it was a means of competing with the other imperial powers of nineteenth-century Europe, especially Great Britain, which held India, Malaya, and Burma.

There is truth in these American perceptions, but it is only a fraction of the truth.

French motives for the conquest and control of Vietnam and the rest of French Indochina were doubtless perfumed with the odor of spiritual crusade and imperial glory and were likely more solidly grounded in the realities of global geopolitics. Nevertheless, what first and last drove the colonization on a daily basis was economics. The Industrial Revolution had transformed Western Europe into a continent of industrial producers and industrial consumers. Like the other nations of the continent, France needed new sources of raw materials and new markets for the consumption of the goods manufactured from them. French Indochina was not only rich in materials; it was strategically positioned as a gateway to the even richer resources and bigger markets offered by China. In France, missionaries, imperialists, politicians, and plutocrats all could agree that French Indochina was worth owning, whatever their particular reason for valuing it.

A view of a Saigon street, circa 1915.

COLONIAL TRANSFORMATIONS

ONLY WHEN MEDIEVAL CHINESE ADMINISTRATORS became so greedy, corrupt, or incompetent that their avarice competed with that of indigenous elites did Vietnam's nobles rebel and seek independence. The fact is that a thousand years of Chinese domination often brought significant benefit to Vietnam in the form of opportunities for the rich to become richer. Much the same was true of French domination. Colonization created major business opportunities for a minority of Vietnamese, who grew wealthy as bankers, merchants, and landowners. The injection of European money set off a land boom—though almost exclusively in the South, where land was both plentiful and extremely fertile. Much as the elites of medieval Vietnam had embraced the culture and trappings of China, so the emerging elites of nineteenth- and early twentieth-century Vietnam avidly adopted the culture and trappings of France. Saigon evolved into the Paris of Southeast Asia.

Vietnamese plantation laborers pose for a photograph taken sometime between 1890 and 1920, at the height of French colonial dominion.

"The Empire is peace."

★★★

—French president Louis-Napoleon Bonaparte, October 15, 1852, anticipating the proclamation of December 2, 1852, that would create the Second Empire and make him emperor

One effect of the French influence was to deepen the division that had long existed between the South and the North. Inherently less conservative and more open to outside influence, the South embraced Western culture, whereas the conservative, tradition-worshipping North shunned it. Moreover, French investors found the comparatively more prosperous South far more congenial to investment than the North. Thus, the new Vietnamese class of bankers, entrepreneurs, merchants, and landlords created by colonization, a minority throughout the country, was concentrated chiefly in the South. North and South, Vietnam remained primarily a land of poor rural peasants; however, whereas the South was developing a prosperous minority of urban and landowning classes, the North was not. Colonization would increasingly widen the gulf between the poor and rich Vietnam. It would also make that gulf a function not only of economics but also of geography, inexorably exacerbating the North-South divide.

Prosperity

A late nineteenth-century visitor to Saigon who was old enough to have known the city before midcentury would have been shocked by its remarkable transformation. It now had boulevards lined with Parisian Second Empire–style buildings. It had restaurants and cafés, at which Vietnamese men and women, attired in what at least passed for the latest Parisian fashions, dined and drank. It had bustling shops proffering Western goods. It had knots of schoolchildren, all attired in neat uniforms, chattering brightly in French—the language they were learning at the French schools, which were by far the best schools in the city.

The municipal theater and the human-drawn "Oriental hansom cab" were symbols of French colonial rule in Vietnam. This image from Saigon dates to about 1915.

Alienation

On the boulevards and principal streets of central Saigon, the striking visibility of this new class of westernized Vietnamese was deceptive. They were a minority. In total gross national income, Vietnam doubtless benefited from French colonial domination. In individual income, however, most Vietnamese did not benefit, and some 90 percent, the peasantry, suffered greatly.

Between the merchant and landowning elite and the dispossessed peasants was another class. Call them the intellectual minority. Some were scholars, writers, and journalists; a few were bureaucrats "retired" or "discharged" from the new government or even still employed in it; most were teachers. All in this class were united by a sense of pessimism, discontent, and alienation. On the one hand, domination by a foreign power seemed to them not only unjust but wrong, even unnatural. On the other hand, much that France had introduced to the country—technology, commerce, a display of sophistication and self-confidence—threw into relief the inadequacies of pre-colonial Vietnam. This in-between class of intellectuals saw that while the present was certainly undesirable the past had hardly been better.

For a time, the intellectual class wallowed in a kind of collective malaise, but, as the nineteenth century gave way to the twentieth, the feeling of *helpless* alienation was transformed into *restless* alienation. Many among this intellectual class had received a French education, which introduced them to the political thought of Europe, including the revolutionary rhetoric of the mid-nineteenth century and the emerging ideas of Karl Marx and Friedrich Engels, the architects of Communism. If the present was bad but the past no better, they began to speculate, why not figure out how to make a different and more acceptable future? There was much dispute about what form that future should take, but on one conclusion all agreed: the foreigners—the French—would sooner or later have to go.

Desperation

Together, the merchant and landlord elite and the intellectual elite constituted no more than 10 percent of colonial Vietnamese society. The rest of the population were peasants. For them, life had never been easy, but colonization made it harder than ever; what is more, by widening the gulf between the peasant majority and the elite minority, colonization added blatant injustice to the injury that was chronic poverty.

In pre-colonial Vietnam, subsistence farming had been a way of life, in which small farm families had access to small plots of land. To be sure, life was hardly easy, but at least a family could rely on having enough to eat and, usually, a little something left over to sell. The French colonial administration, however, acted to centralize land ownership, concentrating it in the hands of what today would be called "agribusiness" in order to increase yields for export. New laws made it easy for individuals and firms to purchase land traditionally cultivated by peasants and to obtain in large blocks as-yet unclaimed lands. The colonial government imposed taxes on produce, inconsequential to big producers but ruinous to small farmers, and added taxes on other staple commodities such as salt and opium. Even those small farmers who had ownership deeds to their land found it impossible to make a living and therefore sold their holdings just to survive.

"Hell on earth."

✴✴✴

—Vietnamese laborer's description of life on a rubber
plantation, quoted in Ngo Vinh Long's *Before the Revolution: The
Vietnamese Peasants under the French* (1991)

Peasant farmers who either sold their land or were pushed off of it could seek wage-labor work in French-built factories, mines, rubber plantations, or shipping ports, or they could set up as tenant farmers or sharecroppers under some large landlord. Failing this, they could hire themselves out as farmhands for a meager wage. French authorities trumpeted the roads, bridges, and railroads the empire built, but these disproportionately served the elites, not the peasants. They also boasted of the industrial sector they brought to the country, pointing to this as a source of employment. In fact, those factories were Dickensian sweatshops, and work on large farms or rubber plantations resembled penal servitude more than an opportunity to make a living. Located in remote regions, the rubber plantations were virtually slave labor camps from which the only certain escape was death, whether from disease, privation, overwork—or murder. Those who made a run for it either fell victim to the jungle or were hunted down and, if caught, executed. Of these, the most fortunate were hanged. Many, however, were tortured to death, often slowly, by stabbing with poles of sharpened bamboo.

REFORM MOVEMENT

FROM TIME TO TIME THROUGHOUT THE SECOND HALF of the nineteenth century, minor uprisings and demonstrations flared but were quickly put down by French colonial gendarmes, marines, and soldiers. A cohesive independence movement failed to develop largely because no charismatic leaders emerged—certainly none capable of uniting urban intellectual and rural peasant—and no one seemed to offer a plan for compelling change once the French were evicted. The idea of returning to the pre-colonial status quo and abandoning the technological and other improvements the French had introduced was hardly attractive. Nor was the restless urge for sovereignty and self-determination driven by a program of social justice.

It was not until the beginning of the twentieth century that a new generation of nationalist intellectuals emerged. The most important of these was Phan Boi Chau, who was born Phan Van San in Vietnam's north-central province of Nghe An in 1867. The province was poor, and so was Chau's family, but Phan Van Pho, his father, was a teacher descended from a family of scholars. The son imbibed from him a love of Vietnamese classical literature and classical Chinese political

NUMBERS
Occupational Hazard

During the late nineteenth and early twentieth centuries, more than one in four Vietnamese rubber plantation workers died on the job.

Phan Boi Chau, pictured here on a "memorial card" published after his death in 1940, was a pioneer of Vietnamese independence from French rule.

philosophy, especially that of Confucius. At the same time, the young Chau witnessed the colonization of his province, which occurred in earnest during the 1870s. The grim spectacle awakened in him what he called a passion for those "who were ready to die for the righteous cause." When the French conquest of northern Vietnam was completed by 1883, the sixteen-year-old Chau drew up a plan for driving the French out of the North. He made copies of it and posted them along a principal local road, with an appeal for the formation of resistance units. Authorities responded by simply tearing down the posters.

In 1885, when he was eighteen, Chau joined the emerging Can Vuong movement, which aimed at ousting the French and putting a genuine and independent Vietnamese emperor on the throne. The court of the child-emperor Ham Nghi assembled in Nghe An for the purpose of organizing resistance. The student Chau worked to recruit his classmates into something he called the Army of Loyalist Examination Candidates, but French troops attacked Nghe An and dispersed the embryonic force before it could take to the field.

After the collapse of his "army," Chau retreated to his books, studying ancient military strategy, including Sun Tzu's *The Art of War* and works of early Vietnamese generals. He continued to follow the Can Vuong movement and gradually entered into a circle of other students, teachers, and intellectuals bent on reform and independence. After several unsuccessful attempts, Chau passed so-called mandarin examinations in 1900, which gave him, he felt, added credibility as a political reformer. He decided to recruit members of the now-moribund Can Vuong movement and others to work toward winning the support of the Vietnamese royal family and to obtain finance from outside the country, especially from Chinese and Japanese revolutionaries. He began to merge his Confucianism with the ideas of such Western thinkers as Voltaire, Rousseau, and Darwin. He also studied history, both Asian and Western, and became an admirer of such Western nationalists as Italy's Count Camillo Benso di Cavour, Germany's Otto von Bismarck, George Washington, and Abraham Lincoln. In 1903 or 1904, he wrote a tract called *Letter from the Ryukyus Written in Tears of Blood*, in which he called for a total "transformation and revitalization of national character." This drew a fair amount of attention, including from Phan Chu Trinh, an early nationalist who admired Chau's ideas but believed the best hope for Vietnam lay in pushing the French to honor their claim that they intended to prepare Vietnam for eventual independence. Phan Chu Trinh's moderation was disappointing to Phan Boi Chau, but it was at least more encouraging than the outright rejection he received from the Vietnamese old guard of the bureaucratic elite. In 1904, Chau founded the Vietnam Reformation Society (the Viet Nam Duy Tan Hoi, sometimes translated as Vietnam Modernization Association), with the aid of Prince Cuong De, a direct descendant of Gia Long. In 1905, Chau moved to Japan, hoping to find financial donors to the society. For the next three years, he sought support in Japan while also writing increasingly bold political tracts, including *History of the Loss of Vietnam, New Vietnam,* and *A Lament for Vietnam and Yunnan.* The Japanese government, unwilling to offend France, declared Chau persona non grata and deported him in 1909. Chau moved for a time to Hong Kong, then to Siam (modern Thailand), trying in vain to raise money and collect weapons. Returning to China, he came under the influence of the Chinese nationalist Sun Yat-sen.

The Movement Drifts

Chau's personal situation grew increasingly desperate. By 1910, he was little more than a hard-drinking homeless beggar until a small influx of cash in November 1910 enabled him to move again to Siam, where he and a group of his followers set up a communal farm. In 1912, responding to the Wuchang Uprising against the moribund Qing Dynasty in China, Chau abandoned the Vietnam Reformation Society and founded the Vietnamese Restoration League (Viet Nam Quang Phuc Hoi), which was patterned after Sun Yat-sen's successful Chinese republican party. Chau's aim was to eject the French from Vietnam, but the connection to Sun Yat-sen attracted followers who also wanted to replace the monarchy with a republic.

Because the Vietnamese nobility was a key constituent of Chau's support, funding became more of a problem than ever, and Chau decided to take more aggressive action. He would launch terrorist attacks. The only weapons available to him were a few hand grenades, which his operatives used against minor officials. These ineffectual attacks succeeded only in giving French authorities an excuse to arrest Phan Boi Chau. At first the Chinese government protected him, but in 1914, Chinese authorities jailed him on suspicion of aiding rivals for power in China.

DETAILS, DETAILS
Educated for Orthodoxy

As late as the twentieth century, the Vietnamese administrative bureaucracy was staffed by those who had passed an imperial or "mandarin" examination. The system had been imported from China, where it had been established in 605, during the Sui Dynasty, and was intended to create a bureaucratic meritocracy run by scholars rather than hereditary nobles. In Vietnam, the mandarin system did ensure an educated bureaucratic class, but it also created a cultural uniformity, which was often narrow and unimaginative. On the other hand, the uniformity tended to promote a national rather than parochial identity in local government bureaus and offices.

NUMBERS

Far from Home

Of some 100,000
Vietnamese sent to Europe
in World War I, more
than 30,000 were killed
during the conflict and
60,000 were wounded or
otherwise injured.

European War and Vietnamese Revolt

Imprisoned during most of World War I, Chau turned to writing during much of 1917. In the meantime, his more moderate ally, Phan Chu Trinh, gained support in Saigon and founded a more mainstream political organization, the Constitutionalist Party, which demanded an increase in political and economic opportunities from the colonial administration.

The Great War itself also had an impact on Vietnamese politics. France sent 50,000 Vietnamese troops and an equal number of workers to Europe. Losses among the troops were heavy, creating in Vietnam a mixture of outrage and patriotic pride along with widespread confidence that the Vietnamese could fight on a par with the best soldiers in Europe.

If conditions were hard on Vietnamese troops and workers sent to Europe, the Vietnamese home front also reeled under burdensome wartime taxes. Throughout the country, revolts erupted—all of which were quickly and brutally suppressed. The most serious wartime revolt took place in May 1916, when the sixteen-year-old king, Duy Tan, broke out of enforced confinement to his palace and joined a soldiers' uprising. Leaders of the revolt were arrested and summarily executed, and Duy Tan was officially deposed and sent into exile.

Duy Tan, the Vietnamese child king shown here, participated in an unsuccessful revolt against the French in May 1916, when he was sixteen. As a result, he was deposed and exiled to Réunion Island in the Indian Ocean.

Phan Boi Chau Embraces Socialism

After Phan Boi Chau was released from prison in 1917, he wandered throughout Japan and China but failed to get traction for his movement. In desperation, he considered actually collaborating with the French, reasoning that the Socialist Party, which assumed control of the French government following the end of World I, would be more sympathetic to Vietnamese independence. He soon abandoned the idea of working with the French under any circumstances and in 1921 leaped over moderate socialism and directly into radical Communism. He traveled to the Soviet Union for study and was deeply impressed. In 1924, he began corresponding with another rising Vietnamese nationalist, Ho Chi Minh, who had recently left Moscow for China. Ho Chi Minh was receptive to collaborating with Chau, but in 1925 Phan Boi Chau was arrested in Shanghai by agents of the French colonial government. He had been betrayed by his trusted secretary, Nguyen Thuong Hien. Chau was sentenced to life imprisonment on old charges of having supplied weapons that were used to kill a Vietnamese governor and two French army majors; however, French authorities bowed to a public outcry and commuted his sentence to house arrest in Hue.

FORGOTTEN FACES
Phan Chu Trinh

Born in the central Vietnam province of Quang Nam in 1872, Phan Chu Trinh was the son of a prosperous landowner and scholar. He might have led a contented provincial life had his father not been killed in the so-called Scholar's Revolt of 1885. (The French didn't kill him; his comrades did—fearing that he had betrayed the revolt.)

A thirteen-year-old orphan, Phan Chu Trinh was tutored by his older brother and in 1901 passed the mandarin examinations and entered the bureaucracy. Resigning in 1905, he agitated for the replacement of the monarchy with a democratic republic, believing the French occupation to be preferable to a return of the Nguyen Dynasty. Although he hoped to collaborate with Phan Boi Chau (whom he met in 1903), Trinh's willingness to collaborate with the French as a step toward republican democracy put him at odds with Chau, who embraced the monarchy in order to eject the French.

Phan Chu Trinh appealed to French governor-general Paul Beau in 1906 to make good on France's declared mission to "civilize" Vietnam and to bring it all the benefits of the modern industrialized West. The next year, in Hanoi, Trinh opened Dong Kinh Nghia Thuc (Tonkin Free School, or Free School of the Eastern Capital), a progressive, anti-monarchical school in which the brutality of the French administration was attacked but the goals of French-inspired modernization and enlightenment were embraced. Trinh tried to inculcate national unity by requiring students to renounce their elitism and embrace the peasant masses. He also opened the school's doors to peasants.

Dong Kinh Nghia Thuc proved short lived. During a tax revolt in 1908, Trinh was arrested and the school shuttered. Authorities handed down a death sentence, which provoked liberal outrage in France. The sentence was therefore commuted to life imprisonment in the penitentiary on Con Son (Iles Poulo Condore) in the Con Dao Archipelago off the coast of southeastern Vietnam. He was released in 1911 to house arrest but protested that he preferred life in prison to partial freedom. In response, he was deported to France, where the government believed it could monitor him. In Paris, however, he collaborated with other exiles to found "The Group of Vietnamese Patriots" while he supported himself as a photo retoucher. Ailing, he covertly returned to Saigon in 1925, where his death on March 24, 1926, provoked nationwide protests demanding an end to French colonial occupation.

THE RISE OF A NEW LEADER

PHAN BOI CHAU LIVED UNTIL OCTOBER 29, 1940, completely isolated by his house arrest. Leaderless, his former followers nevertheless founded the clandestine Vietnamese Nationalist Party (Viet Nam Quoc Dan Dang) as a more radical alternative to Phan Chu Trinh's Constitutionalist Party. The result was to further divide rather than unite reform activists, and neither the Constitutionalists, advocating positive collaboration with the French, nor the Nationalists, demanding independence, made serious inroads against the colonial administration.

Both Phan Boi Chau and Phan Chu Trinh were dedicated patriots and intelligent political philosophers, but neither had the charisma, organizational genius, and ideological flexibility necessary to create a cohesive national movement. Ho Chi Minh, with whom Phan Boi Chau had so briefly corresponded in 1924, possessed all of these qualities—in addition to what must be described as a phenomenal will to persevere against all odds. Charismatic and radical, Ho was remarkably flexible in terms of ideology, promoting independence without the xenophobia characteristic of many other dedicated nationalists. Ideologically and tactically, he would borrow from whatever sources, Asian or Western, seemed to him most useful. Most important of all, Ho Chi Minh, an intellectual, was able to bridge the divide that traditionally separated the urban elites from the peasant majority. To an unprecedented degree, he unified the nationalist movement.

Born Nguyen Sinh Cung (and also known as Nguyen Tat Thanh and Nguyen Ai Quoc) in the central Vietnamese village of Hoang Tru in 1890, Ho Chi Minh adopted this name around 1940, combining a common surname with a given name meaning, roughly, "enlightened will." He was the child of a mandarin family. His father was a Vietnamese bureaucrat who had resigned in protest against the French takeover. From earliest childhood, Ho Chi Minh absorbed his father's Confucianism and patriotism. Early in 1908, a peasant tax protest spread throughout several provinces. Still a student, Ho joined the peasants, offering to set down their grievances in a form that would carry weight with local officials. This brought him to the attention of the colonial gendarmerie, which prevailed upon Ho's school to expel him.

Ho Chi Minh, in a "carte de visite" (calling card) photograph of about 1946.

Cast out, Ho Chi Minh taught briefly, but, dogged by French threats and harassment, he joined the crew of a tramp steamer—as a cook's helper—bound for Europe and the United States. In 1912 and 1913, he lived in New York City's Harlem and then in Boston, where he made his living as a baker in the exclusive Parker House Hotel. He then set off for Europe and worked variously as a waiter or chef in various London hotels, perfecting advanced skills as a pastry chef under no less a figure than Auguste Escoffier.

Ho Chi Minh in Paris

In 1919 (possibly as early as 1917), Ho moved from London to Paris, where he lived until 1923. Ongoing in 1919 were the peace talks among the victors of World War I, which would result in the Treaty of Versailles and the creation of the League of Nations. A key objective of the talks, the treaty, and the League, especially as envisioned by U.S. president and leading treaty architect Woodrow Wilson, was the principle of self-determination, in particular for what were described as the "smaller countries." Calling himself at the time Nguyen Ai Quoc—"Nguyen the Patriot"—Ho led a cadre of Vietnamese ex-pats in petitioning the treaty-making powers to extend the principles of Versailles to Vietnam. The group did not demand independence but a greater degree of self-determination, including rights for Vietnamese equal to those accorded French citizens and Vietnamese representation in the French parliament.

What Ho did not understand was that, when they advocated self-determination for the smaller countries, the framers of the Treaty of Versailles were thinking of the subject states and colonies belonging to empires of the powers defeated in the war, chiefly Austria-Hungary and Germany, not those belonging to the victors, including Great Britain and France. Ho Chi Minh and his followers were simply ignored.

Turned away by the Western democracies, Ho Chi Minh looked for a different set of values and an alternative ideology. The post–World War I years seemed to offer just that: Communism as advocated by Vladimir I. Lenin and implemented in revolutionary Russia. Ho's first step, in 1919, was to join the growing French Socialist Party. Although the party welcomed him personally, it showed no interest in the plight of colonial Vietnam. Ho Chi Minh therefore turned squarely to

Vladimir Ilyich Lenin, architect of the Bolshevik Revolution and the global Communist movement.

Leninism—for Lenin, in the course of fomenting the Bolshevik Revolution, focused sharply on colonialism and unequivocally advocated an end to it.

Lenin's anti-colonial vision came to Ho as a revelation. It elevated local nationalism to the stage of global history, and it provided a plan for radicalizing the peasantry and harnessing their potential for revolution. In 1920, Ho Chi Minh became a founding member of the French Communist Party, which soon drew the attention of Soviet party officials. They invited Ho to Moscow in 1923.

Ho Chi Minh in Moscow

Expecting in Moscow an intellectual and political paradise, Ho Chi Minh instead experienced profound ambivalence during his sojourn in the heart of the Communist revolution. He was excited about working for the Comintern, the organization Lenin created in 1919 to promote Communism globally, and he was grateful for the opportunity to learn the lessons of Marx and Lenin firsthand. Yet he was repeatedly told that agricultural nations such as Vietnam were by nature reactionary, the very idea of ideological revolution anathema to them. Ho Chi Minh was repeatedly excluded from the inner circle of Moscow political discourse.

Increasingly frustrated in Moscow, Ho simultaneously became aware of the nationalist movements arising throughout Southeast Asia. In 1924, he asked the Comintern to send him back to Asia. Perhaps relieved to be rid of him, the Comintern was more than willing to comply.

Ho Chi Minh in China

The Comintern sent Ho to Canton (Guangzhou), China, where he undertook three missions: to write news articles for the Soviet news agency, to work as an interpreter for Comintern agents, and to unite the many self-exiled Vietnamese nationalists who had settled in southeastern China into a cohesive revolutionary organization. In 1925, Ho founded among these individuals the Revolutionary Youth League, which he intended to serve as the nucleus of both a nationalist movement and a Vietnamese Communist party.

Ho worked carefully with his Revolutionary Youth League, identifying the most intellectually promising members as political leaders. Very soon, some of these individuals left China and returned to Vietnam, where they began to lay the foundation of an indigenous movement. Just when things seemed so promising, in 1927, the Comintern did what it so often did: it made an abrupt policy shift, one that required all local leaders to push a strict ideological program, unmixed with broader motives of nationalism and focused exclusively on industrial workers and the poorest of the peasants. The middle class was to be excluded from the movement. As a result of this new edict, not only was the Revolutionary Youth League disintegrated, but Ho Chi Minh was effectively kicked to the curb. His ambition to create a Vietnamese Communist Party was supplanted in 1930 by a Comintern-sanctioned Indochinese Communist Party with a strictly ideological agenda that failed to take into account local aspirations to self-determination.

Premature Uprisings

The worldwide economic depression that had begun in 1929 with the U.S. stock market crash rapidly swept through Asia, exacerbating the bleak economic conditions of peasant life in Vietnam. The new breed of Vietnamese Communists spawned by the Comintern sought to exploit the general discontent. In the province of Nghe Tinh, peasants not only toppled local government but also established governing "soviets" in imitation of the Bolshevik Revolution. But this uprising, like others during the early 1930s, lacked momentum and served only to galvanize a French crackdown. With ruthless efficiency, colonial authorities rounded up the nascent Communists, imprisoning or executing nine out of ten and setting back the development of Communism in Vietnam by years, if not decades.

DETAILS, DETAILS
Globalism, Old School

The Communist International, better known as the "Comintern," was established in Moscow in 1919 for the purpose of disseminating Communism worldwide, overthrowing what Lenin called "the international bourgeoisie," and creating "an international Soviet republic as a transition stage to the complete abolition of the State." The Comintern endured until May 15, 1943, when it was officially dissolved.

The Yen Bai Mutiny

On February 10, 1930, the Viet Nam Quoc Dan Dang (VNQDD), or Vietnamese Nationalist Party, organized a mutiny of Vietnamese soldiers of the French colonial army's Yen Bai garrison. The VNQDD hoped that this armed uprising would stir a general civilian revolt that would gather sufficient momentum to drive the French out of Vietnam.

Fifty Vietnamese troops belonging to the 4th Tonkinese Rifles Regiment rose up against their French officers at the Yen Bai garrison shortly after midnight on February 10. While they held the officers at bay, some sixty civilians, all VNQDD members, rushed the garrison camp from the outside. The mutiny not only failed to stir a general uprising, it proved unable even to win over the majority of Vietnamese soldiers in the garrison itself. There were desultory attacks throughout the Mekong River Delta, but they were quickly defeated. French authorities cracked down on the Vietnamese Nationalist Party, arresting its leaders and thereby extinguishing what had been the single most important revolutionary group in Vietnam.

Many were arrested, tried, convicted, and either jailed, exiled, or executed. French military commanders dispersed native Vietnamese troops, sending many into service outside of Vietnam. Vietnamese soldiers in Vietnam were replaced with troops from France, Cambodia, and Laos, and from among the Montagnards (the French name for tribal peoples from the Central Highlands of Vietnam). French officials, military and civilian, were cautioned to put no trust in Vietnamese soldiers or bureaucrats. The Yen Bai Mutiny tended to transform Vietnam from a colony to an occupied country.

IN THE SHADOW OF A NEW WAR

MARGINALIZED BY THE COMINTERN, Ho Chi Minh also found himself unwelcome and unsafe in Canton after the anti-Communist coup d'état of Chiang Kai-shek in 1927. Ho returned to Moscow, where his health, always frail, failed him. Diagnosed with tuberculosis, he spent several months convalescing in the relative warmth of the Crimea, then returned to Paris in November 1927. Soon, however, he returned to Asia, arriving in Bangkok in July 1928. Late the following year, he moved back to China and, in June 1931, was arrested in Hong Kong in the aftermath of the Yen Bai Mutiny of 1930.

British authorities in Hong Kong had no desire to offend the Chinese and other Asians by giving in to French demands for extradition and so, announcing that "Nguyen Ai Quoc" had died of tuberculosis, they secretly released Ho Chi Minh in January 1933. He took ship for Milan, Italy, and found work in a restaurant.

By the mid-1930s, the European rise of anti-Communism in the form of fascism—led by Benito Mussolini in Italy, Adolf Hitler in Germany, and Francisco Franco in Spain—stirred deep alarm in Moscow, prompting the Comintern to reverse itself and once again embrace broad alliances between orthodox Communists and more liberal nationalists. At the same time, the leftist government of France, also hoping to stem the rising tide of fascism, ordered colonial authorities in Vietnam to permit the International Communist Party to participate openly in Vietnamese politics. In this climate of renewed opportunity, Ho Chi Minh was welcomed back into not only the Comintern but also its inner circle. While most of the world trembled at the gathering of European war clouds for the second time in the twentieth century, Ho Chi Minh regarded them as a suddenly sun-filled vista beneath a clear blue sky.

TAKEAWAY
Communism and Nationalism: Vietnam's Strange Bedfellows

Vietnamese nationalism took shape slowly in the twentieth century, the movement deeply divided between those who advocated replacing the French with a restored Vietnamese monarchy and those who wanted to transform Vietnam into a democratic republic, even if this meant enlisting the aid of France to do so. The development of international Communism after Russia's Bolshevik Revolution in 1917 fostered the rise of Ho Chi Minh, the first Vietnamese leader to emerge with sufficient charisma and cultural and political skill to unite the independence movement in terms of both ideology and class. As World War II approached, threatening to weaken the French hold on Vietnam, Ho glimpsed opportunity to advance independence.

CHAPTER 3

FROM WORLD WAR TO DIRTY WAR

America Backs into a Secondhand Abyss

GREAT BRITAIN AND FRANCE HAD DEFEATED GERMANY in the "Great War" of 1914–1918, yet they came out of the conflict more profoundly demoralized and debilitated than the loser. Determined to punish Germany with the one-sided Treaty of Versailles, the victors were nevertheless utterly unwilling to enforce the stern provisions of the treaty by any means that might involve renewed fighting. Germany, in contrast, emerged from the war bearing a grudge and craving a rematch. The feeble Weimar Republic, a democracy, failed to take root there, and when Adolf Hitler promised a return to greatness, a majority approved. The dictator rose to power, demanded from the rest of Europe *Lebensraum* ("living space"), and the two European victors of the Great War, seeking to "appease" Hitler, gave him the best part of Czechoslovakia in return for his promise to ask for nothing more.

He did not ask but took.

Having been allowed to annex Austria and then given the German-speaking Sudetenland of Czechoslovakia, Hitler simply took the rest of that country as the Allies stood by. It was only when he made actual war on Poland, beginning on September 1, 1939, that the British and French declared war in return. With all Europe in flames, who had time or inclination even to think of a little Asian country?

FRANCE FALLS—AND FALLS AGAIN

HITLER'S MILITARY PLANNERS CALLED IT *Fall Gelb*—"Operation Yellow": the invasion of Western Europe, which was to culminate in the fall of France. It began at dawn on May 10, 1940, as the German army rolled into and rolled over the three small neutral nations of Luxembourg, Belgium, and the Netherlands. The British responded by sending the relatively small British Expeditionary Force (BEF) across the Channel, and the French rushed troops into Flanders, leaving their more southerly territory exposed. They believed that the Maginot Line, a chain of hardened forts along France's eastern frontier, would hold the Germans at bay. The border with Belgium, it was true, was not defended by the Maginot Line, but France was protected here by the dense Ardennes Forest, which to French military planners seemed a natural border impregnable by modern armored vehicles and mobile artillery.

Marshal Henri Philippe Pétain, gallant hero of Verdun in World War I, ignominiously led the capitulation of France in World War II.

Precisely because he knew that the French considered the Ardennes impregnable and would therefore leave it thinly defended, German commander Erich von Manstein sent his *Blitzkrieg,* his "Lightning War," through it and into France.

Even so, with some five million men, the French army was formidable. Unfortunately, the same could not be said of the French high command, which had never developed a vigorous and efficient network of communications or a cogent plan of active defense. Indeed, from top to bottom, the French army, impressive though it was, entered the fray already exhausted at the mere thought of fighting a second great war in twenty years. The main German attack burst through the Ardennes, simply outflanking the Maginot Line; the forces swept around it, not so much defeating it as rendering it moot. When they did that, the French and British fell back and back some more until they found themselves pushed up against the sea at Dunkirk. From there the remnants of the BEF, and French army survivors, were evacuated to England by a remarkable miscellany of warships, fishing vessels, passenger craft, and yachts.

On June 10, Mussolini's Italy entered the war, invading France from the south eleven days later. In the meantime, the French government fled Paris for Bordeaux just ahead of the advancing Germans, who took the capital on June 14. Three days later, Henri Philippe Pétain, the hero of what would now have to be called the *First* World War, announced that France would request an armistice. Pétain had taken a stand at the Battle of Verdun in April 1916, gloriously exhorting his troops, "*Courage! On les aura!*" ("Courage! We will get them!"), but in 1940 he was an old man of eighty-four, a fitting figurehead for a tired country. The armistice was signed on June 22, 1940, splitting France into a German occupation zone in the north and west, a small Italian occupation zone in the southeast, and an unoccupied zone in the south. Here, from the town of Vichy, Pétain presided over a hollow government whose nominal authority was wholly subject to the pleasure of Germany.

French Indochina was among the outer territories now under Vichy control, but that control was of course even more nominal than Vichy's authority in France itself. The colonial administration was totally cut off from supplies or military reinforcement and was therefore wholly at the mercy of the Vietnamese. Germany's Asian ally, Japan, had already invaded French Indochina. Instead of resisting the invasion, French colonial officials offered their acquiescence in the establishment of Japanese bases in the country, reasoning that this would at least keep the indigenous population in check. In return for this concession, Japan agreed to permit Vichy to retain nominal authority in Vietnam.

Neighboring Thailand—its name had been changed from Siam on June 23, 1939—regarded this arrangement as yet another French capitulation and therefore launched an invasion into French Indochina in October 1940. To the surprise of the Thais, the French responded vigorously—only to fold to Japanese demands that Japan be granted authority to mediate peace. Japanese "negotiators" ordered France to return to Thailand portions of Cambodia and Laos taken from the Thais at the start of the century. It was yet another French humiliation, one from which the Vietnamese nationalists, in particular, took heart.

BIRTH OF THE VIET MINH

POSSESSION OF VIETNAM WAS IMPORTANT TO JAPAN since it gave its army access to China, but with France cooperating, Tokyo was content to let French colonial authorities administer the daily affairs of "French" Indochina, even as Japanese troops were sent to occupy the entire region.

Many Vietnamese nationalists were unsure how to assess the Japanese presence. Did it mean they now had a *second* colonial master?

These troops, photographed in October 1941, were part of the first Japanese military forces sent into French Indochina under a "French-Japanese Protocol" for what was termed the "joint defense" of the colony. In reality, defeated by Japan's ally Germany, Vichy France meekly acceded to the Japanese occupation of Vietnam.

Or a *new* master altogether? Ho Chi Minh took the brightest possible view of the situation. As he saw it, an Asian power had ended European hegemony in Vietnam. Yet just when it appeared that France had been reduced to a paper tiger in his country, French soldiers, in November 1941, crushed a Communist-led rebellion in Cochinchina. When Communist guerrillas turned against some Japanese occupation forces, they were also beaten. Clearly, the French and Japanese did have one common enemy: Communism. Could it be, then, that the International Communist Party, the ICP, which the socialist-dominated French government had allowed into Vietnam before the war, now had *two* enemies, the French *and* the Japanese?

Ho Chi Minh refused to despair. In May 1941, for the first time in thirty years, he returned to Vietnam to lead the ICP Central Committee. Meeting with party leaders in Pac Bo, a mountain village near the Chinese border, he called upon the assembled delegates to refrain from combat and instead to forge ahead with political organizing. He explained that the Vietnamese people wanted both the French and the Japanese out of their country, but because they also understood that both France and Japan opposed Communism, it would be necessary for the ICP to subordinate its ideological agenda to a new nationalist organization dedicated not to Communism but to independence. The organization would be called the

REALITY CHECK

What Did Ho Chi Minh *Really* Want?

During and since the Vietnam War, scholars, politicians, and ordinary Americans have argued about Ho Chi Minh's "true" motives. Some insist that he was first and last a Communist, whereas others believe he was primarily a nationalist, seeking the liberation of his country. The obvious resolution to this argument is to conclude that he was both—or, more accurately, that he believed Vietnam should be both unified and independent under a Communist government. Obvious though this may be, it is not entirely true. Clearly, Ho Chi Minh was a nationalist before he became a Communist, but once he embraced Communism, his ideological commitment took precedence. Nevertheless, he was also a pragmatist, willing to dress his Communist aims in the cloak of self-determination and independence in order to build support. It was never a case of trading one objective for another but of holding Communism in abeyance until his nation was in a position to choose—or be led to— Communism.

League for the Independence of Vietnam: Viet Nam Doc Lap Dong Minh Hoi. The name was quickly shortened to Viet Minh.

Ho was confident that, in the current crisis, with their country occupied by *two* foreign powers, patriotism would garner far more support than ideology. The wisdom of this approach became even more apparent after December 7, 1941, when the United States responded to the attack on its navy at Pearl Harbor by declaring war on Japan. Both before and after the declaration, President Franklin D. Roosevelt frequently spoke of U.S. support for "self-determination" and "anti-colonialism," and, after December 7, he routinely included these among U.S. war aims. Ho Chi Minh therefore had every reason to believe that, absent apparent Communist goals, the Viet Minh would find in the United States a powerful ally against the common enemy, Japan.

> **"The sacred call of the fatherland is resounding in our ears; the ardent blood of our heroic predecessors is seething in our hearts."**
>
> ✶✶✶
>
> —Ho Chi Minh, from "Letter from Abroad," June 6, 1941

MIXED MOTIVES

THE VIET MINH BUILT INTERNAL SUPPORT, and then, gradually, under the leadership of Vo Nguyen Giap, a history teacher who proved to have a brilliant military mind, it began to conduct guerrilla operations against the Japanese from a headquarters hidden in the mountains of the North. By 1943, Ho Chi Minh decided that the Viet Minh had become a sufficient guerrilla presence to interest the United States as a military ally. He sent out feelers to American intelligence officers operating in southern China, proposing an anti-Japanese operational alliance.

Ho Chi Minh read U.S. sentiment correctly. President Roosevelt had already expressed public agreement with Soviet premier Joseph Stalin's belief that the Allies should not spill precious blood in Indochina for the purpose of restoring French colonial rule. In fact, FDR sought to marginalize France so that, after the war, it would be unable to restore the colonial status quo. This was FDR's sincere motive, but, like many beliefs sincerely held, it soon came up against some hard realities.

U.S. president Franklin D. Roosevelt (left), Free French leader Charles de Gaulle (center), and British prime minister Winston Churchill (right) convened at Casablanca in January 1943, to discuss the ongoing conduct of the war against Germany and Japan. FDR and Churchill, formidable partners in the prosecution of the war, differed over the status of Vietnam—the American president favoring an end to French colonial rule and the British prime minister, intent on restoring the British Empire after the war, supporting de Gaulle's desire to restore French imperial rule over Indochina.

One was the position of FDR's staunchest ally and collaborator, British prime minister Winston Churchill. Churchill was something of a Francophile but certainly no fan of Charles de Gaulle, the prickly leader of Free France. All things being equal, Churchill would also have liked to marginalize France. Yet he had every intention of restoring the British Empire after World War II, and he could hardly do this if he argued that France should be deprived of *its* empire.

Not only were Churchill and Roosevelt of different minds concerning the postwar fate of the French Empire, but FDR also had to face pressing manpower needs as the war entered its later phases. Although the United States and its allies were triumphant, both the Germans and the Japanese continued to fight fiercely. After France was liberated in 1944, it became, under the quarrelsome de Gaulle, a vast pool of military manpower. The American president could not afford to marginalize France after all, not if he wanted to use its fighting men—not only in Europe but in the Pacific, where plans were being made for a massive invasion of Japan that would dwarf the D-Day invasion of Europe.

Clearly, then, Roosevelt was already moderating his views on French colonialism when the president died of a cerebral hemorrhage,

Ho Chi Minh (center) and General Vo Nguyen Giap (right) are pictured about 1946, after the end of World War II and in the thick of Vietnam's struggle for independence from France. On the wall behind them are posters of Mao Zedong and Vladimir Lenin.

on April 12, 1945. His vice president, Harry S. Truman, was likewise an anti-colonialist, but, also like FDR, his overriding objective was to win the war, even if that meant making certain promises to Charles de Gaulle.

Birth of an Army

On December 22, 1944, the guerrilla forces spawned by the Viet Minh became the Vietnam People's Army (Quan Doi Nhan Dan Viet Nam), under the command of General Giap. (In practice, the Vietnam People's Army—also known early on as the Armed Propaganda Unit for National Liberation—was virtually indistinguishable from the soldiers of the Viet Minh, and all of Giap's forces, as deployed early in the war for liberation, are usually known as the Viet Minh.) Slowly and steadily, Giap made inroads against the Japanese, continually enlarged the new army, worked to clear more and more northern mountain territory, and soon built a formidable redoubt of national resistance.

Architect of Vietnam's Long War

Born in Quang Binh Province in 1911, Vo Nguyen Giap earned a doctorate in economics at the University of Hanoi and became a history professor. Like many Vietnamese intellectuals, he was both a nationalist and a Communist, and after escaping arrest by the French in 1939, he made his way to China, where he joined Ho Chi Minh's Revolutionary Youth League, precursor to the Viet Minh.

Giap returned to Vietnam in 1942—by which time his sister had been executed by French authorities and his wife had died in prison. Although he had no formal military training, Giap set about organizing a guerrilla war against the Japanese occupation forces. It was only after the Japanese surrendered and World War II ended that General Vo Nguyen Giap led the Viet Minh against the forces of the French reoccupation. He did not perform especially well until Mao Zedong prevailed in China, thereby providing Giap with a friendly base for training and equipping soldiers.

From 1949 through 1953, Giap managed to hold his own against the French, finally provoking General Henri Navarre to build a major base at Dien Bien Phu with the object of blocking Giap's access to Laos. Giap understood that Navarre's plan was to tempt him into a showdown battle at Dien Bien Phu. Surprisingly, Giap gave Navarre what he wanted. But instead of doing what Navarre expected him to do—launch an all-out frontal assault—Giap set up a siege around the isolated French base and built up a surrounding force five times greater than Navarre's before launching his assault on March 13, 1954, forcing a French surrender on May 7 and precipitating the final French withdrawal from Vietnam.

Vo Nguyen Giap continued to command Vietnamese army forces throughout the Vietnam War, this time against the Americans; after the fall of Saigon on April 30, 1975, and the creation of the Socialist Republic of Vietnam, he was named deputy premier and minister of defense. Retiring in 1991, Giap was an environmental activist as late as 2010.

Japan Attacks, the OSS Arrives

For their part, the Japanese in Indochina were concerned about the growing threat posed not only by the Vietnamese army but also by the French. By early 1945, France had been liberated and Germany was in retreat everywhere in Europe. Japan itself was suffering an unbroken series of military reverses in the Pacific. It seemed only a matter of time before French colonial forces actually united with the Vietnamese to make war directly on Japan. To preempt this eventuality, on March 9, 1945, Japan initiated a coup d'état against the French colonial government and rapidly assumed control over what had been French Indochina. In an effort to appease the Vietnamese, Japan proclaimed Vietnam independent—even as it set up a Japanese puppet government under the reigning Vietnamese emperor Bao Dai.

Just as Japanese forces drove out the French, operatives of the U.S.

Office of Strategic Services—the OSS, wartime precursor to the modern Central Intelligence Agency (CIA)—arrived in Vietnam. Their original intention was to collaborate with the French against the Japanese, but the operatives quickly realized that the only viable ally was the Viet Minh. Already, Ho Chi Minh had met in China with legendary U.S. Army Air Forces general Claire Chennault, commander of the fabled guerrilla air combat unit known as the Flying Tigers, and now of the U.S. Fourteenth Air Force. Ho then accompanied an OSS team from China into northern Vietnam and introduced the OSS men to the Viet Minh. The American operatives provided weapons, radio equipment, and training. Then, when Ho fell gravely ill, it was an OSS medic, Paul Hoagland, who treated him and surely saved his life.

The OSS

As the war in Europe threatened to draw in the United States, President Franklin D. Roosevelt became increasingly concerned that the nation lacked a formal covert military intelligence service. He called on William J. "Wild Bill" Donovan, hitherto an unofficial adviser, to prepare a report on the national intelligence needs

Before the United States was thrust into World War II, President Roosevelt tapped William J. "Wild Bill" Donovan to make recommendations for the establishment of a "Service of Strategic Information." On June 13, 1942, the president created the Office of Strategic Services (OSS), naming Donovan to direct it. OSS operatives worked closely with Ho Chi Minh to oppose the Japanese in Vietnam. Donovan is shown here in a 1950 official portrait.

Donovan submitted a "Memorandum of Establishment of Service of Strategic Information" and, on July 11, 1941, was appointed as the "Co-ordinator of Information." The following year, on June 13, 1942, President Roosevelt created the Office of Strategic Services (OSS). Donovan, who had served in World War I, was returned to active military duty (first as a colonel, eventually as a major general) and named head of the OSS.

The OSS mission was to collect (often by covert means) and analyze strategic information as ordered by the Joint Chiefs of Staff and to conduct "special operations" that were not assigned to other agencies. From 1943 until the end of the war, the OSS was especially active in Asia, including with the Nationalist Chinese troops of Chiang Kai-shek and in guerrilla operations in Burma. OSS personnel were instrumental in training and arming what were regarded as indigenous anti-Japanese resistance movements, including Mao Zedong's Red Army in China and the Viet Minh in Vietnam.

The OSS was disbanded on orders of Harry S. Truman in September 1945, but it was soon replaced, in 1947, by the new Central Intelligence Agency (CIA).

INDEPENDENCE DAY

IN THE END, NEITHER THE VIET MINH NOR THE OSS, separately or together, scored any great victories against the Japanese. This was simply because the Japanese, aware that defeat was imminent, tended to avoid contact with these forces. Indeed, emboldened by the absence of interference, the Viet Minh made plans for a general uprising, which was to coincide with the moment of Japan's surrender. In the meantime, Viet Minh personnel launched an effort to relieve a catastrophic famine throughout Vietnam, which had begun in 1944 and was continuing unabated though the spring and summer of 1945. *He who feeds*, the old saying goes, *leads*—and, in the North, where Ho's units were most active, starving peasants learned to welcome the Viet Minh.

Fall of the Rising Sun

At 8:15 on the morning of August 6, 1945, a B-29 of the 393rd Bombardment Squadron, piloted by U.S. Army Air Forces colonel Paul Tibbets and named for his mother, *Enola Gay*, dropped "Little Boy," a fission-type bomb loaded with 130 pounds of the fissionable uranium isotope U-235. Forty-three seconds later, at 1,900 feet above Hiroshima, Japan, the bomb detonated, instantly killing 70,000—perhaps 80,000—men, women, and children, about a third of the city's population.

"If they do not now accept our terms, they may expect a rain of ruin from the air, the like of which has never been seen on this earth. Behind this air attack will follow sea and land forces in such numbers and power as they have not yet seen and with the fighting skill of which they are already well aware."

✦✦✦

—Statement issued on August 6, 1945, by President Harry S. Truman announcing the atomic bombing of Hiroshima, Japan

Ascetic and frail-looking, Ho Chi Minh broadcast on September 2, 1945, a Vietnamese declaration of independence modeled on the one Thomas Jefferson wrote for the United States in 1776.

Three days later, Major Charles W. Sweeney piloted another B-29 of the 393rd, *Bockscar* (or *Bock's Car*), carrying a bomb codenamed "Fat Boy" and headed for Kokura. Finding the target city obscured by clouds, Sweeney diverted to Nagasaki, where, at 11:01 a.m., the clouds over that city broke just long enough for bombardier Kermit Beahan to release his weapon. Somewhere between 40,000 and 75,000 residents were killed by the initial blast, shockwave, or fire.

On August 14, 1945, Emperor Hirohito recorded a message for radio broadcast to his subjects on August 15. "The enemy has recently used a most cruel explosive," he said. "Should we continue fighting in the war, it would cause not only the complete Annihilation of our nation, but also the destruction of the human civilization." He continued: "With this in mind, how should I save billions of our subjects and their posterity, and atone ourselves before the hallowed spirits of Our Imperial Ancestors? This is the reason why I ordered the Imperial Government to accept the Joint Declaration."

Ho Chi Minh had his own proclamation at this time, though it was not broadcast, and it is unclear who beyond the inner circle of the Viet Minh heard it: "The decisive hour has struck for the destiny of our people." Throughout the rest of the month, the so-called August Revolution swept through the North and met surprisingly little resistance even in the South, where the Viet Minh had never been a strong presence. While it is true that a variety of smaller nationalist groups vied with the Viet Minh for leadership of the growing insurrection, by August 19, the Viet Minh was clearly in charge at Hanoi and, on the twenty-third, in Hue. Two days later, Saigon was effectively under Viet Minh control, and on August 30, Emperor Bao Dai abdicated—albeit reluctantly—to the Viet Minh, thereby certifying Ho's authority.

On September 2, 1945, Ho Chi Minh, wispy thin, ascetic, even sickly in appearance, mounted a crudely erected platform in Ba Dinh Square, Hanoi. He began speaking, paraphrasing from the American Declaration of Independence: "All men are created equal. They are endowed by their Creator with certain unalienable rights; among these are Life, Liberty, and the pursuit of Happiness.'" (The full speech is on pages 45–46.) Clearly, by predicating Vietnam's declaration of independence on that of the United States, Ho wanted to enlist the aid of the one major combatant that had emerged from the world war strengthened rather than diminished by that war and thus as the greatest power in the world.

Declaration of Independence of the Democratic Republic of Vietnam, September 2, 1945

" **A**ll men are created equal. They are endowed by their Creator with certain inalienable rights; among these are Life, Liberty, and the pursuit of Happiness."

This immortal statement was made in the Declaration of Independence of the United States of America in 1776. In a broader sense, this means: All the peoples on the earth are equal from birth, all the peoples have a right to live, to be happy and free.

The Declaration of the French Revolution made in 1791 on the Rights of Man and the Citizen also states: "All men are born free and with equal rights, and must always remain free and have equal rights."

Those are undeniable truths.

Nevertheless, for more than eighty years, the French imperialists, abusing the standard of Liberty, Equality, and Fraternity, have violated our Fatherland and oppressed our fellow citizens. They have acted contrary to the ideals of humanity and justice.

In the field of politics, they have deprived our people of every democratic liberty.

They have enforced inhuman laws; they have set up three distinct political regimes in the North, the Center, and the South of Vietnam in order to wreck our national unity and prevent our people from being united.

They have built more prisons than schools. They have mercilessly slain our patriots; they have drowned our uprisings in rivers of blood.

They have fettered public opinion; they have practiced obscurantism against our people.

To weaken our race they have forced us to use opium and alcohol.

In the field of economics, they have fleeced us to the backbone, impoverished our people, and devastated our land.

They have robbed us of our rice fields, our mines, our forests, and our raw materials. They have monopolized the issuing of banknotes and the export trade.

They have invented numerous unjustifiable taxes and reduced our people, especially our peasantry, to a state of extreme poverty.

They have hampered the prospering of our national bourgeoisie; they have mercilessly exploited our workers.

In the autumn of 1940, when the Japanese Fascists violated Indochina's territory to establish new bases in their fight against the Allies, the French imperialists went down on their bended knees and handed over our country to them.

Thus, from that date, our people were subjected to the double yoke of the French and the Japanese. Their sufferings and miseries increased. The result was that from the end of last year to the beginning of this year, from Quang Tri province to the North of Vietnam, more than two million of our fellow citizens died from starvation. On March 9, the French troops were disarmed by the Japanese. The French colonialists either fled or surrendered showing that not only were they incapable of "protecting" us, but that, in the span of five years, they had twice sold our country to the Japanese.

On several occasions before March 9, the Vietminh League urged the French to ally themselves with it against the Japanese. Instead of agreeing to this proposal, the French colonialists so intensified their terrorist activities against the Vietminh members that before fleeing they massacred a great number of our political prisoners detained at Yen Bay and Caobang.

Notwithstanding all this, our fellow citizens have always manifested toward the French a tolerant and humane attitude. Even after the Japanese Putsch of March 1945, the Vietminh League helped many Frenchmen to cross the frontier, rescued some of them from Japanese jails, and protected French lives and property.

From the autumn of 1940, our country had in fact ceased to be a French colony and had become a Japanese possession.

After the Japanese had surrendered to the Allies, our whole people rose to regain our national sovereignty and to found the Democratic Republic of Vietnam.

The truth is that we have wrested our independence from the Japanese and not from the French.

The French have fled, the Japanese have capitulated, Emperor Bao Dai has abdicated. Our people have broken the chains which for nearly a century have fettered them and have won independence for the Fatherland. Our people at the same time have overthrown the monarchic regime that has reigned supreme for dozens of centuries. In its place has been established the present Democratic Republic.

For these reasons, we, members of the Provisional Government, representing the whole Vietnamese people, declare that from now on we break off all relations of a colonial character with France; we repeal all the international obligation that France has so far subscribed to on behalf of Vietnam and we abolish all the special rights the French have unlawfully acquired in our Fatherland.

The whole Vietnamese people, animated by a common purpose, are determined to fight to the bitter end against any attempt by the French colonialists to reconquer their country.

We are convinced that the Allied nations, which at Tehran and San Francisco have acknowledged the principles of self-determination and equality of nations, will not refuse to acknowledge the independence of Vietnam.

A people who have courageously opposed French domination for more than eighty years, a people who have fought side by side with the Allies against the fascists during these last years, such a people must be free and independent.

For these reasons, we, members of the Provisional Government of the Democratic Republic of Vietnam, solemnly declare to the world that Vietnam has the right to be a free and independent country—and in fact is so already. The entire Vietnamese people are determined to mobilize all their physical and mental strength, to sacrifice their lives and property in order to safeguard their independence and liberty.

THE FATE OF NATIONS

THE GOVERNMENT OF THE UNITED STATES made no official response to Ho Chi Minh's declaration of independence. Instead, with the other Allies, it continued to execute an ongoing plan for disarming Japanese garrisons throughout China and Southeast Asia. In Indochina, the plan called for the Nationalist Chinese forces of Chiang Kai-shek to disarm and temporarily occupy northern Vietnam while British forces of Lord Louis Mountbatten's South East Asia Command (SEAC) handled these tasks in the South. Both Allies marched into Vietnam even before Japan's official surrender.

In the North

Chiang sent some 200,000 Chinese troops into Vietnam north of the 16th parallel to accept the surrender of the Japanese occupiers there and to disarm them. Chiang's forces cooperated with the Viet Minh and even actively suppressed French overtures of reentry into Vietnam, going so far as to threaten war to prevent French reoccupation. Thanks to the Nationalist (that is, anti-Communist) army of Chiang Kai-shek, Ho Chi Minh was able to consolidate the Communist Viet Minh's hold on northern Vietnam.

At the end of World War II, Generalissimo Chiang Kai-shek, leader of China's anti-Communist Nationalists, acting at the behest of the Allies, occupied Vietnam north of the 16th parallel to accept the surrender of Japanese occupying troops.

Chiang Kai-shek knew that he would have his hands full contesting Mao Zedong and the Chinese Communist Party for control of China. Years earlier, when President Roosevelt suggested putting all of French Indochina permanently under Nationalist Chinese control in order to end French colonialism there, Chiang rejected the proposal with a single phrase: "Under no circumstances!" He was eager to evacuate the remaining Japanese, establish order, turn the country over to the Vietnamese, and return his troops to China, where they were needed in the ongoing struggle with Mao.

In the South

Circumstances were different in the South. Whereas Chiang used 200,000 troops to carry out his mission north of the 16th parallel, Mountbatten could afford to spare no more than a single division, the 20th Indian, under General Douglas D. Gracey. Mountbatten's chronically undermanned SEAC had responsibility for holding India, for disarming Burma, for reoccupying Malaya, and for temporarily holding the Dutch East Indies (today Indonesia). The hard-pressed Mountbatten allotted Gracey fewer than 10,000 troops to perform the mission the Chinese were doing with 200,000. At first, in fact, Gracey didn't even have anywhere near 10,000, since some three-quarters of the 20th Indian Division were still at sea when the general marched into Saigon, a city torn by riots among rival factions in a part of the country where the Viet Minh was weakest. Whereas the Chinese had enlisted the aid of the Vietnamese to enforce order, Gracey allowed some 4,000 Japanese soldiers to retain their weapons and help suppress the riots. With even greater consequence, he deployed a company of *French* commandos, which he greatly expanded on September 12, when he liberated and armed 1,400 French colonial troops who had been imprisoned by the Japanese.

The newly freed French troops, along with a band of liberated French civilians, cracked down on Vietnamese protestors with maximum violence. Gracey made no attempt to contain them but instead treated the "unruly" Vietnamese as lawbreakers. On September 21, pursuant to the British commander's declaration of martial law, the French troops were assigned to occupy Saigon's city hall, police headquarters, the treasury, and other colonial buildings—over all of which they raised the French tricolor. To make matters worse, British authorities in London designated a Frenchman to serve as "temporary high commissioner" in the South. He apparently took this as a signal of the Allies' ultimate intention to reinstall the prewar French colonial administration and issued official communiqués to this effect. Outraged, the Vietnamese refused to roll over. In Saigon, they staged a general strike and abducted French hostages, many of whom they killed.

FORGOTTEN FACES
Fallen Prophet

Lieutenant Colonel A. Peter Dewey, while leading a U.S. OSS team in Saigon, desperately tried to broker cooperation between the Viet Minh in Saigon and the British and French. Not only did both British and French authorities reject his overtures, General Douglas D. Gracey finally ordered him out of the city.

After warning Washington that Gracey was laying the foundation for the reestablishment of French colonial authority in Vietnam, Dewey added that "Cochinchina is burning, the French and British are finished here, and we ought to clear out of Southeast Asia." On September 26, en route to American headquarters near Tan Son Nhut, Dewey was assassinated by Vietnamese who, at this point, made no effort to distinguish one Westerner from another. Thus Dewey became the first American to warn against U.S. military involvement in Vietnam and also the first American to die in combat there. His name is not included on the Vietnam Veterans Memorial in Washington, D.C.

Before the end of September, at the invitation of SEAC and without objection from the United States, a French Expeditionary Corps landed in Vietnam. On October 5, General Jacques-Philippe Leclerc de Hauteclocque, one of the heroes of the French Resistance against Nazi occupation, arrived to command the troops. Four days later, pursuant to an agreement made between London and Paris, Gracey turned over southern Vietnam to the Expeditionary Corps, and the government of Great Britain formally recognized French sovereignty over *all* Vietnam. Immediately, the Expeditionary Corps fanned out from Saigon, fighting Viet Minh and other Vietnamese forces wherever they found them. To the alarm of the French, they discovered that many units consisted of a thousand or more very determined fighters.

The American Response

On April 12, 1945, Harry S. Truman had become president after the sudden death of FDR. He had been vice president for just eighty-two days, during which he met with the president only twice. Of the overwhelming volume of undiscussed problems that suddenly fell to Truman, French Indochina was not high on the list. What advice he received from the State Department was contradictory. The Far Eastern Bureau told him that the United States should get out of Southeast Asia and stay out. The European Bureau called for the United States to support the reentry of France into French Indochina as a means of helping that nation rebuild its self-respect.

To the limited extent that he had time to think about the region, Truman himself was torn. Like Roosevelt, he was at heart an anti-colonialist, but, as a veteran of the Western Front in World War I —he had captained a field artillery battery—Truman was both a Francophile and a Europeanist. What is more, he listened to Charles de Gaulle, who warned of the dangers of France's strong Communist party and suggested that the nation might go Communist if (among other things) France were prevented from reclaiming its Southeast Asian protectorates. Thus, in October 1945, in response to Leclerc's arrival in Saigon, President Truman unenthusiastically announced that the "U.S. has no thought of opposing the reestablishment of French control in Indochina." He went even further: "no official [U.S.] statement . . . has questioned even by implication French sovereignty over Indochina."

By recognizing (though hardly celebrating) "French sovereignty over Indochina," Truman, on behalf of the American government, effectively canceled out the temporary division between North and South as well as Ho Chi Minh's declaration of an independent Democratic Republic of Vietnam (DRV) and reaffirmed the existence of a single Indochinese entity under French sovereignty. Truman did go on to make clear that the United States had no intention to assist France in regaining control of its colony, but apparently the warning from the late Lieutenant Colonel Dewey (and other OSS operatives) to stay out of Vietnam never even reached the president's desk.

By the winter of 1945, France had 65,000 troops in Vietnam and was about to enter the North. Preparatory to this, on March 6, 1946, French envoy Jean Sainteny signed an agreement with Ho Chi Minh, who represented the DRV. It affirmed that, with the withdrawal of Chinese forces from the North, which was imminent, the French government would recognize "the Vietnamese Republic as a Free State having its own Parliament, its own Army and its own Finances." The DRV would be part of the Indochinese Federation and the French Union, with the North and the South to be reunited according to "decisions taken by the populations consulted by referendum." The Sainteny–Ho Chi Minh agreement stipulated that independence would be the final step in the evolution from the status of Free State; it was also a topic that would be "perfected" in some (vague and undefined) future agreement once a "favorable atmosphere" was attained. Ho Chi Minh was willing to accept a degree of gradualism, but he also recognized that France might require a push to "perfect" the agreement toward this end. He therefore wrote to President Truman requesting his support. Aware of Ho's Communist connections, Truman simply chose not to respond to this or any other of Ho's communiqués.

"DIRTY WAR"

PREDICTABLY, TALKS BETWEEN HO CHI MINH AND THE FRENCH soon stalemated, and, independently of Ho, Vo Nguyen Giap prepared the Viet Minh for war. On November 20, 1946, an argument over the collection of import duties at Haiphong exploded into intense urban combat. In December, the Viet Minh clashed with French forces in Hanoi. This was sufficient to rouse Ho Chi Minh to commitment to all-out war.

"**Those who have rifles will use their rifles; those who have swords will use their swords. Those who have no swords will use spades, hoes, or sticks.**"

★★★

—Ho Chi Minh, exhortation following the combat
with the French at Haiphong and Hanoi

This AP photo from January 28, 1947, shows a "French-Indochinese Union" machine gun crew on a Hanoi rooftop aiming their weapon toward the street below during the Indochina War. Note that the troops wear American-supplied uniforms, indicative of the early post–World War II U.S. support of the French reoccupation of Vietnam.

At first, the French scored one easy victory after another. Despite their defeats, the Viet Minh grew. Ho and Giap formulated a strategy founded on the experience of Mao Zedong during the long civil war in China. They would conduct a fighting retreat into the mountains of the North, from which they would launch sporadic guerrilla attacks aimed at wearing down the French forces. All the while, the DRV would build support and military strength. When critical mass had been reached, when they felt strong enough to do so, they would launch an all-encompassing counteroffensive aimed at retaking all the cities.

The result of this strategy was what the French called the "Dirty War." It was a description of a conflict that was not a succession of neatly conventional "set" battles but, rather, of guerrilla actions in which nothing strategic was ever gained or lost—but in which lives on both sides were certainly sacrificed.

As the bodies piled higher, France stopped negotiating with Ho Chi Minh, branding him as first and last a Communist—thereby seeking to preempt any possible U.S. sympathy, let alone support, for him. In an effort to placate the people of Vietnam and demonstrate to the world an absence of nakedly imperialist motives, France, on March 8, 1949, reinstalled Bao Dai as head of an ostensibly independent entity called the Associated State of Vietnam. Soon were added the similar Associated States of Cambodia and Laos, both under monarchs willing to be French puppets. Thereby French Indochina was reconstituted.

COLD WAR

WHILE FRANCE FOUGHT ITS DIRTY WAR in an obscure corner of Southeast Asia, the United States found itself more and more deeply engaged in a Cold War that was increasingly global in scale.

Back in 1823, President James Monroe issued what came to be called the "Monroe Doctrine," warning European powers that the United States would act aggressively to halt any new attempts to colonize the Americas. In 1947, as the Soviet Union refused to withdraw from Eastern European nations it had occupied during World War II, and as it supported the development of Communist regimes elsewhere in Europe and the rest of the world, President Truman promulgated the "Truman Doctrine." It warned the Soviet Union—when it actively backed a threatened Communist takeover of Greece and Turkey—that the United States would act to halt the spread of Communism wherever in the world it menaced democracy.

The Truman Doctrine was founded on the work of State Department official George F. Kennan (1904–2005), who suggested that the most effective way to combat Communism was to "contain" it by tirelessly confronting the Soviet Union (through economic and political means rather than military force, if at all possible) wherever and whenever it sought to expand its political influence. *Containment* was seen as an alternative, on the one hand, to doing nothing and, on the other, to fighting all-out and thereby igniting World War III, which might well escalate to the catastrophic use of nuclear weapons. The pursuit of containment therefore gave rise to the *Cold War*, conflicts that were certainly hostile but also limited in their "heat." Typically, these were conducted as *proxy wars*, conflicts between third-party countries or entities within these countries (such as Communists versus non-Communists in the Communist insurrec-

President Harry S. Truman delivers his "Truman Doctrine" address, March 12, 1947, putting the Soviet Union on notice that the United States would act to oppose Communist aggression wherever it threatened democratic governments.

tions in Greece and Turkey shortly after World War II). These were seen as ideological struggles between democracy (championed by the United States) and Communism (championed by the Soviet Union).

Truman's response to the Soviet blockade of West Berlin in 1948 was the celebrated Berlin Airlift, a spectacular chain of round-the-clock supply flights into West Berlin that broke the blockade without igniting a major war. In April 1949, airlift operations also prompted the creation of the North Atlantic Treaty Organization (NATO), a defensive alliance of the Western nations against the Communist East. Later that year, however, on October 1, 1949, after the Chinese Communist Party defeated the forces of Chiang Kai-shek's Nationalist Party, the world's most populous nation became the Communist-governed People's Republic of China. Aware that Communist factions were positioning themselves to take power elsewhere in Asia, President Truman, on

U.S. C-47 transports unload their cargo at West Berlin's Tempelhof Airport during the Berlin Airlift of 1948.

February 7, 1950, formally recognized the Associated State of Vietnam as constituted under the French puppet Bao Dai. No more than two weeks later, France, wallowing in its Dirty War, threatened to abandon Vietnam to the Communist Ho Chi Minh if the United States did not furnish the substantial economic and military aid it now demanded.

> **"Question whether Ho (Chi Minh) as much nationalist as Commie is irrelevant. All Stalinists in colonial areas are nationalists."**
>
> ✶✶✶
>
> —U.S. Secretary of State Dean Acheson, note to self, May 1949

Truman had earlier declared his firm intention to supply no such support; now, however, in the context of the Truman Doctrine and the policy of containment, he asked Congress for an immediate appropriation of $75 million. A few months later, on June 25, 1950, forces in another divided Asian nation descended out of Communist North Korea and swept into democratic South Korea. Even as this brought the United States into the first Cold War–era "hot war"—an intense, costly, and bitter conflict—President Truman increased aid to the French in Vietnam, immediately sending eight C-47 transport aircraft directly to Saigon, lest this divided nation also "fall" to the Communists.

HOT WAR

FLOWN INTO VIETNAM BY AMERICAN PILOTS, the eight cargo planes dispatched to Vietnam's southern capital constituted the first U.S. military airpower sent to the region. On August 3, 1950, the first contingent of U.S. military ground personnel—advisers of what was called the U.S. Military Assistance Advisory Group (MAAG)—arrived in Saigon. President Truman insisted that the U.S. military role be limited to supplying aircraft and matériel to the French and to working with French forces in an advisory capacity to improve their military capabilities. There was to be no combat role for American forces—except self-defense, if necessary—and there was no discussion of training, supplying, or otherwise aiding indigenous Vietnamese armed forces.

Having ascended to the presidency prior to ratification of the Twenty-second Amendment, which constitutionally limits chief executives to two terms, Harry Truman could have stood for reelection in 1952. He chose not to, however, and Dwight D. Eisenhower, former supreme Allied commander in the European theater of World War II, defeated Democrat Adlai E. Stevenson by a landslide. Truman prepared to pass both Korea and Vietnam to the new president. In Korea, containment was still containing the Communists, but Truman had given up on the goal of uniting the country under a pro-West democracy and was resigned to containing the Communists in the north of a divided nation. In Vietnam, prospects looked a bit brighter because the French appeared to be achieving some measurable degree of success against Ho Chi Minh—yet they were also steadily losing their stomach for the struggle, and support for the war was rapidly waning among the French people.

Among President Truman's final acts in office was to authorize the deployment to Vietnam of the first sizable contingent of U.S. Air Force personnel (other than those few already attached to MAAG): mostly ground crews to maintain U.S. military aircraft loaned or given to the French. They arrived in-country on January 4, 1953, sixteen days before Dwight D. Eisenhower was sworn in as the thirty-fourth president of the United States.

NUMBERS
Down Payment on the Vietnam War

By 1952, as the Korean War ground on (like France's Dirty War in Vietnam, stalemated), the United States found itself financing fully one-third of the French military effort.

TAKEAWAY
The Drift to War

By weakening France's hold on its colonial empire, World War II gave Ho Chi Minh an opening to lead "French" Indochina to independence but also into alignment with the Communist powers emerging in the postwar world. Torn between its traditional opposition to colonialism and its new opposition to Communism, the United States drifted into what had become a colonial, civil, and ideological struggle in Vietnam.

Retired five-star general and World War II Supreme Allied Commander, Europe (SACEUR) Dwight David Eisenhower campaigns in Baltimore for the presidency of the United States in 1952.

CHAPTER 4

PROPPING UP THE DOMINO

America Stakes Its Claim on Southeast Asia

WHEN DWIGHT D. EISENHOWER WAS INAUGURATED ON JANUARY 20, 1953, these four facts about the war in Vietnam were of greatest concern and consequence to the United States:

First, America was now financing more than 40 percent of the French war effort and was also supplying MAAG advisers, U.S. aircraft, and U.S. Air Force personnel to service the planes.

Second, the French people were tired of the war and increasingly opposed to it. Already, stevedores along the docks of Marseilles had gone on strike rather than load ships bound for French Indochina, and a large contingent of French army draftees had mutinied to avoid being shipped out to Vietnam. In response, the French National Assembly did not call for the prosecution of the mutineers but instead passed a law barring the use of conscripts in Indochina.

Third, Dwight D. Eisenhower disliked French colonial imperialism even more than Truman had.

Fourth, Eisenhower, who had come into office partly on a promise to end the war in Korea, feared "losing" Vietnam to the Communists far more than he disliked French imperialism.

THE MARCH TO DIEN BIEN PHU

IN APRIL 1953, THE VIET MINH mounted a major offensive in western Tonkin, crossing into Laos and menacing Thailand for the purpose of achieving two objectives. The first was to secure guerrilla bases in Laos as well as infiltration and supply routes into southern Vietnam via Laos. The second was to persuade the nearest significant power in the region, Thailand, that as long as the French remained in Vietnam, Thailand would be in danger of attack. Ho Chi Minh and Vo Nguyen Giap were determined to turn up the pressure on France to leave.

President Eisenhower ordered U.S. Air Force C-119 "Flying Boxcars" like this one to fly supplies to French troops in Vietnam. Regular military crews flew the aircraft from U.S. air bases in Japan to Nha Trang on the south-central Vietnamese coast. From here, civilian contract pilots and French air force pilots flew the planes to Cat Bi Airfield in the North. This allowed Ike to publicly claim that no U.S. military personnel were flying in combat zones.

The French did no such thing. Instead, military officials requested the loan of USAF C-119 transports to airlift heavy equipment into Laos. President Eisenhower wanted to comply, but he was wary of committing uniformed Air Force pilots to what was in effect a combat mission, flying cargo directly into a war zone. He therefore spun out the first filament in what would become an increasingly complex web of deception. The president ordered military crews to fly the C-119s to Nha Trang on the south-central coast of Vietnam, where American civilian contract pilots and French military pilots would take over for the final flight to Cat Bi Airfield near Haiphong in the North. In this way, Eisenhower could "honestly" deny the participation of U.S. military personnel in combat or combat supply operations.

A Change of Plan

The "Dirty War"—also called the First Indochina War, the French Indochina War, the Anti-French War, and several other names— had begun in December of 1946 (see pages 50–52). The first general in command, the World War II hero Jacques-Philippe Leclerc de Hauteclocque, quickly decided that the war in Southeast Asia was unwinnable, and he approved the proposal of Jean Sainteny, a World War II French resistance hero and son-in-law of two-time pre–World War II

Affairs of "Honor"

The French saying *Plus ça change, plus c'est la même chose* ("The more things change, the more they remain the same") rarely found a more apt application than to the war in Vietnam. What France's prime minister René Mayer called for in 1953—an "honorable political solution" to the Vietnam situation—is virtually identical to the "peace with honor" U.S. president Richard M. Nixon claimed to have achieved with the Paris Peace Accords (January 27, 1973) two decades later.

French prime minister Albert Sarraut, to negotiate with Vietnamese leaders. This prompted Admiral Georges Thierry d'Argenlieu to sputter that he was "amazed—yes, that is the word, amazed—that France's fine expeditionary corps in Indochina is commanded by officers who would rather negotiate than fight." And when the negotiations quickly broke down, Leclerc was replaced by a parade of new commanders— Jean-Étienne Valluy, Roger Blaizot, Marcel Carpentier, Jean de Lattre de Tassigny, and Raoul Salan—who in their turn came, saw, and were conquered. At last, in May 1953, General Henri Navarre, a not particularly distinguished veteran of the two world wars, arrived. He carried with him a plan, the "Navarre Plan," to bring the Dirty War to an end.

> ## "Anti-Communism will be a useless tool as long as the problem of nationalism remains unsolved."
>
> ★★★
>
> —General Jacques-Philippe Leclerc de Hauteclocque, in a report written in 1947 after his return to Paris from Vietnam

It was not exactly a plan for glorious victory, but French prime minister René Mayer, who appointed Navarre, had not asked him for victory, just for the "military conditions" that would lead to an "honorable political solution" to the situation in Vietnam. What the Navarre Plan offered was a way to hand off prosecution of the war from French soldiers to French-allied Vietnamese troops, so that even if France didn't exactly win, at least the war would end—so far as France was concerned. In the intensifying antiwar climate of France, Mayer regarded this as triumph enough.

Navarre believed that, up to now, the Viet Minh had fought the war on their terms, striking against the French whenever and wherever they wanted to. His plan was to compel the Vietnamese forces to fight an open, stand-up, all-or-nothing battle against French soldiers. Better equipped and better trained for such conventional combat, the French would defeat the bulk of the Vietnamese army, thereby so severely degrading it that it would be capable of prosecuting no more than a low-level guerrilla war. With the intensity of the combat thus reduced, the French military could bow out and turn over the entire affair to loyal Vietnamese forces, which, Navarre believed, would be quite capable of containing whatever remained of the Viet Minh.

Operation Castor

Navarre intended to provoke open battle by cutting off the enemy from the rear, severing the Viet Minh units in Vietnam from their Laotian supply lines and, simultaneously, cutting off the Viet Minh holed up in Laos. With their supply lines threatened and an entire force cut off, Navarre reasoned, the main contingent of the Viet Minh would have no choice but to try to break through with an all-in frontal attack against the French. Navarre was confident that, out in the open, they would be no match for French marines, soldiers, foreign legionnaires, artillery, and tanks.

To interdict the Laotian pipeline, Navarre proposed what he called a "hedgehog" operation, in which a heavily fortified, heavily armed fortress position would be established. When the Viet Minh made contact with it and tried to attack it, the "hedgehog" would throw its cruelly painful barbs.

> **"I would like to emphasize that . . . insofar as the free world is concerned, the French Union forces at Dien Bien Phu are fighting a modern Thermopylae."**
>
> ✴✴✴
>
> —U.S. Undersecretary of State Walter Bedell Smith, April 19, 1954

The point chosen to entrench the hedgehog was at Dien Bien Phu. The name translates roughly as "big frontier administrative center" and originally designated a World War II Japanese base and airstrip (now abandoned) in a remote northwestern valley that extended some eleven miles from north to south and about three miles wide at its widest. Here, Navarre decided to position twenty infantry and artillery battalions—some 10,800 men—under the field command of Colonel Christian de la Croix de Castries.

French Foreign Legion paratroops are dropped into Dien Bien Phu in November 1953, prior to the siege by North Vietnamese forces.

Except for Navarre himself, no one liked the plan. In fact, every one of Navarre's principal subordinates protested what they considered the idiocy of being deliberately used as bait, trapped in a remote location, cut off from all overland reinforcement, for the purpose of tempting an enemy attack. Navarre categorically rejected all criticism. He dubbed his plan "Operation Castor," which some military historians have translated into the English "beaver" but which Navarre intended as a reference to the mythological Gemini twin, Castor (his brother, Pollux, would lend his name to a subsequent French military operation), whose name in classical Greek does mean "beaver." It was launched at 10:35 on the morning of November 20, 1953, by parachuting or airlifting the first of the 9,000 French troops who would be inserted into the Dien Bien Phu region over the next three days. By the end of the month, the total planned strength of 10,800 had been established in the valley.

FORGOTTEN FACES
Christian Marie Ferdinand de la Croix de Castries

Born into an old and distinguished family of military officers on August 11, 1902, Christian Marie Ferdinand de la Croix de Castries was marked from the beginning for an army career. Enlisting in the ranks when he was only nineteen, he distinguished himself sufficiently to earn a coveted place in the elite cavalry school at Saumur from which he graduated in 1926 with a lieutenant's commission.

Shortly after Saumur, de Castries abruptly and surprisingly turned away from his military heritage to become a professional equestrian sportsman. He spent the rest of the 1920s and the 1930s in this pursuit but rejoined the army at the outbreak of World War II. With many others, he was captured by the Germans during the Battle of France in 1940, but unlike most of his fellow French POWs, he managed a daring escape and joined the Allies in North Africa. De Castries fought there, then in Sicily and mainland Italy, as well as the south of France. He was with the Allied armies that invaded southern Germany.

Promoted to lieutenant colonel, de Castries remained in the French army and was sent to French Indochina in 1946. Wounded in combat there, he returned to France for a prolonged hospitalization, received promotion to full colonel, and went back to Indochina. General Henri Navarre assigned him to command the garrison at Dien Bien Phu in December 1953, and, in the field, during the course of battle, he was promoted to brigadier general.

De Castries and his men endured a fifty-six-day siege by overwhelmingly superior Viet Minh forces, which finally overran Dien Bien Phu on May 7, 1954. De Castries formally surrendered the next day and was held as a prisoner of war for the next four months until an armistice was concluded in talks at Geneva. He retired from the French army in 1959 and died on July 29, 1991. The defeat of de Castries, an example of the very best and most gallant among the French officer corps, put a human face on the end of French hegemony over its Indochinese colony.

From left to right, General Henri Navarre, commander in chief of French forces in Indochina, General René Cogny, commander in chief of French forces in North Vietnam, and Colonel Christian de Castries, commander-in-chief of the Dien Bien Phu garrison, review an honor guard at Dien Bien Phu in February 1954.

Despite misgivings, the initial deployment had gone very well for the French. But now it was General Giap's turn.

Seeing that the French had men at Lai Chau, near the Chinese border, and at Dien Bien Phu, he quickly reasoned that, if attacked, the French would fall back from Lai Chau to throw everything into the defense of Dien Bien Phu. He then saw quite clearly through Navarre's plan to draw him into a frontal attack against the strongest French point. Giap's response, therefore, was a refusal to blunder into Navarre's "hedgehog."

Instead of attacking Dien Bien Phu directly, he launched diversionary attacks in Laos and against Lai Chau and vicinity. This forced some 16,000 potential reinforcements to divert from Dien Bien Phu to meet these attacks. Once the French had been diverted, Giap stealthily withdrew from all of the fronts and consolidated his forces in the hills surrounding the French valley fortress. In addition to massing his infantry—some 48,000 men—Giap formed a ring around Dien Bien Phu with some two hundred pieces of heavy artillery.

Ike's Anxiety

Navarre's French subordinates were not the only veteran military men worried about Operation Castor. U.S. military observers and Dwight Eisenhower, a career military strategist, were also becoming increasingly anxious as they took note that the Viet Minh were menacing Hanoi and Haiphong, areas from which Navarre had withdrawn forces to bolster Dien Bien Phu. They also began to hear reports of the Viet Minh massing around Dien Bien Phu itself.

The American president responded by authorizing an increase in U.S. military aid short of actually committing personnel to combat. World War II–vintage B-26 twin-engine medium bombers and RB-26 reconnaissance aircraft were immediately sent to Vietnam. The problem was not a shortage of aircraft, however, but a lack of French ground personnel. Reluctantly, therefore, on January 31, 1954, President Eisenhower ordered three hundred USAF airmen to Tourane and the Do Son Airfield near Haiphong in northern Vietnam. This contingent was the first substantial commitment of United States military personnel to the combat zone in what was now a hot war in Vietnam. The president downplayed what he had authorized, explaining in a press conference that he was just sending "some airplane mechanics . . . who would not get touched by combat." At best, this was a distortion; at worst, a lie. What was doubtless true, however, was the fervency of Eisenhower's hope that none of these men would in fact "get touched by combat."

Giap Strikes

On March 13, 1954, Giap's massed artillery opened fire, quickly cratering the two airstrips on which the defenders of Dien Bien Phu depended, rendering them unusable. Under cover of the barrage, Giap then closed in on the French valley fortress, steadily tightening the ring of infantry that encircled Dien Bien Phu, which, without its airstrips, could be supplied only by airdrop—food and equipment parachuted in at great risk.

Giap laid violent siege to the French garrison. The added American logistical support notwithstanding, it became apparent daily that the French situation was moving from dangerous to hopeless. Brigadier General (he had been promoted in the field) de Castries had set up seven advance strong points to defend the principal enclave at Dien Bien Phu, each outpost bearing a girl's name. (Some claimed he had named them after his mistresses, but unless de Castries's girlfriends happened to have names beginning with the first seven letters of the alphabet, this assertion was almost certainly baseless.) One by one, as the days passed and the fighting continued, each "girl" fell to the advancing Viet Minh siege.

As for the French counterfire from the vaunted "hedgehog"—the collection of artillery that was supposed to inflict such stunning pain—it proved so ineffective that Colonel Charles Piroth, commander of the French artillery batteries, committed suicide, leaving behind a note begging forgiveness for the "dishonor" his failure had brought upon his comrades and his country.

The Domino Theory

Sensing that the French were on the verge of surrender, the American president contemplated direct U.S. military intervention, principally in the form of air strikes against the Viet Minh. On April 7, he held a press conference in which he offered a rationale for fighting Communism in Vietnam. "You have a row of dominoes set up," he explained, "you

NUMBERS
Ike Doubles Down

President Eisenhower had authorized the massive sum of $385 million to help the French execute the "Navarre Plan,"of which he nevertheless disapproved as tactically unsound. Presumably, his hope was that an abundance of supplies and ammunition would allow the French to withstand the siege long enough to discourage Giap. Acting uncharacteristically like an increasingly desperate gambler, the American president responded to a long shot by doubling down on it.

knock over the first one, and what will happen to the last one is the certainty that it will go over very quickly."

The press corps, newspapers, radio, television, all took up this awkwardly phrased figure of speech. In this, the so-called domino theory was born, and it would loom through the end of the decade and into the next two as a rationale for continued and ever-deepening United States involvement in Vietnam.

From President Dwight D. Eisenhower's Press Conference of April 7, 1954

Robert Richards, Copley Press: Mr. President, would you mind commenting on the strategic importance of Indochina to the free world? I think there has been, across the country, some lack of understanding on just what it means to us.

The President: You have, of course, both the specific and the general when you talk about such things. First of all, you have the specific value of a locality in its production of materials that the world needs.

Then you have the possibility that many human beings pass under a dictatorship that is inimical to the free world.

Finally, you have broader considerations that might follow what you would call the "falling domino" principle. You have a row of dominoes set up, you knock over the first one, and what will happen to the last one is the certainty that it will go over very quickly. So you could have a beginning of a disintegration that would have the most profound influences.

Now, with respect to the first one, two of the items from this particular area that the world uses are tin and tungsten. They are very important. There are others, of course, the rubber plantations and so on.

Then with respect to more people passing under this domination, Asia, after all, has already lost some 450 million of its peoples to the Communist dictatorship, and we simply can't afford greater losses.

But when we come to the possible sequence of events, the loss of Indochina, of Burma, of Thailand, of the Peninsula, and Indonesia following, now you begin to talk about areas that not only multiply the disadvantages that you would suffer through loss of materials, sources of materials, but now you are talking really about millions and millions and millions of people.

Finally, the geographical position achieved thereby does many things. It turns the so-called island defensive chain of Japan, Formosa, of the Philippines and to the southward; it moves in to threaten Australia and New Zealand.

It takes away, in its economic aspects, that region that Japan must have as a trading area or Japan, in turn, will have only one place in the world to go—that is, toward the Communist areas in order to live.

So, the possible consequences of the loss are just incalculable to the free world.

More immediately, as the siege at Dien Bien Phu ground on, some U.S. military advisers even counseled using tactical (relatively low-yield) nuclear weapons. Maybe it was this suggestion that gave the president second thoughts about military intervention—though there were also plenty of other reasons for him to stay his hand. For one thing, the British refused to approve. For another, the French refused either to employ significant numbers of indigenous troops or to guarantee that they would ever grant Vietnam its independence. Finally, there was the U.S. Congress and the people of the United States. Having just extricated the nation from the shooting war in Korea, neither group wanted to commit to involvement in a new Asian war. And no one seriously believed that the involvement would be strictly limited to air attacks. The consensus was that once the flag had been "committed" in Vietnam by the introduction of air power, the use of land forces would follow—inevitably.

The Last Girls Fall

And so President Eisenhower, the government of the United States, the "Communist World," and the "Free World" watched as Vo Nguyen Giap led his forces to the most spectacular twentieth-century victory of any subject nation against a colonial power. On May 7, he made a breakthrough thrust with 25,000 of his Viet Minh. In rapid succession the three innermost strongpoints with girls' names were overrun.

Communist forces raise the Viet Minh flag over a hardened French position at Dien Bien Phu, on May 7, 1954. Colonel Christian de Castries formally surrendered on the following day. The defeat was a humiliation for French arms and imperial ambitions alike.

NUMBERS

Castor's Toll

At the formal surrender of
Dien Bien Phu on May 8,
1954, the Viet Minh tallied
11,721 prisoners, 4,436
of whom were wounded.
The siege had consumed
56 days.

"C'est fini."

★★★

—Major Jean Nicolas, commanding the garrison of "Isabelle,"
the last French outpost to fall at Dien Bien Phu, May 7, 1954

By five in the afternoon, only the southernmost outpost, Isabelle, remained in French hands, as did the central Dien Bien Phu position, manned by perhaps 3,000 Frenchmen. De Castries knew he could not hold out long and radioed General René Cogny, who was coordinating the execution of Operation Castor from his headquarters (HQ) in Hanoi. "The Viets are everywhere," de Castries said. "The situation is very grave. The combat is confused and goes on all about. I feel the end is approaching, but we will fight to the finish." Cogny, one of those who had warned in vain of the defects in Navarre's plan, responded calmly: "Of course you will fight to the end. It is out of the question to run up the white flag after your heroic resistance."

Before the sun set, de Castries's radio operator broadcast a final transmission. Viet Minh, he declared, were just outside the headquarters bunker. "The enemy has overrun us. We are blowing up everything. Vive la France!" Isabelle fell late that same night. Of the seventeen hundred men who held that position, only seventy evaded death or capture by making a successful run into Laos.

*French and colonial
Vietnamese POWs,
including the wounded,
march out of the Dien Bien
Phu area, July 28, 1954.*

THE GENEVA SOLUTION

MAY 8, 1954: DIEN BIEN PHU SURRENDERED, French prime minister Joseph Laniel appealed for a general ceasefire, and international talks on Indochina commenced in Geneva. These were planned and scheduled before Dien Bien Phu, at a time when the French had anticipated a decisive victory against the Viet Minh, which would put them in a powerful negotiating position when the talks began. That they started on the very day of French surrender came as a particularly cruel irony.

Observed through the lens of the Viet Minh's smashing victory over the very best the French had to offer—elite French marines, battle-hardened French army troops, and soldiers of the fabled French foreign legion all wielding the most advanced weapons American cash and industry could buy them—the outcome of the Geneva talks would seem a foregone conclusion. Simple common sense dictated that the Democratic Republic of Vietnam, or DRV, had unquestionably won its independence.

The problem was that, through some two thousand years of history, "simple common sense" had played virtually no role in the affairs of Vietnam. Moscow, Beijing, and Washington (which had already invested a total of $3 billion in the French bid to defeat Ho Chi Minh) each had a set of demands. Even Paris—the day after the total humiliation of Dien Bien Phu—wanted to retain a foothold in "French" Indochina. As for the DRV Geneva delegation, headed by Pham Van Dong, a longtime confidant of Ho Chi Minh, its aspirations also exceeded the bounds of common sense. Dong opened the talks by demanding international recognition of the independence—and unity—not just of the northern and southern Vietnam but of neighboring Laos and Cambodia as well. Toward this end, Dong called for the inclusion of Laotian and Cambodian Communist officials in the Geneva talks.

The American Position

To the Eisenhower administration, this opening gambit proved the validity of the "domino theory." The "loss" of Vietnam to Communism meant the subsequent probable "loss" of Laos and Cambodia, which, Eisenhower and his advisers argued, would knock over Thailand, Malaya, and Indonesia. Once these were within the Communist sphere, what of Japan, the Philippines—and even Australia?

REALITY CHECK

Heroic Stupidity

The French defeat at Dien Bien Phu is often cited as an example of the superiority of Vietnamese "guerrilla tactics" over Western "conventional tactics" in a jungle setting. This is an easy, convenient, and quite misleading oversimplification. General Vo Nguyen Giap defeated the French at Dien Bien Phu for three reasons. First, he saw through the Navarre Plan and exploited its weaknesses. Second, he deployed at least five times the number of French defenders; this was hardly a "guerrilla" force but, rather, a large, well-trained, well-equipped conventional army. Finally, the Navarre Plan and Operation Castor were so ill-conceived as to be doomed from the beginning. The Viet Minh success was not a guerrilla triumph but instead a victory of superior numbers, well led, over inferior numbers who had been positioned in a place incapable of prolonged defense. In short, Dien Bien Phu was the defeat of gallant stupidity by superior numbers, prudent planning, and skillful leadership.

REALITY CHECK
The Possibilities of Compromise

During much of the 1950s and well into the 1960s, the American politicians and public perceived the Communist countries as members of a single monolithic "bloc," committed to world domination. The willingness of the Soviet Union and China to compromise over Vietnam, even after the crushing Communist victory at Dien Bien Phu, is evidence that the position of the Communists was neither monolithic nor rigidly ideological. The death of Joseph Stalin in 1953 had ushered into the Kremlin a regime that hoped to improve relations with the West. Even the Chinese sought an end to their nation's isolation from the West. Both Russia and China needed to devote resources to improving their domestic economies, not to fighting wars. They had motives for good-faith negotiation. The least willing to embrace that good faith were the United States and, as it turned out, the leaders of what became North Vietnam and South Vietnam.

Indeed, President Eisenhower's secretary of state, the hard-line anti-Communist John Foster Dulles, took steps to ensure that the United States would play a role in the talks but would not be legally bound by any formal agreement reached. He took the United States to Geneva not as a "principal" in the negotiations but only as an "interested nation," and, as if that were not a sufficient demonstration of American contempt for the proceedings, Dulles pointedly refused to shake the hand of Chinese prime minister Zhou Enlai, the chief delegate of the People's Republic of China. Moreover, once the talks got under way, Washington contemplated options for intervening internationally so that the war would not end. In secret, U.S. military commanders met with their French counterparts to plan U.S. airstrikes in aid of a possible French reentry.

Reality and Compromise

Despite U.S. willingness to continue the war (and interest in this on the part of the French military), the rest of those involved at Geneva wanted a settlement. Great Britain, still economically crippled by the costs of World War II, had no desire to back a major conflict and therefore eagerly embraced its role as co-chair, with the Soviet Union, of the Geneva conference. In mid-June, French elections put a new prime minister into office, Pierre Mendès France, who was so committed to a peace settlement that he set July 20 as a deadline and solemnly pledged to step down if he failed to meet it.

If the United States wanted to prolong the war in Vietnam, it would have to do so alone and against the will of the world. Fortunately for the Americans, the major Communist powers, the Soviet Union and the People's Republic of China, were not nearly as unyielding as the DRV negotiators. Soviet and Chinese delegates readily approved a French proposal to compromise by *temporarily* dividing Vietnam into northern and southern halves, pending a referendum on unification under some form of independent government. In the North, the DRV would govern. In the South, Bao Dai's government would hold sway. As for Laos and Cambodia, these would remain separate from Vietnam, pending further negotiation and popular referendum.

That the Soviets, Chinese, British, and French were willing to compromise was a major advance. Now the problem was to sell the compromise—a "temporarily" divided Vietnam—to the DRV victors of Dien Bien Phu. They were predictably outraged by the notion. Yet they were, it turned out, also and always realists. Zhou Enlai explained to Ho Chi Minh and Vo Nguyen Giap that they would likely have to face the United States if the Geneva talks collapsed. The United States military, he reminded them, was not the French military. Zhou pressed further. He asked General Giap how long it would take him to defeat France if it remained in Vietnam, even if the United States did not actually fight in the war. Giap answered frankly: three to five more years. It would be longer, of course, if the Americans actually pitched in or even took over the war.

The conclusion, hard as it was to swallow, was inescapable: Tolerate the partition of Vietnam for the present. Build strength. Work toward unification from a position of strength. Ho Chi Minh accepted this familiar strategy of patient progress and set about persuading his followers.

"Accord" at Geneva

On July 21, 1954, the Geneva Accords were finalized. Vietnam would be divided along the 17th parallel. All French forces would withdraw south of this line and would serve to support the government of Bao Dai in South Vietnam. The Viet Minh, never strong or numerous in the South, would withdraw entirely north of the 17th parallel and would support the government of the DRV. A strict peace would be observed between North and South.

The Geneva Accords specified the reunification of the divided country by a national popular referendum to be conducted in 1956. In an effort to enforce the strictly temporary status of the north-south division, the Accords called the two halves of the country "regroupment zones" rather than "territories" and specifically denied that the 17th parallel was a "political or territorial boundary." Moreover, the Accords barred both the North and the South from entering into any international alliances or admitting any outside power to establish military bases or bring military equipment into either zone.

DOUBLING DOWN

TRUE TO ITS SELF-PROCLAIMED "INTERESTED COUNTRY" status at Geneva, the United States declined to sign the Geneva Accords, but State Department officials pledged that the United States would not "disturb" the

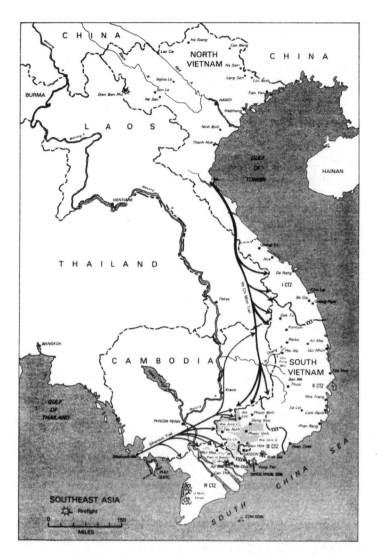

North and South Vietnam, as specified in the Geneva Accords, divided along the 17th parallel, and its regional neighbors. Note the prominence of the Ho Chi Minh Trail through Laos and Cambodia, the main line of Communist infiltration and supply into the South.

agreement by force or by threat of force. Although the American far right bewailed yet another "loss" to the Communists—first China, then North Korea, now North Vietnam—President Eisenhower's secretary of state, John Foster Dulles, counseled his fellow anti-Communists "not to mourn the past but to seize the future opportunity to prevent the loss of northern Vietnam from leading to the extension of Communism throughout Southeast Asia and the Southwest Pacific."

In effect, Dulles sought to define the outcome of Geneva not as the loss of half of Vietnam but as a victory in the struggle to "contain" Communism by keeping it out of the southern half. Even more important, he saw it as a reason to "double down," as it were, in Southeast Asia: to respond to an apparent loss by raising the stakes. He therefore led the effort to create in Southeast Asia a counterpart to Europe's NATO. It would be called the Southeast Asia Treaty Organization (SEATO), which would consist of the United States, Great Britain, France, Australia, New Zealand, Thailand, the Philippines, and Pakistan, all proclaiming their joint opposition to Communist aggression. That joint opposition, however, was more theoretical than actual; for, unlike the NATO compact, SEATO was strictly a paper agreement. There was no standing military commitment to a SEATO force. There was no actual deterrent. And that was not the only weakness of SEATO. Neither India nor Indonesia nor any other "unaligned" (neither pro-West nor pro-Communist) Asian country had signed on to SEATO. As for Laos, Cambodia, and southern Vietnam, the Geneva Accords barred their entering into any alliance, so they didn't sign, either. Overwhelmingly, then, SEATO was a Western alliance, which made it seem less like an Asian self-defense league than a Western imperialist political organ.

But the Eisenhower administration did not rely solely on SEATO to stem the tide of Communist expansion in Southeast Asia. In accordance with the terms of the Geneva Accords calling for the removal of outside military personnel, the U.S. Air Force evacuated its personnel from Vietnam and assisted in the medical evacuation of wounded French troops and prisoners released by the Viet Minh. Even as it pulled these men out, the United States proposed adding to the Military Assistance Advisory Group (MAAG) staff in Saigon. When the international commission charged with enforcing the Geneva armistice disapproved this buildup, the United States redesignated 350 advisers as a "Temporary Equipment Recovery Mission" and publicly assigned them to inventory and remove surplus equipment. In this guise, the commissioners approved their presence, whereupon they were quietly assigned to MAAG, first as logistical advisers and then, in open defiance of the international commission, as MAAG's Combat Arms Training and Organization Division.

MAAG was being reoriented to do what the French had consistently refused to do: build, train, and ultimately equip an indigenous pro-Western South Vietnamese army. The French, offended by the high-handed manner in which the United States seemed determined to displace them as the dominant Western power in Southeast Asia, began indignantly pulling their army out. Far from being a problem for the United States, the Eisenhower administration saw this as a positive development because it removed the last taint of colonialism from the Vietnam situation. The U.S. mission was being realigned as a force to build South Vietnam into a pro-Western bastion in Southeast Asia. No longer would critics both inside and outside the United States be able to claim that the sweet land of liberty was defending colonial oppression. Now, clearly, the United States would be seen as supporting the "self-determination" of a people who wanted to be "free" and independent rather than "Communist" and beholden to a Communist "bloc." With the

French withdrawing, MAAG would be the nucleus from which the American role in building South Vietnam would expand.

A TALE OF TWO COUNTRIES

WHILE HO CHI MINH PLACED HIS FAITH IN THE OUTCOME of the upcoming reunification referendum, the United States set about helping South Vietnam build for itself precisely what the Geneva Accords expressly forbade: an identity as a separate, sovereign nation.

It would not be easy.

Peace between North and South was tenuous and hostility plentiful. On the face of it, the DRV in the North had the much harder situation. Always the poorer, less fertile half of Vietnam, it was reeling economically under the devastating effects of warfare that had disrupted rice production along the Red River Delta. Before the Geneva Accords, the North made up its food shortfalls with rice from the South. Now Saigon called a halt to all trade with the North. As famine loomed, so did fear of Communism among the nonpeasant classes— the urban professionals, the businessmen, the Catholic minority. They began to flee southward across the 17th parallel. The outflow of some of the North's best-educated, wealthiest, and most productive citizens weakened an economy already in critical condition, greatly reducing the already-modest industrial production of a mostly agricultural region.

The DRV government made a show of moderation in an effort to calm anti-Communist fears. There would be respect for private property, leaders promised, and absolute freedom of religion. Yet even as these reassurances issued from Hanoi, radical officials in the field took matters into their own hands, forcing land reform not merely by expropriating property but also by executing landlords and anyone else who protested, resisted, or seemed capable of protest or resistance.

Despite the hunger, the want, the turmoil, and the terror in the North, the charismatic appeal of Ho Chi Minh remained strong. The focus of a cult of personality, he personified age-old Vietnamese aspirations to nationalism. The unity of the beleaguered North only increased. The departure of the middle class and the Catholics came at great economic cost, yet it also purged the region of an inherently dissident element. The land reform, though terribly violent, did put

NUMBERS

Communist Crackdown

In a reign of terror between 1954 and 1956, radical Communist land reformers in North Vietnam rounded up and executed at least fifteen thousand people, many of whom were loyal supporters of the Viet Minh.

land in the hands of more than half the families of the North, people who had never before had land to work and who now had land and a commitment to the forces that had given it to them.

Life was more comfortable in the South, but, by contrast, it lacked any semblance of political stability—let alone allegiance to any one leader. Emperor Bao Dai was unpopular. Warlords belonging to religious sects dominated the Mekong Delta, and an organized crime syndicate held sway over Saigon. Before they departed, the French army was still politically powerful on a day-to-day basis. And not *all* of the Viet Minh had left the South in obedience to the Geneva Accords.

Authority was severely fragmented in the South, which lacked the sense of national identity and unity that prevailed in the North. If the United States were to convert this chaos into a country, and a pro-Western democracy at that, a single viable leader—one who was anti-Communist, receptive to direction from the United States, competent, and reasonably popular—had to be found. The United States chose Ngo Dinh Diem.

OUR MAN IN VIETNAM

AS A LEADER, NGO DINH DIEM HAD FAR MORE LIABILITIES than assets—but those assets, few though they were, greatly appealed to the diplomats in the Eisenhower administration, who, in June 1954, backed his appointment as Emperor Bao Dai's prime minister. He was the son of an imperial Vietnamese official who had been removed from office because he was an anti-colonialist. Like his father, Diem was a nationalist, an enemy of French colonial rule, but he opposed Communism as vehemently as he opposed the French. To the Americans, this combination of traits gave him a most appealing pedigree. Add to this his devout Catholicism. It was a major drawback in overwhelmingly Buddhist Vietnam, but Diem's religion was a strong draw for American policy makers, who saw Christianity as the natural and implacable foe of Communism. A Catholic backslide into the camp of Ho and Mao? Never!

As for the liabilities, they were legion. Diem had spent most of his career as a mandarin in the Vietnamese colonial bureaucracy. He earned a modest reputation as a nationalist and an anti-Communist, but when his profile became sufficiently high to merit real attention, he fled Vietnam in 1950 to escape assassination by agents of Ho Chi Minh.

During his self-imposed exile, Diem attempted to win political support from General Douglas MacArthur, at the time head of the U.S. military occupation government in Japan, but could not even win a meeting with him. He did, however, meet with a Michigan State University political scientist named Wesley Fishel, who saw in Diem the kind of anti-colonial, anti-Communist package that some American diplomats were describing as the "third force." So far, Southeast Asia had seen an anti-colonial but pro-Communist force and an anti-Communist but pro-colonial force. What the United States looked for was nationalist leadership that was also pro-democracy instead of pro-Communist—the *third* force.

Fishel made connections that introduced Diem to officials in the State Department. To this was added a meeting with the politically powerful American Catholic cleric Francis Cardinal Spellman. At last, in 1951, Diem cadged an audience with Secretary of State Dean Acheson, then, at Cardinal Spellman's invitation, took up residence at Maryknoll Seminary in Lakewood, New Jersey. Here he remained for the next three years, garnering, with Spellman's help, support from anti-Communist Catholic groups and lecturing at East Coast universities on the subject of how the United States was the only power capable of "saving" Vietnam from Communist domination. In the meantime, Fishel obtained for Diem an appointment as consultant to the Government Research Bureau of Michigan State University, which ran a number of U.S. government–sponsored international "assistance programs." Diem and Fishel created the Michigan State University Vietnam Advisory Group.

Diem was on the rise, but that rise was not taking place in Vietnam. Absent from the country, he did not build a grassroots following or, for that matter, any particular loyalty at all. After Dien Bien Phu, however, Bao Dai, who was desperate for a source of foreign support, took notice of Diem's American rise. He quickly named Diem's youngest brother, Ngo Dinh Luyen, to the Geneva Conference delegation. The Eisenhower administration in turn interpreted this as a signal of Bao Dai's receptivity, and the administration backed Ngo Dinh Diem to become Bao Dai's prime minister.

The French, among others, were appalled. Those who had known Diem as a functionary in the colonial government considered him incompetent, and French prime minister Mendès France pronounced him a "fanatic." When he landed at Tan Son Nhut airport outside of Saigon on June 26, 1954, only a small knot of Catholic supporters turned out to greet him.

"Diem impresses one as a mystic who has just emerged from a religious retreat into the cold world."

✸✸✸

—C. Douglas Dillon, U.S. ambassador to France, commenting on Ngo Dinh Diem's appointment as prime minister in the government of Bao Dai

America's ambassador to France, C. Douglas Dillon, warned that if Diem *seemed* an acceptable leader it was "only because the standard set by his predecessors is so low." Even President Eisenhower had second thoughts and pondered dropping support in 1955. But then it became apparent that Diem's appointment had an unexpected bonus. The exodus from North to South, something of a flood before his appointment, became a tsunami after it, due to a dramatic increase in Catholic migration. Some 60 percent of Catholics who had been living in the North crossed into the South within the space of a few months. This not only gave Diem the base of local support he had sorely lacked but it also augmented what was already a compelling propaganda bonanza for the "free world" and its champion, the United States.

An Election Rigged and an Election That Never Was

The influx of refugees was so impressive in the months following Diem's appointment as prime minister that American officials became hopeful that their Catholic candidate might just attract sufficient support to actually win the reunification elections in 1956. To increase the likelihood of this outcome, U.S. colonel Edward G. Lansdale organized a flotilla of ships to expedite the North Vietnamese exodus, dubbing the operation "Passage to Freedom." Lansdale also directed a team of CIA agents in an infiltration north of the 17th parallel, where they committed acts of sabotage such as contaminating precious fuel supplies and wrecking printing presses. They also disseminated "disinformation," including rumors of imminent Chinese invasion and (to increase the already overwhelming Catholic exodus) rumors of an impending anti-Catholic purge.

North Vietnamese refugees are transferred from a French landing ship to the USS Montague *at Haiphong in August 1954. Bound for the South, the* Montague *was part of a refugee flotilla organized by U.S. Army colonel Edward G. Lansdale as part of an operation he dubbed "Passage to Freedom."*

While American officials worked vigorously to prop Diem up, the new prime minister suddenly showed himself surprisingly capable of strong action on his own. Using his U.S.-equipped army, he cracked down on the criminal gangs that ran Saigon, pushing the worst of them out of the city—a feat that won him genuine popular gratitude and support. Next, he managed either to co-opt or forcefully suppress the religious sects whose leaders functioned as local warlords throughout the Mekong Delta.

Doubtless emboldened by his own success in these measures, Diem moved against his own titular boss, the Emperor Bao Dai. With American backing and encouragement, Diem proposed transforming South Vietnam into a democratic republic. Announcing his conviction that a majority of the people supported both the idea of a republic and himself as its president, Diem called a national referendum.

Naturally, the 1955 referendum was rigged. Everyone, including the Americans, had expected that. The *degree* to which it was rigged, however, was stunning. Greeted upon his entrance into Vietnam just a year earlier by a meager handful of Catholics, Diem managed to "secure" both the establishment of a republic and his own election by a majority of 98.2 percent of the ballots cast. Meekly abdicating, Bao Dai (his throne name meant "Keeper of Greatness") left Vietnam and lived out the rest of his eighty-four years in Paris.

The removal of Bao Dai eliminated one obstacle to Diem's rise to power. Another, far more formidable, still loomed: the upcoming referendum of 1956. As it became all too apparent that there were not enough Catholics in Vietnam to ensure that Diem would win over Ho Chi Minh and thereby unify Vietnam under a non-Communist government, the Eisenhower administration pondered how to evade the referendum without hypocritically betraying the democratic principles on which the United States was founded and stood.

It was a seemingly insoluble dilemma, which Diem solved very easily. He refused to talk to the North about how the vote would be conducted. When Hanoi protested to officials in Great Britain and the Soviet Union charged with enforcing the Geneva Accords, they declined to support the protest. The United States had quietly indicated its lack of support for the referendum, and one thing the United Kingdom and USSR had in common was a mutual desire not to unnecessarily offend the United States.

Once he was certain that Hanoi had no international support, Diem simply canceled the referendum in his country, noting that South Vietnam had never signed the Geneva Accords (but failing to note that there been no "South Vietnam" to sign them). Having rigged an election to create a republic and make himself its president, Diem now offered a further justification for canceling the referendum. Such "elections," he declared, would be "meaningful only on the condition that they are absolutely free"—an impossible condition under Ho Chi Minh's dictatorship. Thus came into being the Republic of Vietnam, creature, ally, and political hope of the United States of America.

NUMBERS
It Just Didn't Compute

In 1955 in Saigon, 605,025 ballots were cast in favor of creating a republic and of electing Diem its president. In 1955 in Saigon, the total number of registered voters was 450,000.

TAKEAWAY
Liberation, Division

The smashing Viet Minh victory at Dien Bien Phu effectively drove France out of Indochina but failed to result in the creation of an independent Vietnam under the leadership of Ho Chi Minh. Instead, the major powers of the world agreed to "temporarily" divide Vietnam between Ho Chi Minh in the North and the pro-Western emperor Bao Dai in the South, pending a reunification referendum. The United States, seeking to prevent the "loss" of another Asian state to Communism, supported the creation of an anti-Communist bastion in South Vietnam under the leadership of the problematic but highly compliant anti-Communist nationalist Ngo Dinh Diem.

PART TWO

INSURGENCY

CHAPTER 5

THE TORCH IS PASSED

From "Miracle" to "Twilight Struggle"

I N 1954, GETTING THE UNITED STATES INVOLVED IN VIETNAM was a hard sell for the Eisenhower administration. Both Congress and the American people were skeptical at best. Throughout much of 1955, Ngo Dinh Diem didn't make the selling any easier. Unpopular and unprepossessing, he seemed a very slim reed on which to hang the hope of democracy in Southeast Asia.

But as 1955 became 1956 and marched toward 1957, Diem appeared to be turning South Vietnam around. Saigon was being cleansed of organized crime, and the religiously oriented warlords of the Mekong Delta provinces had either been subordinated to the Saigon government or quietly eliminated. Thanks to an influx of American cash, the South Vietnamese economy was doing reasonably well—far better, certainly, than the semi-starvation that characterized the North. Politicians and the press alike were portraying the contrast between South and North Vietnam much as they portrayed the contrast between the rest of the "free world" and the "Communist bloc." There was West Berlin, prosperous and irrepressible, and there was East Berlin, in shades of unrelieved gray, still half buried in the bombed-out ruins of the world war, and hungry, always hungry. There was entrepreneurial Saigon, a city of freedom, and there was primitive Hanoi, marching in grim lockstep to the cadence of Ho, Mao, and the Kremlin.

Life magazine came out with a portrait piece on Diem headlined "The Tough Miracle Man of Vietnam," and any number of politicians were pointing to what they called the "Vietnam miracle." When President Eisenhower invited Diem for a state visit to Washington, he welcomed him in May 1957 with a speech lauding him as "an example for people everywhere who hate tyranny and love freedom." Even the young Democratic senator from Massachusetts, John F. Kennedy, called South Vietnam the "cornerstone of the Free World in Southeast Asia, the keystone to the arch, the finger in the dike."

President Eisenhower (left) and his secretary of state, John Foster Dulles (standing next to him), welcome South Vietnam's president Ngo Dinh Diem, who has arrived at National Airport, Washington, D.C., on a 1957 state visit.

SENSE AND SUBSTANCE

THERE WAS SUBSTANTIAL TRUTH IN THE AMERICAN PERCEPTION of South Vietnam. In Saigon, business was good—and, at long last, free from criminal extortion. In the countryside, the farms were producing at a comfortable subsistence level and beyond. The Diem government was far from pure by American standards. For one thing, "President" Diem was really Dictator Diem, and he wasted no time in putting members of his family, especially his brother Ngo Dinh Nhu, into every key position. Yet Americans could well believe that the alternative to dictatorship and nepotism was chaos. If Diem was a dictator, at least he wasn't a *Communist* dictator—and maybe a new nation needed a bit of dictatorship to give it the stability necessary for the arduous trek toward eventual democracy.

The bottom line seemed to be that, by any visible measure, the people of South Vietnam lived better than the people of North Vietnam. And in 1957, the year after Hungary had struggled hopefully but in vain to escape from behind the Iron Curtain, the year in which (on October 4) the Union of Soviet *Socialist* Republics would beat the *democratic* United States into space with *Sputnik I*, Americans craved whatever evidence they could point to demonstrating the superiority of capitalist democracy over Marxist totalitarianism and predicting the ultimate triumph of the "free world" over that of the "Soviet bloc." What made the stakes in South

PREVIOUS PAGES: Army of the Republic of Vietnam (ARVN) troops off-load from an American-supplied H-21 helicopter about twenty miles north of Saigon, April 17, 1963.

DETAILS, DETAILS

"One Small Ball in the Air"

On October 4, 1957, TASS, the Soviet news agency, announced: "As a result of great, intense work of scientific institutes and design bureaus the first artificial earth satellite has been built." It was called *Sputnik 1*, and by the time it burned up in Earth's atmosphere on January 4, 1958, it had made 1,440 orbits, transmitting a simple beep-beep-beep signal that could be heard on radios everywhere on Earth. It was a 23-inch-diameter ball, weighing 184 pounds, from which four antennas projected. Eisenhower tried to dismiss it as "one small ball in the air," but Americans—and those in the "free" and "Communist" worlds— were well aware that the United States had yet to loft a similar "ball" and had had one failure after another in even launching a rocket beyond Earth's atmosphere.

Vietnam so high was the rapid pace at which the post–World War II planet was decolonizing. Independence was sweeping across Asia and Africa—both above and below the Sahara—and each new state seemed a fruit ripe for whichever ideological camp had sufficiently long reach to pluck it. Experience had already shown that once a people fell under the domination of the Soviets or the Chinese, everything they saw and heard of the world was filtered, stage managed, or wholly manufactured by some politburo. It was important, therefore, to demonstrate the benefits of democratic capitalism wherever possible and to do so before another country fell into the all-controlling, all-consuming Communist grip.

The nations the United States perceived as being in play were those of the so-called Third World—states officially aligned with neither the Communist bloc nor the Western democracies. American policy makers believed that success in places like South Vietnam would help win these over. But capitalist democracies like the United States came into the game with a strike already against them. Most of the states of the Third World had recently emerged—or were still emerging—from the exploitive colonial grip of other capitalist democracies. The advocates of Marxism had no such record and promised something new.

The Making of a Client State

So the United States tried very hard in South Vietnam. Initially, the main thrust was not military but an implementation in Southeast Asia of what had worked so well in Europe—a kind of Marshall Plan approach in which the United States showered South Vietnam with the bounty of capitalism, including economic aid and all the benefits of America's experience of modern civilization. During the 1950s, American civilian technical specialists and experts far outnumbered the U.S. military mission in Vietnam. Washington's Saigon-based diplomatic corps rapidly grew into the largest in the world, dwarfing all other U.S. embassies and consulates, and the investment in U.S. aid exploded, so that by the second half of the 1950s, South Vietnam, just half of what had been a small nation to begin with, was the fifth largest recipient of American foreign aid.

The Marshall Plan was a rational model for creating a pro-Western bastion in Southeast Asia and a showcase for the benefits of free-market

Successfully orbited on October 4, 1957, the **Sputnik I** *satellite was a triumph for the Soviet Union and a bitter Cold War humiliation for the United States.*

democracy. The trouble was that South Vietnam was not Europe and was not, really, even a country. Ruled by a dictator and his family, it was at best a political fragment with aspirations to statehood. Everyone, from Diem on down, tended to use the American bounty they were given not to build a prosperous and enduring democratic nation but to acquire the trappings of such a nation. The aid money was spent lavishly on consumer goods, everything from refrigerators and washing machines to mopeds and stylish Western clothes, not on the creation of sustainable enterprises and industries. The thinking was strictly short term, and the results, though impressive because they were highly visible, were superficial and hollow. The sense created was of a prosperous nation on the rise. The substance was ephemeral, the whiff of middle-class prosperity in a geopolitical entity that produced little, exported virtually nothing, and therefore relied entirely on U.S. aid to finance all that it now enjoyed.

ARVN

When Diem refused to conduct the reunification referendum mandated by the Geneva Accords, Eisenhower administration officials gritted and braced for what they feared would be an inevitable Korea-style invasion from the North. When this failed to materialize, the president and his advisers were grateful for having dodged a bullet but were determined

The United States supplied military equipment as well as training to help the French create a loyal Vietnamese army to oppose the Viet Minh. This photograph, from June 1954, shows a class of Vietnamese army officers learning to operate a .50-caliber machine gun.

DETAILS, DETAILS
A Contraction Is Coined

Beginning about 1956, the Saigon press began using the terms *Viet Nam Cong san* ("Vietnamese Communist") and *Viet gian cong san* ("Communist traitor to Vietnam"). The first was a more or less neutral term for a Vietnamese Communist, whereas the second was a derisive term for a specifically *South* Vietnamese Communist. Within short order, both terms were conflated as well as contracted to *Viet Cong*, to describe Communist guerrilla insurgents in and from South Vietnam. Intended to be pejorative, the designation was adopted by the Viet Cong themselves.

not to rely on good fortune indefinitely. President Eisenhower decided to commit the United States to a sustained and serious military advisory role with the aim of achieving what the French had consistently refused even to attempt: to build an effective, independent, wholly indigenous South Vietnamese military—the Army of the Republic of Vietnam (ARVN). In the run-up to the Korean War, the Truman administration, fearful of provoking the Chinese and Soviets into a major war, had trained and equipped a limited defensive army for Syngman Rhee's South Korea. The Eisenhower administration, in contrast, was anxious to build a large and credible ARVN equipped with the latest U.S. weapons and provided with state-of-the-art training centers and operational bases.

What no amount of weapons and no degree of training could make up for was the low quality of leadership within the ARVN and, consequently, the chronically depressed morale in the ranks. Diem wanted a powerful military, but he also feared it. He therefore appointed top commanders on the basis of their demonstrated loyalty to him, not their demonstrated skill as military leaders. Among the reasons for the loyalty of the high-ranking ARVN officers was Diem's willingness to turn a blind eye toward their exuberant corruption, black marketeering, graft, and general abuse of power.

Viet Cong

Well equipped and handsomely uniformed, the ARVN was nonetheless hollow at the core, and so it was not surprising that the North Vietnamese insurgency into the South increased during the closing years of the 1950s.

In September 1959, a new military insurgency surfaced in the South. It was not an infiltration from the North but a grassroots *southern* Communist movement. Officially, it was known as the Liberation Army of South Vietnam, or the National Liberation Front for South Vietnam, but became best known as the Viet Cong.

The Viet Cong was primarily a Communist guerrilla insurgency indigenous to South Vietnam, although it seems also to have absorbed elements of the Viet Minh—both those who had been operating in the South as well as those from the North. Indeed, throughout the war, the relationship between the Viet Cong and the regular army of North Vietnam, what Hanoi called the People's Army of Vietnam (and the U.S. designated the North Vietnamese Army), was often controversial, confusing, and confused. The precise relationship between the Viet Cong and the government in Hanoi was equally unclear. Saigon and Washington denounced it as a "dirty" front for Hanoi, illegally operating in South Vietnam. The official history of the Vietnam War, written by the victors years after the war, defines it as a part of the People's Army of Vietnam. Whatever one chose to call it or however one chose to define it, the Viet Cong, in September 1959, ambushed two ARVN companies in the Plain of Reeds just southwest of Saigon. This was not so much the start of a guerrilla war in South Vietnam as it was an attack bold enough to force Saigon and Washington to acknowledge that such a war was already well under way.

Determined to put some spine into the ARVN, President Eisenhower, in the last year of his second term, authorized an expansion of the MAAG to 685 advisers, including newly created U.S. Special Forces teams, who were assigned to create and train elite Vietnamese ranger battalions. The hope was that these rangers would be better able not only to defend against guerrillas but also, as an elite organization, to create pride throughout the ARVN ranks, raise morale, and attract a better class of officer.

SHOCKS TO THE SYSTEM

THE VIET CONG AMBUSH OF SEPTEMBER 1959 deeply disturbed the Eisenhower administration, prompting stepped-up military aid, but it was an even greater shock to Diem. Back in 1955, he had moved very vigorously against the Viet Minh in South Vietnam, rooting out these insurgents and would-be insurgents in a campaign conducted under the slogan "Denounce the Communists." With the tacit approval—or at least noninterference—of the United States, Diem sent ARVN and police units on sweeps throughout the countryside, eventually rounding up some 25,000 known and suspected "subversives." They were sent to "detention camps," from which many never returned. Torture for purposes of interrogation as well as punishment was universally applied, and executions were numerous and mostly unrecorded.

These repressive measures were highly effective, at least in the short term. The Viet Minh was all but wiped out below the 17th parallel. The Democratic Republic of Vietnam (DRV) itself estimated that nine in ten

Le Duan, a founding member of the Indochinese Communist Party in 1930 and an aggressive North Vietnamese Communist leader, rejected "peaceful coexistence" with the democratic West and called for a showdown war with the United States in his 1956 essay, "The Road to the South." He is pictured here in 1967, when he served as the first secretary of the North Vietnam Labor Party.

of its operatives in the South were captured or killed between 1955 and 1958. This was sufficient to frighten would-be Communist supporters in the South—those who had been aiding and succoring the Viet Minh—enough to stop their activities.

Why was Diem so successful in neutralizing the indigenous insurgency during 1955–58? There were at least two reasons. First, he was ruthless. Second, Hanoi left the Viet Minh cadres in South Vietnam pretty much to their own fate. The Hanoi government was determined to pursue the plan Ho Chi Minh had laid out. The first step was to finish building a Communist government in North Vietnam before embarking on the unification of North and South under Communism. This meant avoiding war, not provoking it. Not only was this Ho's position but it was that of the Soviet Union as well. Under Premier Nikita Khrushchev—compared to Stalin, a moderate—the Soviet Union pursued a policy of "peaceful coexistence" with the West. It wanted no war.

Yet neither Ho Chi Minh's policy nor the stated wishes of Moscow could prevent Hanoi from hearing the anguished appeals for aid from southern Communists. Could Hanoi let its faithful comrades suffer and die? Even more important, could Hanoi afford to completely lose the Communist Party presence south of the 17th parallel?

Enter Le Duan. A founding member of the Indochinese Communist Party in 1930, he went on to create the Viet Minh organization in South Vietnam and, in 1956, wrote an essay, "The Road to the South," which not only rejected "peaceful coexistence" but also actively called for war with the United States, if that is what it took to achieve reunification of North and South Vietnam under a Communist government. Later that year, in response to the essay, Hanoi declared that reunification was indeed important but that it was for the present a political rather than a military goal. Nevertheless, Hanoi officials did approve a policy of armed self-defense for their southern comrades. Despite severe losses in 1956, small groups of southern-based Viet Minh fighters staged hit-and-run raids against provincial government outposts and, rallying under the slogan "Death to Traitors," targeted for assassination whatever officials of the Diem government they could gain access to.

The Ho Chi Minh Trail

Its name made it sound primitive, like something out of the frontier American West, but the so-called Ho Chi Minh Trail (that was the American name for it) was a sophisticated complex of networked truck roads, river routes, and bicycle/foot paths running from North Vietnam into South Vietnam via the jungles of Laos and Cambodia. The North Vietnamese called it the Truong Son Strategic Supply Route, naming it after the mountain range in central Vietnam.

This network of infiltration, exfiltration, and supply was a masterpiece of logistical engineering—in the estimation of the U.S. National Security Agency, "One of the great achievements of military engineering of the 20th century." It was elaborated from ancient footpaths long used for village-to-village trade, and, at the height of its development, it ran through forbidding mountains, dense rain forests, and triple-canopy jungles. It came under Hanoi government control in 1959 under the administration of the North Vietnam Army's 559th Transportation Group, commanded by a Colonel Vo Bam.

During the early 1960s, stories circulated that the Ho Chi Minh Trail was traversed exclusively by elderly men and women carrying cargo on rickety bicycles or on their backs. This did happen, but the main mode of transport was by rugged Soviet-built trucks. By April 1965, under a new commander, General Phan Trong Tue, the 559th Group consisted of 24,000 troops, and the trucks, bicycles, and people traversed more than 600 miles of roads and paths connecting many supply and ammo dumps, encampments, field hospitals, and command facilities. The entire length of the system was meticulously concealed by dense jungle growth and ingenious artificial camouflage. Bridges were even built just below the surface of the water.

For much of the Vietnam War, the Ho Chi Minh Trail would be the target of an intensive

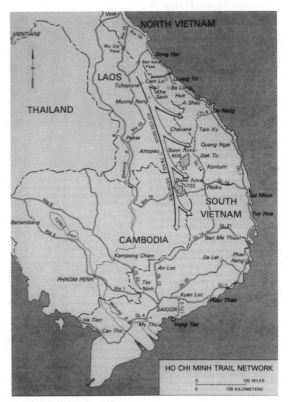

Highly schematic and simplified, this map offers some suggestion of the network structure of the Ho Chi Minh Trail, the extraordinarily efficient and durable route by which North Vietnamese forces infiltrated the South through decades of war.

American air campaign, which, in an effort to "interdict" the trail, would ultimately drop more ordnance on portions of it and territories adjacent to it than all the bombs dropped during World War II by *all* sides. Yet no American action ever succeeded in decisively depleting or delaying the infiltration of troops and supplies from the North to the South.

NUMBERS

In the Time of the Assassins

During the first half of 1960, an average of more than 150 South Vietnamese government officials were falling to assassins' bullets *every month*.

Still, Hanoi persisted in a "North first" policy until a January 1959 Communist Party meeting in which Le Duan and others finally persuaded delegates that Beijing and Moscow were now more receptive to armed conflict in the South. Even more important, while Diem's army and police patrols were taking a devastating toll on the Viet Minh, their aggression was so indiscriminate that neutral and even loyal South Vietnamese were being harassed, imprisoned, tortured, and sometimes executed. Throughout the countryside, the peasantry was becoming increasingly alienated from the Diem government. In acting so ruthlessly against the Communist insurgents in the South, Diem was actually creating a peasant population ripe for conversion to the Communist cause.

The January 1959 meeting ended with the conclusion that "revolution in South Vietnam" would require a "violent struggle." Accordingly, Hanoi authorized construction of a network of roads and trails from the North, moving south through Laos, and then into South Vietnam. Collectively, this network came to be called the Ho Chi Minh Trail and would serve the Viet Cong throughout the Vietnam War as an avenue of infiltration, supply, reinforcement, and exfiltration. The September 1959 ambush was the first dramatic use of the trail. By the end of the year, the Viet Cong instigated uprisings against the Diem government in the central Quang Ngai Province and, even more notably, in the Mekong Delta village of Ben Tre.

THE MIRACLE FADES

AS ANTIGOVERNMENT MOMENTUM BUILT in South Vietnam, Hanoi convened another major Communist Party meeting in September 1960. The upshot of this conclave was a decision to actively challenge Diem, whose support from the people and military alike was eroding daily. Toward this end, party leaders decided on the same strategy Ho Chi Minh had used before and during World War II. They would subordinate the Communist agenda to more ideologically neutral nationalist goals in a bid to attract support from the broadest possible coalition of political, religious, and ethnic groups.

While Hanoi set about organizing a nationalist movement to unify North and South Vietnam, a cabal of disaffected ARVN officers launched a coup d'état against Ngo Dinh Diem on November 11, 1960. They had three principal motives: First, the coup organizers

were disgusted by the extreme politicization of the ARVN, in which promotion and command were based on loyalty to Diem rather than military merit. Second, they found the political power and influence of Diem's brother Ngo Dinh Nhu and his sister-in-law Tran Le Xuan (Madame Nhu) intolerable. An opium addict, Ngo Dinh Nhu made a fortune from the international drug trade and general corruption. He personally commanded ARVN Special Forces, which functioned as his private army, and, as head of the Can Lao Party, he was in effect chief of Vietnam's much-feared secret police. His wife, Madame Nhu, popularly known as the Dragon Lady, was widely perceived as exercising a particularly sinister influence over her brother-in-law, Ngo Dinh Diem. Finally, there was the absolute autocracy and corruption.

South Vietnam's president Ngo Dinh Diem (second from right) poses with his family on June 27, 1963 (back row, from left): niece Ngo Dinh Le Thuy (age seventeen); wife of Ngo Dinh Nhu, Tran Le Xuan (known as "Madame Nhu"); Diem's brother, Archbishop Ngo Dinh Thuc; Diem's brother, Ngo Dinh Nhu, the corrupt head of the secret police; and to Diem's left, Nhu's son, Ngo Di.

FORGOTTEN FACES
Ngo Dinh Nhu

Born on October 7, 1910, Ngo Dinh Nhu became the confidant and adviser of his older brother, Ngo Dinh Diem. Although he held no official position in the civil government or Diem administration, Nhu was widely perceived as the power behind the throne and, in fact, the mastermind of his brother's dictatorship.

Nhu had absolute authority over ARVN Special Forces, which amounted to his personal army, and he was the head of the covert Can Lao Party, which was less a political organization than it was a secret police force analogous to the Gestapo of Nazi Germany. (It was no coincidence that Nhu professed great admiration for Adolf Hitler.)

Nhu was essentially the link between the Diem government and a vast criminal enterprise based largely on opium (to which Nhu was addicted) and the narcotics made from opium, especially heroin. Using the apparatus of the South Vietnamese police and military, Nhu conducted a global drug trafficking operation and built a secret fortune for himself and the Ngo family.

Much like his nearly monkish brother, Nhu was a studious young man and a pious Catholic. Trained in France as a librarian and archivist, he hardly seemed capable of ruthless political strategy and criminal enterprise, yet it is doubtful that his brother could have risen to control South Vietnam without his aid, advice, and sources of illicit finance. It was Nhu who masterminded the execution of the rigged elections of 1955, which transformed South Vietnam into a republic and elevated Diem to the presidency. It was Nhu who shaped the Can Lao into a force that rooted out disloyalty both within and without the inner circles of the regime.

By 1959, Nhu repeatedly overplayed his hand, mounting an unsuccessful attempt to assassinate Cambodia's Prince Sihanouk when he refused to submit to Diem's incursions into his nation's sovereignty, becoming a loudmouthed braggart, and reveling in outrageous threats against the Buddhist majority within South Vietnam. As he had been indispensable to his brother's rise, so he became an instrument of his fall, serving to make the Ngo family and the Diem regime obnoxious to South Vietnamese and Americans alike. Refusing to recognize the growing hatred that engulfed him and his brother, Nhu was utterly unprepared to defend against the 1963 coup that not only toppled the Diem regime but also resulted in his death, as well as that of the president.

Led by Lieutenant Colonel Vuong Van Dong and Colonel Nguyen Chanh Thi, the 1960 coup had the element of surprise, but it was ineptly executed so that Diem was able to stall the plotters and thereby gain time for rescue by loyal ARVN forces. A clash between these units and the rebel units resulted in combat on the streets of Saigon in which more than four hundred people—mostly civilian onlookers—were killed. In the wake of the coup attempt,

Diem accused the Eisenhower administration not only of failing to support him but also of sending CIA operatives to assist the rebels. Even as he argued with his American patrons, Diem cracked down on anyone and everyone who made the slightest criticism of his government. He shook up the ARVN hierarchy, demoting those whose loyalty he questioned and promoting those of whose loyalty he was certain, thereby compounding the politicization of an already-corrupt military.

The internal turmoil of South Vietnam was exacerbated at this time by a crisis in neighboring Laos, whose anti-Communist government was being challenged by the Pathet Lao, a Marxist political movement that closely associated itself with the Vietnamese Communists. The hour seemed right, therefore, to create a broad coalition that would unite anti-Diem nationalists with more orthodox Communists. On December 20, 1960, some fifty representatives from an array of anti-Diem groups secretly assembled near the Cambodian border to create the National Liberation Front (NLF). Like the Viet Minh as originally founded by Ho Chi Minh, the NLF presented itself as an organization of *national* rather than *social* revolution. Its Communist connections were downplayed and even held in abeyance. The NLF effectively absorbed the Viet Minh as well as the Viet Cong, and, as far as the outside world was concerned, the NLF and the Viet Cong were one and the same.

Communist Pathet Lao troops during a military exercise in Laos, 1959.

The creation of the NLF had profound implications for Vietnam. Hitherto, the principal struggle had been between the Communist North and the Western-dominated South, with varying degrees of Communist insurgency penetrating below the 17th parallel. Now the Vietnam War was a combination of a cross-border conflict, in which Hanoi set out to

DETAILS, DETAILS
Coup Fallout
Fourteen ARVN officers and thirty-four civilians were arrested and imprisoned following the 1960 coup attempt. In 1963, an additional seven officers and two civilians were sentenced in absentia to execution. They were never caught, and those who had been jailed in 1960 were released after the 1963 coup in which Diem was assassinated.

REALITY CHECK
The Struggle to Define the Cause

As the United States contemplated deepening involvement in Vietnam during the early 1960s and as the war ground on through the later 1960s and 1970s, then even after it ended in 1975, American politicians, diplomats, and political scientists argued over the true nature of the war. Was it a proxy war between the great Communist powers (China and the Soviet Union) and the great democratic power (the United States)? Was it a cross-border contest for domination between North and South? Or was it, first and last, a civil war between those who supported Diem and those who hated him? The most realistic assessment of the Vietnam War was that, after 1959, it was all of these, which is why the conflict was complex, confusing, and often confused.

Attempts to overthrow the chronically unpopular and exuberantly corrupt Diem regime were frequent. In this photograph from November 11, 1960, rebel soldiers train their rifles against the presidential palace. These troops were part of a band of some five hundred South Vietnamese paratroops and marines who hoped to ignite a coup d'état that would win the support of most of the Army of the Republic of Vietnam. It did not, and, two days later, troops loyal to Diem succeeded in crushing the rebellion.

reunify Vietnam on its own Communist terms, and a civil war between *South* Vietnamese factions.

Diem, the man Americans wanted to see as the architect of the "Vietnam Miracle," met the challenge of civil war in ways that served only to intensify it. As Viet Cong activity spread throughout the South, the Diem government stepped up the peasant relocation program it had first instituted in 1959. Having given up on destroying the Viet Cong below the 17th parallel, Saigon had decided instead to remove peasants from Viet Cong influence. This was to be accomplished by forcibly relocating them from their ancestral villages and farms to special "agrovilles," heavily fortified villages that were intended to exclude Viet Cong infiltrators but were, in fact, little better than concentration or labor camps, with conditions that recalled, to those old enough to remember them, the forced-labor rubber plantations of the French colonial period.

Even as Diem uprooted and attempted to isolate large segments of the provincial population, he issued Decree 10/59, which gave officials throughout the country absolute authority to arrest, try, imprison, and execute anyone deemed subversive. The corruption, brutality, and sheer arbitrary abuse of power licensed by Decree 10/59 radicalized far more peasants than it arrested, imprisoned, or killed. Under threat, many saw the Viet Cong as their best hope of salvation. For many, the choice between the NLF and Diem seemed quite literally a choice between life and death.

Pay Any Price, Bear Any Burden

Running as a Republican, Dwight David Eisenhower had defeated Democrat Adlai Stevenson in 1952 in part by promising to end, and end honorably, the war in Korea that had begun during the administration of Democrat Harry S. Truman. In the mid-1950s, President Eisenhower looked for a way to ensure that he would not pass to the next president an unresolved war in Vietnam. From 1956 to 1958, there seemed reason for optimism that Ngo Dinh Diem had created a miracle, and Eisenhower looked forward to ending his second term in office with South Vietnam well established as a democracy friendly to the United States.

The events of 1959 and 1960 first diminished and then dashed this optimism, and Democratic senator John F. Kennedy of Massachusetts challenged Republican vice president Richard Nixon in part on what he deemed the failure of the Eisenhower administration to stem the tide of Communist aggression in Southeast Asia and elsewhere.

Kennedy was an anti-Communist (his younger brother, Robert, had even served a stint as legal counsel to the notorious red-baiting *Republican* senator from Wisconsin, Joseph McCarthy), but Nixon's Cold War credentials were stronger and longer established than those of Senator Kennedy. Nevertheless, the failure of the Eisenhower administration to build a viable democracy in South Vietnam helped JFK achieve a razor-thin victory over his Republican opponent.

John F. Kennedy is inaugurated as the thirty-fifth president of the United States, January 20, 1961. His celebrated speech that day was intended to prepare the nation for "the role of defending freedom in its hour of maximum danger."

The new president's inaugural address, on January 20, 1961, was a blend of idealism and defiance bordering on the bellicose as he spoke of the "torch" having "been passed to a new generation of Americans—born in this century, tempered by war, disciplined by a hard and bitter peace, proud of our ancient heritage—and unwilling to witness or permit the slow undoing of those human rights to which this Nation has always been committed, and to which we are committed today at home and around the world." He issued what was both a pledge and a warning: "Let every nation know, whether it wishes us well or ill, that we shall pay any price, bear any burden, meet any hardship, support any friend, oppose any foe, to assure the survival and the success of liberty." He spoke of seeking peace but not by tempting adversaries "with weakness. For only when our arms are sufficient beyond doubt can we be certain beyond doubt that they will never be employed." He evoked memories of the "graves of young Americans who answered the call to service [whose resting places] surround the globe" and announced that "the trumpet summons us again—not as a call to bear arms, though arms we need—not as a call to battle, though embattled we are—but a call to bear the burden of a long twilight struggle, year in and year out."

The rhetoric soared, but the ambiguity was and remains profoundly disturbing: a trumpet summons that is not a call to arms ("though arms we need") and not a call to battle ("though embattled we are") but is in fact a call to fight a "twilight struggle." Was this phrase intended as a synonym for the kind of "limited war" that had come to characterize the Cold War period? If so, limited though it might be, the war promised to be very, very long, "year in and year out."

Why accept such a vision, such a burden?

The new president offered a reason: "In the long history of the world, only a few generations have been granted the role of defending freedom in its hour of maximum danger. I do not shrink from this responsibility—I welcome it. I do not believe that any of us would exchange places with any other people or any other generation." In the first few minutes of his presidency, John Fitzgerald Kennedy was preparing his nation for sacrifice. Would it be in Europe—West Berlin? In the Americas—Cuba? Or would the bloody altar be in Southeast Asia—Vietnam?

TAKEAWAY

America in Vietnam— the Torch Is Passed

The Eisenhower administration embraced Diem as the "miracle man" who would build South Vietnam into bulwark of democracy in a region threatened by Communist "aggression." By the end of the Eisenhower presidency, it was increasingly apparent that the Diem miracle was failing, and to the cross-border struggle between North and South Vietnam was added a civil war in the South between those who supported and those who hated Diem. Assuming the presidency in January 1961, John F. Kennedy prepared to commit the United States to an even bigger role in Diem's fatally flawed republic.

CHAPTER 6

VICTOR CHARLIE

The Vietnam War Enters the Kennedy Era

B Y THE TIME PRESIDENT JOHN F. KENNEDY TOOK OFFICE in January 1961, the Viet Cong in South Vietnam had already rebounded from a decimated, apparently moribund handful in the late 1950s to some 14,000 fighters. They waged a combination guerrilla war and campaign of terror and assassination, successfully targeting thousands of civil officials, government workers, and police officers. The new president commissioned a study in the spring of 1961, which concluded that South Vietnam had entered "the decisive phase in its battle for survival." Accordingly, on April 29, 1961, President Kennedy authorized an additional 100 MAAG advisers as well as the creation of a combat development and test center in South Vietnam. He also asked for increased economic aid. Less than two weeks later, on May 11, the president committed 400 U.S. Special Forces troops to raise and train a force of South Vietnamese "irregulars" in areas controlled by the Viet Cong, particularly along the border.

The Special Forces, an elite army organization trained in small-unit tactics—guerrilla warfare—had been in existence since the U.S. Army created the Rangers in 1942. President Kennedy would give the soldiers a higher profile, new status, and a new item of uniform: the Green Beret. For their part, these "Green Berets" would soon come to respect the skill, courage, and determination of the Viet Cong. That name, bestowed by Saigon in an effort to denigrate them, was further reduced by Green Berets to "VC," which, in the phonetic alphabet used by U.S. and NATO forces, became "Victor Charlie." "Charlie" made them sound

EXECUTIVE
PR IS-T

April 11, 1962

TO THE UNITED STATES ARMY:

Another military dimension -- "guerrilla warfare" -- has necessarily been added to the American profession of arms. The literal translation of guerrilla warfare -- "a little war" -- is hardly applicable to this ancient, but at the same time, modern threat. I note that the Army has several terms which describe the various facets of the current struggle: wars of subversion, covert aggression, and, in broad professional terms, special warfare or unconventional warfare.

By whatever name, this militant challenge to freedom calls for an improvement and enlargement of our own development of techniques and tactics, communications and logistics to meet this threat. The mission of our Armed Forces -- and especially the Army today -- is to master these skills and techniques and to be able to help those who have the will to help themselves.

Pure military skill is not enough. A full spectrum of military, para-military, and civil action must be blended to produce success. The enemy uses economic and political warfare, propaganda and naked military aggression in an endless combination to oppose a free choice of government, and suppress the rights of the individual by terror, by subversion and by force of arms. To win in this struggle, our officers and men must understand and combine the political, economic and civil actions with skilled military efforts in the execution of this mission.

"The green beret" is again becoming a symbol of excellence, a badge of courage, a mark of distinction in the fight for freedom. I know the United States Army will live up to its reputation for imagination, resourcefulness, and spirit as we meet this challenge.

CVC/mad

On April 11, 1962, President Kennedy sent a message "TO THE UNITED STATES ARMY," noting that the "'green beret' is . . . a badge of courage, a mark of distinction in the fight for freedom," and expressing confidence that Special Forces soldiers and officers would "live up to [their] reputation for imagination, resourcefulness, and spirit" to meet the challenge of "guerrilla warfare" in Vietnam. JFK understood that, since the end of World War II, the thrust of U.S. military development had been to fight strategic (nuclear) war against the Soviet Union, not insurgencies such as the one under way in Southeast Asia.

DETAILS, DETAILS
America's Best

Since at least the days of World War II, "Rangers" and "commandos" carried a certain mystique, but the unpopularity of the Vietnam War made it difficult for most Americans to celebrate the exploits of the Green Berets—at least until Staff Sergeant Barry Sadler wrote (with historian-lyricist Robin Moore) "The Ballad of the Green Berets" while he was recovering from a leg wound sustained as a medic in Vietnam. The song debuted on the *Ed Sullivan Show* on January 30, 1966, and was the number one U.S. hit for five weeks that year. Two years later, it was featured in *The Green Berets*, a film starring John Wayne. In the hook lyric, a dying Green Beret implores, "Put silver wings on my son's chest / Make him one of America's best."

innocuous enough, but "Victor"—at least in the hindsight of history—came to look like a grim prediction.

HANOI AND WASHINGTON

HANOI EYED THE TRANSITION from Eisenhower to Kennedy with great anxiety. The government of the North was now committed to violent revolution in the South, but at the same time, northern leaders were wary of intensifying the guerrilla raids and assassinations to a degree that would provoke the new American president to full-scale intervention. The first few months of the Kennedy administration had seen an increase in U.S. forces in the South, but so far they were designated as advisers rather than combatants. While most histories of the Vietnam War portray Hanoi as almost suicidal in its commitment to the war by 1961—quite willing (as JFK declared of his own nation) to "pay any price, bear any burden, meet any hardship"—there was in fact sharp disagreement among top leaders. Some advocated a return to the "North first" policy. Others called for maintaining a low level of guerrilla and terrorist violence to gradually wear down the South without provoking a wider war. Still others, led by Le Duan, urged defiance of the United States in the belief that it would never commit to a long and costly war in a place so distant from itself and of such relatively minor economic consequence.

As for President Kennedy, he was above all else determined to reinvigorate American foreign policy, which he believed had suffered from a kind of hardening of the arteries under eight years of Eisenhower. He intended to wage the Cold War, the struggle against Communist global expansion, far more vigorously than his predecessor. Nowhere was this more the case than in the "Third World": those "developing nations" spawned by the postwar decay of European empire that had declared allegiance neither to Washington nor Moscow/Beijing. Kennedy and his advisers saw the Third World as the new "battlefield" of the Cold War.

The withdrawal of the old European powers had opened the door to American influence in Asia, Africa, and Latin America, but the end of empires also left a lingering anti-Western bitterness that included the United States and threatened to push the Third World into the camp of the "Sino-Soviet bloc." The hard fact was that the Soviet premier Nikita Khrushchev also saw the value of the Third World, and in

January 1961, the very month in which JFK took office, the Soviet premier announced the Kremlin's support for what he defined as "wars of national liberation." Like Ho Chi Minh, Khrushchev was careful to employ rhetoric that downplayed any motive of spreading Communist ideology. Instead, he referred only to the broader issues of nationalism and self-determination.

Best and Brightest

Much as Franklin Roosevelt in the 1930s had assembled a "brain trust" to formulate a strategy for recovery from the Great Depression, Kennedy brought together a cabinet and set of advisers that journalist-historian David Halberstam would later characterize (with bitter irony) as "the best and the brightest." For secretary of state, Kennedy drafted Dean Rusk, a Rhodes scholar and State Department veteran who had served as the president of the Rockefeller Foundation. For secretary of defense, he lured Robert McNamara from his brand-new presidency of Ford Motor Company (he was the first CEO who was not a Ford). A World War II strategist and former Harvard Business School professor, McNamara was expected to take a rationally cost-effective, hyper-efficient approach to defense. Kennedy also tapped Harvard—his alma mater—for his national security advisor, McGeorge Bundy, who, at forty-one, was that university's dean of faculty. Bundy brought along with him as special deputy Walt Whitman Rostow, a distinguished economist and political theorist.

President Kennedy meets for talks with Soviet premier Nikita Khrushchev in Vienna during June 1961. The Soviet leader came away from the encounter with an impression of a president he judged to be inexperienced, tentative, and weak.

The Best and the Brightest

✳✳✳

—Title of David Halberstam's 1972 history of the origins of U.S. involvement in the Vietnam War

These highly educated men were dedicated to the president's campaign to win over to the capitalist West the emerging nations of the

Historian David Halberstam called them—with some bitterness of irony—"the best and the brightest":
President Kennedy's distinguished cabinet, pictured here at their swearing-in, in the East Room of the White
House, on January 21, 1961. From left to right: Secretary of State Dean Rusk, Secretary of the Treasury
C. Douglas Dillon, Secretary of Defense Robert S. McNamara, Attorney General Robert F. Kennedy, Postmaster
General J. Edward Day, and Secretary of the Interior Stewart Udall. First Lady Jacqueline Kennedy and the
President stand next to Udall. To the president's left is Representative to the United Nations Adlai E. Stevenson,
and Secretary of Agriculture Orville Freeman. Secretary of Commerce Luther Hodges is hidden behind Supreme
Court Chief Justice Earl Warren (who administers the oath). On the far right are Secretary
of Labor Arthur Goldberg and Secretary of Health, Education, and Welfare Abraham Ribicoff.

Third World. Using the postwar Marshall Plan as a model, they backed a vast investment in foreign aid and enthusiastically supported the boldest expression of President Kennedy's internationalist idealism, the Peace Corps. Their hope and intention was to win loyalty in the developing world by fostering peace, prosperity, and great goodwill. Yet even as the best and the brightest set this peace initiative into motion, they engineered a radically redesigned buildup of the American military.

Flexible Response

As had been the case after World War I, the United States rushed after World War II to dismantle the vast military machinery it had built to fight a conflict unprecedented in scope. Under presidents Truman and Eisenhower, the army, navy, air force, and marines were all reduced in size. Both presidents, however, recognized a need to build a "nuclear deterrent" against the Soviet Union, which developed its own atomic weapons much sooner after World War II than anyone in the West had expected. Nuclear and thermonuclear weaponry was hardly cheap, and the idea of engaging in an "arms race" with the Soviets—in which the finish line was Armageddon—was hardly comforting. Yet Truman and, even more, Eisenhower saw an upside to focusing military development on "strategic" (nuclear and thermonuclear) rather than "tactical" (conventional) forces. First, while everyone thought the weapons were horrific and invited the end of civilization, the idea of dropping out of the atomic arms race and conceding nuclear superiority to the Soviets and the Chinese was simply unthinkable. On this basis alone, the case for transforming the U.S. armed services into a "strategic" force was compelling. But there was more. Costly as strategic weapons were, they were much cheaper than developing, arming, and maintaining large conventional forces. Politicians and top military brass agreed: strategic weapons gave America more bang for the buck.

When Kennedy and his advisers entered the White House, they saw the downside to the strategic transformation. While the American military was now very well prepared to fight World War III, it was ill-prepared for the smaller, so-called brushfire wars, the proxy conflicts that characterized the Cold War period. Continuing the policy of "containing Communism" required a military capable of fighting limited, relatively low-tech, low-intensity wars in the Third World countries of Asia, Africa, and Latin America. President Kennedy therefore advocated developing a military capable of "Flexible Response," which meant building the competence to fight every kind of war, from Armageddon down to sniping in the jungle. As the president and his advisers saw it, Flexible Response was necessary not only to prevail in places like Vietnam but also to prevent wars like Vietnam from escalating into nuclear nightmares. Just as everything looks like a nail to the man who has nothing but a hammer, an American military equipped only to fight atomic wars would sooner or later see every war as an atomic war.

The symbolic elevation of the U.S. Army Special Forces to the status of Green Berets was the first big step Kennedy authorized in the creation of Flexible Response. It was, however, personnel of the United States Air Force (USAF) who were the first to be assigned to "permanent duty status" in Vietnam. The irony was inescapable. Of all the service branches, the USAF was the most thoroughly equipped for strategic warfare (it had the nuclear-capable heavy bombers and intercontinental ballistic missiles) and the least ready to conduct tactical operations. Nevertheless,

DETAILS, DETAILS
Kennedy's Peace Offensive

Formed on March 1, 1961, less than two months into the Kennedy presidency and even as the new president was escalating the American commitment to the war in Vietnam, the Peace Corps was intended to provide civilian technical assistance in developing nations, to help the Third World understand American culture and political values, and to help Americans understand and appreciate the culture and political values of the Third World. The Peace Corps was at its height during the very period in which the United States escalated the Vietnam War. Although it received widespread support from the public and politicians alike, critics on the left charged that it was at best a cynical counterpoint to U.S. aggression in Vietnam and elsewhere in the Third World, while critics on the right condemned it as a haven for "draft dodgers."

This U.S. Air Force C-47 prepares to take off from the runway at Tan Son Nhut air base on a nighttime flare-dropping mission to provide visibility to "allied ground security forces."

the sixty-seven men assigned to a mobile combat reporting post—a state-of-the-art radar installation secretly airlifted to Vietnam during September 26–October 3, 1961—were the leading edge of a "regular" U.S. military presence "in-country," as service members termed a posting to Vietnam. On October 5, another 314 airmen and officers followed, all assigned to Tan Son *Nhat* Airport, which would become home to the massive and highly sophisticated tactical air control system of what would become Tan Son *Nhut* Air Base. This installation and its personnel were soon complemented by a USAF photo reconnaissance mission, including flight crews, photo processing specialists, and support personnel, housed at a base in Don Muang, Thailand.

AMBIVALENCE AND COMMITMENT

EVEN AS JFK SENT SOLDIERS AND AIRMEN to South Vietnam, he was far more concerned about the developing crisis in neighboring Laos, whose pro-Western government—established in 1954 with U.S. aid and ever since then supported (like South Vietnam) in large part with American funding—was locked in a struggle with the Pathet Lao Communist movement. President Eisenhower had advised the young president-elect that he would doubtless have to send troops to Laos, lest the country become one more fallen domino. Despite the "pay any price, bear any burden" resolve expressed in his inaugural address, however, President Kennedy withheld a military commitment, questioning whether that tiny country was worth spilling American blood to save. Even more tellingly, he wondered whether the U.S. Army was even capable of fighting the kind of guerrilla war that was in the offing there. Instead of sending troops, JFK announced in April that the United States would enter into multinational talks in search of a peaceful settlement in Laos. The outcome, in July, was a coalition government, a combination of Communist and non-Communist elements, along with a solemn pledge of absolute neutrality.

The princes of Laos (left to right), Boun Oum, Souvanna Phouma, and Souphanouvong, meet in summit on December 14, 1961, prior to issuing an official declaration of Laotian neutrality in the war in Vietnam. Despite the declaration, the Pathet Lao, formed in 1960 by Prince Souphanouvong, actively collaborated with the Viet Minh, Viet Cong, and North Vietnam Army throughout the war.

A Combat Presence?

No one, West or East, believed the Laotian settlement was permanent. Kennedy and his advisers, however, did think it would buy time to create a stronger position in South Vietnam, while the Pathet Lao and its backers—China, the Soviet Union, and North Vietnam—thought along much the same lines, believing that the combination of coalition and neutrality would reduce or at least delay U.S. intervention in the region. Even the bellicose Le Duan, since 1960 the chief of the Vietnamese Communist party, expressed the hope that the United States would offer a similar settlement deal to North Vietnam. This would buy time for the continued low-level struggle in the South without fear of U.S. intervention.

Le Duan was destined to disappointment. The Laotian settlement actually put political pressure on President Kennedy to stand firmly behind the Ngo Dinh Diem regime in South Vietnam. The young president's father, Joseph P. Kennedy Sr., U.S. ambassador to Great Britain during the prelude to and outbreak of World War II, had earned everlasting scorn for having championed British prime minister Neville Chamberlain's now infamous policy of "appeasing" Adolf Hitler and having urged President Roosevelt to come to terms with the Führer,

DETAILS, DETAILS

Target: Laos

The Pathet Lao ("Lao Nation") was formed in 1950 by Laotian prince Souphanouvong, who united his followers with the Viet Minh in a revolt against French colonial domination of Indochina. Prince Souphanouvong had spent many years in Vietnam, was married to a Vietnamese woman, and was deeply committed to Ho Chi Minh. Despite the official proclamation of Laotian neutrality in 1961, the Pathet Lao continued to cooperate with the Viet Minh and, later, both the North Vietnam regular army (NVA) and the Viet Cong. After the Vietnam War ended in 1975, the Pathet Lao abolished the monarchy and established the Lao People's Democratic Republic, essentially a client state of Vietnam. With the collapse of the Soviet Union and global Communism during the late 1980s and early 1990s, Laos remained Communist but became far more independent of Vietnam.

who he believed was destined to defeat Britain and win the war. After Laos, some sniffed the noxious odor of "appeasement" clinging to Ambassador Kennedy's son. Worse, in April 1961, President Kennedy withdrew military support for the ill-fated Bay of Pigs invasion planned by the CIA and executed by anti-Castro Cuban exiles to provoke a counterrevolution against the Communist government of Cuba. The Bay of Pigs operation had been planned during the closing days of the Eisenhower administration, but Kennedy, inheriting it, had approved it only to abandon it in mid-execution when it appeared hopeless. The collapse of the attempt to "liberate" Cuba was a terrible humiliation for the new administration, and the president was not about to appear to back down again, this time in South Vietnam.

> **"There are just so many concessions that one can make to Communists in one year and survive politically. We just can't have another defeat this year in Vietnam."**
>
> ★★★
>
> —John F. Kennedy, speaking to U.S. ambassador to India John Kenneth Galbraith, quoted in Mark Atwood Lawrence, *The Vietnam War: A Concise International History* (2008)

Jungle Jim

On October 11, 1961, Kennedy ordered the first actual combat detachment to Vietnam. While the official designation of the unit was the 4400th Combat Crew *Training* Squadron, it was, in fact, an elite U.S. Air Force organization of 124 officers and 228 airmen equipped with 16 C-47 transport aircraft, 8 World War II–vintage B-26 medium bombers, and 8 T-28 single-engine pilot-training aircraft. Code-named Farm Gate, the operation was informally nicknamed Jungle Jim. While personnel did train South Vietnamese pilots, it was really an "air commando" unit—the air force equivalent of the army's Green Berets, its all-volunteer personnel handpicked for four qualities: physical prowess, "emotional hardiness," all-around combat skill, and, rather more vaguely, a thirst for adventure.

The B-26: An Aging Veteran Recalled to Service

The B-26 used by the U.S. Air Force in the Vietnam War was a twin-engine light attack bomber built by Douglas Aircraft Company during World War II.

It was originally designated as the A-26 Invader to distinguish it from the B-26 Marauder medium bomber built by the Glenn L. Martin Aircraft Company and used even more extensively during World War II. (The "A" designation signified "attack," a tactical ground-support mission, whereas the "B" signified "bomber," a broader bombing function.)

From 1948 until its retirement from the USAF in 1965, the Invader was redesignated as the B-26, the Martin Marauder having retired in 1945. That the twenty-year-old, obsolescent B-26 Invader was the principal ground-attack bomber of the USAF fleet at the start of U.S. combat involvement in the Vietnam War speaks volumes about the unpreparedness of the *strategic* (nuclear) air force to conduct a *tactical* (nonnuclear) war. Although the USAF would adapt the massive B-52 Stratofortress strategic jet bomber to tactical

Better equipped to fight a thermonuclear war than a war of insurgency that called for close tactical air support of ground troops, the U.S. Air Force made do with such obsolescent World War II–vintage aircraft as this B-26K medium bomber.

missions in Vietnam and would use such fighter jets as the F-100 Super Sabre, F-105 Thunderchief, and F-4 Phantom II for ground support, it was 1972 before a modern purpose-built ground-attack/close-air support jet, the Fairchild Republic A-10 Thunderbolt II, first flew. It was introduced into service in 1977, two years after the Vietnam War had ended.

Even now, with this elite and unconventional unit, the administration's ambivalence was still very much in evidence. Trained as an unconventional combat unit, Farm Gate/Jungle Jim nevertheless was officially assigned nothing more than a training mission—yet personnel were not explicitly ordered to avoid combat. This lack of clarity was perceived not as a call to exercise initiative but as a most vexing ambivalence and ambiguity at the highest levels of government. For nearly three months, Farm Gate/Jungle Jim personnel doggedly trained Vietnamese crews and also undertook hazardous and frustrating aerial reconnaissance missions, often firing in self-defense and almost certainly, on occasion, offensively. On

December 26, 1961, the unit finally received explicit authorization to undertake combat missions—but only when the Vietnamese Air Force was unable to. This introduced a degree of clarity into the mission but not sufficiently to prevent Farm Gate/Jungle Jim from suffering serious problems of morale. The frustrating situation would prove prophetic of the tenor of the entire war.

Walt Whitman Rostow, deputy special assistant to the president for national security affairs, shown here in April 1961, accompanied JFK's national security advisor McGeorge Bundy and military adviser General Maxwell Taylor on a fact-finding tour of South Vietnam in October 1961. Their report resulted in the escalation of the U.S. military role from purely advisory to "a limited partnership and working collaboration" with the military forces of South Vietnam.

Fact Finding

On October 11, the very day he authorized Farm Gate, President Kennedy dispatched McGeorge Bundy's special deputy, Walt Rostow, in company with General Maxwell Taylor, to South Vietnam to personally survey the situation there and make a report to unambiguously answer the question: *Should the United States commit to a direct combat role or merely continue its advisory and training mission?*

Rostow and Taylor flew into Vietnam, took a look, flew out, and made their recommendations. They were, on balance, cautiously conservative. The pair recommended continuing U.S. Air Force reconnaissance flights and also creating a permanent tactical air-ground system to coordinate aerial reconnaissance and combat missions more effectively with ARVN forces on the ground. The system would include stepped-up training and, most significantly, would explicitly give Farm Gate/Jungle Jim a freer hand to conduct still-limited combat missions. This, then, marked an explicit shift from a purely advisory role to a combat mission for U.S. forces and was therefore a policy change with profound consequences. Nevertheless, Rostow and Taylor added a caveat, advising the president not to commit what they termed "substantial" U.S. *ground* combat forces. Thus, in keeping with the prevailing ambivalence, Rostow and Taylor effectively recommended one step forward into combat and two steps in retreat from it. As Kennedy framed it, when he approved the recommendations in November 1961, U.S. policy in South Vietnam was no longer purely advisory but had become a "limited partnership and working collaboration."

FORGOTTEN FACES
General Maxwell Taylor

Relations between Kennedy and military high command were always uneasy—despite the young president's renown as a war hero; he had famously saved most of his crew after his U.S. Navy boat, PT-109, was cut in two by a Japanese destroyer in the South Pacific.

Nonetheless, the brass saw him not only as the son of a pro-appeasement defeatist father but also as the commander-in-chief who had betrayed the "freedom fighters" at the Bay of Pigs. For his part, Kennedy deeply distrusted what he saw as the strategic military's hair-trigger attitude toward nuclear weapons. JFK's most trusted adviser, his brother Robert F. Kennedy, whom the president had appointed attorney general, was on excellent terms with one top commander, General Maxwell Taylor—going so far as to name one of his sons Matthew Maxwell Taylor Kennedy. Through "Bobby" Kennedy, Taylor won the confidence of the president, who recalled him to active duty to serve in the newly created post of military representative to the president. With Taylor as his liaison to the military, JFK effectively circumvented the Joint Chiefs of Staff. To address the problem of White House–military trust more permanently, Kennedy named Taylor as chairman of the Joint Chiefs on October 1, 1962. In some ways, this would ease the awkwardness of White House–military relations, yet the appointment also created enduring enmities between the White House and senior levels of military command.

President Kennedy confers with his military adviser, Joint Chiefs of Staff chairman General Maxwell Taylor, and Secretary of Defense Robert S. McNamara on October 2, 1963. Before the end of the following month, President Kennedy would be assassinated.

PROJECT BEEFUP

THE MOST IMMEDIATE AND VISIBLE CONSEQUENCE of JFK's adoption of the Rostow-Taylor recommendations was a dramatic increase in the flow of U.S. aid and matériel into South Vietnam. In what was dubbed Project Beefup, military assistance more than doubled from 1961 to 1962.

President Kennedy could hardly hide these dramatic increases from Congress and the public, but even as his administration approved an incrementally expanding combat role for U.S. personnel "in-country," including the deployment by aerial spray of chemical defoliants and

NUMBERS

Beefing Up

By June 30, 1962, there were 6,419 American soldiers and airmen in South Vietnam. By the end of 1962, the number would top 9,000.

herbicides (to reduce the jungle canopy and deny the VC concealment) as well as the use of napalm (flaming jellied gasoline) against VC bases and hideouts, the president told more than one press conference that no American *combat* forces were operating in South Vietnam. Pressed, he did admit that the U.S. "training units" were naturally authorized to return fire if fired upon. The fact was that the Kennedy administration now authorized Farm Gate/Jungle Jim to take a more active role in the fighting, mainly by accompanying (and often leading) ARVN troops on combat missions—missions to which both U.S. and ARVN troops were transported by U.S. Army helicopters flown by U.S. Army pilots.

Doubt and Decision

The combat activities of Farm Gate/Jungle Jim, never officially acknowledged by the Kennedy administration, were a very poorly kept secret. The American press, as well as that in North Vietnam, routinely reported on U.S. combat operations. In the United States, the result was a growing divide between those who supported the expanded U.S. military role and those who opposed it. Some in government, including a few men in the Kennedy administration itself—most notably Undersecretary of State George W. Ball—warned that Vietnam was inherently a lost cause.

UNDERSECRETARY OF STATE GEORGE W. BALL TO PRESIDENT KENNEDY: Within five years we'll have 300,000 men in the paddies and jungles and never find them again.

THE PRESIDENT (LAUGHING): Well, George, you're supposed to be one of the smartest guys in town, but you're crazier than hell. That will never happen.

✱✱✱
—Cabinet meeting, 1962

Even as a few officials began to push back against stepping deeper into what some were already calling the "quagmire" of Vietnam, President Kennedy now seemed to shed his earlier ambivalence. Usually thoughtful and having surrounded himself with "the best and the brightest," JFK became almost airily dismissive of critics of his evolving Vietnam policy, even chiding his undersecretary of state, George Ball, as being "crazier than hell" for predicting that the U.S. presence in Vietnam would dramatically increase in five years to 300,000 men lost "in the paddies and jungles." Instead, the president came to be convinced that Eisenhower's domino theory was correct: that if South Vietnam were allowed to fall to Communism, the rest of Southeast Asia would follow, ultimately endangering even the Philippines and Australia. Also, and even worse, JFK was sure that the international credibility of American military might be damaged and the nation's global political commitments would be shattered. The president who had earlier questioned whether Laos was worth spilling American blood now concluded that the security of the entire "free world" depended upon the security of neighboring South Vietnam.

Accordingly, Kennedy pushed ahead with a military commitment to South Vietnam. In the fall of 1961, he authorized joint U.S.–South Vietnamese naval patrols south of the 17th parallel to interdict North Vietnamese maritime supply operations. The administration further expanded USAF missions. Beginning in January 1962, 243 officers and airmen executed an airlift operation dubbed Mule Train, which flew large quantities of cargo and personnel into Vietnam. U.S. Army helicopters and helicopter crews of the 57th and 8th Transportation Companies routinely ferried mixed U.S.-ARVN troop units into and out of combat zones. By March 1962, six officers and six enlisted intelligence specialists from the 6499th Support Group were aiding Vietnamese intelligence-gathering efforts, and at about this time the use of chemical defoliants was dramatically expanded in the USAF's Operation Ranch Hand.

With increased exposure to fire, the body bags began to fill. On February 2, 1962, a slow-moving twin-engine USAF Fairchild C-123 "Provider" cargo aircraft crashed, either the target of VC ground fire or VC sabotage. The three crewmen killed were the first air force fatalities in South Vietnam. Nine days later, a World War II–vintage Gooney Bird, twin-engine SC-47, crashed during a propaganda leaflet-dropping mission, killing six airmen and two soldiers. The American press read these casualties as stark evidence of the nation's growing combat role in the far-off war.

U.S.-trained, U.S-equipped ARVN troops patrol the marshy delta in search of Viet Cong insurgents, 1961.

1962: Hopeful Signs or Wishful Thinking?

President Kennedy's intention was to support Diem and the ARVN to the point at which the South Vietnamese government and military were capable of successfully fighting against the North without U.S. combat participation. During much of 1962, the president had some reason for hope that this approach was working. Using American-supplied weapons, including tanks and artillery, and relying on U.S.-supplied and U.S.-flown helicopters, ARVN forces, even acting without supplementary U.S. combat infantry, made inroads against the VC in the South.

President Kennedy was also gratified by President Diem's Strategic Hamlets program, in which peasant populations were concentrated in villages specially fortified against the incursion and influence of Viet Cong and other Communist activists. By the end of 1962, Diem had built more than six hundred strategic hamlets, each surrounded by a moat, like medieval castles, and ringed with a barrier of sharpened bamboo. Another three hundred or more were under construction by the start of 1963. President Kennedy approved of this initiative, apparently unaware that, to the displaced peasant farmers, life in the strategic hamlets was a miserable existence of forced labor in what amounted to concentration camps.

The South Vietnamese military sought to combat the Viet Cong insurgency by fortifying a series of "strategic hamlets" across the countryside. Ostensibly designed to keep the VC out, trenches and sharpened bamboo obstacles were even better at keeping villagers in, effectively transforming much of the rural South into a series of concentration camps. This image appeared in State Department Publication No. 7724, which the U.S. Department of Defense put in a new cover for issue to U.S. military personnel. It was part of an effort to explain to American soldiers, sailors, and airmen just why they were being sent to Vietnam, a place most of them had never heard of.

During the course of 1962, thanks to the infusion of U.S. equipment, advisers, and funding, the ARVN had grown to a force of 300,000 men, which was now greater than the strength of the North Vietnam Army (NVA)—the North's "regular" army—which stood at 280,000. JFK pointed to this growth as evidence that South Vietnam was rapidly building a credible independent military force. What he apparently failed to consider was that the overwhelming majority of these troops were garrison soldiers, little more than guards assigned to defend the South's industrial and transportation infrastructure, continually the target of VC raids and sabotage. Still, before the end of 1962, ARVN numbers approached 400,000, and, in July 1962, a hopeful U.S. president directed his secretary of defense, Robert McNamara, to begin planning for the phased withdrawal of U.S. forces.

1963: The Tide Turns

As it turned out, and as events of 1963 would show, the evidence of ARVN progress in 1962 was ultimately hollow. The Strategic Hamlets program did keep the VC at bay, but its coercive nature alienated the South Vietnamese peasantry from the Diem regime. In the end, Strategic Hamlets was doubtless more effective in converting South Vietnamese peasants to Communism than any Viet Cong effort

REALITY CHECK
The Big What-If

Much has been made of President Kennedy's July 1962 order to Secretary McNamara to begin planning the drawdown of U.S. troops in Vietnam. Some historians have pointed to this as evidence that JFK had concluded by this time that the war was unwinnable and that it was time to begin cutting U.S. losses. The evidence argues against this, however. When he directed the planning for withdrawal, Kennedy was actually in a hopeful mood. Far from thinking the war a lost cause, he was pleased with what he saw as measurable ARVN progress against the Communist insurgency. When his hopes for South Vietnamese military self-sufficiency soured beginning in 1963, the president scrapped the planned U.S. drawdown and instead stepped up the U.S. commitment. This hardly suggests a policy of cutting losses but, rather, an intention to win.

would have been. Moreover, even as the ARVN grew, Northern activists persisted in stirring the pot of South Vietnamese provincial discontent. As for those much-touted ARVN military victories, while it is true that there were a few major VC offensives in 1962, what Diem and Kennedy interpreted as an enemy on the run was actually an enemy lying low, conducting a war of harassment, terror, and attrition while avoiding the kind of open battles that might knock them out of the war. The fact was that while the ARVN seemed to have seized the initiative, the strength of the VC south of the 17th parallel actually increased in 1962, thanks to the effectiveness of the Ho Chi Minh Trail. Some 10,000 VC fighters and (for the first time ever) heavy artillery had been infiltrated into the South.

The Kennedy administration's optimism ended with the New Year. On December 28, 1962, an American intelligence unit picked up signals from a radio transmitter indicating a VC force in the Mekong Delta hamlet of Ap Tan Thoi, in Dinh Tuong Province, near what was the headquarters of the ARVN 7th Infantry Division. Quickly, U.S. advisers helped the ARVN and the South Vietnamese Civil Guard plan a preemptive encirclement of Ap Tan Thoi with some fifteen hundred troops. Support would be furnished by U.S.-supplied artillery and armored personnel carriers, plus U.S.-manned helicopters.

The attack stepped off on January 2, 1963, with the Civil Guards in the lead. They got as far as the hamlet of Ap Bac, southeast of Ap Tan Thoi, when they were ambushed by elements of the Viet Cong 261st Battalion. The ARVN 11th Infantry Regiment joined the fight in northern Ap Tan Thoi, only to be met with overwhelming fire from a relatively small number of well-entrenched VC. Fifteen U.S. helicopters rushed in with ARVN reinforcements and were met with highly effective Viet Cong ground fire, which shot down five of the craft and badly damaged the others.

By the afternoon of January 2, the situation had turned desperate. Civil Guard and ARVN troops, along with U.S. helicopter crews, were trapped southwest of Ap Bac. Their only hope of rescue was the ARVN 4th Mechanized Rifle Squadron, which, however, was slow in coming and, when it finally arrived, had stunningly little effect on the VC positions. Late in the afternoon, ARVN air-dropped in its 8th Airborne Battalion. These paratroopers, the best soldiers ARVN could field, were quickly pinned down. Only the onset of night and the stealthy withdrawal of the vastly outnumbered VC—350 men against more than 1,500—saved the combined ARVN-U.S. force from annihilation or capture.

Ap Bac revealed the strength of VC as fighters. Even worse, from an American perspective, it exposed the terrible weakness of the ARVN, whose troops simply folded under fire—despite U.S. aid and equipment. The battle kicked off a year of increased Viet Cong attacks throughout much of South Vietnam, especially in the Mekong Delta where the VC escalated the intensity and scope of attacks from raids and guerrilla actions to full-scale battles.

MARTYRS AND TYRANTS

IF 1962 HAD PRODUCED A RISE IN ARVN INITIATIVE, a hopeful development from the American perspective, 1963 revealed its unintended consequences. U.S.-ARVN aggression against the Viet Cong produced even more aggression from the VC in return. As the war turned against them, Ngo Dinh Diem and his brother Ngo Dinh Nhu somehow found a way to make a very bad situation even worse.

Like Dwight D. Eisenhower before him, John F. Kennedy turned a blind eye to the corruption, moral bankruptcy, outright crimi-nality, and irremediable unpopularity of the Diem regime. Both presidents recognized that Diem was shameless in his nepotism, that family, friends, and "business" associates occupied the most impor-tant civil and military offices. They also understood that, while the economy of South Vietnam had expanded with American aid, the only beneficiaries of the prosperity were members of a small urban minority, whereas the vast rural majority was as poor as always—and far more resentful than ever before. Still, through most of the 1950s, then again in 1962, Diem seemed to prove effective against the Communist insurgency. JFK's vice president, Lyndon Baines Johnson, even went so far as to pronounce Diem the "Winston Churchill of Southeast Asia."

Now, in 1963, as the Viet Cong successes multiplied, the people of the South increasingly turned against Diem. He and his brother responded by acting fiercely against political protests by representa-tives of the country's Buddhist majority. Friction between Catholics and Buddhists was hardly new to Vietnamese culture and politics.

NUMBERS
A Humiliating Toll
At the Battle of Ap Bac, January 2, 1963, the Viet Cong fielded approximately 350 men against an ARVN-U.S. force of more than 1,500. VC casualties were 18 killed and 39 wounded. ARVN losses were 83 killed and more than 100 wounded; U.S. losses were 3 killed, 8 wounded, 5 helicopters destroyed, and 9 damaged.

The regime of South Vietnam's Ngo Dinh Diem was openly pro-Catholic (Diem's brother was an archbishop) and aggressively anti-Buddhist. Diem's policies motivated many Buddhist protests, including this hunger strike by Buddhist nuns in early June 1963.

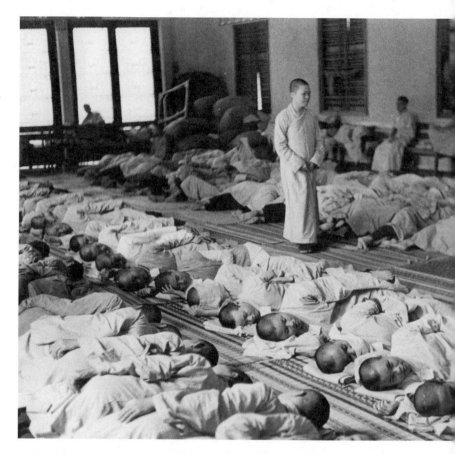

A devout Catholic, Diem had exacerbated the long-existing tension by showing blatant preference to Catholics in every way he could, especially in matters of law, commerce, and political appointment. He made no attempt to disguise his intention to marginalize the Buddhist majority however and whenever possible. Acting in part at the instigation of his brother, Diem cracked down violently on Buddhist protests in the spring of 1963. On May 8, 1963, he authorized ARVN troops in the ancient city of Hue to fire on demonstrators who were agitating for nothing more than the right to display traditional Buddhist prayer flags. Several protestors and bystanders were killed or wounded. In response, Buddhist activists called for an end to persecution and demanded that Diem issue a proclamation of religious equality. Ngo Dinh Nhu spoke for his brother: there would be no government concessions of any kind.

Martyrdom

On June 10, 1963, members of the American press corps in Saigon were told by a representative of local Buddhist activists that "something important" would occur the next morning in the street outside the Cambodian Embassy. The tip made little impact, except on a handful of journalists, including *New York Times* correspondent David Halberstam and Associated Press Saigon Bureau chief Malcolm Browne, both of whom showed up outside the embassy on June 11.

> **"Before closing my eyes and moving towards the vision of the Buddha, I respectfully plead to President Ngo Dinh Diem to take a mind of compassion towards the people of the nation and implement religious equality to maintain the strength of the homeland eternally."**
>
> ✶✶✶
>
> —from note Thich Quang Duc wrote before immolating himself on June II, 1963

A procession of some 350 monks and nuns, following behind an Austin Westminster automobile, approached the reporters' position. They carried banners protesting Diem's persecution policy and demanding religious equality. The car and the procession behind it halted at the intersection of Phan Dinh Phung Boulevard and Le Van Duyet Street. Thich Quang Duc, a sixty-six-year-old Vietnamese Mahayana Buddhist monk, emerged from the Austin with two younger monks. One carried a cushion, which he placed in the intersection. The other opened the vehicle's trunk, took out a five-gallon gasoline can, and, after Thich Quang Duc assumed the lotus position on the cushion, poured the contents of the can over him, as if administering a ritual cleansing. Thich Quang Duc manipulated his prayer beads and began to chant "*Nam Mo A Di Da Phat*" in homage to the Amitabha Buddha. He then calmly struck a match and dropped it on his gasoline-soaked robes.

"Flames were coming from a human being," Halberstam reported, "his body was slowly withering and shriveling up, his head

The most shocking Buddhist protest against Diem's oppressive religious policies came on June 11, 1963, when Thich Quang Duc, a Buddhist monk, allowed himself to be doused in gasoline, then set himself ablaze at a busy Saigon intersection.

blackening and charring. In the air was the smell of burning human flesh; human beings burn surprisingly quickly." The reporter noted the "sobbing of the Vietnamese who were now gathering." As for himself, he was "too shocked to cry, too confused to take notes or ask questions, too bewildered to even think."

"Let them burn and we shall clap our hands."

✳✳✳

—Madame Nhu, wife of Ngo Dinh Nhu, after describing the self-immolation of Monk Thich Quang Duc, June 11, 1963, as a "barbecue"

Though the number of reporters who witnessed the self-immolation was small, an AP photographer was present and recorded the unreal, all-too-real image. Halberstam may have been too shocked to ask questions, but most of the rest of the world was not. In the United States and especially within the Kennedy administration, the questions flew furiously. William Trueheart, acting U.S. ambassador to South Vietnam, immediately informed Diem's secretary of state, Nguyen Dinh Thuan, that an agreement between the government and Buddhists was needed *now*. This demand was followed by a stern note from Secretary of State Dean Rusk warning that the Kennedy administration would announce that it could no longer "associate itself" with the Diem government unless full concessions were made to the Buddhists. On June 16, Diem signed an agreement to end persecution and grant the Buddhists full religious equality.

Downfall

The concession, which Diem and his brother would violate almost immediately, was both too little and much too late. As friction between the Diem government and the United States increased, President Kennedy, on September 2, 1963, appeared on national television in an interview with the dean of TV news anchors, Walter Cronkite.

"Mr. President," Cronkite asked, "the only hot war we've got running at the moment is of course the one in Viet-Nam, and we have our difficulties here, quite obviously."

President Kennedy responded:

> I don't think that unless a greater effort is made by the [Diem] Government to win popular support that the war can be won out there. In the final analysis, it is their war. They are the ones who have to win it or lose it. We can help them, we can give them equipment, we can send our men out there as advisers, but they have to win it— the people of Viet-Nam—against the Communists. We are prepared to continue to assist them, but I don't think that the war can be won unless the people support the effort, and, in my opinion, in the last 2 months the Government has gotten out of touch with the people.

The president went on to cite the "repressions against the Buddhists," calling them "very unwise" and adding: "Now all we can do is to make it very clear that we don't think this is the way to win." Cronkite asked the president if he thought the Diem government

This formerly "TOP SECRET" memorandum of a State Department meeting on August 31, 1963, indicates that the United States was eager to support a coup d'état to overthrow the Diem regime. It also reveals that Vice President Lyndon Johnson had been left out of the strategic loop and was totally unaware of the Kennedy administration's coup plans.

"has time to regain the support of the people," to which Kennedy responded, "I do. With changes in policy and perhaps with personnel, I think it can."

Many historians have cited this interview as evidence that JFK, so enthusiastic about the prospects of South Vietnam the year before, had now decided to begin the end of U.S. involvement, at least in active combat. It was, he said, "their war. They are the ones who have to win it or lose it," and the "help" he now offered them he deliberately described as "equipment" and "advisers." As for the future of Diem, "changes in . . . personnel" seemed to be a pointed hint.

Perhaps President Kennedy intended this interview with America's most popular and trusted newsman to be the first signal of his new intentions with regard to the war in Vietnam. We can never know. What is now known, however, is that, even as he spoke to Cronkite, Kennedy had secretly approved a CIA-backed military coup d'état in South Vietnam. On his orders, the State Department had transmitted to Ambassador Henry Cabot Lodge Jr. in Saigon "Cable 243" after Diem's raids on Buddhist pagodas across South Vietnam during the night of August 21. The cable declared that Ngo Dinh Nhu "has maneuvered himself into a commanding position" and announced that the "US Government cannot tolerate situation in which power lies in Nhu's hands. Diem must be given chance to rid himself of Nhu and his coterie and replace them with best military and political personalities available." Lodge was directed to inform Diem accordingly. "If, in spite of all your efforts, Diem remains obdurate and refuses," the cable continued, "then we must face the possibility that Diem himself cannot be preserved." Lodge replied to Rusk that the "chances of Diem's meeting our demands

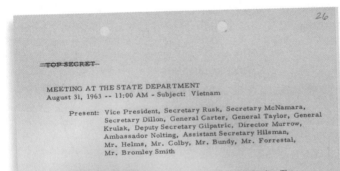

are virtually nil," and Cable 243 and Lodge's reply to it have been taken as acknowledgment of the Kennedy administration's approval of the overthrow of the erstwhile "tough miracle man of Vietnam."

Diem under Siege

As ARVN generals broadcast to South Vietnam their announcement of the coup d'état, President Ngo Dinh Diem telephoned U.S. Ambassador Henry Cabot Lodge Jr. at the embassy. Lodge reported the conversation to Washington:

Diem: Some units have made a rebellion and I want to know what is the attitude of the U.S.?

Lodge: I do not feel well enough informed to be able to tell you. I have heard the shooting, but am not acquainted with all the facts. Also it is 4:30 A.M. in Washington and the U.S. government cannot possibly have a view.

Diem: But you must have some general ideas. After all, I am a chief of state. I have tried to do my duty. I want to do now what duty and good sense require. I believe in duty above all.

Lodge: You have certainly done your duty. As I told you only this morning, I admire your courage and your great contributions to your country. No one can take away from you the credit for all you have done. Now I am worried about your physical safety. I have a report that those in charge of the current activity offer you and your brother safe conduct out of the country if you resign. Had you heard this?

Diem: No. You have my phone number.

Lodge: Yes. If I can do anything for your physical safety, please call me.

Diem: I am trying to reestablish order.

A later account from an embassy staffer added significant material to the report Lodge had sent to Washington:

Lodge: Well, you are a chief of state. I cannot give you advice, but personally, and as a friend, and as somebody who is concerned about your health, my suggestion would be you think seriously of getting away. Now, if I can be of any help on that, I'm prepared to send my driver with an officer of mine to escort you to safety. And we can get you on my jet aircraft, and I'm sure I can deliver on that. One of my officers will ride in the front seat of my limousine with the chauffeur.

Diem: No, I cannot agree to fleeing, because this is all a tempest in a teapot; it's a couple of hothead generals who don't speak for the army, and I know that the real troops are loyal to me and will soon have this all straightened out.

Lodge: Well, Mr. President, that is your decision, certainly. I cannot advise you one way or the other. But as I've said, if I can ever be of any assistance in looking after your security, I would certainly do so.

Diem: Well, I want you to tell Washington that this is being done, and that I want them to land the BLTs [battalion landing teams], the two marine BLTs on the aircraft carriers offshore. I want them to land and protect the palace.

Every inch the suave statesman, U.S. ambassador to South Vietnam Henry Cabot Lodge Jr. confers with President Diem on August 26, 1963, even as the U.S. State Department was planning to support an anti-Diem coup d'état.

NUMBERS
Butcher's Bill, 1962

As of the end of December 31, 1962, 27 U.S. servicemen had been killed in the Vietnam War and 65 more wounded. Five were being held as POWS by the Viet Cong. Vietnamese, North and South, Communist and non-Communist, military and civilian, were dying at the staggering rate of 2,000 each week, some the direct victims of combat, others of starvation and disease resulting from the chronic state of war. By mid 1963, 16,652 Americans were serving in South Vietnam.

On November 1, 1963, the coup commenced. While fighting raged in the streets of Saigon, Diem telephoned Ambassador Lodge, who advised Diem to leave immediately, and even offered to provide transportation (see the transcription on the previous page).

According to one U.S. Embassy staffer, Diem politely refused to "agree to fleeing, because this is all a tempest in a teapot," the work of "a couple of hothead generals who don't speak for the army." According to Diem's bodyguard, the South Vietnamese president sputtered into a rage that was anything but polite:

> Mr. Ambassador, do you realize who you are talking to? I would like you to know that you are talking to the president of an independent and sovereign nation. I will only leave this country if it is the wish of my people. I will never leave according to the request of rebellious generals or of an American ambassador. The US government must take full responsibility before the world for this miserable matter.

Early the next morning, on November 2, 1963, the Gia Long Palace, his official residence, was overrun, and Ngo Dinh Diem surrendered to the military leaders of the coup. He again telephoned Ambassador Lodge, who offered asylum but now informed him that he could not arrange transportation until the following day.

Was Lodge deliberately cutting Diem loose? Probably.

Did he know the fate that awaited him? Possibly.

According to one account, as he had long feared rebellion, Diem had ordered the construction of a secret escape tunnel out of Gia Long Palace. After packing a suitcase full of U.S. currency, he and his brother Nhu fled through it and reemerged in a wooded area, where they were picked up by a waiting car. Others insist that there never was a tunnel and that the brothers simply walked quietly out of the palace. In either case, they did not get very far before "rebel" officers intercepted them, placed them under arrest, and then put them in an armored personnel carrier (APC). Their destination, the officers said, was Tan Son Nhat Airport, but somewhere en route—apparently at a railroad crossing—the president and his brother were shot, pointblank, inside the APC, with a semi-automatic weapon. After death, their bodies were riddled with more bullets, and then stabbed over and over again.

With the Diem regime no more, a military junta proclaimed a provisional government, which the United States hastened to recognize on November 8. An almost exultant Ambassador Henry Cabot Lodge Jr., listening to the cheering crowds outside his embassy window, fired off a cable to Washington: "The prospects now are for a shorter war." The Viet Cong may have had similar thoughts. Seeking to exploit a fluid situation, they intensified their attacks.

As for the thirty-fifth president of the United States, his life would be ended just twenty days after Diem's, not in the obscurity of a dark railroad crossing on the outskirts of Saigon but in the bright sunlight of a motorcade through downtown Dallas. He had yet to announce any decision about increasing the U.S. combat presence to meet the heightened threat in Vietnam, or standing pat, or beginning a withdrawal from what he had told Walter Cronkite and the American people was, "in the final analysis," Vietnam's war.

TAKEAWAY
Kennedy's War

After initial ambivalence about committing more military resources to Vietnam, President Kennedy significantly escalated U.S. financial and military aid and was gratified, in 1962, by apparent ARVN progress against the Viet Cong. The following year, however, showed a dramatic increase in Viet Cong attacks and an even more dramatic reduction in popular support for the Diem regime, culminating in a coup d'état covertly supported by the CIA and the Kennedy administration. Ngo Dinh Diem and his brother Ngo Dinh Nhu were not only overthrown but also assassinated. On the verge of deciding his own next move in Vietnam, John F. Kennedy, thirty-fifth president of the United States, was gunned down on a Dallas street.

With JFK's assassination, Vietnam turned into "Johnson's War." In this photograph, the president's widow, Jacqueline Kennedy, and the president's brother, Attorney General Robert F. Kennedy, walk away from the casket during the funeral at Arlington National Cemetery on November 25, 1963.

PART THREE

JOHNSON'S WAR

CHAPTER 7

THE PEACE CANDIDATE

Vietnam Becomes Johnson's War

RUSHED OUT OF PARKLAND MEMORIAL HOSPITAL AFTER JOHN F. KENNEDY was pronounced dead there at one o'clock Dallas time, Vice President Lyndon Baines Johnson was driven to Love Field, where he boarded Air Force One. The aircraft remained on the tarmac as a casket carrying the remains of President Kennedy was taken aboard and as Federal Judge Sarah T. Hughes, a Johnson family friend, boarded to administer the oath of office. As JFK's widow looked on with others in the crowded passenger cabin of the Boeing 707, Johnson became the thirty-sixth president of the United States at 2:38 p.m., two hours and six minutes after the shots were fired in Dealey Plaza, Dallas. The aircraft then departed, landing at Andrews Air Force Base outside of Washington, D.C., in the early evening. The new president stepped off the plane, stood before a row of microphones set up on the apron, and read from a statement hastily prepared by staffers Jack Valenti, Bill Moyers, and Liz Carpenter during the flight.

"This is a sad time for all people," he began. "We have suffered a loss that cannot be weighed. For me, it is a deep personal tragedy. I know that the world shares the sorrow that Mrs. Kennedy and her family bear." Then came the part some viewers found disarmingly honest, comparing it to

Truman's famous confession after FDR's sudden death—"I felt like the moon, the stars, and all the planets had fallen on me"—and others found disquieting for its absence of confidence and inspiration. "I will do my best. That is all I can do. I ask for your help—and God's."

TRANSITIONS

LYNDON BAINES JOHNSON, THE POLITICAL PRODUCT of a rural Texas childhood, worked his way through Southwest Texas State Teachers' College, taught school to mostly poor, mostly Mexican children, and entered politics via President Franklin Delano Roosevelt's New Deal, as head of the Texas division of the National Youth Administration in 1935. He quit in 1937 to run for Congress and was elected to the House of Representatives on a strong New Deal platform. Personally driven and highly ambitious—those who knew him said he had a positive "lust" for power—Johnson was nevertheless a man who cared deeply about the welfare of the kind of children he had taught and the class of people the Depression-era New Deal was intended to aid. When he was thrust into the presidency on November 22, 1963, his focus was on domestic rather than on foreign policy—an area from which the Kennedy brothers had largely excluded him. (Neither of them much liked LBJ; he was chosen as JFK's running mate mainly to appease southern and western voters.) Indeed, it was in the domestic arena that, as president, Johnson intended to make his enduring mark. He saw the "Great Society," the series of welfare initiatives beginning in 1965 with Medicare and Medicaid, as the chief legacy of his administration.

Yet there was another side to Lyndon Johnson. A sitting congressman on December 7, 1941, when the Japanese attack on Pearl Harbor propelled the United States into World War II, he sought and secured a commission in the U.S. Naval Reserve and then asked Undersecretary of the Navy James Forrestal for a combat assignment. Instead, he was sent to inspect domestic shipyards until President Roosevelt tapped him early in 1942 to be his personal representative in the Southwest Pacific theater. While performing this mission, he was awarded the Silver Star, a decoration third in rank after the service crosses and the Medal of Honor. Although the medal came directly from the hands of General Douglas MacArthur, it was a controversial award. Johnson and others had reported that the B-26 bomber transporting him from one island base to another had been attacked by Japanese fighter aircraft, but still others (including the flight crew of that B-26) claimed

PREVIOUS PAGES: *LBJ meets with his National Security Council, February 7, 1968. Left to right: The president, Secretary of Defense Robert McNamara, Secretary of the Navy Paul Nitze, and a figure who appears to be General Earle Wheeler, chairman of the Joint Chiefs of Staff.*

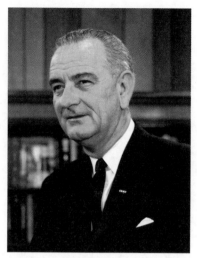

Lyndon Baines Johnson, thirty-sixth president of the United States. Note the small horizontal bar on his left lapel, the civilian emblem of the Silver Star he was awarded during World War II. He served in a noncombat role, and the decoration, of which he was very proud, was bestowed under what many consider controversial, even questionable, circumstances.

that the plane had turned back to base with engine trouble and had never come under attack. Whether it was merited or not, Johnson wore the decoration proudly and, throughout civilian life, was rarely seen in public without a miniature Silver Star lapel pin displayed on his suit-coat. Clearly, there was some part of Lyndon Baines Johnson, the president who aimed to create a beneficent social welfare program even more ambitious than the New Deal, that revered military might and relished martial glory.

Hanoi Turns Up the Heat

Months before the assassination of President Kennedy, Hanoi had begun intensifying offensive operations below the 17th parallel. The overthrow of Diem prompted the Communists to turn up the heat even more. Ambassador Henry Cabot Lodge had reported to Washington that the coup against the Diem regime happily boded "a shorter war." Kennedy took heart, but only fleetingly. For even before JFK's assassination, it was already becoming apparent that the military junta, which had complained so bitterly that Diem's cronyism and corruption were fatally weakening the war effort, now maneuvered to *avoid* taking the military initiative against the Viet Cong. The junta instead concentrated on building political support in the South so that it could negotiate an end to the war from a stronger popular position than Diem had commanded. In other words, instead of serving the intention of the United States, which was to reduce the Communist footprint in Southeast Asia by winning the war in Vietnam, the new South Vietnamese government was proving itself far less interested in victory than in simply ending the war short of abject defeat.

For its part, Hanoi decided that time was now of the essence. As North Vietnamese leaders saw the situation following the fall of Diem, the new government of South Vietnam had far more popular support than that of the toppled leader, and the United States was far more likely to increase its aid to a popular, less corrupt government. Some in Hanoi urged an immediate invasion across the 17th parallel, using North Vietnam regular army (NVA) troops. While a majority of party leaders rejected this, Hanoi did approve significantly strengthening the Viet Cong insurgency. The objective was to gain control of as much of South Vietnam as possible before the anticipated influx of more American forces.

The Generals Turn Up the Heat

If the hawks were in the ascendancy in Hanoi, it was also true that President Johnson was more inclined toward an aggressive combat policy in Vietnam than President Kennedy had been. Despite popular mythology, which purports to read JFK's mind and to find that mind turning toward withdrawal from Vietnam, there is no hard evidence that he was on the verge of doing so. What is apparent, however, was that JFK was far more willing to share his doubts publicly about commitment in Vietnam than LBJ was. Vietnam loomed larger for Johnson than it did for Kennedy. After just one week in office, Johnson exhorted his cabinet and advisers to "let no day go by without asking whether we are doing everything we can to win the struggle there." That Silver Star lapel pin meant something. A Roosevelt liberal in matters of domestic policy, LBJ was consistently—as representative, senator, and vice president—a "Cold Warrior" and hard-line anti-Communist in very nearly a conservative Republican mode. He wholeheartedly believed in Eisenhower's domino theory.

In the hindsight of history, we know that the massive escalation of the Vietnam War would ultimately conflict with, erode, and cripple the Great Society. Yet, at the end of 1963 and into the early years of the presidency he won in his own right in 1964, it seemed to Lyndon Johnson that hanging tough in Vietnam warded off accusations from the political right that he was soft on Communism and thereby actually helped him garner positive support for his bold domestic agenda. In 1963–64 and into 1965, Johnson envisioned absolutely no conflict between butter and bullets.

"I believed the loss of China had played a large role in the rise of [Republican red-baiting Senator] Joe [Joseph R.] McCarthy. And I knew that all these problems, taken together, were chickenshit compared with what might happen if we lost Vietnam."

★★★

—Lyndon Johnson to historian Doris Kearns Goodwin, quoted in *Lyndon Johnson and the American Dream* (1976)

LBJ and Secretary of Defense Robert McNamara (in the white shirt, to the president's left) confer with the Joint Chiefs of Staff at the president's much-beloved Texas ranch in December 1964. LBJ (left) leans on the table; General Curtis E. LeMay (center) faces the camera.

In any event, the military top brass did everything it could to encourage the hawkish direction of the new president's thoughts. The relentlessly aggressive U.S. Air Force general Curtis LeMay, together with the Joint Chiefs of Staff, hammered at Johnson to expand the war as quickly as possible and to do so by taking that war to the North, including the bombing of Hanoi. Secretary of Defense Robert McNamara objected to so drastic an escalation, which he feared would bring Chinese or Soviet intervention or provoke Soviet aggression elsewhere in the world, such as West Berlin. He advised President Johnson to confine operations to below the 17th parallel but recommended relaxing the rules for combat air engagement within South Vietnam, giving a free hand to USAF pilots to fly combat missions as necessary instead of deferring to South Vietnamese crews.

FORGOTTEN FACES
Curtis LeMay

Born in 1906 in Columbus, Ohio, Curtis Emerson LeMay grew up with a passion for two things: the military and flying. When he failed to obtain an appointment to West Point, he enrolled at Ohio State University, leaving to join the army in 1928 without graduating but after having completed the ROTC program. In September, he enrolled as a cadet in the Air Corps Flying School; he earned his wings on October 12, 1929.

As a second lieutenant (he was commissioned in January 1930), LeMay served with the 27th Pursuit Squadron, based in Michigan and, over the next three years, completed the civil engineering degree he had begun at Ohio State, earning his diploma in 1932.

During the Great Depression, LeMay worked with the New Deal–era CCC (Civilian Conservation Corps) and flew the airmails when President Roosevelt assigned Army Air Corps pilots to airmail operations in 1934. Promoted to first lieutenant in June 1935, LeMay attended an over-water navigation school in Hawaii. In 1937, he transferred from fighter aircraft ("pursuit ships," as they were then called) to bombers. It was a fateful move.

Attached to the 305th Bombardment Group at Langley Field, Virginia, LeMay drew the attention of top Air Corps brass for his work in developing aerial techniques for locating ships at sea. Recognized as a bold innovator, he was assigned as one of the very first army pilots to fly the new Boeing B-17 Flying Fortress bombers, and he led a flight of them on a goodwill tour to Latin America during 1937–38. On his return, he enrolled in the Air Corps Tactical School (1938–39) and was promoted to captain in January 1940. Assigned to command a squadron in the 34th Bombardment Group later that year, he was promoted to major in 1941.

After the United States entered World War II in December 1941, LeMay's rise became meteoric. In January 1942, he was promoted to lieutenant colonel, and just three months later to colonel. He assumed command of the 305th Bombardment Group in California in April and brought the unit to the United Kingdom as part of the Eighth Air Force, America's first major combat contribution to the war in continental Europe.

LeMay's work was central to the Army Air Forces' mission in the European theater. It was he who spearheaded the development of precision bombing doctrine, which included intense and comprehensive study of targets prior to missions and the hazardous tactic of abandoning evasive maneuvering while over targets. When

The World War II career of U.S. Air Force general Curtis E. LeMay culminated in his command of the XXI Bomber Command, which was responsible for the atomic bombing of Hiroshima and Nagasaki and, before that, the even more destructive and deadly fire-bombing of Tokyo. In the Cold War era, LeMay built the Strategic Air Command (SAC) into the primary nuclear weapons arm of the United States. As a member of the Joint Chiefs of Staff during the Vietnam War, he would talk of bombing North Vietnam "back into the Stone Age."

FORGOTTEN FACES Curtis LeMay (continued)

LeMay's techniques were applied to Eighth Air Force sorties, the number of bombs dropped on target doubled. LeMay was assigned command of the 3rd Bombardment Division in June 1943 and in September was promoted to temporary brigadier general, followed by a step up to temporary major general in March 1944. High command recognized his value as an innovator and therefore sent him to China to lead the 20th Bomber Command against the Japanese. In January 1945, he was transferred to command of the 21st Bomber Command, based on Guam, and revolutionized bombing tactics using the new B-29.

The giant Boeing Superfortress, the biggest bomber in World War II, was the most advanced bomber aircraft in the world. It was equipped with even more defensive guns than the B-17 and, with its fully pressurized cabin, was designed to fly higher and faster. Yet B-29 crews were not getting their bombs on target. LeMay took charge, analyzed the problems, and immediately stripped the B-29s of their defensive guns, as well as gun crews and ammunition, so that each ship could carry substantially more bombs. As if this weren't sufficiently radical, he ordered these aircraft, built for high altitudes, to bomb from low altitudes to increase accuracy and also to break formation—this at a time when every pilot was taught that a crew's only safety lay in strict formation flying, that stragglers were invariably slaughtered.

It was slaughter that aircrews anticipated, thanks to LeMay's new tactics. In fact, not only did accuracy rates improve remarkably but so did crew survival rates. LeMay's 21st Bomber Command devastated the four largest Japanese cities, including Tokyo, with combined high explosive and incendiary attacks, which were far more destructive than the later atomic bombing of Hiroshima and Nagasaki—operations that were also under LeMay's overall command. He was the highest-ranking American officer to be directly associated with nuclear weapons in actual combat.

After the war, the Air Force turned to LeMay to take charge, first, of planning the great Berlin Airlift of 1948–49 and then to create and to lead, beginning in October 1948, the Strategic Air Command (SAC). In this capacity, LeMay not only ushered the United States Air Force into the jet age with B-47 and B-52 bombers but also into the space age by introducing intercontinental ballistic missiles (ICBMs) into the strategic arsenal. Both of these transitions made the Air Force the nation's principal nuclear arm, and more than any other single commander, it was LeMay who shaped the postwar American military into a nuclear and thermonuclear force, even at the expense of its conventional ("tactical") capabilities.

Promoted to general in October 1951, LeMay was the youngest man to hold four-star rank since Ulysses S. Grant. He was named vice chief of staff of the Air Force in 1957 and chief of staff in 1961. Unapologetic about his advocacy of building a massive "nuclear deterrent," LeMay also made no

The Boeing B-47 Stratojet—seen here at its 1947 roll-out, designated "XB-47" for "Experimental Bomber"—was the world's first all-jet-powered aircraft capable of carrying nuclear weapons. Retired in its combat configuration in 1969 and in an electronic warfare configuration in 1977, it was the precursor to the B-52 Stratofortress, first flown in 1952.

excuses for his right-wing political beliefs, which frequently put him at odds with both presidents Kennedy and Johnson and, even more, with the secretary of defense who served both administrations, Robert S. McNamara. LeMay retired from the U.S. Air Force on February 1, 1965. He drew outraged public criticism in 1968 for becoming the running mate of segregationist third-party presidential candidate George Wallace and for reportedly advocating the use of nuclear weapons to end the Vietnam War by bombing the North "back into the Stone Age." LeMay subsequently claimed that he had been misquoted, explaining that he had "never said we should bomb them back into the Stone Age," only that "we had the capability to do it." LeMay retired from public life—and the public eye—after Wallace was defeated. He died in 1990.

JOHNSON ASSESSES, DECIDES, DELAYS

AS THE NEW YEAR APPROACHED, PRESIDENT JOHNSON presented a resolute public face, repeatedly affirming the U.S. commitment to the war. In December 1963, he sent McNamara on a fact-finding trip to South Vietnam. The defense secretary returned with the profoundly disturbing assessment that the Viet Cong controlled far more southern territory than even the most pessimistic U.S. officials had reported. The Strategic Hamlets program, which had given hope to President Kennedy, was clearly a shambles and a failure, he reported, and in Saigon and other cities, lawlessness and a general collapse of public morale reigned. During his service as defense secretary, Robert McNamara was criticized as much as he was praised for his emotion-free rationality. One journalist reported a description of McNamara as a "'human IBM machine' who cares more for computerized statistical logic than for human judgments," and others called him an "IBM machine with legs." What President Johnson saw in him was an adviser given neither to blind panic nor blind optimism. When McNamara now told his president that, in the absence of some big change, South Vietnam would collapse in sixty to ninety days, LBJ took him very seriously.

Under Kennedy, Washington had already backed one coup. Now Johnson decided to support another. The record of ARVN general Nguyen Khanh was not very encouraging. Eager to see France swept out of the country, he joined the Viet Minh in 1945, only to switch allegiance

Modern major general-MᶜNamara style

The product of Harvard Business School, Robert McNamara had been recruited as President Kennedy's secretary of defense shortly after he had become the first non–Ford family member to be named president of Ford Motor Company. Coolly rational in demeanor, he was once denigrated as an "IBM machine with legs," a point this 1965 Gib Crockett political cartoon illustrates.

to the French-backed puppet State of Vietnam by joining the Vietnamese National Army. In this capacity, he fought *against* the Viet Minh. In November 1960, he helped Ngo Dinh Diem defeat a military coup—though detractors pointed out that he waited until Diem seemed assured of victory before he threw in his support—and he did not participate in the 1963 coup that overthrew Diem. As a result, deeming him untrustworthy, the post-Diem ARVN high command sought to isolate Khanh by putting him in a provincial command near the 17th parallel.

Despite Khanh's demonstrations of naked ambition and cynical careerism, the Johnson administration welcomed his promises to renew and reinvigorate the war effort. When, in January 1964, he launched a coup against the military junta led by General Duong Van Minh, Washington approved. Indeed, Khanh initially proved to be a skillful politician. Accepting the post of prime minister, he allowed Minh—who was fairly popular with the public and much of the ARVN—to remain in office as a figurehead president. The coup, completed on January 30, was therefore bloodless, for which Washington gave thanks.

While Johnson and his advisers waited to see whether Khanh would deliver on his promise to wage a more effective war, calls for disengagement from Vietnam via negotiation became increasingly numerous. Editorial writers and members of Congress—overwhelmingly from Johnson's own party—called for peace. Within the administration, Undersecretary of State George Ball continued (as he had under President Kennedy) to predict a hopeless quagmire and to urge negotiations. He pointed to a communiqué received in February 1964 from David Nes, Ambassador Lodge's number two in Saigon, warning that the peasants of South Vietnam were "exhausted and sick of twenty years of civil conflict," whereas the Viet Cong were "a grass roots movement . . . disciplined, ideologically dedicated," and, most important of all, "easily identifiable with the desires of the peasantry." Moreover, Nes concluded, the VC were "of course ruthless." The conclusion Nes led up to was that the United States could never expect to achieve anything like victory in South Vietnam. And when LBJ looked beyond his own administration, turning to America's closest allies in the Cold War, including Canada and the United Kingdom, he received a startlingly cold shoulder in response. No other Western nation wanted to become involved in what LBJ himself was already calling "just the biggest damn mess I ever saw."

LBJ's Reelection Strategy

There can be no doubt that Johnson was deeply worried about Vietnam. Amid the misgivings expressed by the press and others and in the face of rebuffs from allies, he sent out vague peace feelers to Hanoi. When these were spurned, the hitherto cautious Robert McNamara became the first administration official to advocate formulating a comprehensive air strike plan against North Vietnam. Military advisers were called in, and they persuaded Johnson that General Khanh's promises and good intentions would not turn the situation around. Only a substantial infusion of U.S. ground troops would put iron into the ARVN spine. While this would apply pressure to the VC in the South, a bombing campaign above the 17th parallel would apply pressure directly to Hanoi.

The president was inclined to agree; however, 1964 was an election year, and his Republican opponent was Senator Barry Goldwater of Arizona, a conservative hawk, who had recently retired from the U.S. Air Force Reserve with the rank of major general, continuing to pilot B-52 bombers late into his military career. Goldwater advocated a very aggressive policy in Vietnam, including bombing Hanoi. A majority of the American electorate viewed Goldwater as an extremist and feared that, as commander-in-chief, he would not hesitate to use nuclear weapons in Vietnam. Johnson portrayed himself as the peace candidate and Goldwater not merely as the war *candidate* but also as a war *monger*. To dramatize the difference between them, LBJ put the Hanoi bombing campaign on the shelf, along with any substantial increase in troop commitment, until after the November elections. He did authorize a modest increase in U.S. personnel "in-country" but was careful always to call them "advisers" rather than "soldiers," "airmen," or "combat forces." Even more significantly, in June 1964, the president tapped General William Westmoreland, a seasoned veteran of World War II and Korea who had extensive experience with airborne (paratrooper) and airmobile (troops ferried into combat by air) warfare, to replace General Paul D. Harkins as top U.S. commander in Vietnam. Increasingly notorious for his invariably optimistic reports on the military situation in South Vietnam, Harkins was perceived as being increasingly out of touch with reality in the field. Westmoreland, in contrast, was widely regarded as a no-nonsense, results-oriented, "muddy boots" commander. He was also, already, an outspoken advocate of expanding America's combat role in the Vietnam War.

LBJ campaigns for election in his own right, 1964. He ran against Republican conservative Barry Goldwater's reputation as a "fanatic" war hawk who would not scruple to ignite World War III by using atomic weapons against Vietnam. Goldwater supporters in the crowd hold up flyers with his image.

"An American General with a swagger stick and cigarette holder . . . who would not deign to soil his suntans [khaki uniform] and street shoes in a rice paddy to find out what was going on."

✳✳✳

—Neil Sheehan, UPI Saigon bureau chief, on General Paul D. Harkins, top U.S. commander in Vietnam from 1962 to June 1964

Still, Johnson remained supremely disciplined in exercising self-restraint prior to the election. On November 1, 1964—two days before the general election—Viet Cong briefly overran Bien Hoa Air Base, killing four U.S. Air Force airmen, wounding seventy-six (some sources report seventy-two) others, and wrecking aircraft and buildings. The

Joint Chiefs of Staff were quick to recommend immediate and severe reprisals. *President* Johnson pondered the recommendation, but *Candidate* Johnson deferred a decision.

Tonkin

Come election day, Lyndon Baines Johnson won a spectacular 61.1 percent of the popular vote, piling up 486 electoral votes against Barry Goldwater's 52. With the election handily won, the president believed he now had a free hand to expand the war in Vietnam. It had been made even freer by events before the election.

On July 31, 1964, the U.S. Navy destroyer *Maddox* set out on a reconnaissance mission in the Gulf of Tonkin, off the coast of North Vietnam. On August 2, the ship reported itself under attack, "in international waters," by North Vietnamese patrol boats and withdrew to South Vietnamese territorial waters. Here, *Maddox* was joined by another destroyer, the USS *Turner Joy*. The "battle," however, had produced no U.S. casualties and negligible damage to *Maddox*: a single ding created by the impact of a single machine-gun bullet.

Two days after this incident, on August 4, U.S. navy patrol craft intercepted what radio operators interpreted as communications signaling another North Vietnamese naval attack. The intelligence was relayed to *Maddox* and *Turner Joy*, which went on high alert. When a radar operator identified blips that seemed hostile, the two destroyers unleashed a two-hour barrage in the direction and at the range of the radar contacts.

Although no one on board either ship actually sighted an enemy, the radar contacts were reported and relayed to the White House. Johnson, McNamara, and their aides put the August 4 report together with the gunfire exchange of August 2. The presidential race notwithstanding, LBJ ordered immediate retaliatory air strikes against North Vietnam, albeit limited to North Vietnamese "gunboats" and facilities supporting them. On the evening of August 4, a grim-faced President Johnson appeared on all three national television networks to describe the attacks and the retaliatory measures he had authorized. Declaring that "We Americans know, although others appear to forget, the risk of spreading the conflict," he assured both American TV viewers and, presumably,

A North Vietnamese torpedo boat runs past the USS Maddox *during the first incident in the Gulf of Tonkin, August 2, 1964. The gunboat directed machine gun fire against the American destroyer, inflicting negligible damage. The photograph was furnished to Congress by the U.S. Navy.*

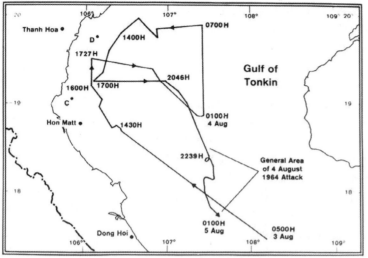

This official U.S. Navy map, furnished to the U.S. Congress, tracks the course of the destroyers **Maddox** *and* **Turner Joy** *before, during, and after the reported second attack by North Vietnamese gunboats in the Gulf of Tonkin on August 4, 1964.*

the North Vietnamese, "We still seek no wider war."

On television, the president spoke of the August 4 incident as a repeat of the August 2 attack, this time "by a number of hostile vessels . . . with torpedoes," not just machine guns. He reported the navy's belief that "at least two of the attacking boats were sunk." In the meantime, after the president addressed the nation, Secretary McNamara testified to Congress that the North Vietnamese attacks had been entirely unprovoked, even though he knew (but did not reveal to Congress) that the *Maddox* was employed on a so-called DESOTO ("*DEHAVEN Special Operations off Tsingtao*") mission, a "signals intelligence" (SIGINT, or electronic eavesdropping) operation in "hostile" (not, as claimed, *international*) waters. The purpose of DESOTO missions was to provide intelligence to guide South Vietnamese strikes north of the 17th parallel.

McNamara lied to Congress about the August 2 attack, which was neither unprovoked nor in international waters. As for the August 4 "attack," he told Congress that the administration possessed "unequivocal proof" that it had occurred. There was no such proof, however, and McNamara knew it. Nevertheless, following his testimony and the delivery, on August 5, of a message from the president, Congress formulated the so-called Gulf of Tonkin Resolution, authorizing the president "to take all necessary steps, including the use of armed force, to assist any member or protocol state of the Southeast Asia Collective Defense Treaty [SEATO signatory] requesting assistance in defense of its freedom." A few legislators were alarmed by giving the president what they called a "blank check" to conduct a war without consulting with Congress, let alone securing the constitutionally mandated declaration of war from Congress. The Senate debated the resolution on August 6–7, which was passed by both houses on August 7.

From the Senate Debate of the Tonkin Gulf Resolution, August 6–7, 1964

Mr. Nelson: [Gaylord Nelson, D-WI] . . . Am I to understand that it is the sense of Congress that we are saying to the executive branch: "If it becomes necessary to prevent further aggression, we agree now, in advance, that you may land as many divisions as deemed necessary, and engage in a direct military assault on North Vietnam if it becomes the judgment of the Executive, the Commander in Chief, that this is the only way to prevent further aggression"?

Mr. Fulbright: [J. William Fulbright, D-AR] As I stated, section I is intended to deal primarily with aggression against our forces. . . . I do not know what the limits are. I do not think this resolution can be determinative of that fact. I think it would indicate that he [the president] would take reasonable means first to prevent any further aggression, or repel further aggression against our own forces . . . I do not know how to answer the Senator's question and give him an absolute assurance that large numbers of troops would not be put ashore. I would deplore it. . . .

Mr. Nelson: . . . My concern is that we in Congress could give the impression to the public that we are prepared at this time to change our mission and substantially expand our commitment. If that is what the sense of Congress is, I am opposed to the resolution. I therefore ask the distinguished Senator from Arkansas if he would consent to accept an amendment [that explicitly says Congress wants no extension of the present military conflict and no U.S. direct military involvement].

Mr. Fulbright: . . . The Senator has put into his amendment a statement of policy that is unobjectionable. However, I cannot accept the amendment under the circumstances. I do not believe it is contrary to the joint resolution, but it is an enlargement. I am informed that the House is now voting on this resolution. The House joint resolution is about to be presented to us. I cannot accept the amendment and go to conference with it, and thus take responsibility for delaying matters.

Mr. Gruening: [Ernest Gruening, D-AK] . . . Regrettably, I find myself in disagreement with the President's Southeast Asian policy. . . . The serious events of the past few days, the attack by North Vietnamese vessels on American warships and our reprisal, strikes me as the inevitable and foreseeable concomitant and consequence of U.S. unilateral military aggressive policy in Southeast Asia. . . . We now are about to authorize the President if he sees fit to move our Armed Forces . . . not only into South Vietnam but also into North Vietnam, Laos, Cambodia, Thailand, and of course the authorization includes all the rest of the SEATO nations. That means sending our American boys into combat in a war in which we have no business, which is not our war, into which we have been misguidedly drawn, which is steadily being escalated.

This resolution is a further authorization for escalation unlimited. I am opposed to sacrificing a single American boy in this venture. We have lost far too many already. . . .

Mr. Morse: [Wayne Morse, D-OR] . . . I believe that history will record that we have made a great mistake in subverting and circumventing the Constitution of the United States. . . . I believe this resolution to be a historic mistake. I believe that . . . future generations will look with dismay and great disappointment upon a Congress which is now about to make such a historic mistake.

REALITY CHECK

Creating a Cause for War

Years after the Gulf of Tonkin Resolution was passed, the supposed "facts" on which it was based were brought increasingly into doubt. In 1995, former Secretary of Defense Robert McNamara admitted that he had lied to Congress in 1964. He affirmed that the gunfire in the August 2 attacks had been real but explained that both he and the president knew the reports of the August 4 attack were mistaken. Crews of both American destroyers had believed they were under attack, but this impression was based either on malfunctioning radar equipment or the misinterpretation of "false echo" radar artifacts.

On November 30, 2005, the National Security Agency (NSA) declassified documents that included a confidential 2001 article in which NSA historian Robert J. Hanyok concluded that NSA intelligence officers had "deliberately skewed" evidence to show that North Vietnamese ships had attacked on August 4, 1964.

Given a "blank check," Johnson folded it neatly and tucked it into his wallet. Ordering immediate reprisals for the reputed attacks in the Gulf of Tonkin was one thing, but vastly expanding the war on what was virtually the eve of the face-off at the polls was quite another. Johnson wanted to draw a contrast with Goldwater, not commit an act worthy of him. He therefore waited—although, covertly, he authorized further DESOTO support for South Vietnamese hit-and-run sabotage raids against facilities in the North.

Johnson need not have worried that the Gulf of Tonkin Resolution in itself would scare off voters. Overnight, his approval rating jumped thirty points. Far from creating concern among the president's supporters, the combination of the resolution and the retaliatory strikes immediately neutralized Goldwater's criticism of LBJ's Vietnam policy. The incumbent candidate looked strong and from this position of strength could solemnly assure the American electorate that "We are not about to send American boys nine or ten thousand miles away from home to do what Asian boys ought to be doing for themselves."

The Uncertainty of Triumph

As Johnson saw it, obtaining the Gulf of Tonkin Resolution was a victory in prelude to an ultimate triumph: the landslide defeat of Barry Goldwater. Yet turning back to Vietnam itself, there was hardly any triumph to be found. With each passing day, General Khanh was on his way to becoming every bit as unpopular as both Diem and the junta that followed him. Struggling simply to retain some semblance of power, Khanh attempted to rule via a triumvirate and then with the aid of a "High National Council" that barely gave the appearance of a bona fide civilian government. In fact, neither he nor anyone else was able to govern efficiently during 1964, let alone prosecute the war effectively. Throughout South Vietnam, malaise, cynicism, war weariness, and resentment of the American presence increased relentlessly.

Just when the situation seemed incapable of getting any worse, it did.

The retaliatory air strike against the North that proved so popular with American voters did nothing to chastise Hanoi. On the contrary, Communist leaders responded in September by doing what they had never done before. They dispatched NVA units—the regular North Vietnamese Army—across the 17th parallel. It was an infiltration rather than a full-scale invasion, but it made its point. The war had reached a new level of escalation, and to demonstrate that it was in the fight to the finish, whatever the United States might do, Hanoi openly appealed to Beijing and Moscow for long-term support.

NUMBERS

Governments Come, Governments Go

After the assassination of Ngo Dinh Diem in November 1963, through the end of 1965, at least eleven governments, some civilian, some military, some in between, would come and go in South Vietnam, none capable of surviving long, even with U.S. support.

Written in 2001 by National Security Agency (NSA) historian Robert J. Hanyok, this article concluded that the reported August 4, 1964, attack against U.S. destroyers in the Gulf of Tonkin was a fabrication. The article was not declassified until November 30, 2005.

TOP SECRET//COMINT//X1

Cryptologic Quarterly

(U) Skunks, Bogies, Silent Hounds, and the Flying Fish: The Gulf of Tonkin Mystery, 2-4 August 1964

ROBERT J. HANYOK

(C//SI) The Gulf of Tonkin incidents of 2 to 4 August 1964 have come to loom over the subsequent American engagement in Indochina. The incidents, principally the second one of 4 August, led to the approval of the Gulf of Tonkin Resolution by the U.S. Congress, which handed President Johnson the carte blanche charter he had wanted for future intervention in Southeast Asia. From this point on, the American policy and programs would dominate the course of the Indochina War. At the height of the American involvement, over a half million U.S. soldiers, sailors, airmen, and marines would be stationed there. The war would spread across the border into Cambodia and escalate in Laos. Thailand assumed a greater importance as a base for supporting the military effort, especially for the air war, but also for SIGINT purposes of intercept and direction finding.

(U) At the time, the Gulf of Tonkin incidents of August were not quite so controversial. According to the Johnson administration, the issue of the attacks was pretty much cut and dried. As the administration explained, our ships had been in international waters – anywhere from fifty to eighty miles from the DRV coastline by some calculations, during the alleged second attack – and were attacked twice, even though they were innocent of any bellicose gestures directed at North Vietnam. Secretary of Defense Robert McNamara had assured the Senate that there had been no connection between what the U.S. Navy was doing and any aggressive operations by the South Vietnamese.[1] Washington claimed that the United States had to defend itself and guarantee freedom of navigation on the high seas.

(U) However, within the government, the events of 4 August were never that clear. Even as the last flare fizzled in the dark waters of the South China Sea on that August night, there were conflicting narratives and interpretations of what had happened. James Stockdale, then a navy pilot at the scene, who had "the best seat in the house from which to detect boats," saw nothing. "No boats," he would later write, "no boat wakes, no ricochets off boats, no boat impacts, no torpedo wakes – nothing but black sea and American firepower."[2] The commander of the *Maddox* task force, Captain John J. Herrick, was not entirely certain what had transpired. (Captain Herrick actually was the commander of the destroyer division to which the *Maddox* belonged. For this mission, he was aboard as the on-site commander.) Hours after the incident, he would radio Commander-in-Chief, Pacific (CINCPAC) telling them that he was doubtful of many aspects of the "attack."

(U) It would be years before any evidence that an attack had not happened finally emerged in the public domain, and even then, most reluctantly. Yet, remarkably, some of the major participants in the events still maintained that the Gulf of Tonkin incident had occurred just as it had been originally reported. Secretary of Defense Robert McNamara, in his memoirs *In Retrospect*, considered the overall evidence for an attack still convincing.[3] The U.S. Navy's history of the Vietnam conflict, written by Edward J. Marolda and Oscar P. Fitzgerald (hereafter referred to as the "Marolda-Fitzgerald history"), reported that the evidence for the second attack, especially from intelligence, including a small amount of SIGINT, was considered conclusive.[4]

Derived From: NSA/CSSM 123-2
24 February 1998
Declassify On: X1

TOP SECRET//COMINT//X1

Page 1

Toward Christmas Eve and After

Reelected by the people and empowered by Congress, Lyndon Johnson was free to expand the war. Yet even as North Vietnam was securing war matériel from both China and the Soviet Union, America's traditional allies were becoming increasingly strident in their calls for the United States to disengage. Britain, Canada, and now Japan all rebuffed requests for assistance in the war. France's president, Charles de Gaulle, proposed negotiations to neutralize Vietnam, just as Laos had been neutralized. When U.S. diplomats pointed out that "neutral" Laos was actively aiding North Vietnam, de Gaulle admitted that his proposal was certainly imperfect but claimed that it was better than escalating a war that could not be won.

It was in Laos that LBJ took his first truly aggressive post-election step. In December, he approved limited aerial attacks on the Ho Chi Minh Trail in Laos. He voiced agreement with his military advisers that this would be merely the first phase of a two-phase bombing campaign. The second phase would be a sustained program of bombardment of North Vietnam. He agreed, but he worried, because he understood that sustained air combat operations would require U.S. air bases in South Vietnam, and U.S. air bases would require *ground* forces to defend them. There could be no such thing as conducting a purely air war. Planes had to land, had to be serviced, aircrews had to be domiciled, and everything and everyone had to be protected from attack. With the South Vietnamese government chronically unstable and the ARVN chronically unreliable, Johnson found himself unable to pull the trigger on committing a large number of U.S. combat personnel on the ground.

Much closer to home, Johnson's own vice president, former Minnesota senator Hubert Horatio Humphrey, sent the president a memo in which he claimed that the same overwhelming electoral victory LBJ was using to justify escalating the war would be better used to justify withdrawing from it. The lofty approval ratings, Humphrey suggested, made Johnson invulnerable to attacks from right-wing conservatives. What is more, by not only continuing but also escalating what might well be an unwinnable war, Johnson would not mollify, let alone win over, conservatives and would ultimately lose the support of Democrats of all political stripes, from liberal to moderate.

The Brinks Hotel, Saigon (today Ho Chi Minh City), was being used as a billet for U.S. and South Vietnamese military officers when it was bombed by Viet Cong saboteurs on Christmas Eve 1964 at 5:45 p.m., the height of "happy hour" in the hotel's crowded bar.

Happy Hour

Amid pressures to pull back, LBJ continued to escalate, albeit cautiously. Then, on December 24, 1964, Viet Cong saboteurs loaded some two hundred pounds of high explosives into the trunk of a car, rigged the bomb with a timer, and parked the vehicle on the grounds of the Brinks Hotel, where many unmarried U.S. Army officers were billeted. The hotel had a bar that served as an Officers' Club. The timer was set to detonate at 5:45 p.m., the middle of "happy hour" on Christmas Eve. The blast killed two—including a lieutenant colonel and a staff sergeant—and injured thirty-eight U.S. officers and at least twenty-five Vietnamese civilians.

The Joint Chiefs of Staff urged—practically demanded—reprisals. If LBJ was going to expand the war, this was surely the occasion for it. Yet, dismayed by the failure of the retaliatory air strikes he had been certain would demoralize and intimidate Hanoi, he held back, much to the outrage of the military brass.

The Battle of Binh Gia

Christmas 1964 came. Christmas 1964 went. On December 28, there was a new attack, as some 1,800 Viet Cong struck the hamlet of Binh Gia in Phuoc Tuy Province, quickly overwhelming a South Vietnamese "Popular

REALITY CHECK
Hope in the Crosshairs

The Viet Cong bombers took care to plan the explosion at the Brinks Hotel to detonate precisely when they knew the bar would be most crowded. That was bad enough. Some military figures and historians believe they also intended the blast to kill or injure Bob Hope, the legendary radio, film, and television comedian who had been a favorite of shows staged in combat zones by the USO since World War II. Hope was indeed expected to arrive at the hotel on December 24, though it is uncertain whether or not the bombers knew this. In any case, fortunately for the entertainer and his entourage, a baggage mix-up at Tan Son Nhut Air Base delayed his arrival.

Force" militia unit. Using U.S. helicopters and pilots, ARVN commanders airlifted two ranger battalions to relieve the militia. They also were quickly overwhelmed. On December 30, South Vietnamese marines were sent in, came under attack that evening, but managed to repel the attackers with the aid of U.S. Army helicopter gunships. More ARVN marines joined the battle on January 1, 1965, along with ARVN airborne troops supported by U.S. Air Force bombers. The combination of these forces finally succeeded in compelling the withdrawal of the Viet Cong, who had lost at least 32 killed but had killed 201 ARVN and U.S. personnel, wounding 192 more. Some 68 were classified as missing in action.

Maxwell Taylor, President Kennedy's military adviser, whom LBJ had appointed as the new U.S. ambassador to South Vietnam earlier in 1964, had consistently opposed calls by the Joint Chiefs for retaliation and escalation. The sheer audacity of the VC assault on Binh Gia now prompted him to join the Chiefs in calling for the bombing of North Vietnam.

Finding Facts

Despite what was now almost universal pressure on him to retaliate and escalate, President Johnson continued to hesitate. The government of South Vietnam was less stable than ever, and Johnson seriously questioned whether there was any ruling structure there worth fighting for—or even possible to fight for. Eisenhower had spoken of preventing the fall of a domino. Johnson beheld a South Vietnam so insubstantial that he wondered less about a falling domino than if a domino even existed.

Agonizing, President Johnson decided that he needed more information and therefore sent national security advisor McGeorge Bundy on a fact-finding mission to Saigon in February 1965. Almost immediately upon his arrival, Bundy found his first fact—or, rather, that fact found him.

Tipping Point Pleiku

On February 7, 1965, the Viet Cong 409th Battalion kicked off the Communist spring offensive in spectacular fashion with an attack on the U.S. airfield at Camp Holloway near the town of Pleiku in the Central Highlands of Vietnam. The camp was home to some four hundred soldiers of the U.S. Army 52nd Combat Aviation Battalion. Also posted here was the U.S. advisory compound of II Corps, MACV. Base security was the responsibility of an ARVN force, including an elite Ranger battalion, five Regional Force companies, and an armored squadron. The base itself was heavily fortified with multiple concertina-wire fences more than thirty feet high. Both U.S. and ARVN commanders were confident that no attack could penetrate.

Nguyen Thanh Tam, the VC commander, devised a multipronged assault, with separate combat groups assigned to destroy aircraft on the ground with a mortar barrage, to shell the MACV compound, to engage all of the defensive forces, and to break through the multilayered fences while preserving an avenue of retreat. Highly enterprising VC combat engineers employed explosives to breach the fences and planted land mines to protect the attackers' line of retreat. From the beginning, the plan was to hit, hit hard, and run away.

The attack stepped off at 1:50 a.m. on February 7. The vaunted defensive measures were overcome with startling ease. Following massed fire from Soviet- and Chinese-made AK-47 assault rifles, the attackers penetrated Camp Holloway and wreaked havoc while units outside the perimeter rained down mortar shells on the MACV compound and the airfield. After a mere five minutes of sustained attack, the VC began their withdrawal.

Bundy had come to Vietnam thinking he would be faced with a daunting task of evaluating risk and reward. The shocking attack on Pleiku—a base considered virtually impregnable—suddenly made his job easy. In concert with Ambassador Taylor and General Westmoreland, Bundy cabled President Johnson an unequivocal recommendation to bomb North Vietnam.

Operation Flaming Dart began on February 7, the very day of the Pleiku raid, with an airstrike against a major NVA barracks. Over the next several days, through February 24, Flaming Dart employed USAF and Vietnam Air Force aircraft and crews in attacks on various NVA bases and facilities throughout the North. Far from chastening the Communists, the attacks brought renewed VC reprisals, including a devastating strike against the U.S.-ARVN barracks at Qui Nhon, in which twenty-three U.S. airmen and seven Vietnamese troops were killed on February 10.

NUMBERS
Pleiku Catastrophe
Of 400 U.S. Army personnel in Camp Holloway, 9 were killed and 109 (some sources report 126) wounded. Ten aircraft were completely destroyed and another 15 badly damaged but capable of being repaired.

LBJ's national security adviser McGeorge Bundy surveys the devastation of a February 7, 1965, Viet Cong attack on the U.S. airfield at Camp Holloway in the Central Highlands town of Pleiku. MACV commander General William Westmoreland stands to Bundy's left.

NUMBERS

Bigger Than World War II

Operation Rolling Thunder would fly some 304,000 combat sorties in which 2,382 aircraft, including a large fleet of B-52s, dropped approximately 643,000 tons of munitions over 6 months. One thousand eighty-four U.S. Air Force officers and airmen were killed, captured, or declared missing, and 938 U.S. aircraft were lost. North Vietnamese casualties are estimated at 52,000 military deaths and up to 182,000 civilian deaths. Perhaps 120 North Vietnamese aircraft were destroyed. For comparison, during World War II, Allied aircraft (U.S., British, and—briefly—French) flew a total of 301,757 combat sorties in the European theater between 1940 and 1945.

Operation Flaming Dart had no strategic impact on the North but resulted only in a pattern of U.S.-ARVN strikes alternating with VC counterstrikes. This failure prompted President Johnson to double down on the air campaign against North Vietnam by authorizing a truly massive program of sustained aerial bombardment.

A ROLL OF THUNDER

IT WAS CALLED OPERATION ROLLING THUNDER, and it sent into Northern Vietnamese skies, among other aircraft, the biggest bombers in the Air Force inventory, B-52 Stratofortresses, planes built to deliver thermonuclear annihilation against the Soviet Union but pressed into service now to drop ton after ton of "big iron"—conventional high-explosive bombs—against multiple targets above the 17th parallel. The operation began on March 2, 1965, continuing in what planners described as a "slowly ascending tempo" until May 11, when raids were suspended while LBJ sought peace talks with the North Vietnamese. Rebuffed, the president ordered the resumption of bombing on May 18. Rolling Thunder operations would continue, with periodic recesses intended to invite negotiation, through November 1, 1968.

The commencement of so ambitious an offensive operation as Rolling Thunder made a large commitment of American combat troops to the ground war nearly inevitable. General William Westmoreland filed his first request even before Rolling Thunder flew its first mission, asking at the end of February for two U.S. Marine battalions to guard the U.S. air base established at Da Nang, a port city on the coast of the South China Sea. The president did not question, much less challenge, the request.

At 5:45 on the morning of March 8, 1965, less than a month after Westmoreland asked for the marines, the four ships of Amphibious Task Force 76 closed to within 4,000 yards of the Da Nang shore and anchored in the harbor. Fifteen minutes later, the order was given to "land the landing force." The operation was carried out in high surf with choppy waves, which made it hazardous. Nevertheless, by the end of the next day, a total of 3,500 marines and their equipment were onshore. By the end of the year, more than 38,000 U.S. Marines would be serving, in combat, in-country.

Even as the marines were landing at Da Nang, President Lyndon B. Johnson, having just committed the first major American air and ground combat forces to the war in Vietnam, wrestled with his cabinet, advisers, and military commanders to decide not just how the war would be fought but to what purpose. Up to this point, with boots already crunching sand a world away from the White House, the basic objectives of a "Vietnam War" had yet to be defined.

Marines of the 9th Marine Expeditionary Brigade land at Da Nang, March 8, 1965. The U.S. ground war in South Vietnam begins in deadly earnest.

TAKEAWAY
America's "Peace Candidate" Goes to War

With the general election of 1964 approaching and at pains to present himself as the "peace candidate" versus his opponent, the unapologetic war hawk Barry M. Goldwater, President Lyndon B. Johnson delayed making a major, irreversible commitment of American combat forces to Vietnam. Holding a "blank check" from Congress, written to him after the so-called Gulf of Tonkin Incident in August 1964, and having won a landslide election to the presidency in his own right, LBJ continued to defer a major combat commitment to a seemingly ungovernable South Vietnam until a series of stunning Viet Cong military successes moved his hand to initiate in March 1965 the massive bombing of North Vietnam and the landing of thousands of United States Marines. Vietnam was now Johnson's war.

CHAPTER 8

AN INCH AT A TIME

Johnson's War Becomes America's War

"ROLLING THUNDER" WAS INTENDED AS NOTHING MORE OR LESS than the standard macho and martial operational code name calculated to stir pride in pilots and crews, but the phrase also spoke volumes about the attitude of the Johnson administration toward fighting this war in 1965 and 1966. It implied a continuous action of formidable size and long duration. It suggested the roar of hundreds of giant bombers in flight, and it summoned to the imagination the effect of carpet bombing a large area day in and day out. Perhaps most significantly of all, the name evoked a storm, powerful and yet remote.

A great but impersonal force—that is what LBJ wanted to wield in Vietnam. Since the days of the French Empire and Japanese occupation, war in Vietnam had been a guerrilla conflict, the combat up close and personal. That is how the Viet Minh and now the Viet Cong wanted it. Guerrilla war was war on *their* terms. The president meant to change those terms. Americans—the military, the politicians, the public—were uncomfortable with guerrilla warfare. Despite the existence of the U.S. Marines (trained in small-unit tactics) and JFK's Green Berets (a counterinsurgency force),

U.S. military strategists remained wedded to fighting the American way—with high technology, including big planes and big bombs.

STRATEGIC PERSUASION

NO AIRCRAFT IN THE U.S. AIR FORCE ARSENAL was bigger or could drop more "big iron" than the Boeing B-52 "Stratofortress"—to use the aircraft's official name, which no actual

member of the "B-52 community" ever used. The hulking monster—nearly 160 feet long, a wingspan of 185 feet, an empty weight of 185,000 pounds, bomb load of 70,000 pounds, powered by *eight* turbofan jet engines—was universally called, by those who flew and serviced them, "BUFF." It was an acronym for *Big Ugly Fat Fucker*, unconvincingly sanitized by USAF public relations hacks as *Big Ugly Flying Fellow*.

As with the name "Rolling Thunder," it is difficult *not* to see the use of the B-52 in Vietnam as an emblem of American conceptions and misconceptions about the war. It was, after all, the ultimate projection of U.S. military technology and power, the nation's principal atomic weapons platform, directed against insurgent fighters in a small jungle nation. The incongruity is striking.

The origin of the B-52 can be traced to 1945, when the United States Army Air Forces formulated a requirement for a long-range heavy bomber powered by turbine engines—not jets originally but turbo-props—to replace the piston-powered B-29. From the beginning, the principal purpose of the aircraft was to carry atomic weapons, a task for which the B-29, though it had been modified to attack Hiroshima and Nagasaki, was just barely adequate. A design emerged in 1948, equipped with turboprops, and the United States Air Force, newly independent from the U.S. Army, ordered prototypes in that propeller configuration. Before production began, however, the Air Force ordered a change to full jet power, and the first B-52A, jet powered, was airborne by August 1954.

Under the direction of Strategic Air Command (SAC) commanding officer General Curtis E. LeMay, the B-52 became the backbone of the United States nuclear deterrent. The development of the Boeing KC-135 Stratotanker (based on the design of what became the famed Boeing 707 passenger jetliner), which LeMay also oversaw, meant

A B-52 flies over Vietnam, October 1966. Designed and built for a strategic mission— the deployment of thermonuclear weapons— the Stratofortress was awkwardly pressed into a tactical role in the Vietnam War. Its only modification: a jungle-green camouflage paint job to replace the original sleek silver of bare metal. The B-52 would not only become the mainstay of the U.S. nuclear air fleet but also would be used extensively to drop tens of thousands of tons of ordnance against Vietnam and its neighbors. It still plays a major role in U.S. air power some sixty years after its first flight.

Napalm was essentially gasoline that had been "jellied," so that it would adhere to its target as it burned: a building of wood or bamboo, a child of flesh and blood. Nearly four hundred thousand tons of napalm was dropped on Vietnam. The tonnage dropped on Cambodia is unknown, but total U.S. bomb tonnage used against that country totaled 2.7 million, of which a significant percentage was napalm. Three million tons of U.S. ordnance was dropped on Laos—making it the most bombed country per capita in the world—again including a large proportion of napalm weapons.

that the B-52 could be refueled in flight, a capability that put virtually any target on the planet within range, therefore making the B-52 the supreme strategic weapon.

Everything about BUFF—size, power, payload capacity, range, and endurance—made it the most formidable strategic aircraft in the world. Its very existence was an expression of Cold War doctrine, a cocked weapon pointed at a single enemy, the Soviet Union, which in a thermonuclear world was seen as the *only* enemy that mattered. Now "Big Ugly" was being sent into a tactical war in Vietnam, assigned a tactical mission, delivering ton upon ton of napalm and high-explosive munitions. It is little wonder that President Johnson found it easy to believe that the pounding of Rolling Thunder would beat Hanoi into submission—or at least send the Communist leaders to the conference table. To South Dakota senator (and later political rival) George McGovern—himself a World War II B-24 bomber pilot—LBJ crowed, "I'm going up old Ho Chi Minh's leg an inch at a time." In a jungle country like Vietnam, the B-52 might not be able to deliver total annihilation, but it surely would, Johnson reasoned, create an attrition no government could long compel its people to endure.

The Eternal Bomber

No combat aircraft has proved more enduring than the B-52. Born in a design created at the end of World War II, the "A" version first flew in 1954, and the B-52B model entered service the following year. A total of 744 B-52s were built.

The last aircraft, a B-52H, was delivered in October 1962, and today, a half-century after the end of production, eighty-five aircraft of this model remain active in the USAF inventory, with another nine in reserve. Continually updated with modern avionics and other technology, the B-52H is projected to continue in service *beyond* 2045, a century after initial drawing-board concepts. As today's B-52 crews quip, "We ain't in your father's Air Force, but we may be flying your father's airplane."

Aerial refueling gives the B-52 a range limited only by crew endurance; its unrefueled combat range exceeds 8,800 miles. Nearly 160 feet long, the B-52 has a wingspan of 185 feet. Its eight Pratt & Whitney TF33–P-3/103 turbofan engines each create 17,000 lbf (pound force), enabling the 185,000-pound bomber to lift 70,000 pounds of bombs and a crew of five (aircraft commander, pilot, radar navigator, navigator, and electronic warfare officer) at a climb rate of 6,270 feet per minute to a service ceiling of 50,000 feet and a top speed of 650 miles per hour.

This B-52 of the 20th Bomb Squadron was an "H" model, the most advanced iteration of the aircraft. It is the only version of the remarkable B-52 that is still flown today, and it will probably continue in service at least until 2045, by which year the basic design will be nearly a century old.

The View from Washington

While Rolling Thunder pounded, President Johnson and his advisers scrambled to formulate their definitive war aims. Although LBJ had vowed to go up Ho's leg an inch at a time, he inched back from the original objectives of Truman, Eisenhower, and (as far as can be determined) Kennedy. The goal was no longer to unify Vietnam as a pro-Western republic but merely to maintain the independence of a non-Communist South Vietnam by proving to Hanoi that they could not win below the 17th parallel. The president hoped to achieve this through "strategic persuasion," the euphemism used for incessant bombing intended to greatly reduce the flow of North Vietnamese infiltration into the South, to inflict daily casualties on the VC and NVA, and to raise the morale and resolve of the South Vietnamese government, people, and armed forces.

> **"I sleep each night a little better, a little more confidently because Lyndon Johnson is my President. For I know he lives and thinks and works to make sure that for all Americans and indeed, the growing body of the free world, the morning shall always come."**
>
> ✱✱✱
>
> —Jack Valenti, "special assistant" to the president,
> June 8, 1965, reported in *The Congressional Record*

What rational leader or set of leaders could believe that a small, poor, mostly rural, rather backward nation like North Vietnam could survive a prolonged encounter with a superpower capable of hurling sortie after B-52 sortie against it?

The View from Hanoi

Inch by inch up "old Ho Chi Minh's leg." Doubtless, President Johnson did not think of it when he said this to Senator McGovern, but the operative word in his homely expression was the adjective *old*. In 1965, Ho was seventy-five. Never in good health, having suffered a serious bout of TB, having nearly died during World War II (when he was saved by an American OSS medic), the leader of the Vietnamese revolution and Communist party was a frail figurehead by the mid-1960s—he would die in four more years—and the real leader at this time was Le Duan, the Communist extremist who believed war with the United States was not only inevitable but also a desirable step on the road to unification of Vietnam under a Communist regime.

To Johnson and his advisers, Le Duan, first secretary of the Communist Party, would not have appeared to be a "rational leader" but, rather, a Communist "fanatic." In point of fact, however, Le Duan presented to his Hanoi colleagues a highly reasonable rationale for continuing to endure the bombs. To begin with, he knew that conducting air raids, no matter how intensive or prolonged, was insufficient to conquer the North. If the United States was serious about winning, it would, sooner or later, have to commit large numbers of troops to a ground war. Le Duan understood that the American military was a strategic and not a tactical machine and that it was not well prepared to prosecute a long guerrilla war in a land the VC knew intimately and the Americans knew not at all. He also believed that the American people would not tolerate a long war, whereas the Viet Cong and the people of North Vietnam could be persuaded (or compelled) to hold out for however long was necessary. America, he believed, would count and mourn every soldier it lost, whereas North Vietnam (as he put it) "will not count the cost." The Americans had B-52s, yes, but the North Vietnamese people had an inexhaustible capacity for enduring pain and absorbing punishment. Le Duan believed that his people possessed a far more powerful weapon than any airplane.

CALLING OUT THE CAVALRY

ROLLING THUNDER PRODUCED NO IMMEDIATE EFFECT on the course of the war. Although the Ho Chi Minh Trail was hit hard, VC infiltration into the South continued. Johnson waited, poring over statistics, straining to hear every word of his daily briefings, looking for some indication of progress.

In the meantime, as he had feared it would, the landing of the U.S. Marines at Da Nang—necessary to protect the air bases from which the Rolling Thunder raids were being launched—only brought more

LBJ walks the White House lawn with the Joint Chiefs of Staff, April 8, 1965.

calls from the Joint Chiefs and from General William Westmoreland to prepare to fight a major war on the ground. Before March 1965 ended, the Joint Chiefs requested three additional U.S. Army divisions—about 40,000 soldiers—and sought authority to use them offensively anywhere throughout the South.

Anatomy of an Army

During the Vietnam era, the United States Army was organized in this manner:

Army, consisting of 2 to 4 *corps*, totaling 80,000 to 200,000 soldiers, and commanded by a general

Corps, consisting of 2+ *divisions*, totaling 20,000 to 45,000 soldiers, and commanded by a lieutenant general

Division, consisting of 2 to 4 *brigades* or *regiments*, totaling 10,000 to 15,000 soldiers, and commanded by a major general

Brigade, consisting of 2+ *regiments* or 3 to 6 *battalions*, totaling 3,000 to 5,000 soldiers, and commanded by a brigadier general

Regiment, consisting of 2+ *battalions*, totaling 3,000 to 5,000 soldiers, sometimes operating as part of a *brigade* and sometimes as an independent unit, and commanded by a colonel

Battalion, consisting of 2 to 6 *companies* (or artillery *batteries*), totaling 300 to 1,300 soldiers, and commanded by a lieutenant colonel

Company (or artillery *battery*), consisting of 2 to 8 *platoons*, totaling 80 to 225 soldiers, and commanded by a major or captain

Platoon, consisting of 2+ *squads* or *patrols*, totaling 26 to 55 soldiers, and commanded by a first (sometimes second) lieutenant

Squad or *patrol*, consisting of 2+ *fireteams*, totaling 8 to 13 soldiers and commanded by a sergeant (sometimes a corporal)

Fireteam, totaling 4 soldiers and commanded by a corporal or sergeant

Fire and maneuver team, totaling 2 soldiers and commanded by any noncommissioned officer or a private first class

A War of Compromise

As the war ground on into the late 1960s, Johnson's growing legion of detractors would begin to argue that the president had broken from reality, specifically from the reality that the Vietnam War was unwinnable. One can find evidence to support this view, as well as evidence against it. In early 1965, however, President Johnson, far from breaking with the war's realities, was growing increasingly aware of them. As Rolling Thunder continued, he came to the unwelcome conclusion that North Vietnam was not going to be brought to the negotiating table by aerial bombardment alone—at least, in all probability, not before South Vietnam, with its perpetually dysfunctional government, collapsed. LBJ, McNamara, Bundy, and other advisers were inclined to accept the contention of General Westmoreland and the Joint Chiefs that the air war had to be fought in parallel with an aggressive ground war. What is more, Westmoreland had a direct and simple objective. Since even massive bombing was not putting an end to traffic along the Ho Chi Minh Trail, a large ground force was clearly necessary to sever the Communists' carotid artery into the South.

Johnson pondered. What worried him was that the war, which had initially bolstered his credibility with the electorate and freed his hand to pursue his domestic "Great Society" program—including in 1964 passage of the momentous Civil Rights Act—was now damaging it, and badly. The sheer cost of conducting the war was already eating into funds he wanted to ask Congress to devote to his domestic agenda. To commit more ground troops would certainly increase those costs. Defense Secretary McNamara also pondered. His chief concern was that infusing more troops into combat and sending them into Laos or anywhere near the border with North Vietnam would prompt China to intervene, as it had done during the Korean War.

Johnson and McNamara responded to Westmoreland and the Joint Chiefs with a compromise. They would give the Chiefs and their in-country commander the 40,000 soldiers requested. The president would

Drawn in 1965 by Herblock (Herbert Block), one of the great political cartoonists of his day, "Kindly move over a little, gentlemen" portrays LBJ as a western barkeep, politely asking two cowpokes ("Military Establishments" and "Arms Costs") to make room for a ragged child labeled "Health, Education and Welfare."

also authorize offensive operations—but these would be strictly limited to what McNamara referred to as "enclaves" immediately surrounding major U.S.-ARVN bases along the South Vietnamese coast. There would be no offensive *ground* operations targeting the Ho Chi Minh Trail, though the bombing would continue there. In effect, the Johnson administration was authorizing Westmoreland to conduct an "active defense"—defensive operations with offensive components—rather than the full-out offensive war he wanted to fight.

> ## "The greatest fear of U.S. imperialism is that people's wars will be launched in different parts of the world."
>
> ★★★
>
> —Lin Biao (Piao), vice premier of the People's Republic of China and vice chairman of the Communist Party of China, September 3, 1965

A War of Secrets

Westmoreland gave his attenuated mission a name, the Central Highlands Campaign, but neither he nor the Joint Chiefs were satisfied with what the administration had authorized. They believed they were being sent to war with their hands tied. Thus the main phase of U.S. combat in the Vietnam War was launched in what high command considered bad faith. (Indeed, the feeling that it was being hobbled by civilian politicians would haunt the military throughout the entire Vietnam War.)

Lyndon Johnson had no desire to alienate the military or the pro-war faction of Congress. He was, however, even more fearful of alienating those either already opposed to the war or inclined to oppose it. What is more, even though he had won election by a landslide, he had no desire to alarm the American public. Therefore, even as he expanded the war (albeit in ways that fell short of what the military wanted), the president worked to keep the expansion as secret as possible. He continued to define the bombing of North Vietnam, massive though it was, as nothing more than "retaliation" for VC attacks against the South. He never announced Operation Rolling Thunder for what it was, the biggest sustained bombing offensive since World

War II. As for the growing commitment of combat troops, the president could not hide this, but he hardly trumpeted it, either. Instead, he waited for a reporter to ask about it at a routinely scheduled press conference weeks after he had authorized the forces. In effect, then, America's full-scale entry into the Vietnam War was never announced but was instead casually mentioned in a routine press conference to which few Americans paid attention.

Olive Branches All Around

Half commitments and half truths never create total satisfaction. LBJ's attempts to soft-pedal an offensive escalation brought criticism from the left as well as the right. Protests arose from liberal politicians as well as from a small segment of the public. The most vocal objections were heard in academia. At some colleges and universities, students protested and professors staged "teach-ins," and on April 17, 1965, the first major public antiwar demonstration was conducted as more than fifteen thousand protestors marched in Washington, D.C. Among the international community, Canada and the United Kingdom, which up until now had merely declined to aid in the war effort, became more strident in calling for the United States to appeal for negotiations with North Vietnam. In this, they were joined by United Nations Secretary General U Thant and by UN delegates of various Third World ("non-aligned") nations. On the right, hawkish conservatives complained that the president was conducting the escalation with neither sufficient vigor, volume, nor speed.

Seeking to answer his critics and hoping to damp down controversy on the left as well as the right, the president made a highly publicized speech at Johns Hopkins University on April 7, 1965, in which he sought to mollify, if not satisfy, both sides. He announced what he called his absolute willingness to participate in "unconditional discussions" toward a peaceful resolution of the war in Vietnam. Then he upped the

This Washington, D.C., protest against the Vietnam War—the first major public antiwar demonstration—was relatively early: April 17, 1965. The demonstrations would get bigger, more numerous, and sometimes violent.

DETAILS, DETAILS

Academic Arguments

"Teach-in" was a phrase coined in 1965 on the model of "sit-in," which itself was coined to describe one of the nonviolent protest techniques employed by Mohandas Gandhi in South Africa early in the twentieth century. Students for a Democratic Society (SDS, founded in 1962) organized the first teach-in at the University of Michigan, Ann Arbor, on March 24–25, 1965. Although sponsored by students, principal participants were faculty members. During May 21–23 of the same year, a much bigger teach-in was organized at the University of California, Berkeley, by the Vietnam Day Committee (VDC), which had been founded by a former graduate student, Jerry Rubin, and Berkeley professor Stephen Smale, among others. As many as 30,000 students, faculty, and others participated, including child-rearing guru Dr. Benjamin Spock, socialist activist leader Norman Thomas, and novelist Norman Mailer. Portions of the event were broadcast on radio and recorded, later released on a set of Folkway LPs.

The "teach-in" antiwar protest at the University of California, Berkeley, during May 21–23, 1965, was widely covered by the media and was even commercially recorded by Folkways Records.

ante by proposing to invest a billion dollars in a non-military economic development program for both North and South Vietnam. He suggested that it be modeled on something he—and other Americans of his generation—knew very well: the Tennessee Valley Authority, an American New Deal program created in 1933 to address economic development, including flood control, electricity generation, river navigation, and various aspects of agricultural development in a region particularly hard hit by the Great Depression. Johnson proposed a kind of peace offensive, much as the Marshall Plan in Europe had been. And lest he leave the right wing out of the picture, he closed his speech by reiterating his commitment to protecting an independent South Vietnam.

In the immediate aftermath of the speech, Pham Van Dong, prime minister of North Vietnam, proposed a four-point basis for negotiations. These conditions included the withdrawal of U.S. forces from South Vietnam, honoring of the 1954 Geneva Accords, elections to install a new government in South Vietnam, and ultimate reunification. On the one hand, they were demands Dong knew would be unacceptable to the Americans; on the other, Dong broadly hinted that they were negotiable. President Johnson did not respond immediately, but in May, he ordered a five-day suspension of Rolling Thunder, a gesture apparently intended to demonstrate his openness to talks—although it was unclear for whose benefit the demonstration was staged. Many observers believed the bombing pause was, like the Johns

Hopkins speech, intended more to assuage critics of the war than it was to lure Hanoi to the conference table.

The hard fact was that the Johnson administration believed the United States had little to gain from a negotiated settlement at this point. The ARVN and the civil government of South Vietnam were so fragile and unpopular that negotiation risked effectively turning the South over to the North. Only when the South grew stronger could meaningful negotiations take place, administration officials argued. And the South would grow stronger only through significant military victories.

A majority of North Vietnamese leaders believed the main advantages were with the Communist cause and that it would therefore be a terrible mistake to make peace now. Almost certainly, the tipping point was reached by a push from outside Vietnam. The year 1964 had seen a decline in Soviet aid to North Vietnam because the Soviets were seeking to improve relations with the United States. By early 1965, however, friction between the Soviet Union and China had come to outweigh the Kremlin's fear of offending the United States. The more important motive for action now seemed to be finding ways to prevent China from dominating Southeast Asia. This, then, was no time to pull back from Vietnam. Alexei Kosygin, the Cold War hard-liner who had replaced the more moderate Nikita Khrushchev as Soviet leader (Chairman of the Council of Ministers) in October 1964, made a state visit to Hanoi in February 1965 and pledged full "support and assistance." At about this time as well, China's Mao Zedong, despite his fear of engaging in war directly against U.S. forces, answered requests for aid from Hanoi by declaring it China's "principle" to "do our best to provide you with whatever you need and whatever we have." Both the Soviets and the Chinese made good on their promises. The Soviets sent massive amounts of military weapons and other supplies, and the Chinese sent weapons and more general supplies as well as support and labor forces but not combat troops.

The Cavalry Arrives

Although Johnson and McNamara gave the military establishment less than it wanted, one of the bold innovations the administration enthusiastically approved was the transformation of the 1st Cavalry Division—a storied U.S. Army unit created in 1921 and made famous by

---

REALITY CHECK
Antiwar Hanoi

While most North Vietnamese leaders opposed negotiation in 1965 and 1966, contrary to popular mythology, Hanoi was not unanimous in its opposition. The peace faction in Hanoi was a minority, but it was a significant one. While Le Duan remained steadfast in his belief that the North Vietnamese people could endure bombing, some government leaders were gravely concerned about the damage the bombing was doing to the North Vietnamese economy. Le Duan and his war faction countered this argument by predicting that the imminent collapse of the South Vietnamese government would prompt the withdrawal of the United States. He held, however, that even if this did not occur, the people of the United States would never allow a prolonged commitment of U.S. forces in so foreign and distant a conflict.

The People's Republic of China supplied weapons of all kinds to the North Vietnamese Army and the Viet Cong, including this 7.62 mm Type 54 pistol, a Chinese copy of the Soviet TT-33 introduced in 1933. The export version of the weapon was designated M20 in a lame attempt to disguise its origin. Note the damage to the barrel, caused by a U.S. 5.56 mm rifle round at the Battle of Phouc Loc, December 3, 1967. The weapon was recovered from the body of a Viet Cong officer.

Shoulder patch of the 101st Airborne "Screaming Eagles," who traded in their parachutes for deployment from Huey helicopters in Vietnam.

its distinguished service in the Pacific theater during World War II and in the Korean War—into the 1st Cavalry Division (Airmobile), a.k.a. 1st Air Cavalry.

The "air cavalry" concept was a bold step toward closing the tactical gap created in American military readiness by the long Cold War concentration on developing strategic forces. The idea was to translate the speed and mobility of traditional cavalry into terms of American military high technology. Instead of riding horses into battle, the troopers of the new 1st Cavalry Division (Airmobile) would ride helicopters. The division was initially equipped with more than 400 of these modern "mounts," including the single-rotor Bell UH-1 troop carrier helicopter, universally known as the Huey; the well-armed attack version, the AH-1 Cobra; as well as a fleet of much larger, twin-rotor CH-47 Chinook helicopters, used primarily for carrying cargo and equipment. The 1st Air Cavalry was deployed extensively in the Central Highlands Campaign during late 1965 and early 1966. Using small helicopters to insert and extract troops in clearings surrounded by trackless jungle quickly proved the viability of the airmobile concept. The helicopters provided a way to outmaneuver the VC, to get *into* advantageous positions, and to *get out of* ambushes. In short order, the 101st Airborne Division—the "Screaming Eagles" of World War II fame—traded their parachutes for Hueys and, working in concert with the 1st Air Cavalry, developed the tactics and doctrine that would be used in the Vietnam War for the next five years.

CREDIBILITY

MAY 1965 BEGAN WITH a new Communist offensive in which the Viet Cong were heavily reinforced by the NVA. As usual, the ARVN responded weakly and seemed, to many observers, clearly on the edge of complete collapse, notwithstanding years of American training, equipping, and funding. The U.S. Military Assistance Command, Vietnam (MACV) responded to the new VC-NVA actions by authorizing massive naval gunfire support on May 14, 1965, a pounding that supplemented aerial bombardment. Did this succeed in driving back the Communist offensive? It is difficult to say because the North's signature tactic was the hit-and-run offensive. There was never an attempt to take and *hold* territory. Instead, the damage was done, the terror inflicted, and the troops withdrawn to fight another day.

Bell UH-1D "Huey" helicopters airlift members of the 2d Battalion, 14th Infantry from the Filhol Rubber Plantation area to another staging area in Operation Wahiawa, May 16, 1966. The Huey was to the Vietnam-era U.S. infantryman what the horse had been to the cavalryman of the late nineteenth-century "Indian Wars" in the American West.

Another Junta

In June, the month following the big VC-NVA offensive, a new military junta came to power in South Vietnam, led by Air Vice Marshal Nguyen Cao Ky and ARVN general Nguyen Van Thieu. Their rise had been made possible by the removal of U.S. support for General Khanh after he refused, in January 1965, to crack down on Buddhist protests against the expansion of the war and even made overtures toward negotiating directly with the North. When Ky and Thieu took over in June—with Ky becoming prime minister and Thieu a figurehead president—they imposed rigid censorship, suspended most civil liberties, and responded to Buddhist and other opposition groups by officially ignoring them while unofficially threatening to shoot any "troublemakers." Ky and Thieu organized their relatively few civilian supporters into armed paramilitary squads to enforce acquiescence to the regime. Believing that a crumbling South Vietnam needed a strongman dictatorship, at least in the short run, the United States supported the new government and its decidedly anti-democratic policies in the wan hope that the repressive measures would at least interrupt (though almost certainly not permanently end) the debilitating cycle of coup and countercoup.

Cam Ranh Air Base, South Vietnam, October 26, 1966: President Lyndon Johnson (left) is seen with General William Westmoreland, South Vietnamese President Nguyen Van Thieu, and Prime Minister Nguyen Cao Ky. The ARVN officer in the background is unidentified.

Even more important, while Ky and Thieu had little popular support, they did have a broad military constituency, which meant—as far as the Johnson administration was concerned— that they stood a chance of remolding the ARVN into a credible force. Still, no one in the administration or the U.S. military believed that the newest junta would long endure, and therefore new calls arose for rapidly escalating the war against the Communists before South Vietnam simply crumbled. Seconded by the Joint Chiefs of Staff, General Westmoreland requested 150,000 additional ground troops.

A Taste of Victory

Westmoreland backed up his request for more troops with a demonstration intended to show what the army could do if given the men, the means, and the mission. On June 28, 1965, the U.S. 173rd Airborne Brigade airlifted two battalions of its own 503rd Infantry Regiment and two ARVN battalions into combat in Bien Hoa Province, just twenty miles northeast of Saigon. This, the first major U.S. ground operation, produced mixed results, but it was followed during August

18–21, 1965, by Operation Starlite, in which more than five thousand U.S. Marines attacked the Viet Cong 1st Regiment south of Chu Lai in Quang Ngai Province, scoring an unambiguous victory by trapping the VC and destroying their major base at Van Tuong, also south of Chu Lai.

From Limited War to Limited Debate

The Bien Hoa fight and Operation Starlite bracketed a series of White House debates during July, in which President Johnson met with his cabinet, advisers, and key legislators to decide, in essence, whether to prosecute a major war in Vietnam. Both sides, pro and con, were represented, with Undersecretary of State George Ball predictably arguing against expanding the war on the grounds that the United States military was ill-equipped to fight a protracted guerrilla conflict in a distant and alien place and that there was, in the final analysis, no viable South Vietnamese government to fight for—nor was there likely to be. Secretary of State Dean Rusk and Secretary of Defense Robert McNamara spoke in favor of expansion. They did not attempt to refute Ball's objections but pointed to a motive for war they believed simply overrode them. As Rusk put it, "If the Communist world finds out we will not pursue our commitments, I don't know where they will stay their hand."

The reason for a wider war was the old domino theory, and the reason for acting on that theory was not so much to defend South Vietnam as it was to uphold the political and military credibility of the United States in a "bipolar world," a world in which power was seen as contested between the democratic-capitalistic West (championed by the United States) and the totalitarian-Communist East (led by the Soviet Union and China). Why was the fate of South Vietnam important? Rusk

Secretary of Defense Robert McNamara (seated at right), Secretary of State Dean Rusk (hand to chin), and General Earle Wheeler, chairman of the Joint Chiefs of Staff (leaning on desk) confer with President Johnson at a regularly scheduled 12:30 p.m. National Security meeting on Vietnam, July 26, 1965. The president's look of intense concentration would become increasingly anguished as the war dragged on.

and McNamara would explain that if the United States surrendered the proxy war against the Communists in South Vietnam, the free world would have two choices: give up and allow the other dominoes to fall to Communism or face the Soviets and/or the Chinese directly in World War III, with its prospect of thermonuclear Armageddon. McNamara concluded his case for escalation with a customarily cool calculation. Lose South Vietnam and, he predicted, Cambodia, Laos, Burma, and Thailand would all quickly fall under Communist governments. This would lead to the "loss" of Malaysia within the space of perhaps three years, and such countries as Greece and Turkey, both of which had active Communist parties, would likewise be imperiled. Thus Europe's "Iron Curtain" would be extended all the way south to the Aegean and Adriatic, a major stride toward the Communist encirclement of Western Europe.

No one denied the position represented by George Ball and others; however, the perceived enormity of the global consequences of "surrender" cut off debate. President Johnson asked hard questions, and the answers did not end his doubts. Nevertheless, the prospect of going down in history as the American president who lost the Cold War and surrendered to global Communism moved him to agree to a significant portion of the troop increase Westmoreland and the Chiefs asked for. He would not, however, authorize an immediate infusion of 150,000 young men but would instead send 50,000 now and another 50,000 by year's end. He let the top commanders know that he was further inclined to authorize more troops later, if conditions warranted it. Moreover, he removed McNamara's "enclave" restrictions, giving Westmoreland permission to operate anywhere and everywhere in South Vietnam. While the president stopped short of offering the military carte blanche, his decisions in July transitioned Vietnam from a "limited war" to a "war," and, what is more, a war in which the role of the United States dramatically shifted from adviser to principal combatant.

BODY COUNT

GENERAL WESTMORELAND WAS ABLE TO DELIVER POSITIVE RESULTS in the ongoing Central Highlands Campaign, which culminated in the Battle of Ia Drang Valley during October 23–November 20, 1965. In hard, sustained fighting, the 1st Cavalry Division (Airmobile) defeated combined VC and NVA forces that had massed in western Pleiku

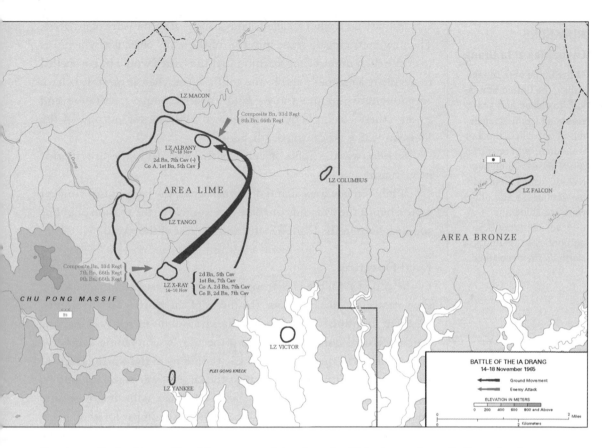

Province. Both sides suffered heavy casualties, but the U.S. air cavalry achieved a major strategic victory in that it spoiled the Communists' attempt not merely to hit and run but also to control this region, thereby cutting South Vietnam in half.

Ia Drang may be interpreted as the first significant *strategic* gain for the United States in the Vietnam War. Unfortunately for the United States, there would be few more. The fact was that the U.S. overall war aims were not conducive to achieving traditional strategic gains, which are territorial in nature. In fact, since the declared objective of the war had shifted from unification of Vietnam under a non-Communist government to merely preserving the independence of the South, American military planners needed a way to show progress in a war that was no longer aimed at "expanding" control north of the 17th parallel. Instead of charting progress in terms of territory held (ostensibly, all of the territory below the 17th parallel was already held by South Vietnam), the

Ia Drang battle map showing two enemy attacks against U.S. forces. Circled positions marked "LZ" are landing zones for Huey helicopter transports.

NUMBERS

Casualties at Ia Drang

At the Battle of Ia Drang Valley, the United States lost 305 killed and 524 wounded (some sources report 234 killed and 245 wounded), with unknown ARVN losses. Combined NVA-VC losses reported by Vietnamese authorities were 554 killed and 669 wounded, but U.S. authorities estimate 1,519 North Vietnamese killed.

REALITY CHECK

The Futility of Attrition

In terms of body count, U.S.-ARVN forces were highly successful in conducting a war of attrition in Vietnam. Overall, three Communist fighters died for every two U.S.-ARVN soldiers killed. In terms of strategic progress, however, the war of attrition failed for the simple reason that the North Vietnamese were willing to absorb disproportionately heavy losses. As Ho Chi Minh had told the French in the early 1950s, "You can kill ten of our men for every one we kill of yours. But even at those odds, you will lose and we will win."

U.S. military used what it called "body count" as its measure of progress. The new metric made sense in terms of the war's objective, which was to create such unremitting attrition that the North would be compelled to negotiate a favorable end to the conflict. Yet whereas most wars have been fought to gain something—land, imperial conquest, liberation, and so on—the focus on body count seemed to define the purpose of the Vietnam War as producing death, period.

So *killing* was the noble objective of the defender of the "free world" in Vietnam?

While it made logical and doctrinal sense, the body count concept would haunt the war and contribute inexorably to the erosion of public support, both in the United States and the rest of the world.

Dual Doctrine

By the end of 1965, the U.S. troop increases had resulted in tactical and even strategic victories against the forces of the North. This heartened President Johnson, who, following the advice of his secretary of defense, pursued a dual doctrine in fighting the war by combining aggressive ground tactics in the South with heavy bombing in the North. The year ended with a major air strike against the large power plant at Uong Bi, fourteen miles north of Haiphong, and 1966 began with a major ground operation, called Marauder, which was the first combat foray of a U.S. unit, the 173rd Airborne Brigade, into the long-contested Mekong Delta. During January 1–8, the 173rd defeated one VC battalion and destroyed the headquarters of another in the Plain of Reeds.

Operation Marauder was followed by Operation Crimp during January 8–14, sometimes called the Battle of Ho Bo Woods. In this operation, the 3rd Infantry Brigade and 173rd Airborne, both under the U.S. 1st Infantry Division, were joined by the 1st Battalion of the Royal Australian Regiment (which was attached to the U.S. 173rd Airborne). The largest single "Allied" ground operation in South Vietnam up to that time, Crimp fielded approximately 8,000 soldiers against a much smaller number of combined VC and NVA forces, estimated at 1,000 to 5,000 men. The objective of Operation Crimp was to disrupt infiltration routes ("crimp" them), and the U.S.-Australian troops did discover and destroy a complex of tunnels, the most important of which were found at Cu Chi on January 9, 1966. Construction of these had begun in 1945, during the war between the Viet Minh and the French, and were expanded beginning in the early 1960s. It was Australian combat engineers (called "sappers"), who explored the Cu Chi tunnels most thoroughly and discovered a complex that included such specialized structures as "fighting tunnels"—which allowed immediate passage to the surface, while also providing cover and concealment—meeting "rooms," headquarters/command facilities, and storage areas (mostly for food). The Cu Chi tunnels stretched from the Cambodian border, where they met the Ho Chi Minh Trail, to Saigon itself. The tunnels were so well built that they had withstood bombing and shelling, periodic during the 1950s and intensive by the mid-1960s. The tunnels at Cu Chi were said to accommodate 5,000 soldiers, some of whom lived underground for as long as six months at a time. U.S. forces lost 14 killed and 76 wounded during Operation Crimp. Australian losses were 8 killed and 29 wounded. North Vietnamese killed included a confirmed body count of 128 with an additional 190 estimated, and 92 VC and NVA troops were captured.

An Australian soldier of the 1st Battalion of the Royal Australian Regiment inspects a VC tunnel during Operation Crimp, January 1966.

This cross-section of a Viet Cong tunnel was photographed on display at Cu Chi, a Vietnamese tourist site that today preserves some of the tunnels for their historical value.

A Coalition of Sorts

The United States found few allies in the Vietnam War. Traditional allies, such as Canada and the United Kingdom, stayed out, as did France, the nation the United States had originally sought to aid in the war during the 1950s.

Australia entered the war on August 3, 1962, with 30 military advisers, and remained in-country until June 1973, contributing during these eleven years some 50,000 ground troops, naval personnel, and airmen and suffering the loss of 496 killed and nearly 2,400 wounded in what was the longest war in the nation's history. New Zealand also fought in Vietnam, entering in May 1965 and remaining until 1973. The small nation's contingent totaled 3,890 men, of whom 187 were wounded and 37 killed.

South Korea was the United States' staunchest ally in the Vietnam War, contributing a total of 320,000 soldiers to the conflict between 1964 and 1973—with peak troop levels reaching 50,000 in 1968. (As early as November 1961, South Korea offered troops; President John F. Kennedy demurred.) The United States reimbursed South Korea $235,560,000 for its contribution, growing the country's gross national product (GNP) fivefold during the war. Five thousand South Korean soldiers were killed and 11,000 wounded.

The Philippines first deployed a small contingent of 28 military personnel, including nurses and 6 civilian medical workers, to South Vietnam in 1964. During 1966 to 1968, the Filipino contingent would grow to 182 officers and 1,882 enlisted soldiers, all of whom served in the Philippine Civic Action Group–Vietnam (PHILCAG–V), a logistical and medical unit rather than a combat force.

Thai forces served in small numbers in South Vietnam during 1965 to 1971 and in covert ground operations in neighboring Laos between 1964 and 1972. Beginning in November 1967, the U.S.-backed Republic of China (Taiwan) secretly operated a logistical unit and, less covertly, provided training for ARVN and other South Vietnamese military personnel. Taiwanese commandos were also active in the war.

Although Canada was officially a non-belligerent in the war, it contributed troops to the International Control Commission, charged with monitoring the 1954 ceasefire agreement. Some historians believe that members of these forces actually aided the United States. A much larger Canadian contribution to the war effort came from individual Canadians who volunteered to serve in the U.S. armed forces—some 30,000 in all, of whom 110 were killed in action and 7 remain listed as missing in action. One Canadian, Peter Charles Lemon, U.S. Army, received the Medal of Honor for actions on April 1, 1970, at Tay Ninh.

Within the Central Highlands of Vietnam, the Degar tribes, better known by the name the French applied to them, Montagnards ("people from the mountains"), served extensively alongside U.S. troops in the mountains, contributing perhaps 40,000 fighters to the war.

These victories were followed during January 19–February 21 by Operation Van Buren, in which the 1st Brigade of the 101st Airborne Division, the 2nd Republic of Korea Marine Brigade, and the 4th ARVN Regiment drove Communist forces out of Phu Yen Province in the central coastal region.

These troops of the 327th Infantry, 101st Airborne Brigade, part of Operation Van Buren, advance across an open rice paddy in search of Viet Cong, January 23, 1966. Operation Van Buren drove Viet Cong forces out of Phu Yen Province in the central coastal region and cut off their supplies of rice—for a time.

NUMBERS

From North to South

The rate of North Vietnamese infiltration of the South averaged 1,500 men per month in 1965. This rose to 4,500 per month in 1966 and to 6,000 per month by 1967.

Defying Logic in the Ground War

The American successes of 1965 and early 1966 were a function of increased troop numbers and of a revision of mission doctrine. The latest operations executed a newly articulated doctrine called "search-and-destroy," in which highly mobile patrols seized the initiative by seeking out the enemy, engaging him wherever found, and killing him. Enemy body count rose precipitously, and there is no question that killing VC and NVA troops cleared them out of a given piece of territory.

It soon became apparent, however, that *clearing* a territory and *holding* a territory were two very different objectives. Search-and-destroy claimed a region, which was held for precisely as long as U.S. or U.S.-ARVN troops remained in it. Search-and-destroy doctrine, however, was not about holding or occupying territory. It required forces to be continually on the hunt and therefore continually on the move. No sooner did a unit move out of an area, having piled up so many bodies there, than the enemy returned to it. Nothing was gained except attrition—a deadly price the North continued to show itself willing to pay. This seemingly limitless capacity for accepting loss defied the logic of war as President Johnson and his generals understood it. Infamously, but always in private, LBJ would vent his frustration to his advisers, wondering out loud how "that damn piss-ant little country" could hold out in the face of such disproportionate losses.

Defying Logic in the Air War

As bewildered as the American president was by the failure of tactical success on the ground to produce enduring strategic progress, he was even more chagrined by the disappointing results of Operation Rolling Thunder and other bombing operations against the North. The objective of the air war was threefold: to interdict North Vietnamese infiltration of the South; to create a level of attrition in the North that would drive the Communists to negotiate a peace favorable to the South; and, in the shorter term, to raise South Vietnamese morale by demonstrating America's commitment to "their" war.

Some historians believe the bombing did give some South Vietnamese hope, but none argue that it succeeded in diminishing

Soviet-supplied surface-to-air missiles (SAMs) and missile launchers were part of a large, complex, and skillfully used North Vietnamese antiaircraft defense system. The missiles targeted high-flying U.S. warplanes, often forcing pilots to descend to lower levels, where antiaircraft artillery (also Soviet-supplied) could shoot them down. In this undated photograph, a North Vietnamese SAM crew poses in front of their launcher.

the flow of troops and supplies down the Ho Chi Minh Trail or that it drove the North to anything approaching surrender. To make such an argument would be to deny reality. While the bombing unquestionably devastated the North, the flow of troops and supplies from 1965 to 1967 only increased, and while tens of thousands of North Vietnamese were killed by American bombs, either directly or because of the privation they wrought, Hanoi held firm.

Nor did the North passively absorb punishment from the air. Thanks to the work of Chinese logistical troops and technical experts and shipments of advanced Soviet-made anti-aircraft weapons, including artillery and surface-to-air missiles (SAMs), North Vietnam built a remarkable system of air defense. By the end of the 1960s, the system was the largest in the world, and, by the end of the war in 1975, it was responsible for shooting down more than 950 U.S. aircraft (938 of them in the course of Operation Rolling Thunder alone), killing 2,584 airmen and making POWs of an additional 356.

Of course, most of the bombers made it past the anti-aircraft defenses and dropped their bombs. The North Vietnamese defended themselves with an elaborate network of underground tunnels and shelters—*twenty million* individual and communal shelters excavated in the course of the war. The civilian population was organized into rigidly disciplined, highly dedicated work battalions, which rushed out to repair damage virtually the moment the roar of the bombers had faded away. In a country with so little infrastructure to begin with, rebuilding what was lost could be accomplished with remarkable speed.

"CROSSOVER"

TO HIS CREDIT, GENERAL WILLIAM WESTMORELAND WAS NOT SATISFIED with merely compiling a body count. His strategy of attrition had an end point, a goal. It was to reach what he called the "crossover point," the statistical moment at which the rate of enemy loss would cross over the rate at which the enemy could replace its losses. Reach that crossover, and the Vietnam War would begin to end.

The problem?

As 1966 drew to a close—a year in which United States forces "in-country" grew to a total of 385,000 plus 60,000 sailors on sea duty just offshore—General William Westmoreland could neither calculate nor guess, let alone see, the crossover point.

TAKEAWAY

Commitment and Escalation

The years 1965 and 1966 saw continued, arguably increasing, instability in South Vietnam and the beginning, in the United States, of an organized antiwar movement. Nevertheless, instead of discouraging the Johnson administration from escalating the American commitment to the war, these factors tended to intensify the perceived urgency of such escalation, lest South Vietnam collapse before the North sat down to negotiate a peace favorable to U.S. objectives. Escalation produced measurable U.S.-ARVN tactical victories but no discernible strategic progress, as the commander in charge of U.S. forces in Vietnam, General William Westmoreland, struggled toward the "crossover point," that point at which enemy losses exceeded the enemy's capacity to replace them, hitherto a point both elusive and unknown.

CHAPTER 9

MAIN FORCE

Johnson's War Becomes Westmoreland's War

THE LARGE-SCALE U.S. OPERATIONS OF THE FIRST HALF OF 1966, beginning with Marauder, Crimp, and Van Buren, were typical of what American commanders called the "main force" war. The name came from the fact that Viet Cong fighters were of two general types. There were the local VC groups, which included hardened guerrillas as well as young (typically teenage) recruits—inexperienced and often forced to enlist by peer or parent pressure or threats from local Communists—and there were VC units made up of professional, uniformed soldiers, more like NVA troops than their comrades in local VC units. The Americans designated these highly trained full-time formations the "main force," and it was against them that the major U.S. search-and-destroy operations were directed. Hence the phase of the Vietnam conflict known as the "main force war."

On the face of it, fighting the main force war made tactical and strategic sense. The VC main force was certainly the most formidable of the Communist military formations—bolder and more imaginative than the NVA and far more experienced and reliably committed than the local VC units. The U.S.-ARVN objective was to engage and overwhelm the insurgents wherever they surfaced in numbers. Never very comfortable fighting a guerrilla ("unconventional") war—as Johnson administration dissidents like Undersecretary of State George Ball relentlessly pointed out—U.S. military leaders chose during most of 1966 and 1967 to fight instead the kind of conventional conflict familiar to them. The result of this approach had two consequences. First, the numbers of military operations proliferated but to no strategic purpose other than to meet force with overwhelming force wherever and whenever possible and thereby add to body count. Second, the almost exclusive focus on main force VC largely ignored the broader Viet Cong insurgency. Even as the approach took a heavy toll on Viet Cong and NVA troops, the North managed to build up its military capabilities throughout this period.

CAMPAIGNS OF ATTRITION

GENERAL WILLIAM WESTMORELAND WAS NOT DEAF to a growing legion of critics, both inside and outside of the Johnson administration, who warned that concentrating on the VC main force allowed insurgent political organizing activity to continue practically unabated throughout the South. He did not deny or attempt to refute this charge but responded that he was using American troops in the most efficient manner possible, namely, to create the attrition of enemy forces. There was truth to this, in that inflicting losses—engaging and killing large enemy concentrations—was what the American army was trained to do. Westmoreland's rationale, however, was not purely military. To administration officials, he argued that shifting his mission from attrition, destroying the VC main force, to pacification, which was essentially population control, would require far more American boots on the ground than the American public would ever allow. Thus, his approach to the Vietnam War was never exclusively military. It was also political, aimed at getting as many troops as he could without, however, totally alienating the American electorate. In this way, General Westmoreland came to embody the predicament of the post–World War II American commander. Given a military mission, he was continually constrained by *political* considerations.

To further justify his approach, General Westmoreland explained that his objective was to intensify the rate of attrition toward the "crossover point," the point at which the losses he was inflicting would finally outpace the enemy's ability to replace them. The sooner the crossover was reached, he contended, the sooner the Viet Cong would be forced to negotiate and, with that, would necessarily have to end the insurgency. In the meantime, while U.S. forces pursued the objective of attrition, Westmoreland would dispatch the ARVN to carry out, as best it could, the mission of population control by building security throughout the countryside—the process benignly, even soothingly, termed "pacification."

> **"Declare the United States the winner and begin de-escalation."**
>
> ✶✶✶
>
> —Senator George Aiken (R-VT), October 19, 1966

Operation Masher, January 28, 1966: Soldiers of 2d Battalion, 7th Regiment, 1st Cavalry Division (Airmobile) prepare for the ride to An Khe Airfield at the commencement of the operation.

Operation Masher

Beginning on January 28 and extending to March 6, 1966, some 20,000 U.S. Army, ARVN, and Republic of Korea (ROK—that is, South Korean) troops were sent on an extensive sweep of Binh Dinh Province on the central coast in what was billed as a "nation-building" mission—a campaign of "pacification." It was, however, a particularly ambitious search-and-destroy mission, an exercise in attrition—despite receiving a name change early on from Operation Masher (appropriate to destruction) to Operation White Wing (more in line with nation building). During the course of forty-two days, Masher/White Wing engaged one VC and two NVA regiments, killing (according to U.S. body count) 2,389 of the enemy for a loss of 228 U.S. troops killed and 834 wounded; 10 ROK troops were also killed in action.

American military officials declared that Masher/White Wing had annihilated the 3rd NVA Division—an assessment undercut when the unit later reappeared, intact, elsewhere on the battlefield. This unfounded claim, along with the utter incongruity of the operation's declared "nation-building" purpose and its high body count, was not the only profoundly disquieting aspect of the operation. On February 12 and March 17, the ROK Army's Capital Division killed 1,200 unarmed South Vietnamese civilians in and around the village of Tay Vinh in the Tay Son district of coastal Binh Dinh Province. On February 26, the Capital Division and another ROK Army unit, the Tiger Division, killed unarmed civilians in Go Dai hamlet, cutting down 380 villagers in the span of an hour. Killing civilians was not a declared aspect of "main force" doctrine, but it would prove central to the "pacification" mission.

In March, the troops of Masher/White Wing joined forces with U.S. Marines, who were moving into the northern provinces of South Vietnam, where they were almost continually engaged with the enemy from March through October. In late May, the NVA 324B Division crossed the 17th parallel—now universally referred to as "the DMZ," the demilitarized zone—where it was engaged by a U.S. Marine battalion in the beginning of the Battle of Dong Ha. This clash developed into the largest battle of the war up to that time. The bulk of the 3rd Marine Division, about 5,000 men, rushed north to reinforce the beleaguered battalion. Beginning in late June, the

REALITY CHECK
Acceptable Atrocity?

The Tay Vinh and Go Dai massacres did not create the public outrage generated by the My Lai Massacre, which was perpetrated on March 16, 1968, and exposed by reporter Seymour Hersh in November 1969. That it did not was almost certainly due to the massacres having been carried out by South Korean rather than American forces. Today, it is shocking to read General Westmoreland's observation, made in the 1974 Vietnam War documentary film *Hearts and Minds*, that the "Oriental doesn't put the same high price on life as does a Westerner. . . . We value life and human dignity. They don't care about life and human dignity." During the "Vietnam era," such beliefs were not shocking but common. Indeed, it was the American experience of the Vietnam War that did much to purge the nation and its people of such ethnocentricity.

Operation Hastings, July 1966: Marines of Company H, 2d Battalion, 4th Marine Regiment wade through a stream en route to rendezvous with the main body of their battalion at Dong Ha.

marines coordinated with ARVN troops, offshore U.S. naval gunfire, and USAF air strikes in what was dubbed Operation Hastings. During three weeks of heavy fighting, from the middle of July into early August, the marines and ARVN forces managed to drive the NVA back into North Vietnam.

Operation Birmingham

While Operation Hastings was ramping up near the DMZ, Operation Birmingham, which followed Masher/White Wing in April and May, was conducted closer to Saigon. Some 5,000 troops of the U.S. 1st Infantry Division and the ARVN 5th Regiment sought out the Viet Cong 9th Division with the object of defeating it and thereby gaining control of Route 13, which traversed the South Vietnamese border with Cambodia. Supported by helicopters and armored vehicles, the infantry swept across an area north of Saigon in search of the VC main force, but for three weeks, from April 24 through May 17, the operation killed no more than 119 VC, for a loss of 54 U.S. casualties, killed or wounded. At the end of the very next month, on June 30, VC fighters hit American soldiers hard along Route 13. Stunned by the ferocity of the attack, U.S. commanders called in an artillery barrage and air support, which suppressed the Viet Cong, but not before the attack took a heavy toll on U.S. ground troops.

Operation Attleboro

Operation Hastings focused on the DMZ, and Operation Birmingham focused on Route 13, just north of Saigon. South of Saigon, the Dau Tieng district stretched from the South Vietnamese coast to the border of Cambodia. Just northwest of this district, Operation Attleboro was carried out from September 14 through November 24, principally by the 196th Light Infantry Brigade (which had been formed at Attleboro, Massachusetts). The 196th was joined by the U.S. 4th Division, ARVN forces, South Vietnamese Popular Forces (the equivalent of militia), and Nung tribal fighters in what became the largest air mobile operation to date. The Viet Cong staged a fierce counterattack on November 8 but were driven back by artillery and air assault. Once this resistance was neutralized, U.S. forces advanced on a VC base camp, where two million pounds of rice and large weapons and ammunition caches were captured. The operation was hailed by Army spokesmen as a "severe blow" against the Viet Cong supply system into the South.

"We started the end of War Zone C as a sanctuary for the VC. War Zone C will never be the same."

✸✸✸

—General Fred C. Weyand, on the success of
Operation Attleboro, during an interview
at Long Binh headquarters,
South Vietnam

Prime Beef, Red Horse, and the Long Haul

By the end of 1966, U.S. Air Force construction units called "Prime Beef" teams (BEEF: *Base Engineer Emergency Force*) rushed to completion fully outfitted air bases at Tan Son Nhut (the main Saigon airport), Bien Hoa, Da Nang, Nha Trang, Pleiku, and Binh Thuy, building everything from aircraft revetments to barracks to perimeter fences and guard towers as well as aircraft runways. Simultaneously, USAF "Red Horse" (*Rapid Engineer Deployable Heavy Operational Repair Squadron Engineers*) teams provided such services as major civil engineering projects necessary to make the air bases self-sufficient over the long haul. The message was clear: it would be a long war, and to fight it meant transforming the predominately rural landscape of South Vietnam into a collection of bases and airfields.

The system of USAF air bases in South Vietnam, at the height of U.S. involvement in the war, 1968.

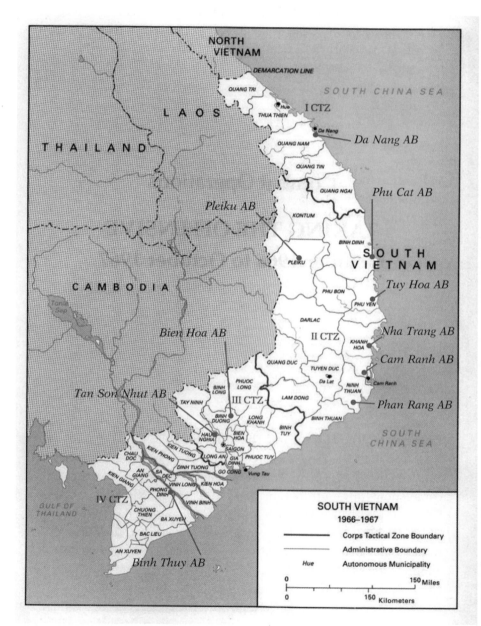

EYEWITNESS

MORTAR ATTACK AGAINST TAN SON NHUT AIR BASE, APRIL 13, 1966

The U.S. air base at Tan Son Nhut, adjacent to the South Vietnamese capital city of Saigon, was the frequent target of VC attacks, including one on April 13, 1966. That insurgents could attack the base almost at will demonstrated how little control U.S. and ARVN forces had even over territory closest to the capital. Trained mainly to perform technical functions, Air Force personnel were poorly equipped to repel ground attack, as Staff Sergeant Allan Rubin recalled years later:

"I was stationed at Tan Son Nhut from Mar 66 to Mar 67. I was . . . the midnight E-5 [staff sergeant] in charge of the ops [operations] building just outside the base. The night we were mortared I was sitting at the back gate opening to the airfield in my shorts with some buddies drinking beer when all hell broke loose. We jumped into the ditch, and watched some of [South Vietnamese prime minister Nguyen Cao] Ky's [propeller-driven Douglas A-1] Skyraiders get hit and a couple jets.

"I remember crawling to a bunker next to the barracks and we were all saying prayers. . . . [G]uys were crawling out of the NCO club 'cause our MPs were shooting down the road at anything that moved. They even shot at the ambulance trying to get in the compound. . . . [W]hen the armorer finally made it to the arms room sometime later, he was handing out rifles and belts of ammo, [but] there were no loaded clips. Also we set up a machine gun position at the opening at the rear of the compound . . . in the morning they realized they had put the ammo belt in the machine gun backwards. . . .

"By the way, Ssgt [Staff Sergeant] Daugherty was in my bunker when the mortars began to fall. We were in the last bunker west . . . I remember that when the lull in the shelling began, Ssgt Daugherty thought it was over and said he was going to go to the arms room for a weapon. I remember telling him, along with others with me, to stay put and wait awhile, but he was adamant. He exited the bunker and began running down the sidewalk when the shelling started again and he was killed instantly when a shell struck the sidewalk where he was running.

"I further remember that all I could think of was I needed a cigarette and I stupidly crawled out of the bunker and into my barracks to retrieve them, then crawled back to the bunker. I probably should have been a statistic also, but we did do some dumb things when we were younger. The rest of the guys sure appreciated having the cigarettes though. . . . After the shelling, as we all left the bunkers, someone stupidly lit off a string of firecrackers and we all dove for the bunker again."

Tan Son Nhut Air Base under attack in April 1966. Viet Cong mortar fire ignited numerous fuel fires on the base, including this one being battled by airmen pressed into service as firefighters.

JANUARY 1967

AS 1966 ENDED AND 1967 BEGAN, AMERICAN progress could be fairly judged this way: General Westmoreland had saved South Vietnam from what had seemed, in 1965, imminent and certain collapse. His search-and-destroy missions against the VC main force had taken a heavy toll on the Communists—significantly heavier than the toll they were taking on his forces. Attrition had blunted, though hardly halted, the momentum and tempo of North Vietnamese operations against the South. In truth, the most Westmoreland could honestly claim at the start of 1967 was to have turned certain defeat into bloody stalemate. As for the "crossover point," it continued to prove elusive.

If attrition were measured only in dead bodies, Westmoreland had reason to feel some hope. If, however, it were measured by the strength of an active army, he had no cause for encouragement. The fact was that Hanoi was expanding its armies. One resource North Vietnam had was young men, nearly a quarter million of whom reached draft age every year, and the Communist government did not scruple to conscript them. And that was just in the North. While troops were drafted there, they were also zealously recruited throughout the South. In the early days of the American phase of the war, volunteers came forth eagerly. By 1967, more and more local VC units consisted of young men who were pressed into service by threats and violence. Doubtless, morale suffered as a result, and *Time* magazine, on December 9, 1966, ran a story titled "Encouraging Returns," announcing the defection to the side of the Saigon government of 17,726 Viet Cong—"a full 6,600 ahead of the total for all of 1965."

And yet the Communist armies continued to grow, and they continued to infiltrate the South, and they continued to fight—hard.

Despite the aggressive vigor of U.S. operations, two NVA divisions launched spectacular artillery assaults across the DMZ, battering the northernmost bases of the American forces, at Khe Sanh, the Rockpile, Cam Lo, Dong Ha, Con Thien, and Gio Linh. The Americans responded with air assaults.

NUMBERS
Attrition's Toll

From 1965 to 1967, an estimated 179,000 VC and NVA troops were killed, more than three times the number of combined U.S.-ARVN losses.

Hanoi's Allies

Like the United States, North Vietnam had allies in the war, of which the People's Republic of China and the Soviet Union were the most important. The PRC extended diplomatic recognition to the Viet Minh's Democratic Republic of Vietnam in 1950, supplying weapons and military advisers to aid in the war against the French. Indeed, the 1954 Geneva Accords were negotiated by French prime minister Pierre Mendès France and Chinese premier Zhou Enlai. It was Chinese rice that allowed North Vietnam to draft large numbers of young men, taking them from the rice paddies, beginning in 1960. Chinese premier Mao Zedong began supplying rifles in large numbers in 1962 and, three years later, sent anti-aircraft artillery and crews as well as engineering battalions (whose mission was to repair air raid damage). After relations between China and the Soviet Union suffered a crisis in 1968, China demanded that North Vietnam cut relations with the Soviets. When Hanoi refused, China began a withdrawal from North Vietnam, which culminated in 1970.

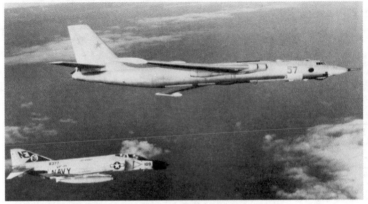

Under Leonid Brezhnev, the Soviet Union operated intelligence ships that gave Hanoi early warning of U.S. air raids beginning in the mid-1960s. The USSR also supplied medicine, small arms, tanks, fixed- and rotary-wing aircraft, artillery, and surface-to-air missiles (SAMs). As many as 3,000 Soviet troops were stationed in North Vietnam during the conflict.

In this rare photograph, a U.S. Navy F4B-6-MC Phantom II from the carrier USS Coral Sea intercepts a Soviet Myasishchev 3M bomber (NATO code name "Bison-B") off the Vietnamese coast sometime between July 29, 1966, and February 23, 1967.

In addition to China and the USSR, North Korea contributed to the Communist war effort by sending a fighter squadron to North Vietnam, which operated from early 1967 through most of 1968. North Korea also contributed two anti-aircraft artillery regiments, weapons, ammunition, and uniforms.

Finally, it is known that Cuba contributed some personnel, but neither the Cuban government nor the present Vietnam government has revealed the extent of Cuba's involvement. U.S. Senator (and former presidential candidate) John McCain, a U.S. Navy aviator who was a prisoner of war (POW) in North Vietnam from October 26, 1967, to March 14, 1973, reported that Cuban personnel participated in torture and interrogation programs. Other U.S. POWs have made similar reports.

CAMPAIGNS OF PACIFICATION

ON JANUARY 8, 1967, THE U.S. 1ST AND 25TH INFANTRY DIVISIONS, the 11th Armored Cavalry Regiment, and the 173rd Airborne Brigade were joined by ARVN forces in Operation Cedar Falls, which was intended to clear the so-called Iron Triangle, an area of Binh Duong Province that had become a VC stronghold. Located immediately north of the South Vietnamese capital, it was, as one American commander called it, a "dagger pointed at the heart of Saigon." A total of 30,000 U.S. and ARVN troops participated in the operation, making it the biggest single ground campaign in the entire war.

Combat was concluded on January 28, by which time (according to U.S. officials) 750 VC had been killed, 280 taken prisoner, and 540 had "defected" to the South. Six thousand civilians were forcibly deported to "relocation camps" officially called "New Life Villages," a grim feature of the "pacification program." In addition, large numbers of arms and ammunition, along with rice sufficient to feed 13,000 troops a year, were captured, as were a variety of military documents. A complex of tunnels and bunkers were destroyed, and a significant portion of the jungle in the area was chemically defoliated.

Operation Cedar Falls, January 1967: U.S. armor—M113 armored personnel carriers (foreground) and M4SA3 Sherman tanks (background)— rumble along a rough road between a rubber plantation and the edge of the jungle.

Hearts and Minds

U.S. officials proclaimed the Operation Cedar Falls—in which U.S. casualties were 72 killed and 337 wounded, and ARVN losses, 11 killed and 8 wounded—a complete success. Statistically, this appeared to be the case, and there can be no doubt that, in the short term, the operation dealt a very heavy blow to the Viet Cong. This said, the forced deportation of 6,000 South Vietnamese, whose belongings were seized and whose homes were destroyed, was hardly a moral triumph and almost certainly qualifies as an atrocity if not a war crime. More to the point, in strategic terms, it deepened the ongoing alienation of so many South Vietnamese peasants from the government of South Vietnam. In a speech of January 16, 1964, President Johnson had spoken of winning the "hearts and minds" of the South Vietnamese. He would reiterate this phrase (sometimes as "minds and hearts") twenty-seven more times through August 19, 1968. Ostensibly, the phrase described not only the American effort in the war but also the objective of the ARVN pacification program. Yet much that was done as part of Operation Cedar Falls served only to alienate and lose minds and hearts, to drive South Vietnamese peasant families into the arms of the Communists. Beyond this massive failure of strategic pacification, the tactical effects of Operation Cedar Falls were short lived as the Viet Cong returned to the Iron Triangle quite quickly, and while they could not completely rebuild their base there, they readily reasserted their dominance before the end of 1967.

Junction City

Operation Cedar Falls was followed, beginning on February 22, by Operation Junction City. While Cedar Falls was the biggest ground action of the war, Junction City was the biggest U.S. airborne (paratroop) operation since the ill-fated Operation Market-Garden (September 17–25, 1944) of World War II and was the only major paratroop action in the Vietnam War.

The objective of Junction City was to clear NVA and VC units from the region northwest of Saigon and, secondarily, to take or destroy the NVA-VC headquarters in the area, which was believed to control most Communist military and political activity in South Vietnam as well as the southerly portions of neighboring Laos and Cambodia. Some 30,000 U.S. and ARVN troops operated in Tay Ninh Province for eighty-two days, until May 14, suffering 282 killed and 1,576 wounded but killing, according to U.S. commanders, 2,728 of the enemy. While the Communist troops were

Operation Junction City, February 22–May 14, 1967: A C-130 Hercules cargo transport airdrops supplies to U.S. airborne troops.

pushed out of the area of the operation, the headquarters was evacuated before it could be captured.

As usual, the enemy returned to the region after U.S. and ARVN
forces had moved on, making Operation Junction City all too typical of
the most ambitious "main force" search-and-destroy missions under-
taken by the United States. Tactical gains were significant, but strategic
gains—progress measurable by more than body count—was nil.

> ## "[The Viet Cong] seem like ghosts. All the six spearheads of our forces have been attacked while we don't know exactly where their main force is. . . . It's so strange."
>
> ✳✳✳
>
> —ARVN staff officer, quoted in *I Engaged in Intelligence Work* (Hanoi, 2006) by Dinh Thi Van

PHOENIX RISING

HIGH-RANKING OFFICERS, including General Westmoreland, measured
victories by body count, but commanders and troops on the ground were
repeatedly frustrated by the absence of more enduring strategic progress.
To them, the war became increasingly surreal. During long operations
and patrols, conditions in "the boonies," as troops called the jungle,
were miserable, perpetually hot, perpetually wet, perpetually dangerous.
Back at the base camps, however, life was strangely comfortable, with
decent food, entertainment (including regular visits from the USO), and
excellent medical care. Saigon offered an array of attractions, ranging
from nightclubs and gambling to an abundance of prostitutes. On the
other hand, even rearward bases were subject to VC raids. These were
unnerving, to be sure, but worst of all was the sense of nothing changing.
As one soldier put it, "You go out on patrol maybe twenty times or more,
and nothin', just nothing. Then, the twenty-first time, zap, zap, zap, you
get hit, and Victor Charlie fades into the jungle before you can close with
him." As if the invisibility of the enemy were not bad enough—the sense
that you were not only fighting shadows but fighting them on *their* terms,
not yours, as well—there was the randomness of death by other means.
The earth in patrol areas was often thickly sown with booby traps and

land mines. Even in the total absence of enemy troops, an unlucky step could trigger an explosion, often by a tiny shoe mine, which didn't kill a man but did take off his foot.

During 1965 and 1966, General Westmoreland's "crossover" strategy had been a wager that the Communists would succumb to attrition before the South Vietnamese government crumbled under the weight of its own internal rottenness. By 1967, the terms of the wager were shifting: Would the crossover point be reached before *American* soldiers and the *American* people became too discouraged and demoralized to tolerate the war any longer?

Frustration quickly led to the American soldiers' disdain for the ARVN and distrust of the Vietnamese civilian population—a sizable portion of which was, indeed, cooperating with the Communists. Although he himself had divided strategic responsibility between the United States, which took on the burden of the "main force" war, and the ARVN, which was responsible for pacification, General Westmoreland brought the pacification program under direct U.S. supervision by mid 1967.

As the ARVN conducted it, pacification included military components as well as education, land reform, communications, agriculture, and other civil programs, in addition to forced relocation to "New

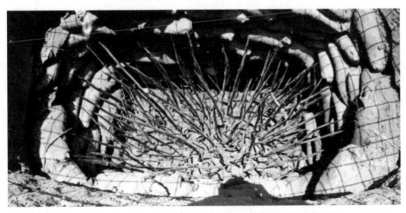

This simple but effective Viet Cong booby trap, a "classic" punji pit, contains thirty-inch sharpened bamboo "punji" sticks, designed to penetrate and close in on a man's leg, causing severe injury on entry as well as when he attempted to pull his leg out of the pit. The punji sticks were usually smeared with human feces, so that the puncture and tear wounds they caused were sure to become infected, severely disabling the victim, taking him out of the battle, and tying up the services of medics and evacuation personnel.

DETAILS, DETAILS
Lethal Weapons

Sometimes and in some places, the hazards weren't even explosive. The Viet Cong excelled at making the most out of the least of resources. A familiar booby trap was the punji stick, a sharpened bamboo spike planted upright in the ground, camouflaged by undergrowth, grass, or even crops. The point of the stick was often smeared with feces so that, when it was stepped on, it would not only create a deep and disabling puncture wound but would also likely cause a serious infection, possibly bringing death, certainly necessitating care, and sometimes requiring amputation. While many punji booby traps were simple, others were more ingenious. The spikes might be placed at the bottom of a lightly covered pit, through which the victim would fall, impaling himself. Some punji pits placed the spikes in the walls of a leg-sized pit rather than the bottom, the sharpened points angled downward, so that it was impossible to remove one's leg without severely tearing it.

REALITY CHECK

Phoenix in Congress

In 1971, the Phoenix program would become the subject of a series of Congressional hearings, in which reports of atrocity were heard. At these hearings, MACV repeatedly responded by asserting that the program was conducted in compliance with South Vietnamese law as well as the laws of land warfare—though (officials admitted) it was possible that individuals may have violated these laws from time to time. William E. Colby, a CIA official who later served as CIA director under Presidents Nixon and Ford, had responsibility for the program in 1971 and justified its methods by citing its effectiveness. "North Vietnamese and South Vietnamese Communists," he testified to Congress, "state that in their mind . . . the toughest period that they faced . . . was the period from 1968 to 1972 when the Phoenix program was at work." Colby did not speculate on the effect Phoenix had on winning the "hearts and minds" of the South Vietnamese people.

Life Villages" and other quasi-concentration camps. The object was to destroy the Viet Cong infrastructure, village by village, and develop an anti-VC self-defense capability within each village.

When General Westmoreland determined that he could discern no measurable progress, he took over the program. On July 9, 1967, the Military Assistance Command, Vietnam (MACV) issued Directive 381–41, which created the Intelligence Coordination and Exploitation for Attack on VC Infrastructure (ICEX). By the end of the year, ICEX was dubbed the "Phoenix" program. Under U.S. direction, ARVN and U.S. forces, plus the Special Police Branch of South Vietnam's National Police Field Force and Provincial Reconnaissance Units (PRUs), worked to end indigenous support for the Communists by rounding up, interrogating, torturing, and generally terrorizing suspected civilian sympathizers. Rules and evidence requirements were promulgated, but for the most part, Phoenix ignored these, relying almost exclusively on brutal interrogation methods; long, arbitrary detentions; and extra-judicial executions. Indeed, few detainees were ever released.

An American intelligence officer, K. Milton Osborne, testified before Congress (in 1971) that a South Vietnamese interrogator inserted a "6-inch dowel into the canal of one of my detainee's ears," and then "tapp[ed] [it] through the brain until dead." He also reported the "starvation to death (in a cage), of a Vietnamese woman who was suspected of being part of the local political education cadre in one of the local villages" and the widespread use of "electronic gear such as sealed telephones attached to . . . women's vaginas and men's testicles" used to administer electric shocks during interrogation. In addition, Phoenix agents routinely murdered suspects as well as their family members—on the assumption that the family could never be trusted.

THE THUNDER ROLLS ON

LIKE THE GROUND WAR, THE AIR WAR WAS PRODUCING MANY CASUALTIES, but also much doubt and frustration, by the end of 1967. As Rolling Thunder and other air missions targeted the Ho Chi Minh Trail, air crews estimated in 1966 that they were destroying just 18 percent of the trucks that traveled it. When the bombing program was intensified in 1967, the North Vietnamese responded by creating an elaborate system of anti-aircraft defense, using artillery as well as SAMs (surface-to-air missiles).

45

Vietcong Infrastructure strength. These goals have been re-fined in order to focus the action on the higher level and more significant Vietcong Infrastructure. The Phoenix program is not a program of assassination. In the course of normal military operations or police actions to apprehend them, however, Vietcong Infrastructure are killed as members of military units or while fighting off arrest. The Phoenix program has been widely publicized in Vietnam as a program to protect the people against terrorism and participation by local leadership and population has been encouraged. "Wanted" posters have been circulated to enlist public assistance in the apprehension of Vietcong Infrastructure, although the posters point out to the individual that he may rally under the Chieu Hoi program and be free of any punishment. The following figures give the results of the program over the past several years:

PHOENIX OPERATIONS AGAINST VCI

	Captured	Rallied	Killed	Total
1968	11,288	2,229	2,559	15,768
1969	8,515	4,832	6,187	19,534
	Sentenced	Rallied	Killed	Total
1970	6,405	7,745	8,191	22,341
1971 (May)	2,770	2,911	3,650	9,331

In his 1971 testimony, Ambassador Colby described the U.S. role in the Phoenix program.[85]

The United States through CORDS has provided advice and assistance to the Phoenix program. This currently includes approximately 637 U.S. military personnel working with the Phoenix centers at the district, province, region, and national levels. It also includes a very few U.S. civilian personnel. Of course, advisors with the military units, the National Police, the Chieu Hoi program, et cetera, advise and assist their respective service in its normal role, which includes support of the Phoenix program.

In his concluding remarks, Ambassador Colby defended the U.S. role in the Phoenix program.[86]

The Phoenix program is an essential element of Vietnam's defense against Vietcong Infrastructure subversion and terrorism. While some unjustifiable abuses have occurred over the years, as they have in many countries, the Vietnamese and U.S. Governments have worked to stop them, and to produce instead professional and intelligent operations which will meet the Vietcong Infrastructure attack with stern justice, with equal stress on both words. Considerable evidence has appeared from enemy documents and from former and even current members of the enemy side that, despite some weak-

[85] Ibid., p. 184. Policy and responsibilities for all U.S. personnel participating in or supporting Phoenix operations are provided in MACV Directive No. 525–336, dated May 18, 1970. For text of directive, see hearings, p. 288. On September 12, 1972, Col. David E. Farnham, Office of the Assistant Secretary of Defense for International Security Affairs, advised that as of August 28, 1972, only 125 U.S. military personnel remained as advisors to the Phoenix program and it is the Department of Defense's intention to phase out their advisory role to the Phoenix program by December 31, 1972.
[86] Ibid., p. 184.

NUMBERS

Winning Hearts and Minds

By 1972, when the program was officially discontinued, Phoenix agents had reportedly "neutralized" 81,740 suspected Communist supporters and collaborators. Of this number, 26,369 had been killed.

A congressional report on Operation Phoenix portrayed it as a benign effort to "win the hearts and minds" of the South Vietnamese people. It was, in fact, a U.S.-supported "pacification" program of systematic terror and torture that served only to further alienate the South Vietnamese peasantry from the Saigon government.

This Soviet-made, shoulder-fired, SA-7 surface-to-air (SAM) missile launcher was highly effective against U.S. helicopters and other low-flying aircraft.

The losses inflicted on U.S. aircraft stirred controversy in military as well as political circles. Some argued that the cost in planes and crews was excessive. Some argued that, despite the cost, the bombing was essential in a war of attrition. Still others countered that the bombing actually served to harden the will of the Hanoi government, not erode it. Eight times in 1967, LBJ called a temporary halt to the bombing of North Vietnamese targets in an effort to lure the North to the conference table. Each time, however, talks failed to develop, the war continued, and troops and supplies rolled from the North into the South.

> "Of course, he [General Vo Nguyen Giap] was a formidable adversary . . . [but] by early 1969, I think, he had lost, what, a half million soldiers? He reported this. Now such a disregard for human life may make a formidable adversary, but it does not make a military genius. An American commander losing men like that would hardly have lasted more than a few weeks."
>
> ★★★
>
> —General William Westmoreland, USA (ret.), to W. Thomas Smith Jr. in *George* magazine, 1998

THE WAR COMES HOME

AS FRUSTRATION, DOUBT, AND DWINDLING MORALE were increasingly serious concerns "in-country" during 1967, that year also came to be seen as a turning point against the war on the American home front. In 1965, opinion polls gave President Lyndon Johnson a spectacular 80 percent approval rating. By the end of 1967, this had fallen to 40 percent and had done so for one reason and one reason alone: the Vietnam War.

Media Offensive—and Defensive

The Johnson administration responded to the decay of public support for the war by waging what White House insiders—apparently unable

to tear themselves away from martial rhetoric—termed a "media offensive." The biggest gun in the campaign was none other than William Westmoreland, whom the president summoned back home for a time to make the case for continuing the war and for pursuing the dual strategy of search-and-destroy ground missions in the South and bombing in the North.

What Westmoreland brought home with him from Vietnam were numbers, and lots of them. He pointed to estimates that the Communists could send about 7,000 troops down the Ho Chi Minh Trail each month and that the Viet Cong could recruit on a monthly basis perhaps 3,500 troops within South Vietnam. In 1966, Westmoreland pointed out, U.S. and ARVN forces claimed that they were killing 8,400 NVA and VC fighters per month. By the summer of 1967, they claimed 12,700. This meant that losses were now outpacing the Communist capacity to replace them. Westmoreland explained that the United States was now, at last, at the "crossover point," which meant that U.S. victory was virtually certain.

General William Westmoreland, overall U.S. commander in Vietnam, addresses a press conference just outside of the White House, April 7, 1968. He is flanked by Secretary of State Dean Rusk (left) and President Lyndon B. Johnson (right). As the war ground on, Westmoreland's credibility with the press evaporated.

Cooking the Count

Body count statistics presented by General William Westmoreland in 1967 indicated that U.S. and ARVN forces were inflicting losses beyond the capacity of the North to replace them.

By Westmoreland's own logic, therefore, the long sought-after "crossover point" had been reached, and the war should therefore have been measurably close to an end that year. That it continued for another *eight* years suggests that Westmoreland's estimates of the enemy's capacity to make good his losses was incorrect or that his body counts were inflated—or some combination of both.

On January 23, 1982, CBS television newsman Mike Wallace interviewed General Westmoreland for an exposé entitled *The Uncounted Enemy: A Vietnam Deception*, which alleged that, along with others, Westmoreland had knowingly underestimated Viet Cong troop strength during 1967 with the purpose of deceiving troops, policy makers, and the public. Westmoreland responded by suing CBS and Wallace for libel. A trial began, only to end suddenly when Westmoreland settled by accepting nothing more than a quiet apology from CBS. The reasons for the settlement remain in dispute, but before the trial was aborted, two former U.S. Army intelligence officers, Major General Joseph McChristian and Colonel Gains Hawkins, had already testified to the validity of the allegations made in the documentary. They affirmed that Westmoreland had ordered alterations in intelligence reports on VC troop strength.

The handsome general known affectionately and respectfully to his colleagues as "Westie," also presented statistics from the ongoing pacification campaigns, including the Phoenix program, which looked highly encouraging. He showed estimates that anywhere from 800,000 to 1,000,000 South Vietnamese villagers had been "liberated" (his term) from Communist control by the end of 1966. He also noted that while the insurgents had closed 70 percent of South Vietnam's roadways and waterways in 1965, by the beginning of 1967, 60 percent of those had been reopened and were under South Vietnamese control.

Americans place great faith in numbers, and Westmoreland's argument was, on the face of it, persuasive. Yet, as daily newspaper and nightly television coverage seemed to show, there was no end to the war in sight, those numbers notwithstanding. By the end of 1967, it seemed to a growing number of Americans that the war was at a bloody stalemate.

That was one word for it—*stalemate*—and it was heard a lot. Another emerging term was *quagmire*. The president himself introduced a new metaphor, when he repeatedly spoke of evidence or proof or indications or hints or glimmers of "light at the end of the tunnel." The numbers Americans heard most often and most clearly were the numbers of American "boys" killed. The total for 1967 was 11,153 (up from 6,143 in 1966, 1,863 in 1965, and 401 between 1956 and 1964).

It was these numbers, not the statistics Westmoreland presented and LBJ touted, that gave rise to the ubiquitous currency of yet another phrase by the end of 1967. It had been coined at least a year earlier by Senator J. William Fulbright of Arkansas, chairman of the Senate Foreign Relations Committee, a longtime friend and political ally of LBJ, the very legislator who had served as the floor manager to facilitate passage of the Gulf of Tonkin Resolution in 1964. In February 1966, Fulbright suddenly broke with the president over Vietnam when he led his committee through six days of televised hearings on the war, explaining that they were necessary because he could not get straight answers from the administration. He said that there was a "credibility gap" between what the administration presented and what he, other legislators, and a growing segment of the American public believed.

Not subject to doubt or dispute was the fact that the Vietnam War, day by day, month by month, was producing more and more casualties on both sides. The question was: Did these add up to anything more than loss? At dinner tables, on street corners, in bars, and in university classrooms and quads, in newspaper columns, and on radio programs and television shows, that question was debated with greater and greater heat.

One casualty of the war was beyond debate. It was the credibility of the United States government under a president who had assumed office with the earnest intention of lifting the torch from the lifeless hands of the leader slain in Dallas and carrying it forward to illuminate a "Great Society" for America but who now dropped bombs and leveled villages in a small green country half a world away.

TAKEAWAY
No End in Sight

The years 1966 and 1967 saw America locked in a war against the "main force" of the Viet Cong in South Vietnam, exacting upon it a heavy toll while continuing to bomb towns and villages in North Vietnam. The bodies of the enemy were piled higher and higher, even as the flag-draped coffins of American "boys" arrived home in a volume that nearly doubled from 1966 to 1967. Frustration, despair, and anger developed on the battlefield and the home front alike as, edging toward 1968, popular and political support for the war melted.

Arkansas Senator J. William Fulbright, turned against "Johnson's war" in February 1966 when, as chairman of the powerful Foreign Relations Committee, he opened a Senate inquiry into U.S. Vietnam War policy. Fulbright is pictured in the foreground. Left to right at the witness table are Colonel Forrest I. Rettgers (Department of Defense Legislative Affairs), David Steiner (aide to David E. Bell, administrator of the Agency for International Development), Bell, and Rutherford M. Poats (another Bell aide).

CHAPTER 10

THE TET PARADOX

A Tactical Triumph Becomes a Strategic Catastrophe

ELEVEN THOUSAND ONE HUNDRED FIFTY-THREE AMERICANS were killed in South Vietnam during 1967. Lyndon B. Johnson, William Westmoreland, American families with soldier husbands and sons, young men of draft age, and boys approaching it, all hoped the New Year would herald a 1968 destined to fill fewer body bags. What the Americans called just another year, 1968, the Vietnamese, raised with a traditional twelve-year animistic calendar, called the Year of the Monkey. The Vietnamese New Year, which would fall at the end of January, was, therefore, *Tet Mau Than*: "Feast of the First Morning of the Year of the Monkey." Tet was always the most important and most popular holiday of the Vietnamese calendar, but for this particular First Morning of this particular Year of the Monkey, Hanoi had very special plans.

RUN UP

HANOI'S PLAN WAS THAT THIS TET WOULD BE THE "FIRST MORNING" of a general uprising throughout South Vietnam. It would be the start of a great offensive that would at long last tip the entire country to the North and to unity under Communism.

To prepare an offensive sufficiently vast in scope to trigger the uprising

Naval aviator Lieutenant Gerald L. Coffee was the pilot of an RA5C Vigilante reconnaissance aircraft shot down on February 3, 1966, over North Vietnam. Captured, he was held prisoner until his release in 1973. Like many other U.S. POWs, Coffee did whatever he could to pass the time and maintain a sense of a world beyond the "Camp of Detention for U.S. Pilots." He drew this cartoon to commemorate the 1968 New Year. The infant year pulls a wagon with a scroll that reads, "New Hope for Peace."

required positioning major Communist forces throughout the South—troops, rocket launchers, and mortars. The commander in charge of the offensive, General Hoang Van Thai, was a combat-savvy veteran who had served as chief of staff to Vo Nguyen Giap during the siege and battle at Dien Bien Phu. Aware that the volume of movement such preparation required was bound to attract attention, he launched in late October 1967 a diversionary action against the ARVN 5th Division, which defended Saigon as well as Highway 13 leading into it. The attack would serve the additional purpose of giving Communist forces in the South an opportunity to rehearse coordinating attacks among several units. The plan was to hit the ARVN 5th at Loc Ninh, a district capital located on Highway 13 near the Cambodian border, about seventy miles north of Saigon. Not only would this operation provide both a valuable rehearsal and diversion, but it would also deceive American and South Vietnamese intelligence officers into concluding that the North was merely carrying out the usual kinds of attacks, nothing overly ambitious or out of the ordinary.

Spearhead

Despite Hoang Van Thai's planning, the first clash was totally unplanned. The Viet Cong 271st Regiment was supposed to spearhead the attack on Loc Ninh, but it instead ran into the 2nd Battalion of the U.S. 28th Infantry at a quiet stream called Ong Thanh on October 17. In a fierce firefight, the Americans were mauled, suffering fifty-six killed in action, including the commanding officer, Lieutenant Colonel Terry Allen Jr. Had the VC commander chosen to linger, he could have wiped out the U.S. unit completely, but he was intent on getting beyond Ong Thanh Stream and into his planned position at Loc Ninh. This decision gave information officers of the Military Assistance Command, Vietnam (MACV) the leeway they needed to report the bloody U.S. *tactical* defeat as a U.S. *strategic* victory, which (they said) succeeded in delaying the arrival of the Communist spearhead unit at what turned out to be the main battlefield. With so little unambiguously good news to report, MACV had become adept at putting the most favorable "spin" on whatever news came its way.

Deciding not to await the arrival of the 271st Regiment, General Thai sent his 88th NVA Regiment against an ARVN command post along the Song Be (*song* is Vietnamese for "river") in a nighttime attack on October 27. The ARVN repulsed the attackers, who, on October 29, moved next against Loc Ninh itself.

FORGOTTEN FACES
Hoang Van Thai

Hoang Van Thai was born in May 1915 in Thai Binh Province. He joined the Communist Party of Indochina in 1938 and served as a squad commander in the resistance against Japanese occupation during World War II.

On September 7, 1945, he was appointed to the General Staff of the People's Army of Vietnam and, at Dien Bien Phu in 1954, was special campaign chief of staff and assistant to the general commander, Vo Nguyen Giap. From 1967 to 1973, he commanded the South Vietnam Liberation Army and was commander during the Battle of Loc Ninh and throughout the Tet Offensive, which the North Vietnamese government deemed a great victory. Hoang Van Thai was appointed deputy chief of the General Staff in 1974 and became a full general in 1980. He was a member of the Central Executive Committee of the Communist Party of Vietnam and was active both in the military and the Communist Party until his death on July 2, 1986.

Loc Ninh

General Hoang Van Thai had chosen wisely in targeting Loc Ninh, which, up to this time, had been largely bypassed in the war. The town was the center of numerous rubber plantations in the surrounding district and was also home to a Green Beret outpost (Detachment A-331, 5th Special Forces), which included, in addition to U.S. soldiers, Vietnamese, Montagnard, and Nung troops. The Nung, an ethnic minority in Vietnam and China, contributed a significant number of mercenary fighters to the anti-Communist cause. The Green Berets esteemed them as highly as they did the Montagnards. The outpost, located near the Cambodian border, a chronic source of infiltration, was tasked primarily with border observation. Yet no one detected Hoang Van Thai's attack, which commenced at 1:15 on the morning of October 29. While one Communist battalion poured fire on the Special Forces camp, another hit the ARVN district headquarters, penetrating the compound in less than an hour. The Communists occupied Loc Ninh for the rest of night and well into the morning and afternoon of October 30, withdrawing after the arrival of U.S. infantry and artillery—albeit not before warning the townspeople that they would return.

They did return.

On October 31—Halloween for the Americans—two Viet Cong regiments attacked (another was held in reserve), striking both the

North Vietnamese general Hoang Van Thai was the commander in charge of the Tet Offensive, which ushered in the fateful year of 1968.

DETAILS, DETAILS

The Kalash

One of the world's first assault rifles, designed in 1944 late in World War II, the AK-47 is still the most widely used weapon of its type in the world, with as many as 75 million having been produced—and another 100 million variants. A gas-operated automatic/semi-automatic weapon, it is capable of firing 600 rounds per minute. The rifle was developed in the Soviet Union by Mikhail Kalashnikov and was formally designated Avtomat Kalashnikova by the Soviet military. More familiarly, it is a "Kalashnikov," "Kalash," or simply an "AK." In 1949, the weapon was universally adopted throughout the Soviet Armed Forces as well as by most of the Warsaw Pact nations—the so-called Soviet bloc in addition to Communist China. The weapon's virtues include simplicity, durability, low production cost, and ease of use. For this reason, it has long been the rifle of choice among Third World nations, emerging nations, revolutionary groups, and terrorist organizations.

The Soviet-designed AK-47 was and remains a great assault rifle. It was standard issue to North Vietnamese and Viet Cong forces. First produced in 1944, the AK-47 is by far the most widely used weapon of its kind in the world. This example was manufactured in the USSR in 1954.

town of Loc Ninh and the nearby Green Beret encampment. The Americans responded with artillery, defeating five separate assaults and inflicting heavy casualties on the VC who (Green Beret recon squads noted) were armed with Chinese-manufactured AK-47 assault rifles.

It was not over yet. On November 2, combined forces of the NVA and the Viet Cong struck again, this time concentrating on the Green Beret camp, which returned fire with artillery and called in a massive "Arc Light" attack, as close air support (CAS) sortie packages carried out by B-52s were called. The combination of artillery and intensive aerial bombardment obliterated two Communist regiments.

The Communists launched a final attack on November 7, by which time Loc Ninh had been heavily reinforced by three battalions of the U.S. 1st Division and additional ARVN forces. After this, the U.S. military declared the Battle of Loc Ninh to have ended. The body count was, as usual, very lopsided. Nine hundred of the enemy had been killed for a loss of 50 Americans and South Vietnamese killed and 234 wounded. The North had absorbed 30,125 artillery rounds, 452 air sorties, and eight full-scale Arc Light strikes. Little wonder that *Time* magazine pronounced the battle a major Communist defeat. As for the White House, President Johnson was able to secure highly favorable press reports on the performance of the ARVN, which supported his contention that the South Vietnamese were earnestly working to improve their military effectiveness. Unknown to *Time*, to Saigon, and to Washington, Hanoi counted Loc Ninh a significant victory that "consolidated" the Communists' "offensive springboard north of Saigon." In Hanoi's view, the tactical losses suffered took nothing away from this strategic achievement.

Dak To

Even while the Battle of Loc Ninh was being fought, NVA and VC troops were positioning themselves in the Central Highlands. From November 3 to November 22, in and around the village of Dak To, a series of major engagements were fought in which the Communists fielded four separate regiments, about 7,000, troops against 16,000 U.S. and ARVN soldiers. The U.S. 173rd Airborne Brigade alone lost 208 killed and 645 wounded, a devastating 27 percent casualty rate. Overall, U.S. losses totaled 376 killed, 15 missing in action, and 1,441 wounded, while ARVN deaths numbered 73, with 18 reported missing. After its soldiers withdrew, Hanoi reported a "resounding victory" in a "siege" from which (presumably based on radio intercepts) the Americans admitted they were "surrounded and cannot evacuate [their] wounded." Despite this claim, combined NVA-VC losses were at least 1,000 killed (the U.S. reported the body count as 1,644) and as

At the Battle of Dak To, members of C Company, 1st Battalion, 8th Infantry Regiment, 1st Brigade, 4th Infantry Division advance down Hill 742 sometime during November 14–17, 1967. General Westmoreland almost certainly inflated the enemy body count to justify the heavy losses U.S. forces sustained in this battle.

many as 2,000 wounded, far greater than the U.S.-ARVN casualty figures, high as these were. This result moved General Westmoreland to respond to a reporter's question, was Dak To the "beginning or end of anything in particular for the enemy," that, yes, it was "the beginning of a great defeat for the enemy."

Khe Sanh

There was one more border battle to come before the all-out Tet Offensive. It was at Khe Sanh, a village just south of the DMZ on Route 9 leading to Laos. Khe Sanh had been held by U.S. Marines since 1962, and they were now reporting a buildup of Communist forces in the surrounding hills. It seemed increasingly clear to U.S. military intelligence that a siege was imminent—an impression that General Thai, still striving to divert attention from the pre-Tet buildup near Saigon, was eager to create. The U.S. NSA (National Security Agency) and CIA were picking up a stream of North Vietnamese radio traffic and fed the intercepts to General Westmoreland and his staff. Westmoreland saw the intercepts as confirmation that a big attack on Khe Sanh was in the offing, but a number of CIA analysts warned that the intercepts more strongly suggested an uprising, an offensive much bigger, wider, and more general than an attack on Khe Sanh. Analysts for the Defense Intelligence Agency (DIA) were even more convinced of this and drew up a paper reporting their conclusion that Hanoi's intention was to lure U.S. forces north, to concentrate them near Khe Sanh, so that the southern lowlands, near Saigon, would be left weakly defended and therefore vulnerable. The report was suppressed by the DIA deputy director, who apparently did not want to incur General Westmoreland's wrath by appearing to second-guess him. He refused to pass it up to MACV, the Joint Chiefs, or to Westmoreland, who, following his own gut, sent heavy reinforcements to Khe Sanh.

"How could you possibly know more [about this situation] than General Westmoreland?"

✱✱✱

—Defense Intelligence Agency deputy director, ordering his analysts to suppress their report predicting the general Communist "uprising" that became known as the Tet Offensive

UNDOING DIEN BIEN PHU

GENERAL WESTMORELAND WAS DETERMINED to achieve at Khe Sanh what the French had sought and failed to achieve in 1954 at Dien Bien Phu. His intention was to dare the Communists to attack the heavily fortified U.S. Marine position in the expectation that they would simply batter themselves to pieces against it. The prospect of creating a Dien Bien Phu in reverse was a powerful lure not only to Westmoreland but also to President Johnson. As the New Year approached, the president was increasingly torn by conflicting claims, advice, recommendations, and demands from the military, his advisers, and his secretary of defense.

The military called for more troops, more bombing, and an expansion of the ground war into Cambodia, Laos, and southern portions of North Vietnam itself. As 1967 drew to a close, Westmoreland and MACV conceded that the war was not yet won, but they also insisted that it was by no means stalemated, as critics asserted. Whereas military intelligence supported Westmoreland's claim that the crossover point had been reached and that progress toward victory was therefore real and quantifiable, civilian intelligence—mostly from the CIA—reported that the military grossly underestimated the strength of the enemy. General Westmoreland reported the presence of 285,000 Communist troops in South Vietnam. The CIA counted more than twice this number, perhaps as many as 600,000. If this was accurate, the crossover point was nothing more than a mirage.

Closer to the Johnson inner circle, both Vice President Hubert Humphrey and Secretary of Defense Robert McNamara were now pointing to severe failures not just in the military picture but in the political situation as well. Humphrey returned from a visit to Saigon convinced that backing the regime of Nguyen Van Thieu was "throwing lives and money down a corrupt rat hole," and McNamara claimed that the effort in Vietnam, far from building U.S. global credibility, was destroying it. "The picture of the world's greatest superpower killing or seriously injuring 1,000 noncombatants a week, while trying to pound a tiny, backward nation into submission on an issue whose merits are hotly disputed," he wrote in a memorandum to the president, "is not a pretty one." To Johnson's supreme consternation, McNamara, who had always been the administration's chief proponent of escalation, now called for a halt to the bombing of the North and to setting an absolute cap on troop numbers while moving heaven and earth to transfer the entire burden of combat to the ARVN, fast. "Vietnamization," he called it.

Finally, McNamara urged the president to further scale back the nation's war aims, which had already been dramatically reduced from the reunification of Vietnam under a capitalist democratic republic to merely preserving the independence of South Vietnam. The secretary now advised making some compromise—a more drastic one—that the North would find compelling. He told the president that this did not have to be presented to the American public as surrender. After all, he explained, the political situation of Southeast Asia had improved in that Mao Zedong's "Cultural Revolution" had created such social, political, and economic chaos in China that the nation was no longer capable of intervening in conflicts beyond its borders. As for Indonesia, it was now in the hands of a right-wing regime, which had beaten down the Communist threat that had loomed so large in the early 1960s. The regional situation had changed; no more "dominoes" were likely to fall, even if the Communists made inroads into South Vietnam.

As usual, LBJ doggedly and desperately attempted to steer something of a middle course between the demands of the military and the doubts voiced from within his own administration. He did not give the military all that it asked for, especially with regard to expanding the ground war into Laos, Cambodia, and north of the DMZ. He also retracted his own earlier demand that Hanoi withdraw all troops from South Vietnam as a precondition to a bombing halt and the opening of full negotiations. Instead, he now invited those negotiations to begin immediately.

Depressed, confused, thwarted, and trapped, the president was hungry for *some* indisputable victory. Westmoreland's idea of rewriting Khe Sanh as Dien Bien Phu with a happy ending gave him a reason for hope.

The Siege Begins

Heavy jungle rains poured down on the U.S. Marine encampment at Khe Sanh on the night of January 2, 1968. Through the sheets of water, marines manning a listening post spotted six men uniformed in black just outside the defensive wire of the main base. The marines called out a challenge. Receiving no response, they fired into the rain, killing five and wounding one, who managed to run off. In response

to the Marines' report of this engagement, Major General Robert E. Cushman Jr., deputy commander of the III Marine Amphibious Force, reinforced Khe Sanh, and the base commander sent detachments to occupy nearby hills.

U.S. Marines (C Battery, 1st Battalion, 13th Marines) defend beleaguered Khe Sanh late in February 1968.

Contrary to the popular perception that all North Vietnamese fighters were fanatically loyal to their cause and country, desertions and defections from the VC and NVA were common, and on January 20, La Thanh Ton, an NVA anti-aircraft lieutenant, showed up at Khe Sanh and laid before the marines everything he knew about a planned series of attacks. Thus warned, the marines prepared, and they fended off the first attempts at incursion, except at one place, where the Communists did break through the defensive perimeter and had to be driven back in hand-to-hand combat. What followed next was a terrific barrage of mortar and 122-millimeter rocket fire into the marine compound, which destroyed most aboveground structures. The worst of it came early in the barrage, when an enemy mortar round detonated the main ammo dump, cooking off many rounds, which exploded into the air, and then fell back onto the base. Shortly after this, another mortar

round blew up a tear gas dump, blanketing the compound in a suf-
focating CS aerosol. Even after the bombardment ended, the resulting
fires continued to be dangerous, especially when, about ten o'clock in
the morning, a cache of C-4 plastic explosive ignited, resulting in many
detonations.

The chaos created by the barrage and the countless secondary
explosions provided an ideal opportunity for the Communists to
launch a penetrating assault. Instead, however, they set up a siege,
which was accompanied by a heavy artillery assault using 100- and
152-millimeter guns, beginning on January 21. The marines hunkered
down under the onslaught, taking some comfort in the approaching
Tet truce, scheduled for January 29 to 31.

Operation Niagara

In the days before the assault on Khe Sanh, an experimental installation of
electronic sensors in southeastern Laos, part of a U.S. Air Force program
initially called Operation Muscle Shoals and subsequently renamed
Operation Igloo White, revealed unusual Communist activity along
the Ho Chi Minh Trail near the DMZ. In coordination with Operation
Niagara I, an intelligence operation combining CIA with military ground
and aerial reconnaissance forces, the Muscle Shoals/Igloo White data
not only suggested that a major North Vietnamese assault was in the
offing—Westmoreland mistakenly believed it was aimed exclusively at
Khe Sanh—but also provided what USAF general William W. Momyer
considered a magnificent opportunity. With so many North Vietnamese
troops massing in an unpopulated northern region near the DMZ, which
was not subject to the bombing restrictions that hobbled air force efforts
both farther south and farther north, the enemy would be a sitting duck

*This cutaway drawing
illustrates an ACOUSID
III, an acoustic and
seismic intrusion detector,
of the type the U.S.
Air Force deployed in
Operation Igloo White
(a.k.a. Operation Muscle
Shoals). Using seismic
sensors and microphones,
the devices were intended
to detect stealthy VC
movement and transmit
warnings to U.S. and
ARVN forces.*

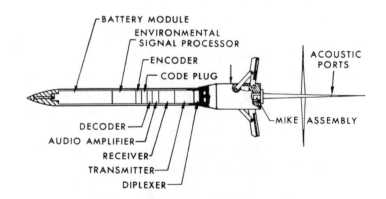

for a massive air assault. Incredibly, the U.S. Marines, who had their own air arm, refused to relinquish to the air force overall command of Momyer's proposed operation. The dispute pitted the army's Westmoreland (Momyer was his deputy commander for air operations) against the navy's commander-in-chief, Pacific (CINCPAC), Admiral U.S. Grant Sharp Jr., who had overall responsibility for the marines. An

Admiral U. S. Grant Sharp Jr., commander-in-chief, Pacific (CINCPAC), led both sea forces as well as the marines. On the eve of Tet and during the long siege of Khe Sanh, he fell into an unseemly turf war with General William Westmoreland.

unseemly interservice dispute heated up, ascending all the way to the level of the Joint Chiefs of Staff and, in the process, consuming valuable preparation time. The impasse was ended only when an exasperated General Westmoreland threatened to resign if air operations were not put in the hands of a single U.S. Air Force commander.

In the face of Westmoreland's threat, Admiral Sharp backed down, and Operation Niagara II, which combined aircraft of the U.S. Air Force, Navy, and Marines all under USAF command, was launched. It is still regarded as the most intensive concentration of aerial firepower in all of military history.

On January 20, Observation Squadron Sixty-Seven (VO-67) began air dropping acoustic and seismic sensors—316 of them by the end of the month. From then through March, some 350 fighter-bombers, 60 B-52s, and 30 observation aircraft operated on a daily basis near Khe Sanh. Ultimately, a total of 9,691 USAF sorties dropped 14,223 tons of ordnance on the enemy. The U.S. Marines flew 7,098 sorties, dropping or firing 17,015 tons of mixed munitions. Naval aviators flew 5,337 sorties, deploying 7,941 tons of ordnance.

Despite the unprecedented rain of death from the sky, the NVA continued to fight the marines for control of the hills outside the base. Combat was not hand-to-hand but, more typically, a duel of opposing artillery and mortars. For the first time in the war, the NVA used Soviet-built tanks (the formidable PT-76) in combat, overrunning a Green Beret camp at Lang Vei on February 7. But by the end of March, battered from the air and the ground, the Communists began to withdraw.

NUMBERS
Niagara II Numbers

Claiming victory at Khe Sanh, the U.S. Air Force reported that, in coordination with naval and marine aviation assets, it had killed or wounded an estimated 9,800 to 13,000 North Vietnamese troops in Operation Niagara II.

TET UNLEASHED

BY MARCH 1968, WHEN GENERAL WILLIAM WESTMORELAND, an infantry man after all, generously credited air power with a great victory in Khe Sanh, two things were true. First, despite the death or withdrawal of many NVA and VC troops, Khe Sanh was still under fire, if not under full siege, and would remain so, according to U.S. commanders, until April 8 or, as Vietnamese historians claimed, July 9. Second, Khe Sanh had clearly become just one front in the much larger battle intelligence officials, unheeded, had predicted. This was the Tet Offensive, and it would end for the Americans in that most puzzling of paradoxes of war: a great tactical victory that was nevertheless a profound strategic defeat.

The Onslaught

Although the siege of Khe Sanh is often viewed as integral to it, the Tet Offensive proper stepped off during the early morning hours of January 30. Despite the Americans' extensive electronic surveillance network and other intelligence and reconnaissance assets, the NVA and VC had managed to infiltrate and position forces throughout the South. The element of surprise was total as, within a matter of hours, five of South Vietnam's biggest cities, including Saigon, came under heavy attack. In the capital, at 2:45 a.m., a twenty-man team—sixteen Viet Cong and four embassy drivers, who may have been infiltrators—blasted a gaping hole into the wall that enclosed the U.S. Embassy compound. A fierce six-hour firefight ensued with the U.S. Marine contingent guarding the embassy. It ended only after all of the attackers had been killed or badly wounded. Simultaneously, the capital's airport, the presidential palace, and the national radio station all fell under attack.

While Saigon was beleaguered, thirty-six of the South's forty-four provincial capitals were attacked, along with sixty-four district capitals. Some 7,500 Communist troops stormed Hue, the ancient imperial capital of Vietnam, a city of great historical and spiritual importance. It was soon completely overrun and occupied.

The Response

There can be no denying that, from the U.S. point of view, the Tet Offensive was a stunning failure of intelligence—or, more accurately, a failure of intelligence analysis and interpretation. To look at a map of South Vietnam as it appeared at the end of January and beginning

REALITY CHECK

Khe Sanh: Who Won?

Both sides declared victory at Khe Sanh. Without question, the U.S. Marines, aided by Operation Niagara II, inflicted far more casualties than they incurred. In April 1968, President Johnson personally issued an order to "hold the base of Khe Sanh at all cost." Nevertheless, in July 1968, the marines and Green Berets withdrew from the base complex, which had been, in any event, totally leveled by a combination of artillery barrage and the explosion of ammo dumps. When the U.S. military moved out, the NVA moved in.

Saigon in flames: the image suggests the ferocity of the Viet Cong attacks during the Tet Offensive of 1968.

of February 1968 is to see the military-geographic equivalent of an undetected cancer gone into hopeless metastasis. From Khe Sanh and Quang Tri near the DMZ in the north, to Ca Mau and Bac Lieu in the country's southern peninsula, desperate battles raged.

Yet, despite being caught so spectacularly flat footed, the "allied" forces—U.S., ARVN, Republic of Korea (South Korea), Australia, and

This map of the Tet Offensive illustrates the enormous scope of the simultaneous Viet Cong attacks, which fell upon the entire length of the country.

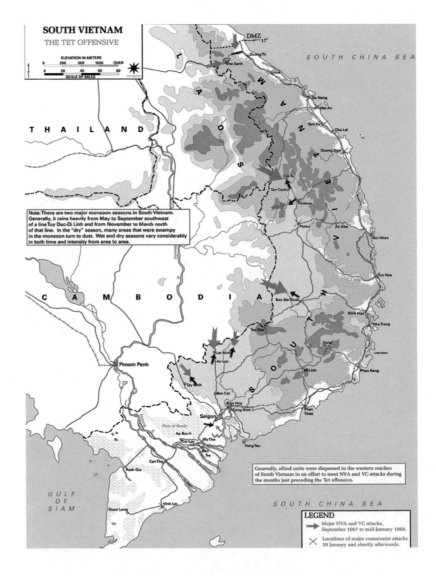

New Zealand—responded with incredible speed, vigor, and effectiveness. Most surprising and gratifying to U.S. military and political leaders was the response of the ARVN. Certainly, a major objective of the Tet Offensive had been to break whatever fighting spirit remained in an already badly demoralized South Vietnam; Tet, however, seemed to produce precisely the opposite effect. Immediately following the initial offensive, some 15,000 ARVN deserters voluntarily *returned* to the army, and 240,000 South Vietnamese civilian young men voluntarily

ARVN Rangers—the elite of the South Vietnamese ground forces—defend a Saigon street. Among other things, the Communists intended Tet to humiliate the ARVN. In fact, the South Vietnamese military met the crisis of Tet with unprecedented courage, determination, and patriotism. The rate of desertion plunged; voluntary enlistment soared.

presented themselves for military service. Not waiting to be drafted, they enlisted.

With the single exception of Hue, the initial gains made by the NVA and VC were rapidly reversed all across the South, usually within days of the initial onslaught. As for body count, approximately 15,515 Communist fighters were killed during January 28–February 3, whereas 416 U.S. and 784 ARVN troops (as well as 3,071 South Vietnamese civilians) died. Thus nearly 15 NVA/VC troops died for every U.S./ARVN soldier killed in the opening phase of the offensive. Even worse for the Communists, the massive offensive failed to trigger the general southern uprising its planners had counted on. This was due less to the mood of the South Vietnamese people than to the speed with which the allied forces ejected the North Vietnamese. As military historians look at it, the Tet Offensive extended through three "phases": Phase 1, January 30–March 28, was the most intense. Phase 2, May 5–June 15, and Phase 3, August 17–August 30, were more extended campaigns in which Communist resistance was stubborn, but Communist losses were very high. The invaders were never able to set up the civil structures and political cadres required to convert the loyalty of the populace. The sole exception—for a time—was in Hue, which was not recaptured by U.S. and ARVN troops until March 2. Here, political cadres worked fast and worked brutally, summarily executing as many as 2,800 South Vietnamese troops and civilians.

REALITY CHECK
The Revolt That Failed

Even now, it remains difficult to determine just why the Communists were unable to incite a widespread uprising against the unpopular Thieu government. The overwhelming military victories of U.S. and ARVN defenders certainly played a role, but it is also important to note that the odds were historically and ideologically stacked against the Communists, regardless of the military situation. Since the end of World War II, both the nationalist and Communist movements had always succeeded more readily in the countryside, among the long-suffering peasants, than in the cities, whose people enjoyed more of the benefits offered by Western-oriented capitalism.

NUMBERS

Tet's Toll

The number of troops involved in executing and countering the Tet Offensive was staggering. Estimates of Viet Cong and NVA forces committed vary from a low of about 323,000 to as many as 595,000, whereas the numbers of combined "allied" forces—which included U.S., ARVN, South Korean, Australian, and New Zealand units—approached one million men. Total casualties from all three phases of the Tet Offensive, January to August 1968, are reported as 111,604 for North Vietnam, including 45,267 killed, 61,267 wounded, and 5,070 missing. For the "allies," total casualty figures are still in dispute but number at least 45,820, including 9,078 killed, 35,212 wounded, and 1,530 missing.

Tactical Triumph, Strategic Catastrophe

By any tactical standard, the U.S.-led allied defeat of the Tet Offensive was a triumph, a remarkable recovery from a terrible lapse in intelligence, and a heavy blow to the armed forces of the North. Both President Johnson and William Westmoreland attempted to seize control of the popular perception of Tet and portray it as an act of Communist desperation, evidence that the North was fatally weakened. The president and his general pointed to the ARVN performance as irrefutable evidence that Vietnamization was beginning to work, that there really was "light at the end of the tunnel," that the war soon could be turned over to South Vietnam, so that American boys could begin to come home.

Yet while the armed forces had converted defeat into victory, Washington was suffering unremitting defeat in its campaign to "spin" Tet. The year just ended, 1967, had seen the balance of public opinion turn against the war. Now, to a growing majority of Americans, Tet said two things: First, despite what Johnson and Westmoreland claimed, the massive Tet attacks hardly appeared to be the work of a moribund enemy. As America's most popular and trusted television news anchor, Walter Cronkite, asked, "What the hell is going on? I thought we were winning the war?" Second, the scope and intensity of the Tet attacks looked like dramatic evidence of North Vietnamese unity and commitment. For many Americans, the NVA and VC were beginning to look like nationalist heroes and freedom fighters, not just a highly determined enemy.

In the days, weeks, and months following the initial onslaught of the Tet Offensive, the American news media showed more evidence of ARVN (and even U.S.) combat brutality than of the atrocities committed by the Communists. The single most stunning image was the photograph by Eddie Adams of the Associated Press (AP), taken on February 1, 1968, showing the chief of South Vietnam's national police, Colonel Nguyen Ngoc Loan, summarily executing a Viet Cong prisoner with a single .38-caliber shot to the head. Everything about the image was obscene: the setting in the middle of an otherwise peaceful Saigon intersection; the businesslike demeanor of the chief; the plaid short-sleeve shirt of the suspect (no uniform), his hands tied behind him; the grotesque contortion of the man's face as the bullet entered his skull. This single image, accurately or not, revealed a hardened enemy to

For the American people, this Eddie Adams photograph of Colonel Nguyen Ngoc Loan, chief of the South Vietnamese national police, summarily executing a VC prisoner at a Saigon intersection became a horrific icon of the war. Was the man with the revolver really America's ally? And was the boy with tied hands really America's enemy?

be no more than a slightly built youngster and, to all appearances, an innocent, helpless victim.

Lyndon Johnson had often characterized the war as a struggle for the "hearts and minds" of the Vietnamese people. In the aftermath of Tet, the president was clearly losing the struggle for the hearts and minds of his fellow Americans.

> ## "Ho! Ho! Ho Chi Minh! The NLF is going to win!"
>
> ## "Hey! Hey! LBJ! How many kids did you kill today?"
>
> ★★★
>
> —Protest chants popular with American antiwar student demonstrators, 1967—69

ANTIWAR MOMENTUM

ALTHOUGH THE PENDULUM HAD SWUNG AGAINST DOMESTIC SUPPORT for the war by the end of 1967, Tet, a terrible tactical defeat for North Vietnam, an indisputable tactical victory for the United States, gave the antiwar movement unstoppable momentum, not only among a growing majority of the American people but also within the Capitol and the West Wing of the White House itself.

The Television War

The Johnson administration had hoped to achieve favorable coverage of the Vietnam War through its own extensive use of television. Whereas the Korean War had taken place during the infancy of TV and was therefore reported mainly by newspapers, Vietnam exploded during the first great heyday of televised news. By the middle of 1965, all of the major networks opened Saigon bureaus, which grew into the third largest each of them maintained, behind only New York and Washington, D.C. Little wonder, then, that historians of television and popular culture have been quick to call Vietnam the "television war" and have gone on to explain that, by 1967–68, the White House lost control of the medium, which from that point on became increasingly responsible for fueling the antiwar movement by bringing into the nation's living rooms graphic images of the horrors of combat.

Without question, there were disturbing images. As early as August 1965, CBS News aired a report showing U.S. Marines igniting the thatched roofs of the village of Cam Ne with Zippo lighters. It was television that broadcast the still photograph of the monk Thich Quang Duc immolating himself at a Saigon intersection on June 11, 1963, to protest Ngo Dinh Diem's persecution of Buddhists, and it was NBC News that broadcast newsreel footage of South Vietnam national police colonel Nguyen Ngoc Loan blowing out the brains of his captive on a Saigon street. All of this was powerful. Yet the fact is that television reporting routinely took pains to *avoid* showing scenes of bloodshed, let alone atrocity, at least up to the period of the Tet Offensive. If anything, White House and military public relations officers were able to guide television reporters to deliver mostly upbeat stories or to simply relay to viewing audiences whatever military spokespeople provided in daily press briefings that became known by 1968 as the "Five O'clock Follies." Indeed, prior to 1968, on-the-scene visual coverage of the war was rare.

It was called the "first television war," and although most American reporters tried to put a positive spin on what they saw, there was no way to rationalize the systematic burning of South Vietnamese villages by U.S. Marines. Here, Morley Safer of CBS News reports in a 1965 broadcast that showed marines applying their Zippo lighters to the thatched roofs of the villagers' "hooches."

More commonly, evening news anchors read reports that were illustrated by maps, and while they dutifully delivered the U.S. casualty figures, these were always accompanied by enemy "body counts," which far outweighed them, thereby reinforcing the impression of military progress.

    After the Tet Offensive, and when President Richard Nixon (elected in 1968) began the slow withdrawal of U.S. ground forces, television news coverage increasingly reflected growing skepticism among journalists about government claims of progress and the always elusive "light at the end of the tunnel." It is difficult to say whether this skeptical view shaped or reflected evolving public opinion. Most likely, the relationship between coverage and public sentiment was reciprocal. Whether it reported or created public opinion, TV coverage tended to validate antiwar sentiment, thereby adding energy to the antiwar momentum. In the early 1960s and even during the "teach-ins" of 1965, television covered U.S. antiwar protest as if it was something of a fringe activity. After Tet and continuing well into the 1970s, television news reports routinely juxtaposed stories filmed

The Zippo lighter was the smallest weapon in America's Vietnam War arsenal. Soldiers and marines often had them personalized with engraving or stamping. Short for fragmentation grenade, "frag" was also the root of the slang word "fragging," which described the act of "fratricide"—the murder of one's fellow soldier. In Vietnam, fragging was epidemic, and the targets were almost always unpopular platoon leaders, who were perceived as all too willing to put their troops in harm's way.

DETAILS, DETAILS
The Smallest Weapon

Sturdy, simple, well-made, with a "classic" design that had changed little since the Zippo Manufacturing Company was founded in Bradford, Pennsylvania, in 1933, the Zippo lighter had been a favorite of U.S. servicemen in World War II and Korea. It was in Vietnam, however, that the Zippo graduated from lighting cigarettes to burning villages. During search-and-destroy as well as pacification missions, U.S. soldiers and marines often razed rural hamlets suspected of harboring VC and Communist organizers. Such operations were carried out with the flip of a Zippo, striking a flame, and applying it to the highly combustible straw roofs of peasant "hooches."

in Vietnam with coverage of antiwar demonstrations and protests at home. This served to elevate the antiwar movement from fringe protest to mainstream political movement.

Protest and the Draft

By 1968 it was commonplace for newspaper and television news commentators to write or speak of "the war in Vietnam" along with a simultaneous "war at home." To be sure, from its beginnings, the antiwar movement had included a wide range of Americans. At first, it was leftist activists (often called "radicals," either approvingly or disapprovingly, depending on who was using the word) who led the movement principally in protest of a war they condemned as unjust and immoral. Many of this first wave of protestors saw the Vietnam War as the product of an unholy alliance between the government and big business—what President Dwight Eisenhower (certainly no radical) had called the "military industrial complex" in his January 17, 1961,

In an antiwar demonstration in Manhattan on April 15, 1967—"income tax" day—a protester burns his draft card, the legally required certificate of Selective Service registration.

farewell address. As the war ground on, the remarkable fact was not that "radicals" were protesting it but that the war itself had radicalized many "ordinary" middle-class people. Increasingly, it divided the nation. Many feared (and some doubtless hoped) that the war would bring a genuine social and political revolution.

Politics, ideology, and morality were important drivers of antiwar protest, but almost certainly, the most potent motive behind the antiwar movement, especially after Tet, was the military draft. Young American men were liable to fight, kill, and quite possibly die in a war that fewer and fewer Americans understood, let alone supported. Moreover, inasmuch as the Vietnam War coincided with much of the civil rights movement (no less a civil rights figure than Dr. Martin Luther King, Jr. began directing much of his energy to protest against the war), many came to believe that the draft was an instrument of racially and economically based social injustice. The Selective Service Act of 1967 classified all men between the ages of eighteen and thirty-five as eligible for conscription but granted various deferments, including those for college students (service was deferred until the student had earned a four-year degree or reached the age of twenty-four, whichever came first). Many believed that this was, in effect, a pass for the children of the white middle class, because fewer African American and Hispanic young men attended college. Antiwar activists commonly asserted that the Vietnam War was being fought disproportionately by members of racial and ethnic minorities.

During the Vietnam War, some 100,000 "draft dodgers" fled the country to avoid service. Of this number, it is estimated that 50,000 to 90,000 crossed into Canada, where they were treated as immigrants because draft evasion was not a criminal offense under Canadian law. Most of the rest became fugitives within the United States. Among those who did serve, substantial numbers deserted before their units shipped out for Vietnam. These young men had a more difficult time evading the law, because Canada provided no haven. While draft evasion was not a crime there, military desertion was, and it is believed that no more than a thousand deserters sought refuge north of the border. Still, while the Canadian government announced that it reserved the right to prosecute deserters, not a single case was ever brought to trial.

It was not until 1977, two years after the end of the Vietnam War, that President Jimmy Carter issued a general amnesty to draft evaders

REALITY CHECK
Feeling vs. Fact
Statistics from the Vietnam era do not support the commonly held belief that African American and Hispanic American young men were drafted in numbers disproportionate to their white counterparts. In fact, these minorities were drafted in numbers roughly corresponding to their representation in the American population. Of those killed in the conflict, 86 percent were white, 12.5 percent were black, and 1.2 percent were members of other races—again, percentages that closely reflected the racial makeup of the nation at the time. Also mistaken was the popular impression that draftees bore the brunt of the fighting. In fact, the army far preferred to deploy volunteers to frontline units in the belief that volunteers naturally made better combat soldiers. Two-thirds of the army personnel who fought in Vietnam were voluntary enlistees, whereas most draftees during this period remained in the United States or were assigned to noncombat roles in Southeast Asia or elsewhere. (Eighty percent of all U.S. military personnel in South Vietnam were support troops, not combat personnel.)

Antiwar demonstrators—among them Coretta Scott King, the activist wife of civil rights leader Dr. Martin Luther King Jr., and famed "baby doctor," Benjamin Spock—protest outside the White House gates on May 17, 1967.

in an effort to heal the national cultural wounds inflicted by the war. Even so, an estimated 50,000 men chose to remain permanently in Canada.

Washington Antiwar

At the commencement of the Tet Offensive, President Johnson authorized the immediate transfer of 10,500 additional troops to Vietnam, but he refused to accede to General Westmoreland's demands for much larger increases. In March 1968, while the most intensive phase of Tet was winding down, a somewhat distorted news story reported that Westmoreland was asking for an immediate commitment of 206,000 more men to the war. This rumor unleashed a storm of outrage among the American public, and antiwar protests became more numerous, bigger, and more boisterous. A widely published poll that month indicated that 70 percent of the American people now favored a "phased withdrawal" of U.S. forces from Vietnam.

LBJ read the polls. Not that he had to. Demonstrators were almost continually chanting beyond the White House fence: *Hey! Hey! LBJ! How many kids did you kill today?* It was deeply wounding to a president who had begun his career as a young man in rural Texas, teaching school to classes of poor Mexican children. He read the polls, and he listened to the protests. By the end of March, he initiated a gradual process of "phased withdrawal" designed to take the United States out of the war, and while he did not give General Westmoreland anything approaching the number of troops he requested, by the end of 1968, the U.S. commitment in-country would peak at 536,000.

Amid protests in the streets and bitter debates between congressional hawks and doves—in which the ranks of the latter grew as those of the former shrank—the president accepted on November 29, 1967 (to become effective February 29, 1968) the resignation of the longtime architect of Vietnam strategy, Secretary of Defense Robert McNamara. Johnson spun the resignation as a positive step in McNamara's career—LBJ had engineered his appointment to the presidency of the World Bank—and he presented him with both the Medal of Freedom and the Distinguished Service Medal. At least one major historian of the Vietnam War, Stanley Karnow, wrote that the *president* asked McNamara to step down because of the secretary's growing opposition to the war he had once advocated so vigorously. McNamara himself, who died in 2009, always maintained that he was uncertain as to whether he or the president had instigated his departure.

McNamara was replaced by Clark Clifford, a Democratic adviser to the White House since the days of Harry S. Truman, who, at the president's request, thoroughly reassessed U.S. policy in Vietnam. Clifford concluded that the United States would not achieve victory in South Vietnam, not even with twice or three times the number of troops—a million to a million and a half men. As the president well knew, the war was taking bigger and bigger bites out of his cherished Great Society social programs. Clifford warned that attempting to sustain the war effort would not only destroy this legacy but cause irreversible damage to the economy as well. He advised sending no more than 22,000

REALITY CHECK
Economic Defeat

Back in 1965, President Johnson's economic advisers assured him that the nation could pay for a limited war in Vietnam and also foot the bill for the Great Society. By 1968, however, these same advisers warned that the $2 billion per month cost of the war could not be sustained and was causing a combination of deficits and inflation. Globally, the U.S. dollar had been sent into decline as foreign investors lost confidence in the currency and bought up gold in unprecedented amounts. Secretary of the Treasury Henry Fowler warned that only major tax increases combined with draconian reductions in Great Society funding could support continued escalation of the war without leading to a national economic collapse. The war in Vietnam was becoming ruinous.

additional troops immediately while relentlessly pressing South Vietnam to assume more of the burden of the war. Johnson accepted these recommendations—though he upped the additional troop count somewhat, to 24,500—and, what is more, also embraced an idea presented by Secretary of State Dean Rusk, who proposed cutting back the bombing campaign as a means of both reducing antiwar protests and signaling to North Vietnam a renewed openness to negotiations.

For all his willingness to begin a slow withdrawal, President Johnson still believed that the response to the Tet Offensive had measurably weakened the Communists, and he hoped to find a way to help South Vietnam take on the major burden of the war and press on to victory. In the meantime, however, the so-called Wise Men, a panel of foreign policy experts Johnson had convened to review the impact of the Vietnam War on U.S. standing in the world, reported that the conduct of the war, especially the bombing of the North, was severely damaging American prestige and American alliances internationally. Added to this were challenges to Johnson's upcoming bid

Secretary of Defense Clark Clifford and Secretary of State Dean Rusk confer in the Oval Office, October 22, 1968.

President Johnson's foreign policy advisers were dubbed the "Wise Men."
Among their jobs was the ongoing assessment of the effect of the Vietnam War
on America's image in the world. Here, the Wise Men meet with the president
for a working lunch in the White House dining room, March 26, 1968. Left
to right: General Creighton Abrams, George Ball, Tom Johnson (standing),
General Maxwell Taylor, McGeorge Bundy, General Matthew Ridgeway, Arthur
Dean (mostly hidden), Henry Cabot Lodge, Dean Acheson, LBJ, General of the
Army Omar Bradley, W. Averell Harriman, Secretary of Defense Clark Clifford,
Cyrus Vance, Walt Rostow, and Secretary of State Dean Rusk.

for reelection (his presidential service after JFK's assassination had
been less than two years, so he was not barred by the Twenty-second
Amendment from running), from Senator Eugene McCarthy of
Minnesota and from Senator Robert F. Kennedy of New York, both of
whom were Democrats running on antiwar platforms.

From President Lyndon Johnson's Televised Address to the Nation, March 31, 1968

Throughout this entire, long period, I have been sustained by a single principle: that what we are doing now, in Vietnam, is vital not only to the security of Southeast Asia, but it is vital to the security of every American. . . . [T]he heart of our involvement in South Vietnam—under three different presidents, three separate administrations—has always been America's own security.

. . . Tonight I have offered the first in what I hope will be a series of mutual moves toward peace. I pray that it will not be rejected by the leaders of North Vietnam. . . .

. . . The ultimate strength of our country and our cause will lie not in powerful weapons or infinite resources or boundless wealth, but will lie in the unity of our people. This I believe very deeply. Throughout my entire public career I have followed the personal philosophy that I am a free man, an American, a public servant, and a member of my party, in that order always and only. For 37 years in the service of our Nation, first as a Congressman, as a Senator, and as Vice President, and now as your President, I have put the unity of the people first. I have put it ahead of any divisive partisanship. And in these times as in times before, it is true that a house divided against itself by the spirit of faction, of party, of region, of religion, of race, is a house that cannot stand.

There is division in the American house now. There is divisiveness among us all tonight. And holding the trust that is mine, as President of all the people, I cannot disregard the peril to the progress of the American people and the hope and the prospect of peace for all peoples.

So, I would ask all Americans, whatever their personal interests or concern, to guard against divisiveness and all its ugly consequences.

Fifty-two months and 10 days ago, in a moment of tragedy and trauma, the duties of this office fell upon me. I asked then for your help and God's, that we might continue America on its course, binding up our wounds, healing our history, moving forward in new unity. . . .

United we have kept that commitment. United we have enlarged that commitment. Through all time to come, I think America will be a stronger nation, a more just society, and a land of greater opportunity and fulfillment because of what we have all done together in these years of unparalleled achievement.

Our reward will come in the life of freedom, peace, and hope that our children will enjoy through ages ahead. What we won when all of our people united just must not now be lost in suspicion, distrust, selfishness, and politics among any of our people. Believing this as I do, I have concluded that I should not permit the Presidency to become involved in the partisan divisions that are developing in this political year. With America's sons in the fields far away, with America's future under challenge right here at home, with our hopes and the world's hopes for peace in the balance every day, I do not believe that I should devote an hour or a day of my time to any personal partisan causes or to any duties other than the awesome duties of this office—the Presidency of your country.

Accordingly, I shall not seek, and I will not accept, the nomination of my party for another term as your President.

But let men everywhere know, however, that a strong, a confident, and a vigilant America stands ready tonight to seek an honorable peace—and stands ready tonight to defend an honored cause whatever the price, whatever the burden, whatever the sacrifice that duty may require.

Thank you for listening.

Good night and God bless all of you.

President Johnson stunned America and the world during his televised speech of March 31, 1968, by announcing a restriction of bombing above the 20th parallel—a peace overture—and by declaring that he would neither seek nor accept "the nomination of my party for another term as your President." Like thousands of his fellow Americans, he had become a casualty of the war in Vietnam.

TAKEAWAY
Tactical Victory, Strategic Defeat

The Tet Offensive, a massive North Vietnamese military operation beginning on January 30, 1968, and intended to trigger a general uprising throughout South Vietnam, was overwhelmingly defeated by U.S., South Vietnamese, and allied forces. Despite suffering a crushing tactical defeat, however, North Vietnam achieved a decisive strategic victory in that the American popular will to continue the war had been broken. The most immediate result was the decision of President Lyndon Baines Johnson not to run for reelection in 1968. For the first time since the early 1960s, the United States was on a path away from war. It would, however, prove long, winding, and bitter.

The president felt himself cornered and, what is more, had come to believe that his presence in the White House had cornered the nation. Accordingly, on March 31, 1968, he secured air time on all three national television networks and appeared before the cameras, a haggard, even a beaten, man. His first announcement came as a surprise. He declared his intention to restrict bombing above the 20th parallel, thereby throwing open the door to a negotiated settlement of the war. His second announcement sent shockwaves. "I shall not seek, and I will not accept, the nomination of my party for another term as your President," he declared. By the end of the telecast, it was clear. Lyndon Baines Johnson had just become the latest casualty of the Vietnam War.

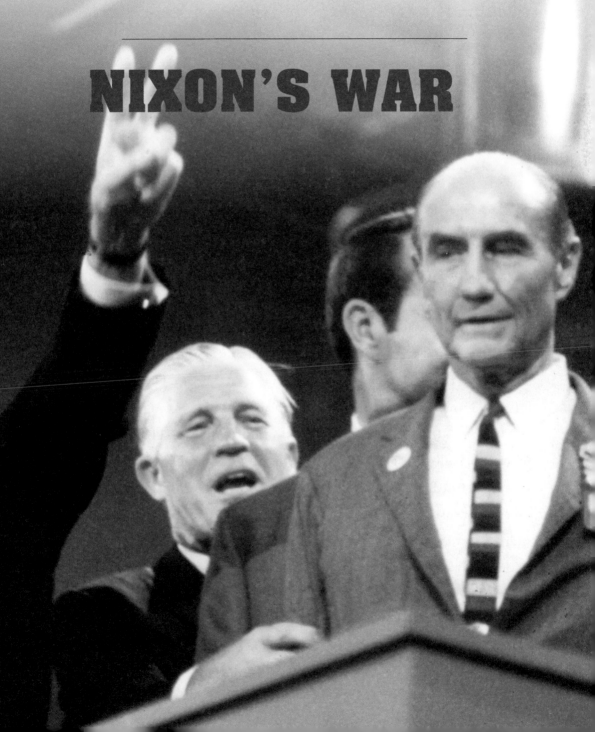

PART FOUR

NIXON'S WAR

CHAPTER 11

"THE WHOLE WORLD IS WATCHING"

A New American President, a New American Strategy

RICHARD MILHOUS NIXON WAS AN UNLIKELY POLITICAL SUCCESS STORY. Charmless, ruthless, and clearly uncomfortable in his own skin, he nevertheless was elected congressman and senator, and he then served eight years as Dwight D. Eisenhower's vice president. Through it all, a peculiar shiftiness clung to him, and he was never able to shake the epithet acquired at the very start of his political career, "Tricky Dick." By contrast, John F. Kennedy was a charismatic political natural, who edged Nixon out in the 1960 presidential election by the thinnest of margins (120,000 votes: 0.02 percent of ballots cast). When Nixon sought a comeback by running against Democrat Pat Brown for California governor in 1962, his defeat by 300,000 votes was crushing. Everyone wrote him off, including Nixon himself, who snarled to reporters at a press conference the morning after the election, "You won't have Nixon to kick around anymore, because, gentlemen, this is my last press conference."

Yet, at the 1968 Republican National Convention in Miami, held from August 5 to August 8, Richard Nixon defeated his two most serious challengers, the moderate Nelson Rockefeller and the conservative Ronald

Richard M. Nixon delivers his State of the Union Address to a Joint Session of Congress, January 22, 1971.

Reagan, on the very first ballot. It was not a victory achieved through misplaced reliance on anything resembling personal likability. Instead, he made a bargain based on hard numbers, devising a so-called Southern Strategy, by which he secured the support of Southern conservatives—especially segregationist South Carolina senator Strom Thurmond—by embracing a states' rights platform that was inherently opposed to the ongoing civil rights movement. Republican convention delegates understood that Nixon had succeeded in wresting the "solid South" from the Democratic grip. Like him or not, they now believed Nixon could win.

"Would you buy a used car from this man?"

★★★

—Widely circulated quip about Richard Nixon attributed to stand-up comic Mort Sahl, c. 1960

PREVIOUS PAGES: Richard Nixon flashes his trademark victory sign to delegates at the Republican National Convention on August 8, 1968, after his nomination as the party's presidential candidate. At the right is South Carolina's Senator Strom Thurmond, a former Democrat who joined the Republican Party in 1964 and was instrumental in advancing Nixon's infamous "Southern Strategy," which exploited anti–African American racism to win over Southern Democrats to the GOP. Michigan governor George Romney stands between Nixon and Thurmond.

FEAR, LOATHING, AND GREAT EXPECTATIONS

ALL ELECTIONS ARE ULTIMATELY ABOUT NUMBERS, of course, but Republican strategists in 1968 understood that this had never been more urgently the case. The nation was deeply divided over the Vietnam War. More specifically, Republicans were well aware that the Democratic Party was more deeply divided than at any time since the eve of the Civil War. There was a vocal and growing antiwar faction, which also identified strongly with the civil rights movement and the Great Society initiatives. There was also a more moderate Democratic faction that disliked the war, to be sure, but favored a gradual "phased withdrawal" rather than an immediate pullout; they tended to be generally less liberal and less engaged with civil rights and the Great Society. Finally, there were the white Southern constituents, many of them increasingly alienated by the party's Northern liberal wing and resentful of having racial integration and civil rights "shoved down their throats" (as they viewed it).

"When the strongest nation in the world can be tied down for four years in a war in Vietnam with no end in sight; when the richest nation in the world can't manage its own economy; . . . when the President of the United States cannot travel abroad or to any major city at home without fear of a hostile demonstration—then it's time for new leadership for the United States of America."

★★★

—Richard M. Nixon, speech accepting the Republican nomination for president, August 8, 1968

If prospects looked hopeful for the Republicans in 1968, there were also great expectations on the part of the Democratic Party's liberal, or progressive, faction. President Johnson's withdrawal from the election left open the very real possibility that the Democratic Convention, to be held in Chicago during August 26–29, after the Republican convention, might actually nominate an antiwar candidate, a leader who would quickly pull the American nation out of the Vietnamese quagmire.

The Peace Candidates

The first of the Democratic antiwar hopefuls to emerge was Senator Eugene McCarthy of Minnesota. That rarest of combinations, a career politician and a published poet, McCarthy had an especially strong appeal to students and the college-educated younger voter, who identified with the emerging "peace and love" message of a generation that was both producing and embracing a new idealism in music, art, literature, and politics. Yet the title of his collected verse, *Cool Reflections: Poetry for the Who, What, When, Where and Especially Why of It All*, speaks volumes about his qualities and limitations as a politician. To many, he seemed aloof and unapproachable, overly

Antiwar Democratic presidential aspirant Senator Eugene McCarthy of Minnesota visits with President Johnson in the White House on June 11, 1968.

intellectual—noble-minded but removed from gritty political reality. Nevertheless, his strong showing at the Democratic primary in New Hampshire encouraged the entry of another antiwar candidate, Robert F. Kennedy, former attorney general in the cabinet of his brother, John F. Kennedy, and subsequently senator from New York.

Where McCarthy was a cool reflector, RFK—the initials came naturally—was passionate and disarmingly charismatic. He had both grown up and come of age politically in the shadow of his older brother. With JFK five years in his grave, however, Robert Kennedy had not only emerged from that long shadow but also had come forth lightly cloaked in his brother's mantle. To many, he seemed JFK reborn. To many, RFK held the promise of redeeming the legacy of his slain brother, a heritage (as they saw it) LBJ had failed to honor. To many, the very first promise of that legacy was clear: end the Vietnam War.

Idealistic but steeped in the White House experience, anointed (in the perception of many) by his brother, handsome, and sufficiently boyish to be identified with the youth movement that had overtaken an increasingly stormy decade, Robert F. Kennedy handily won the Indiana and Nebraska primaries. He went on to California, which he and others saw as the make-or-break contest. Win here, and he might well capture the nomination. Capture the nomination, and it would be a second Kennedy for president, a chance at peace and redemption.

> **"Reality is grim and painful. But it is only a remote echo of the anguish toward which a policy founded on illusion is surely taking us."**
>
> ★★★
>
> —Robert F. Kennedy, speech on U.S. policy in the Vietnam War, February 8, 1968

Ten minutes after midnight on June 5, about four hours after the California primary polls closed, a beaming Kennedy claimed victory in an announcement at the Embassy Room of the Ambassador Hotel, Los Angeles. Eager to get the candidate to the press area, aides

ushered him through the ballroom's jammed kitchen and pantry. Kennedy shook the hands of well-wishers along the way, including that of busboy Juan Romero. The teenager's hand was still in the candidate's grip when Sirhan Bishara Sirhan, a twenty-four-year-old Palestinian refugee with Jordanian citizenship living in California, stepped out from behind a wheeled tray-stacker and, at point-blank range, squeezed off a succession of shots from his .22 caliber Iver-Johnson Cadet revolver. Several people around Kennedy wrestled the assassin to the floor. Juan Romero knelt beside the senator and placed a rosary in his hand while cradling his bleeding head in his palm. Still conscious, Kennedy asked Romero, "Is everybody safe, OK?" The busboy replied, "Yes, yes, everything is going to be OK." Heroic emergency neurosurgery followed to remove the bullet and bone fragments from RFK's brain, but at 1:44 a.m. on June 6, the senator was pronounced dead.

June 5, 1968: Robert F. Kennedy flashes the victory sign to a crowd of well-wishers at the Ambassador Hotel, Los Angeles, immediately after a victory speech following his California primary win. Minutes later, he would be shot and mortally wounded by assassin Sirhan Sirhan.

Questions of Motive

Under arrest, Sirhan Sirhan struggled to explain his motive: "I can explain it," he said. "I did it for my country." Presumably, Sirhan was referring to the long conflict over a Palestinian homeland and saw some connection between that and RFK. As with the assassination of President Kennedy, there have been a number of conspiracy theories hypothesizing scenarios beyond the lone perpetrator Sirhan. Some maintain that the location of Kennedy's wounds suggest the presence of a "second gunman." Although an official review in 1975 found no forensic evidence to support the second gunman theory, it has resurfaced repeatedly, and a suspect, a part-time security guard named Thane Eugene Cesar, has even been proposed. Cesar did admit to pulling a gun at the scene, but its caliber, .38, matched none of the .22 slugs in Kennedy's body.

O thers point to testimony by RFK campaign worker Sandy Serrano that she saw a "girl in a polka-dot dress" running from the scene with a man while shouting, "We shot him! We shot him! We shot Senator Kennedy!" Los Angeles Police Department investigators concluded that Serrano's account was unreliable. Some conspiracy theorists believe that Sirhan was the lone gunman but that he had been brainwashed ("psychologically programmed") to commit the assassination—perhaps (as Irish filmmaker Shane O'Sullivan contended in his 2007 documentary *RFK Must Die*) by rogue CIA officers bent on avenging what they saw as President Kennedy's betrayal of Cuban refugee insurgents during the 1961 Bay of Pigs invasion.

To date, no enduringly compelling evidence has been found to conclusively support any of these theories.

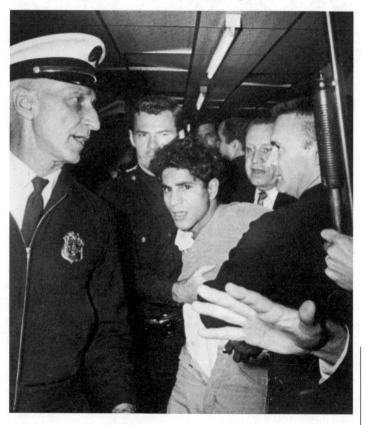

Sirhan Bishara Sirhan is led away from the Ambassador Hotel after shooting Senator Robert F. Kennedy.

Chicago, Summer of '68

The shock, fear, and despair were not limited to Robert Kennedy's supporters. He was, after all, the second Kennedy to fall victim to an assassin, and the second man of peace that very year to be assassinated. Just two months earlier, on April 4, 1968, the Reverend Martin Luther King Jr., the nation's preeminent civil rights leader and, more recently, a high-profile leader of the antiwar movement, had been gunned down on the balcony of the Lorraine Motel in Memphis. That assassination sparked riots in the African American ghettos of Washington, Chicago, Baltimore, Louisville, Kansas City, and other, smaller cities. At the time, RFK was en route to a campaign rally in Indianapolis. Informed of the assassination, he calmly and movingly relayed the news to the gathering, quietly urging them to honor Dr. King's faith in nonviolence. There were no riots in Indianapolis that night or that spring.

The murder of Robert Kennedy left one antiwar Democrat in contention for his party's nomination, Eugene McCarthy. Widely admired, he nevertheless gained little traction and managed to garner just 23 percent of the delegates as the convention got under way in Chicago during August 26–29. Party regulars instead got behind the more "mainstream" candidate, Vice President Hubert H. Humphrey, who soon amassed a commanding lead for the nomination.

Not that this was evidence of a unified party. Like McCarthy, Humphrey was a Minnesota Democrat, though his progressivism was tempered by strains of conservatism. An early and tireless advocate of civil rights, a driving force behind the creation of the Peace Corps in 1961 and passage of the Civil Rights Act of 1964, he had also been a vigorous opponent of Communism during the 1950s, sponsoring Title II of the Internal Security Act of 1950, which provided for the "emergency

Hubert Horatio Humphrey, President Johnson's vice president, won his party's presidential nomination in a Democratic National Convention torn by violence between Chicago police and antiwar protestors. Humphrey pledged to see the war through to a successful conclusion.

President Johnson and his family sat out the Democratic National Convention, watching it on television at the LBJ Ranch near Stonewall, Texas. One of the television screens from that viewing is shown here, from August 28, 1968.

detention" of Communists and subversives, and even calling for federal legislation to make membership in the Communist Party a felony. Within the Johnson administration, Humphrey had begun to oppose escalation of the Vietnam War, yet, as a contender for the presidential nomination, he now proposed prosecuting the war to its conclusion, essentially following through with the Johnson program. More than anything, it was this stance—the perception that HHH would simply continue the war policies of LBJ—that drew some ten thousand antiwar and civil rights protestors to Chicago during the convention. They commandeered two of the city's elegant lakefront green spaces, Grant Park and Lincoln Park, as campgrounds. Their intentions, they said, were peaceful but disruptive. And what they intended to disrupt was any process that would nominate Hubert Horatio Humphrey.

"Dump the Hump!"

★★★

—Anti-Humphrey nomination slogan and chant, August 1968

Among those gathered in the Chicago parks were members of two major antiwar groups, the Youth International Party (known as Yippie), led by "radical" activists Abbie Hoffman and Jerry Rubin, and the National Mobilization Committee to End the War in Vietnam (MOBE), an umbrella organization that included many Yippies, as well as Students for a Democratic Society (SDS) and others. The "hippie scene" along Lake Michigan drew much media attention, even before the convention got under way. An incident on August 22, in which police officers shot and killed a seventeen-year-old youth (not associated with the protests) during a stop for a curfew violation (the boy allegedly drew a pistol that misfired), sparked protests from the groups just then assembling at the parks. No violence resulted, but the demonstrators taunted the police by calling them "pigs" and even proposed to run a pig, named Pigasus (after Pegasus, the winged horse of Greek mythology), for president. Tensions rose, and on the Sunday before the convention opened, a "confrontation"—it was a word that would often be heard during the convention and the protests—erupted between police and demonstrators. On Sunday evening, there were three sharp clashes between baton-wielding police, who were determined to enforce eleven o'clock park curfews, and demonstrators, who were equally determined to defy the curfews. Both sides greatly exaggerated the numbers involved and the scale of the violence, which miasmatic police tear gas served only to render more dramatically warlike.

The Sunday night melee was repeated with minor variations throughout the week of the convention. Television crews covered each and every confrontation, which gave the appearance of an all-out civil war on the streets of Chicago. The police often seemed frustrated and unprofessional in their exercise of force, whereas the demonstrators proved themselves more media savvy, taking every opportunity to chant for the cameras, "The whole world is watching! The whole world is watching!"

The protests and confrontations took place in and near Grant Park and Lincoln Park in downtown Chicago and along the adjacent lakefront to the north; however, the convention itself was held at the International Amphitheatre, more than forty blocks south of this

NUMBERS

More Than a Demonstration, Less Than a Riot

Police claimed that 10,000 protestors rioted on the night before the Democratic National Convention, August 25, 1968, and protestors claimed to have been attacked by 1,000 police officers. Both claims were wildly exaggerated. An official Chicago Police Department report listed 152 officers as wounded—though the reported "wounds" included the likes of a split fingernail. Medical volunteers among the protestors reported treating 500 civilians; however, the total number of injured actually treated in Chicago hospitals during the entire convention week was just 101. There were no fatalities.

Like similar scenes frequently played out during the 1968 Democratic National Convention in Chicago, here helmeted police officers clash with antiwar demonstrators on the night of August 28, near the Conrad Hilton Hotel on the city's elegant Michigan Avenue.

area. Nevertheless, some delegates took the protest inside the convention hall by denouncing (in the words of Senator Abraham Ribicoff of Connecticut) "Gestapo tactics on the streets of Chicago," and television viewers were shocked by live coverage of newsman Dan Rather's attempt to interview a Georgia delegate as he was (apparently) being forced off the convention floor by men without identification badges. While approaching the man, Rather himself was punched in the stomach and knocked to the ground. "He lifted me right off the floor and put me away," Rather recalled. "I was down, the breath knocked out of me, as the whole group blew on by me. . . . In the CBS control room, they had switched the camera onto me just as I was slugged."

In the end, the protests failed to block the nomination of Hubert Humphrey. They may, however, have helped to ensure that his Republican opponent would win the general election. Weeks earlier, in accepting his own nomination, Richard Nixon had denounced the violence that plagued "the nation with the greatest tradition of the rule of law." The words and images flowing out of the Democratic National Convention in the Democratic political stronghold that was the city of Chicago seemed a ratification of these words.

FORGOTTEN FACES
Abbie Hoffman and Jerry Rubin

Abbie Hoffman and Jerry Rubin were the two most highly visible figures of the militant antiwar movement of the 1960s.

Born Abbot Howard Hoffman on November 30, 1936, in Worcester, Massachusetts, Abbie Hoffman was cofounder of the Youth International Party ("Yippie").

A rebellious youth who was expelled from his high school for pummeling a teacher who called him a "Communist punk" because he wrote an essay questioning the existence of God, Hoffman did earn a bachelor's degree in psychology from Brandeis University. One of his mentors there was the renowned Marxist theorist Herbert Marcuse. Hoffman went on to graduate school at the University of California, Berkeley, and became active in the civil rights movement and then in the National Mobilization Committee to End the War in Vietnam (MOBE), under whose aegis he helped organize the 1967 March on the Pentagon. He went on to help found the Youth International Party on December 31, 1967, and led it to prominence in the protests during the Democratic National Convention in Chicago during August 1968.

Along with Jerry Rubin (a fellow Yippie), David Dellinger, Rennie Davis, John Froines, Lee Weiner, Tom Hayden, and Black Panther Party co-founder Bobby Seale, Hoffman was tried for conspiracy and inciting to riot as a result of his activities in Chicago. Hoffman took his flair for political theater of the absurd into the courtroom and was among four of the so-called Chicago Seven (originally, the "Chicago Eight," until Seale's trial was severed from that of the others) to be convicted of intent to incite a riot while crossing state lines. All of the convictions were subsequently overturned, although Seale was sentenced to a four-year term for contempt of court.

Hoffman wrote a number of books, the best known of which was titled *Steal This Book* containing advice on living for free, and was arrested in 1973 on charges of drug use and drug dealing. He skipped bail and lived in hiding until 1980, when he turned himself in. He received a one-year sentence but was released after serving four months. He was arrested in 1986 on trespassing charges in connection with a protest against CIA recruitment on the University of Massachusetts

Left to right: Yippie leaders Jerry Rubin and Abbie Hoffman, who were tried for having conspired to incite riots during the Democratic National Convention. Rubin and Hoffman were part of the "Chicago Seven," who were tried together. An eighth defendant, Black Panthers leader Bobby Seale, was tried separately. The photograph was taken on February 14, 1970, at a news conference during a recess in the trial.

campus. Acting as his own attorney at trial, he quoted Thomas Paine in his defense and secured acquittal. He died three years later, on April 12, 1989, after washing down a bottle of Phenobarbital tablets with liquor.

Among those who attended Hoffman's funeral was Jerry Rubin. Born on July 14, 1938, in Cincinnati, Ohio, he lived for a time in Israel, after the death of his parents within ten months of one another, and then returned to Cincinnati, where he completed high school and graduated from the University of Cincinnati with a degree in sociology. He enrolled as a graduate student at the University of California, Berkeley, in 1964, but he left to devote himself to left-wing social activism. He organized some of the early antiwar protests, co-founded with Abbie Hoffman and others the Youth International Party, and was active in the National Mobilization Committee to End the War in Vietnam. With Hoffman, he spearheaded the protests during the National Democratic Convention in Chicago and was subsequently tried for conspiracy and incitement to riot. His conviction on the incitement charges was overturned on appeal, along with many contempt of court citations.

After the Vietnam War, Rubin became a successful businessman and an early investor in Apple Computer while also running and financing a legal aid office in Los Angeles. Rubin died on November 14, 1994, of injuries sustained in a jaywalking accident.

Law and Order versus Peace with Honor

Given the contrast between the orderly Republican convention and the mayhem of the Democrats in Chicago, it is perhaps surprising that the general election ended as closely as it did: Nixon polled 31,783,783 popular votes (43.4 percent), and Humphrey 31,271,839 (42.7 percent), while third-party candidate George Wallace (running, with former USAF general Curtis LeMay, on an ultra-conservative segregationist platform) captured 9,901,118 votes (13.5 percent). The margin, seven-tenths of 1 percent, suggests just how deeply divided the United States was.

There were those who said that the election of Richard Nixon had not taken place in November but back in August, during the week of chaos in Chicago, and that the plank in the Republican platform that lifted him to the White House had nothing to do with Vietnam and everything to do with "law and order." Perhaps. However, it is apparent that not only did Republicans *unite* behind their candidate but also that their candidate promised voters that *he* had a plan to achieve in Vietnam "peace with honor."

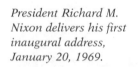

President Richard M. Nixon delivers his first inaugural address, January 20, 1969.

A "plan" *and* "peace with honor"? These were far more than Hubert Humphrey promised. That candidate Nixon refused to divulge any of the contents of his plan certainly raised doubts among many, who never really felt they could trust "Tricky Dick." Yet the mere promise proved sufficient to put him over the top, and on January 20, 1969, the new thirty-seventh president of the United States delivered his inaugural address. He spoke little of the war, but what little he did say seemed to imply an eagerness to reach an end to the fighting. "We are caught in war, wanting peace," he noted, and he spoke of leaving "a period of confrontation" and "entering an era of negotiation."

> **"Let all nations know that during this administration our lines of communication will be open.**
>
> **We seek an open world—open to ideas, open to the exchange of goods and people—a world in which no people, great or small, will live in angry isolation."**
>
> ★★★
>
> —Inauguration address, President Richard M. Nixon, January 20, 1969

JOHNSON'S WAR BECOMES NIXON'S

AS HARRY S. TRUMAN HAD LEFT DWIGHT D. EISENHOWER an unfinished war in Korea, so Lyndon B. Johnson left Vietnam to Richard M. Nixon. Johnson's withdrawal from the presidential race on March 31, 1968, brought word from Hanoi just three days later of a willingness to open talks. Yet neither the Johnson administration nor the Hanoi leadership was actually willing to make any meaningful concessions. For weeks, both sides argued fiercely and fruitlessly over just where talks would take place before they finally settled on Paris. Negotiations began on May 13, only to grind to an immediate halt over North Vietnam's demand that bombing above the DMZ stop immediately and the U.S.

response that bombing would continue until North Vietnam ceased infiltration and withdrew all forces in the South.

Month after month passed in stalemate as Secretary of Defense Clark Clifford and chief U.S. negotiator W. Averell Harriman (former U.S. ambassador to the Soviet Union and New York governor) begged the president to make *some* concession to overcome the inertia. If Johnson were inclined to offer anything, however, he was dissuaded by his secretary of state, Dean Rusk, and his national security advisor, Walt Rostow, who backed the Joint Chiefs of Staff in their claim that the defeat of Tet represented real progress and that now was no time to give ground.

So even as he had managed to convene talks, President Johnson also stepped up the war in the months following Tet. His rationale for Paris was to concede nothing, but instead to strengthen his hand in the talks. If this took both inflicting and incurring more casualties, so be it—and one of the very first casualties was William Westmoreland, who was officially relieved of duty as overall commander in Vietnam on June 10, 1968.

Westmoreland was replaced by General Creighton Abrams, whose mission would depart sharply from Westmoreland's reliance on attrition measured by body count. Instead of merely accumulating kills, Abrams was tasked with physically reclaiming South Vietnam by driving the enemy out of all densely populated areas and intensifying pacification efforts in rural areas. This meant beefing up both the Chieu Hoi (Open Arms) program, which granted amnesty to North Vietnamese defectors, and the Phoenix program, which conducted pacification.

Abrams was also directed to make Vietnamization viable. In part, Johnson wanted to publicly demonstrate a shift of the burden of war from American "boys" to Vietnamese "boys." In more immediate tactical terms, he simply wanted to put more troops on the ground, since only very large numbers would be effective in occupying territory after the VC and NVA had been pushed out of it. It is questionable whether Johnson honestly believed that he had hit on an effective strategy for winning the war. What is beyond doubt, however, is that he found a way to appease hawks, both in Congress and among the public, by escalating the war, while also mollifying doves by shifting responsibility for the war to the ARVN. This meant more money for more weapons, so that the ARVN could expand from 685,000 troops to more than 800,000 as quickly as possible.

FORGOTTEN FACES
Creighton Williams Abrams Jr.

Creighton Williams Abrams Jr. was born on September 15, 1914, in Springfield, Massachusetts, and received an appointment to West Point, from which he graduated in 1936, eighteenth in a class of 276. Commissioned a second lieutenant of cavalry, he was promoted to captain in 1940 and transferred to armor. In Europe, during World War II, Abrams brilliantly commanded the 37th Tank Battalion and, during the critical Battle of the Bulge, he led the column of 4th Armored Division into Bastogne, Belgium, on December 6, 1944, to aid the 101st Airborne Division under siege by a massive German offensive. No less a figure than Third U.S. Army commander Lieutenant General George S. Patton declared, "I'm supposed to be the best tank commander in the Army, but I have one peer—Abe Abrams."

General Creighton W. Abrams, Jr. a renowned tank commander during World War II, succeeded William Westmoreland as MACV commander on June 10, 1968, and presided over the long drawdown of U.S. ground forces in Vietnam during the Nixon years.

At the conclusion of the war, Abrams was appointed director of the Armored School at Fort Knox, Kentucky, serving from 1946 to 1948. Graduated from the Command and General Staff College in 1949, he served during the Korean War, from June 1950 through July 1953, as chief of staff for the I, X, and IX Corps successively. After the ceasefire of 1953, he was tapped to attend the Army War College, and in 1956 he was promoted to brigadier general and named deputy assistant chief of staff for reserve components on the Army General Staff.

Awarded a second star in May 1960, Major General Abrams served in various command and staff posts, including as commander of the Third Armored Division from 1960 to 1962. In the late summer of 1963, Abrams was promoted to lieutenant general and given command of V Corps in Germany. A year later, in September 1964, he received his fourth star and was named army vice chief of staff.

In May 1967, Abrams was named deputy commander of the U.S. Military Assistance Command, Vietnam (MACV), and in June of the following year replaced William Westmoreland as MACV commander. In accordance with directions from President Johnson and the Joint Chiefs of Staff, Abrams departed sharply from Westmoreland's strategy of search and destroy (the object of which was to create attrition by inflicting casualties) and instead adopted a plan of patrol and ambush intended to regain permanent control of South Vietnamese territory. Abrams was required to balance the new strategy against another imperative, Vietnamization—the transfer of the burden of the war from U.S. to ARVN forces. As MACV commander during the Nixon administration, he oversaw the reduction of U.S. ground forces in Vietnam through July 1972, when he was appointed chief of staff of the army—a post he held until his death, from lung cancer, on September 4, 1974. The U.S. Army honored his memory by naming its main battle tank the M-1 Abrams in his honor.

Thus, President Johnson prepared to deliver to the next president a Vietnam War in which talks were in place, the pressure on the enemy had been turned up, and a program was operational to transfer the burden of actual combat to the South Vietnamese. The effect of the stepped-up attacks was being felt by North Vietnam, where many young men of draft age adopted a grim mantra: "Born in the North, to die in the South." Draft evasion—sometimes through such drastic means as self-amputation and other self-mutilation—became commonplace, and the rate of defection and desertion to the South increased markedly. Yet the Communist negotiators in Paris maintained poker faces and yielded nothing.

In the meantime, the toll of the stepped-up pressure was in some ways as great on Saigon and Washington as it was on Hanoi. As mentioned in Chapter 9, blowback from the Phoenix program was increasingly counterproductive. Although the pacification efforts certainly damaged Communist networks throughout the South, they also alienated the South Vietnamese peasants to such a degree that, reduced though the Communist cadres were, they continued to attract supporters and adherents. At the same time, the government of President Nguyen Van Thieu did work to fight corruption and improve efficiency, but, overwhelmed by more than a million refugees created by the Tet Offensive, it found itself buckling under the weight of a social crisis that was sufficiently massive to have strained the resources of even a healthy government, which that of South Vietnam was far from being. While the aftermath of Tet created a civil burden on the South, the encouraging resurgence of the ARVN that had immediately followed the offensive quickly faded. By mid-1968, desertion from ARVN units had reached staggering levels, corruption was rampant at every level, and combat effectiveness simply melted away.

Only in October, as the U.S. general election day drew near and in an effort to boost Humphrey's sagging campaign, did President Johnson at last authorize his negotiators to offer a bombing halt in exchange for Hanoi's agreement to "limit"—not stop, just limit—infiltration into the South and accept South Vietnamese representatives in Paris. President Thieu vehemently objected to *any* concessions, and it is now known that the Nixon campaign secretly encouraged the South Vietnamese president to press his objections, assuring him that it was in his interest to bring about in November the defeat of Humphrey, who (candidate

Nixon's men said) was more committed to ending U.S. involvement in the war than he was in preserving South Vietnam. Although Thieu warned Washington that he would not attend the negotiations, Johnson nevertheless announced on October 31 a total bombing halt above the 17th parallel. At the same time, he secretly assured Thieu that the United States would continue to stand by him. Despite the assurance of a lame duck president, on the next day—just three days before the U.S. election—Thieu announced his government's absolute refusal to participate in the Paris Peace Talks. The collapse of the faltering peace process, coupled with candidate Nixon's repeated claims of a plan—still undisclosed—for achieving peace with honor, almost certainly ended Humphrey's last chance to win.

Nixon and Kissinger

As many who had not supported candidate Nixon predicted, the "secret plan to end the war" failed to materialize after the new president took office. Nixon did, however, take a new approach to the war, an approach aimed at reviving and influencing the course of the stalled Paris Peace Talks.

The new strategy relied heavily on analysis and advice from a new foreign policy adviser, a brilliant former Harvard political scientist named Henry Kissinger. He stepped back from the kind of tactical issues that had so absorbed President Johnson. Instead the adviser focused on creating a grand *global* strategy intended to improve relations with the Soviet Union by means of expanded trade (which the ailing Soviet economy desperately needed) and an arms-limitation agreement (which, by reducing the costs of the arms race, would also benefit that economy). The objective of improved U.S.-Soviet relations was to disengage Moscow from Hanoi, thereby cutting off one of North Vietnam's two sources of economic, matériel, and military support.

That left China. In what Kissinger termed "triangular diplomacy," even as Washington improved relations with the Kremlin, it would also work to normalize relations with Beijing. Well aware of deteriorating relations between the Soviets and the Chinese, Nixon and Kissinger hoped to play the two against one another by offering each the prospect of productive relations with the United States. The condition both Communist nations would have to accept, however, was ending their active support of North Vietnam. Nixon and Kissinger's idea was to persuade both the Soviets and the Chinese that they had a greater stake in achieving and maintaining good relations with the United States than they did in uniting all of Vietnam under a Communist government. Convince them of this, and North Vietnam, cut loose, would have no choice but to negotiate a favorable peace that would allow both it and the South to exist under whatever forms of government each chose. And *that*, the new American president was satisfied, constituted "peace with honor."

The Madman Theory

"Triangular diplomacy" had the ring of sophisticated geopolitical theory one would expect from the likes of Harvard's Kissinger. President Nixon, however, had another component to add, and he called it by a far less academic name. It was "The Madman Theory." Nixon's rise to political power had taken place in the earliest days of the Cold War, during which he earned a reputation as an uncompromising anti-Communist, a hard-liner in dealing with the Soviets and the Chinese. Now that he was president and had his finger on the thermonuclear button, he wanted both Moscow and Beijing to believe that he was as ideologically unbending as ever and that he would not hesitate to escalate Vietnam into a global war if that is what it took to defeat the Communist threat. Even as he extended offers of improved or normalized relations with the Soviets and the Chinese, he was intent on creating the image of an implacable hawk, a president unafraid to make war and to make war bigger. "They'll believe any threat of force Nixon makes," he told Kissinger, characteristically referring to himself in the third person, "because it's Nixon."

Two Tracks Plus One

Neither Nixon nor Kissinger believed that "triangular diplomacy" and "The Madman Theory" in and of themselves would end the Vietnam War. Global diplomacy and personal intimidation comprised just one track of what the two men called a "two-track" approach. The second track was an intensive schedule of uninterrupted military operations both above and below the DMZ. Nixon intended to hit the Communists hard, even harder than Johnson had, while at the same time pursuing diplomatic initiatives that emphasized the mutual benefits of a negotiated resolution.

Partner in Presidential Power

Henry A. Kissinger was born on May 27, 1923, in Fürth, Bavaria, Germany, and moved with his family to the United States in 1938 to escape the Nazi persecution of Jews. He enrolled in an accounting program at City College, New York, but was drafted early in 1943 and sent to basic training at a camp in South Carolina, where he was naturalized as a U.S. citizen.

Kissinger's fluency in German gained him an assignment in military intelligence, and he volunteered for a hazardous combat intelligence assignment during the Battle of the Bulge. He remained in Europe after the war as an instructor in the European Command Intelligence School, first as an army sergeant and then as a civilian employee.

After returning to the United States, he earned a BA (1950), MA (1952), and a PhD (1954) from Harvard University and then joined the faculty of the Department of Government there. From 1958 to 1971 he was director of the institution's Defense Studies program and during this period worked as a security consultant to several U.S. government agencies. He earned a national reputation as an expert on American strategic policy and a persuasive advocate of building a strong nuclear deterrent.

In December 1968, President Nixon appointed Kissinger assistant for national security affairs. From 1969 to 1975, he also served as head of the U.S. National Security Council and was named secretary of state in September 1973, serving until the end of the Gerald Ford presidency, January 20, 1977. Kissinger was instrumental in engineering with Nixon the policy of détente with the Soviet Union and normalized relations with China. He was also a key negotiator of the SALT I arms-limitation agreement with the Soviet Union (1972).

The architect of Nixon's global "triangular diplomacy" strategy, Kissinger was initially a hard-liner in the Vietnam War and urged Nixon to bomb Cambodia, but he was also instrumental in the implementation of the Vietnamization policy and served as America's chief negotiator with the North Vietnamese during the later phases of the Paris Peace Talks, which produced the Paris Accords of January 27, 1973. In 1973, Kissinger shared the Nobel Prize for Peace with his North Vietnamese counterpart, Le Duc Tho—who, however, declined to accept the prize.

Kissinger went on to play a major role in mediating peace in the Arab-Israeli War of 1973 and in reestablishing diplomatic relations between Egypt and the United States, which had been severed in 1967. He remained in office as secretary of state after President Nixon's resignation, serving through the term of President Gerald Ford. After Ford was defeated in his bid for election in his own right in 1976, Kissinger entered the private sector as a highly paid consultant, writer, and lecturer. In 1983, President Ronald Reagan appointed him to head a national commission on Central American affairs.

Henry A. Kissinger, President Nixon's national security advisor, is sworn in as secretary of state by Chief Justice Warren E. Burger, September 22, 1973.

In an effort to accelerate the "Vietnamization" of the war effort, the U.S. expanded training resources for the ARVN. At the Black Horse Training Center, South Vietnam, December 29, 1968, instructors observe recruits in the ARVN 26th Training Company, 18th Division, fire M-60 machine guns.

It was a plausible approach, and Nixon, newly arrived in the White House, was supremely confident of its success. "I'm not going to end up like LBJ," he assured his White House chief of staff H. R. Haldeman, "holed up in the White House, afraid to show my face on the street. I'm going to stop that war. Fast. I mean it!" It would be, he was sure, a matter of no more than a few months.

In the meantime, to ensure that he *could* show his face on the street now, he decided to take immediate steps to placate those at home who opposed the war. In January 1969, days after taking office, President Nixon announced as one of the primary goals of his administration turning the war over to the Vietnamese and bringing U.S. combat troops home. He ordered his secretary of defense, Melvin R. Laird, to make the Vietnamization of the war a top priority. As he said in his "Vietnamization speech," televised November 3, 1969:

We have adopted a plan which we have worked out in cooperation with the South Vietnamese for the complete withdrawal of all U.S. combat ground forces, and their replacement by South Vietnamese forces on an orderly scheduled timetable. . . .

There are powerful personal reasons I want to end this war. This week I will have to sign 83 letters to mothers, fathers, wives, and loved ones of men who have given their lives for America in Vietnam. It is very little satisfaction to me that this is only one-third as many letters as I signed the first week in office. There is nothing I want more than to see the day come when I do not have to write any of those letters.

. . . Let us be united for peace. Let us also be united against defeat. Because let us understand: North Vietnam cannot defeat or humiliate the United States. Only Americans can do that. . . .

Nixon's plan was to substitute intensified U.S. bombing as he carried out a staged reduction in the presence of U.S. ground forces while simultaneously stepping up the training and equipping of ARVN troops to shoulder a steadily increasing share of combat. In effect, this was a "third track" added to the Nixon-Kissinger two-track approach to fighting and ending the war. What the overly confident Nixon did not count on was the third track becoming a "third rail." He believed he could alter global geopolitics, increase military pressure on North Vietnam, *and* end antiwar protests at home. Like both Presidents Kennedy and Johnson before him, Richard Nixon failed to appreciate just how much the North Vietnamese people were willing—or could be forced—to endure. For their part, the Communist leaders in Hanoi interpreted Vietnamization not as a component of a grand strategy to achieve "peace with honor," but as blatant proof that the United States, even under its new "madman" president, had finally lost its will to win. Faced with the prospect of isolation from Moscow and Beijing and suffering under stepped-up bombing raids, North Vietnamese negotiators nevertheless offered nothing. Instead, they hardened into an even more aggressive and unyielding posture at the conference table in Paris. Nixon's war would not be fast—a matter of months—and the American nation would not accept it quietly.

TAKEAWAY
From Victory to Peace with Honor

The assassination of Robert F. Kennedy and the weakness of the primary campaign of Eugene McCarthy took the Democrats' two antiwar candidates out of the running for the presidential election of 1968, leaving the party badly divided and support for Hubert Humphrey, LBJ's vice president, lukewarm. Thanks to this and to a promise of a "plan" to bring "peace with honor" to Vietnam, Republican Richard M. Nixon became the thirty-seventh president of the United States and embarked on a new "two-track" strategy that combined bold geopolitics intended to disengage both Moscow and Beijing from Hanoi with stepped-up military operations on the ground and in the air. This was combined with a commitment to Vietnamization, shifting the burden of war from U.S. to South Vietnamese forces while gradually withdrawing all U.S. ground troops.

CHAPTER 12

VIETNAMIZATION AND
DEMORALIZATION

Nixon's Impossible Mission

As of January 1969, 542,000 U.S. military personnel were serving in South Vietnam. American ground forces were at their peak number. Having announced Vietnamization and the phased withdrawal of American ground forces, President Nixon was determined to apply as much pressure on the North as possible in an effort to offset any impression that the reduction in troops meant a diminishment of the American will to win.

Simultaneous withdrawal *and* intensification, the reduction *and* expansion of the war: these were not just tall orders; they were oxymorons—contradictions in terms. Yet they were the core of Nixon's program to end the war. To his fellow Americans, he intended to give the appearance of disengagement. To both the North and the South Vietnamese, he intended to give the appearance of turning up the heat. To the Soviets and the Chinese, he intended to give the appearance of a "madman" capable of expanding the war globally. In the end, as Nixon saw it, the only way to pull it all off was to lie to everyone.

Putting Cambodia on the Menu

SINCE 1941, PRINCE NORODOM SIHANOUK had governed Cambodia, sometimes as king, sometimes as prime minister. By the early 1960s, his continued leadership had come to depend on his ability to balance his nation among the separate threats posed by his Communist and non-Communist neighbors—plus the United States. He believed that, ultimately, North Vietnam would prevail in the Vietnam War, and he tended to bend his allegiance distinctly leftward. Yet he dared not openly embrace an alliance with Hanoi for fear that the United States would make war on Cambodia. Nevertheless, in 1966, he struck an agreement with Zhou Enlai of the People's Republic of China, supporter of North Vietnam, to allow NVA and VC base areas to be established in Cambodia and, most important, to allow the North Vietnamese military to use Sihanoukville as a port. This agreement notwithstanding, Sihanouk continued to claim total neutrality and relied on the guarantees of neutrality stipulated in the Geneva Accords of 1954.

Prince Norodom Sihanouk, Cambodia's duplicitous leader, torn between superpowers and torn between the bitterly opposed factions in his own country, speaks to reporters in a November 4, 1967, press conference.

President Kennedy winked at Sihanouk's duplicity, but President Johnson authorized a covert armed reconnaissance operation into Cambodia, called Project Vesuvius, with the objective of persuading Prince Sihanouk to end his support for the North Vietnamese military. By late 1968, Operation Vesuvius produced results. Pressured by an American threat to make his violations of neutrality public and thereby use them as a predicate for offensive military action and also wanting to appease the growing right wing within Cambodia, Sihanouk reopened full diplomatic relations with the United States. He also agreed to the creation of a left-right coalition Government of National Salvation of which the pro-Western general Lon Nol would serve as prime minister. This meant that North Vietnam no longer had official sanction to continue to use Cambodia as a base and a port. The NVA and VC did not respond by meekly departing from the country; President Nixon now had what he saw as an opening to act against the Communist troops and supply bases there. If Vietnamization was going to work, the infiltration and supply of NVA and VC troops south of the DMZ via Cambodia had to be stopped.

FORGOTTEN FACES
Lon Nol

Born in Prey Veng Province in Cambodia on November 13, 1913, Lon Nol was educated at the Lycée Chasseloup-Laubat in Saigon, and then returned to Cambodia, where he enrolled in the Royal Military Academy. He entered the French colonial civil service in 1937 as a magistrate, rising by 1946 to the governorship of Kratie Province.

Arising right-wing politician, he became closely associated with Norodom Sihanouk, at the time Cambodia's king. Lon Nol joined the Cambodian army in 1952 and fought against the Viet Minh. After Cambodia became independent from France on November 9, 1953, Lon Nol was instrumental in developing the nation's political right wing and secured appointment from Sihanouk (who was now prime minister) as army chief of staff in 1955. In 1960, he was also elevated to commander-in-chief of the armed forces and defense minister. He served Sihanouk faithfully, using the police to suppress radical Cambodian Communists. Rewarded with an appointment as deputy premier in 1963, Lon Nol threatened Sihanouk's balancing act by forthrightly embracing cooperation with the United States.

As he continued to move to the right and Sihanouk drifted leftward, Lon Nol became prime minister after the parliamentary elections of 1966 put his party in power. Injuries sustained in an automobile accident in 1967 temporarily sidelined him, but he returned to his post as minister of defense and in 1969 was elected prime minister a second time. Digging in against Sihanouk, Lon Nol sanctioned the 1970 coup that deposed Sihanouk and elevated himself to provisional head of state.

A 1970 coup d'état overthrew the increasingly leftist Sihanouk and elevated the pro-Western, right-wing Lon Nol to provisional head of state. As Thailand fell into outright civil war, Lon Nol was elected the first and only president of what was now called the Khmer Republic. This photograph was taken in 1973.

With the country now engulfed in a full-scale civil war, suffering incursions from the North Vietnamese as well as the South Vietnamese ARVN and the United States Army, Lon Nol was elected the first and only president of what was now called the Khmer Republic. He set restoration of Cambodian sovereignty as the goal of the new government, but his administration quickly faltered, and his own health failed. His increasingly incompetent regime was propped up by U.S. aid but inexorably gave ground to the Khmer Rouge—the radical Cambodian Communist movement—and on April 1, 1975, Lon Nol resigned and fled, first to Indonesia and then to the United States, settling first in Hawaii then, in 1979, California, where he died on November 17, 1985.

President Nixon's initial inclination was to order a naval blockade of the Cambodian coast, but the Joint Chiefs of Staff favored direct ground attacks against the "base areas," and they believed that, under the current conditions, Sihanouk would acquiesce to these attacks. By way of preparation, Joint Chiefs of Staff chairman General Earl G. Wheeler recommended bombing what he called the "Cambodian sanctuaries," the NVA and VC strongholds. MACV commander General Creighton Abrams agreed.

A U.S. Air Force B-52 bombs Cambodia during Operation Menu (March 1969–May 1970). Some 40,000 Cambodians, civilians, and Khmer Rouge troops were killed in carpet-bombing raids on Cambodia.

Before Nixon could issue an authorization, however, the NVA and VC launched a new offensive against U.S. bases all over South Vietnam on February 23, 1969. The offensive included rocket attacks on Saigon and various assaults on towns and villages throughout the country. It was a less ambitious version of the infamous Tet Offensive, but the toll it took was heavy enough: 1,140 U.S. service personnel were killed.

The attacks prompted President Nixon to order National Security Advisor Henry Kissinger and military advisers to prepare air strikes against the Communist base areas in Cambodia. His intention was to frame these strikes not as part of an offensive, but merely as reprisals for the attacks in South Vietnam; however, by the time everyone had convened and preparations were under way, weeks had passed. Bombing, therefore, would look less like retaliation and more like a willful attack on a neutral country. Accordingly, President Nixon decided to bide his time and await a fresh provocation. He was certain that one would come.

It did, and soon.

On March 14, NVA and VC forces launched another offensive, this time exclusively against South Vietnamese cities. Just four days later, on the night of March 18, the U.S. air assaults, Operation Menu, began with a raid by sixty B-52 bombers flying out of Andersen Air Force Base, Guam.

"[President Nixon] wants a massive bombing campaign in Cambodia. He doesn't want to hear anything. It's an order, to be done. Anything that flies on anything that moves. You got that?"

✦✦✦

—Henry Kissinger, phone call to his military assistant, General Alexander Haig, concerning the ongoing "Operation Menu," December 9, 1970

The Breakfast Lie

The initial mission of Operation Menu was called "Breakfast," and its target was Base Area 353, which U.S. military intelligence had identified as the headquarters of the Central Office for South Vietnam (COSVN), the nerve center for VC and Communist political operations south of the DMZ. From the beginning, the Nixon administration was determined to keep the incursion into Cambodia secret—so secret, in fact, that Breakfast aircrews were briefed on a fictitious mission over South Vietnam, only to be suddenly diverted, in flight, across the Cambodian border, where they were ordered to drop 2,400 tons of bombs.

The immediate results of Breakfast were so encouraging that, over the next fourteen months, five more phases of Operation Menu were planned and executed: Lunch (against Base Area 609), Snack (Base Area 351), Dinner (Base Area 352), Supper (Base Area 740), and Dessert (Base Area 350). These involved some 3,800 B-52 sorties, dropping 108,823 tons of ordnance.

Strictly Off the Menu

As far as Congress and the American public were concerned, Operation Menu was strictly *off* the menu. The president and his national security adviser enforced absolute secrecy, fearful not only of congressional outrage likely to produce a legislative backlash but also of igniting a new round of antiwar protests, especially on American college campuses. Nixon, who profoundly distrusted the press, was certain that the media would portray him as a fascist brute gleefully bombing a simple, little, neutral Buddhist country. Therefore, like a pair of larcenous accountants, Nixon and Kissinger authorized the U.S. Air Force to keep two sets of books, one reporting the missions as if they were targeting South Vietnamese objectives, the other reporting the results of the actual Cambodian operations.

As for Sihanouk, the United States made no attempt to inform him of the operation, but he did not raise a protest once the bombing had begun. Later, both Nixon and Kissinger would claim that Sihanouk's silence was tacit approval for the Menu operation, but there is no evidence for this. By the summer of 1969, the administration at last confidentially informed five key members of Congress, two Republicans and three Democrats, none of whom protested. Operation Menu remained essentially secret until December 1972, when USAF major Hal Knight revealed it to Democratic senator William Proxmire in a letter requesting, ostensibly for the major's own legal purposes, clarification of U.S. policy with regard to bombing Cambodia. Proxmire responded by opening a major Senate investigation, which concluded that the deception had violated the Constitution in that it usurped the war-making power of Congress.

THE NIXON DOCTRINE

THE SO-CALLED NIXON DOCTRINE IS USUALLY DESCRIBED as the president's policy of substituting increased military aid for U.S. participation in combat in South Vietnam. As it was actually administered, the Nixon Doctrine was more complex than that. While it did involve more aid and fewer U.S. ground troops, the doctrine also called for the general intensification of ground combat and a vast expansion of the air war. We now know that these measures had a severe impact on the Communists, reducing both manpower and morale and greatly accelerating the rate of desertion, defection, and civilian exodus from the North during 1969. Nevertheless, Hanoi managed to maintain the continued availability of the Ho Chi Minh Trail, despite the bombings in Cambodia, and Communist leaders made a cold, hard calculation that the North had more to gain by continuing to fight and to sacrifice than it did by giving up. Even with the effects of attrition, Hanoi reasoned that time remained on its side and that sooner rather than later discontent in the American homeland would force the U.S. president to abandon the war entirely. Thus, beleaguered as their nation was, North Vietnamese

DETAILS, DETAILS
Protest Goes Mainstream

Despite the efforts of the administration to mollify antiwar protestors with Vietnamization, troop withdrawals, and changes in draft policy, opposition to the war continued to expand into Middle America itself. On October 15, 1969, a "Moratorium to End the War in Vietnam," a kind of national strike, was organized by a small group of antiwar activists. At least 100,000 people turned out in Boston, and smaller demonstrations occurred elsewhere. One month later, on November 15, a second moratorium brought a half-million demonstrators to Washington, D.C. At many American universities and colleges, the "moratoria" were repeated monthly. The president made a show of being unfazed: "Now, I understand there has been, and continues to be, opposition to the war in Vietnam on the campuses and also in the nation. As far as this kind of activity is concerned, we expect it, however under no circumstances will I be affected whatever by it."

negotiators in Paris repeatedly rejected U.S. proposals for mutual troop withdrawals from South Vietnam. More provocatively, while the North agreed to the creation of a special secret back channel of communications between U.S. and North Vietnamese negotiators during the talks (so that proposals could be tested in complete confidence, without either side risking public loss of face), Hanoi unilaterally proclaimed a Provisional Revolutionary Government (PRG) to rival and replace the Thieu government in the South.

Triangular Diplomacy Fails, the Domestic Situation Deteriorates

In the meantime, President Nixon's bold efforts to pressure Moscow to trade disengagement from North Vietnam for improved U.S.-Soviet relations stumbled and fell. Afraid of losing face in the Communist world by ending its commitment to the North just as the Chinese were reaffirming theirs, the Kremlin rushed to declare its official recognition of the PRG as the legitimate government of all Vietnam. On the heels of this recognition came an increase in Soviet aid to Hanoi.

Moscow's definitive rebuff was disheartening in itself, but the president was even more discouraged by the dramatic uptick in antiwar demonstrations across the United States, especially on college campuses. Most disturbing to the president was that the protests were both more numerous and more intense than during the LBJ administration. What is more, they were spreading across class lines, creeping further and further into the suburban middle class, the traditional preserve of Republican support.

Reformulating the Doctrine

President Nixon responded to the disappointing results of his approach to the war by attempting to reformulate its ingredients. He dramatically reduced the number of troops in-country, bringing it down to 475,200 by the end of 1969. Within a year of that, further reductions would shrink the number to 334,600.

Of even greater consequence was his reform of the Selective Service System. In order to neutralize one common source of protest, that the draft unfairly targeted the working class and minorities (who could not afford college and who therefore could not obtain

Demonstrators march in Washington during the second Moratorium to End the War in Vietnam, November 15, 1969.

student deferments), the president ordered his secretary of defense, Melvin R. Laird, to create a lottery in which every eighteen-year-old male was assigned priority for call-up based on a random drawing of numbers 1 to 366, corresponding to the days of the year. The first drawing was on December 1, 1969, and the first number drawn was 257, corresponding to September 14; therefore, eighteen-year-olds with September 14 birthdays were number 1 in the lottery. Those whose birthdays correspond to numbers from 1 to 195 ended up being called. As President Nixon had hoped, the lottery system, which remained in place through 1975 (but was not used for call-ups after 1971), did largely remove the draft as a source of protest.

Winding Down the Draft

Secretary of Defense Melvin R. Laird presided over a troop reduction to 475,200 men in 1969. Staged troop withdrawals continued so that by May 1, 1972, there were 69,000 U.S. soldiers in Vietnam.

Secretary of Defense Melvin R. Laird presided over the massive drawdown of U.S. ground forces from Vietnam during the Nixon administration and began the process to end the draft and convert the U.S. military into an all-volunteer force (AVF).

The drawdown coincided with a 95 percent reduction—from January 1969 to May 1972—in U.S. combat deaths compared to 1968, which was the peak year for casualties. Moreover, while the United States increased funding to the ARVN so that it could shoulder the growing burden of the war, expenditures on the Vietnam War were reduced by some two-thirds between 1969 and 1972 because of the dramatic reduction in U.S. troops.

Even as he oversaw the withdrawal of ground forces, Secretary Laird worked toward ending the draft altogether and transforming the U.S. military into an all-volunteer force (AVF). He set June 30, 1973, as the target date for the transition to an AVF. Laird and Nixon agreed that eliminating the draft not only would drain the fuel from the antiwar movement but also would give the government much more leeway in making decisions about war. Call-ups fell from 300,000 in 1969, to 200,000 in 1970, 100,000 in 1971, and 50,000 in 1972. On January 27, 1973, after the Paris Peace Accords were signed, Secretary Laird suspended the draft altogether, five months ahead of his projected schedule.

Typically, even as Nixon appeased dissent with one set of actions, he provoked it with others. While aspects of his war policy were intended to mollify the antiwar faction, other aspects were aimed at destroying it. The president covertly called on both the FBI and the CIA to conduct surveillance of protest groups, to infiltrate them, and, where possible, to undermine and sabotage them. Whereas much of the FBI activity was probably at least marginally legal, the operations conducted by the CIA, explicitly barred by law from most domestic surveillance, were certainly illegal. For his part, the president was convinced that the antiwar movement did not oppose his policies on ideological and moral grounds alone but was directly influenced, funded, and even controlled by a variety of Communist "interests." Ultimately, he believed, Moscow and Beijing were calling the shots. As he put it in a conversation with FBI director J. Edgar Hoover, "hundreds, perhaps thousands, of Americans—mostly under 30—are determined to destroy our society."

The president's war on dissent was not entirely covert. While federal and local police agencies secretly spied on groups and individuals, the Nixon administration mounted a high-profile public relations assault aimed at discrediting "the kind of people" who opposed the war. Nixon's point man in this campaign was Vice President Spiro T. Agnew, whose barbs aimed at the protesters sought to define them as what he called "an effete corps of impudent snobs who characterize themselves as intellectuals," even as he defined an "intellectual" as "a man who doesn't know how to park a bike." Although President Nixon himself avoided such name-calling, he did make it clear that he was appealing to a group of Americans who stood apart from this privileged class of unpatriotic whiners and naysayers. They were the working class, the ordinary American people, the salt of the earth, Middle America, the "great silent majority," who, he claimed, backed him and his efforts.

As illustrated in this 1970 cartoon by Edmund S. Valtman, Vice President Spiro T. Agnew served as President Nixon's "hatchet man," attacking opponents of Nixon's conduct of the Vietnam War. Agnew reveled in his role as Nixon's political attack dog, and even the many Americans who did not admire him admitted that he had a way with words. The fact is, however, that his most celebrated alliterative volleys, including "pusillanimous pussyfooters," "nattering nabobs of negativism," and "hopeless, hysterical hypochondriacs of history," were the work of speechwriters William Safire and Pat Buchanan.

> **"In the United States today, we have more than our share of nattering nabobs of negatism."**
>
> ✳✳✳
>
> —Vice President Spiro T. Agnew, on administration critics in the press, at a speech in San Diego, September II, I970

Invading Cambodia

While President Nixon battled on the American home front, the B-52s of Operation Menu continued to bomb targets identified as North Vietnamese "base areas" in Cambodia. The missions—Breakfast through Dessert—would continue over a total of fourteen months. Destruction there was, and in abundance; but the flow of VC and NVA troops and supplies down the Ho Chi Minh Trail nevertheless continued virtually unimpeded as troops and vehicles used the complex network's many detours, tunnels, and hidden routes to get around areas of bomb damage. Even worse, the raids were having a destabilizing effect on the Cambodian government. While Sihanouk was vacationing in France in January 1970, the pro-U.S. prime minister Lon Nol instigated anti–North Vietnamese demonstrations, unilaterally closed Sihanoukville to Communist supplies, and, on March 12, issued an ultimatum to the North Vietnamese, demanding they withdraw from Cambodia within seventy-two hours. Hearing of this, Sihanouk left France for Moscow and Beijing, hoping to persuade leaders there to pressure Hanoi into pulling back from Cambodia voluntarily.

But it was too late. Sihanouk had already lost control of the Cambodian government. On March 18, 1970, the Cambodian National Assembly ousted him and elevated Lon Nol to the post of provisional head of state. In response, Sihanouk proclaimed a Cambodian government in exile in Beijing and immediately sought what he had dared not seek earlier: outright alliances with North Vietnam (and the Viet Cong) as well as with the militant Communists in Cambodia (the Khmer Rouge) and Laos (the Pathet Lao). Locked in combat in Vietnam, Hanoi nevertheless immediately began sending both weapons and advisers to the Khmer Rouge. Thus armed, Cambodia now erupted into full-scale civil war.

President Nixon responded to the exploding North Vietnamese military activity in Cambodia by prevailing on the Thieu government to send ARVN forces across the border. Nixon proposed augmenting the ARVN invasion with an "incursion" by U.S. ground forces. To this, both Secretary of State William P. Rogers and Secretary of Defense Melvin Laird objected, arguing that a U.S. invasion would torpedo the Paris Peace Talks while igniting a firestorm of protest at home. Henry Kissinger turned against both men, accusing them of "bureaucratic foot dragging." For his part, Nixon briefly pondered his options and quickly resolved to (in his words) "go for broke."

The ARVN invasion began on April 29. Two days later, 30,000 U.S. troops crossed into Cambodia for a follow-up attack. ARVN operations would be conducted through July 22, 1970, and the U.S. "incursion" would be capped at sixty days, from May 1 to June 30.

NUMBERS
Ground War in Cambodia

The ARVN committed 58,608 troops to operations in Cambodia, and the U.S. sent 50,659. Opposing these were approximately 40,000 soldiers of the NVA and VC. ARVN losses were 638 killed and 3,009 wounded; U.S., 338 killed, 1,525 wounded, 13 missing. The United States claimed an enemy body count of 12,354; 1,177 were captured.

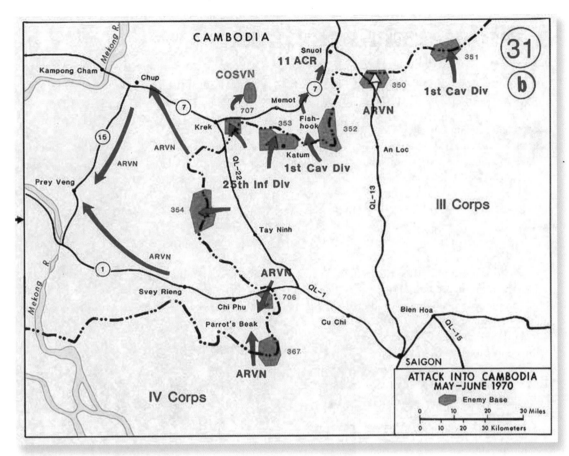

The joint ARVN-U.S. incursion into Cambodia, May–June 1970.

The objectives were to capture enemy weapons and supplies, destroy bases, and kill VC. The haul of weapons and supplies was indeed impressive: 28,500 of all kinds were seized, along with more than 16 million rounds of small-arms ammunition and 14 million pounds of rice. Of the estimated 40,000 Viet Cong believed to be in Cambodia, some 12,000 were killed (according to U.S. claims) and more than 1,000 captured, but the rest withdrew into North Vietnam to fight another day. Both the U.S. military and ARVN would claim victory, though the vital nerve center of the ongoing North Vietnamese infiltration of South Vietnam, the Central Office of South Vietnam (COSVN), was never located and therefore not destroyed.

A Pitiful, Helpless Giant

Unlike in Operation Menu, President Nixon could not keep a ground invasion involving more than 100,000 combined ARVN and U.S. troops secret from either Congress or the American public. Accordingly, he took his case to the nation in a televised speech of April 30, 1970:

"**G**ood evening my fellow Americans:

"Ten days ago, in my report to the Nation on Vietnam, I announced a decision to withdraw an additional 150,000 Americans from Vietnam over the next year. I said then that I was making that decision despite our concern over increased enemy activity in Laos, Cambodia, and in South Vietnam.

"At that time, I warned that if I concluded that increased enemy activity in any of these areas endangered lives of Americans remaining in Vietnam, I would not hesitate to take strong and effective measures.

"Despite that warning, North Vietnam has increased its military aggression in all these areas, and particularly in Cambodia. . . .

"To protect our men who are in Vietnam and to guarantee the continued success of our withdrawal and Vietnamization programs, I have concluded that the time has come for action. . . .

"For the past five years as indicated on this map that you see here North Vietnam has occupied military sanctuaries all along the Cambodian frontier with South Vietnam. Some of these extend up to twenty miles into Cambodia. . . . In cooperation with the armed forces of South Vietnam, attacks are being launched this week to clean out major enemy sanctuaries on the Cambodian-Vietnam border.

"A major responsibility for the ground operations is being assumed by South Vietnamese forces. . . .

"There is one area, however, immediately above Parrot's Beak, where I have concluded that a combined American and South Vietnamese operation is necessary.

"Tonight, American and South Vietnamese units will attack the head-quarters for the entire Communist military operation in South Vietnam. . . .

"This is not an invasion of Cambodia. The areas in which these attacks will be launched are completely occupied and controlled by North Vietnamese forces. Our purpose is not

In a televised speech on April 30, 1970, President Nixon justified expanding the war into Cambodia by insisting, in part, "This is not an invasion of Cambodia. The areas in which these attacks will be launched are completely occupied and controlled by North Vietnamese forces."

to occupy the areas. Once enemy forces are driven out of these sanctuaries and once their military supplies are destroyed, we will withdraw. . . .

"We take this action not for the purpose of expanding the war into Cambodia but for the purpose of ending the war in Vietnam and winning the just peace we all desire. . . .

"The action that I have announced tonight puts the leaders of North Vietnam on notice that we will be patient in working for peace; we will be conciliatory at the conference table, but we will not be humiliated. We will not be defeated. . . .

"My fellow Americans, we live in an age of anarchy, both abroad and at home. We see mindless attacks on all the great institutions, which have been created by free civilizations in the last 500 years. Even here in the United States, great universities are being systematically destroyed. . . .

"If, when the chips are down, the world's most powerful nation, the United States of America, acts like a pitiful, helpless giant, the forces of totalitarianism and anarchy will threaten free nations and free institutions throughout the world.

"It is not our power but our will and character that is being tested tonight. . . .

"I have rejected all political considerations in making this decision. . . . Whether my party gains in November is nothing compared to the lives of 400,000 brave Americans fighting for our country and for the cause of peace and freedom in Vietnam. Whether I may be a one-term President is insignificant compared to whether by our failure to act in this crisis the United States proves itself to be unworthy to lead the forces of freedom in this critical period in world history. I would rather be a one-term President and do what I believe is right than to be a two-term President at the cost of seeing America become a second rate power and to see this Nation accept the first defeat in its proud 190-year history."

WAR HITS HOME

TACTICALLY, BY THE NUMBERS, THE CAMBODIAN INVASION was a significant success. Approximately twelve North Vietnamese soldiers were killed for every ARVN-U.S. battle death. However, as usual in this very long war, enduring strategic success remained elusive. NVA and VC forces were hard hit but still very much intact. Despite the loss of precious weapons and supplies, the Ho Chi Minh Trail remained viable, and both China and the Soviet Union were willing to furnish more of everything needful in war.

Strategic failure was bad enough, but the broader strategic consequences of the Cambodian "incursion" went far beyond failing to achieve decisive military progress. While President Nixon's Vietnamization initiative, troop withdrawals, and modifications of the draft did temporarily diminish the volume of antiwar protests, the invasion of Cambodia renewed them with a vengeance, especially on college campuses where demonstrations became increasingly militant. Protestors now routinely committed major acts of vandalism and outright destruction, including arson of campus buildings associated with the Reserve Officers Training Corps (ROTC) and, on some campuses, military weapons research.

"Confrontations" between students and the police or National Guard occurred with such regularity that news organizations as well as consumers of the news were becoming numb to them. The news coming out of Kent State University in Kent, Ohio, that protestors had set fire to the ROTC building made little national impact, but Governor James Rhodes was sufficiently alarmed to call out some nine hundred Ohio National Guard troops to quell what he deemed dangerous rioting on campus.

Most of the guardsmen were "weekend warriors," many doubtless having sought service in the Guard as an alternative to being drafted into the regular army with the risk of ending up in Vietnam. Nevertheless, even if they had no experience of combat, they at least had some training for it. What they lacked completely was any preparation for crowd and riot control. On Monday, May 4, the fourth day of antiwar demonstrations on campus, Companies A and C of the 1/145th Infantry Regiment and Troop G of the 2/107th Armored Cavalry Regiment received orders to disperse a crowd of some two thousand students gathered on the Kent State University Commons. When the crowd refused the Guard's orders to disperse, the troops discharged tear gas toward them. Inexperienced as they were, the soldiers failed to consider wind direction, and most of the CS gas wafted back over their own ranks. A number of students picked up smoking tear gas canisters and hurled them back at the guardsmen, as they and their fellow students taunted them with rhythmic shouts of "Pigs off campus!"

In the face of the students' refusal to disperse, seventy-seven guardsmen from Company A and Troop G fixed their bayonets and advanced against the crowd, which retreated in a loose mass up a hill. The guardsmen followed. At this point, most of the students had in fact dispersed, and the prudent action would have been for the detachment to stand down, quietly watch, and patiently wait. Instead, the troops seemed confused as to what to do next. They were assembled on an athletic practice field facing a parking lot. Some soldiers suddenly went to one knee, assuming a firing position. They raised their weapons as if to fire, only to lower them

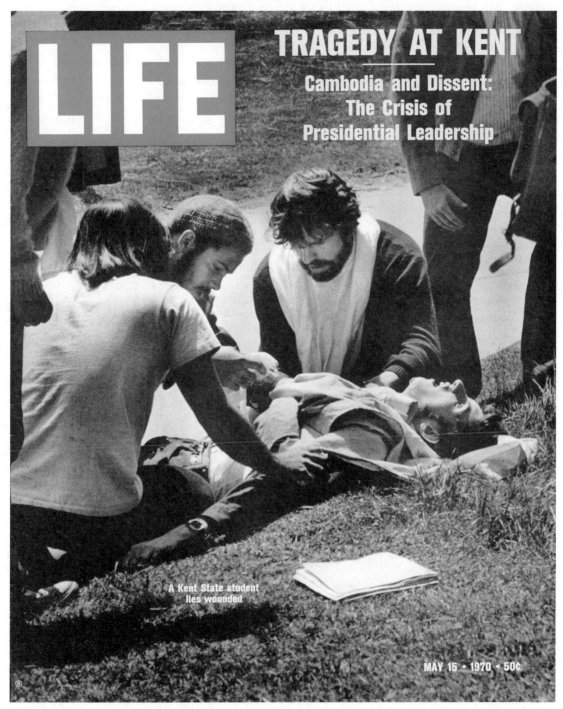

TRAGEDY AT KENT

Cambodia and Dissent:
The Crisis of
Presidential Leadership

A Kent State student
lies wounded

MAY 15 • 1970 • 50¢

The Life *magazine cover of May 15, 1970, is one of the iconic images of the Kent State Massacre, which occurred eleven days earlier. University student Joe Cullum (center, with beard) and others do their best to minister to fellow student John Cleary, who was shot in the chest from 110 feet. Cleary recovered.*

again. At last, after some ten minutes of apparently confused discussion among the soldiers, the guardsmen began moving back to the Commons. In the meantime, some among the remnant of protestors pelted the guardsmen with rocks and with spent or smoldering tear gas canisters.

At twenty-four minutes past noon, according to a student eyewitness, Sergeant Myron Pryor fired his .45 pistol into a knot of students. This prompted (according to National Guard testimony) twenty-nine of the seventy-seven troops present to commence fire with their M-1 rifles. It was later determined that a total of sixty-seven rounds were discharged in thirteen seconds, although some witnesses reported a minute or more of continuous firing. As a result of this assault, four students were killed, one dying instantly, one only minutes after being wounded, and two before the end of the day. Nine more were wounded, one of whom suffered permanent paralysis from the chest down. At least five of those wounded were clearly bystanders caught in the fusillade and not protesters.

Television broadcasts and newspapers carried many pictures of the wounded and slain, but the most emotionally devastating image was captured by a Kent State photojournalism student named John Filo, who would earn a Pulitzer Prize for it. Published by *Life* magazine, the photograph showed Mary Anne Vecchio (who turned out to be a fourteen-year-old runaway, not a student) helplessly screaming for aid while kneeling in horror beside the dead body of student Jeffrey Glenn Miller. The scene looked uncannily like an image out of the Vietnam War itself. To many, its visceral message was unmistakable: Richard Nixon had brought the horrors of that increasingly hated conflict home to the plains of Ohio, heartland of the United States.

The thirteen deadly seconds of that afternoon were dubbed the "Kent State Massacre," and they triggered the largest strike in American history, as more than one hundred college campuses immediately closed for the remainder of the school week. It is estimated that five million American students joined the national student strike over the next days and weeks. More than five hundred colleges and universities were shuttered by mid-May, and before the month was out, the total of closed institutions exceeded nine hundred. Eight of every ten U.S. campuses erupted in violence, and some 35,000 National Guardsmen were called up in sixteen states. The burning and bombing of college ROTC facilities became epidemic—at least thirty were damaged or destroyed. On one campus alone, the University of Wisconsin at Madison, already known as a hotbed of student and faculty "radicalism," twenty-seven fire bombings were reported. Nationwide, May 1970 set a record for arsons that has never been broken in the United States.

Protests were not confined to campuses. On May 9, more than 150,000 marchers converged on Washington, D.C. Not since the Civil War had the capital looked so much like a city under siege, and former Chief Justice of the Supreme Court Earl Warren assessed the aftermath of the Kent State Massacre as the worst crisis in American history since that war of 1861–65.

In the wake of Kent State, President Nixon took tactical measures aimed at appeasing the protesters. He limited incursions into Cambodia to no more than thirty-five kilometers inside the border. He also capped the campaign at two months maximum. None of this, however, even began to address the combined anger and malaise oozing through American communities. It infected the American military itself. During that month of May, more than 500 United States soldiers deserted *each* day. In South Vietnam, some U.S. Army units mutinied, to a man, refusing direct orders to cross into Cambodia. Many soldiers added improvised black armbands to their combat uniforms, tokens of mourning for the slain students, and some of these troops flatly declared their intention to refuse any more combat orders in Vietnam.

For many, whether in or out of uniform, the Kent State Massacre created or affirmed their sense that the war was not just hopelessly stalemated but also had, as far as United States policy was concerned, lost its moral justification and, in fact, had lost *any* rationally definable purpose. First the war engulfed all of Vietnam. Then it engulfed Cambodia. Now, having engulfed America itself, it showed no sign of ending.

TAKEAWAY
War of Lies

In an effort to support Vietnamization and prevent the collapse of the ARVN while U.S. troops were withdrawn from Vietnam, President Nixon sought to definitively stanch the flow of NVA and VC troops and supplies into South Vietnam by attacking North Vietnamese bases and troop formations in neighboring Cambodia. While combined air assaults and an invasion achieved impressive tactical results, both were strategic failures. The new pro-Western regime of Cambodia's Lon Nol became increasingly weak (it would collapse completely early in 1975). Also the bloody invasion of what most Americans perceived as a small, neutral, Buddhist nation created antiwar protests of unprecedented volume and intensity throughout the United States. These culminated in the tragic Kent State Massacre of May 4, 1970, the watershed of opposition to American involvement in the Vietnam War.

CHAPTER 13

THEY WERE ALL THE ENEMY

My Lai, the Soldiers' Battle, the Pentagon Papers

THE STORY OF A WAR TRADITIONALLY UNFOLDS ALONG ITS BATTLEFRONTS. Vietnam, it is true, was sharply divided by a front, the demilitarized zone (DMZ) that ran along the 17th parallel, yet as increasingly war-weary politicians, press, and public remarked time and again, the Vietnam War was a "war without fronts." Or, rather, the battlefront might be anywhere at any time, as the Tet Offensive had so shockingly demonstrated and as U.S. soldiers and South Vietnamese civilians might experience on virtually any day. No place was secure—immune from combat. Whether a jungle outpost a few "clicks" (as U.S. troops called kilometers) south of the DMZ or a GI bar in Saigon, both were subject to attack at any time.

Fighting a war without established fronts was bad enough, but as the Kent State Massacre had shown, a front might explode in South Vietnam, Laos, or Cambodia—or even in the United States, on a preserve of learning nestled in the American heartland. By the 1970s, the Vietnam War had come to resemble a malignancy, spreading at first from a locus remote and obscure, only to be discovered with a sudden chill at the very center of the homeland. Could this war get any more insidious?

PINKVILLE

On SEPTEMBER 6, 1969, Associated Press (AP) wire service teletypes spilled a brief story into newsrooms all across the United States:

> FT. BENNING GA. AN ARMY OFFICER HAS BEEN CHARGED WITH MURDER IN THE DEATHS OF AN UNSPECIFIED NUMBER OF CIVILIANS IN VIET NAM IN 1968, POST AUTHORITIES HAVE REVEALED.
>
> COL. DOUGLAS TUCKER, INFORMATION OFFICER, SAID THE CHARGE WAS BROUGHT FRIDAY AGAINST 1ST LT. WILLIAM L. CALLEY JR., 26, OF MIAMI, FLA., A TWO-YEAR VETERAN WHO WAS TO HAVE BEEN DISCHARGED FROM THE SERVICE SATURDAY.

Just 126 more words, seven sentences, followed these headlines. The questions they raised should have been stunning: "Unspecified number of civilians"? How many? Who? Where? And *how*, how had they been "murdered"? "1st Lt." Calley was actually a second lieutenant. But who, exactly, was William Calley, anyway? The story came across the wires early on a Saturday morning and said Calley "was to have been discharged" that very day. That meant he had been charged one day before he was scheduled to leave the service. What was *that* all about? Yet, at the time, no one on the staff of a major newspaper or broadcast news organization paid any attention to the story, let alone sought answers to these questions.

Interviewed in a *Time* magazine article written later (December 5, 1969), AP general manager Wes Gallagher said he had not received "a single call from an individual paper or from broadcasters" concerning the story. Maybe this was a symptom of collective emotional fatigue among journalists reporting one dismal, brutal, disheartening account after another, always against the relentless din of body count and casualty figures and always concerning places with names still meaningless to most Americans. Or maybe the lack of follow-up was simply because the wire story had been released early on a Saturday morning.

Second Lieutenant William Calley (right) arrives for questioning by U.S. Army officials after being charged with six specifications for premeditated murder for the deaths of 104 civilians in the My Lai Massacre. With him is his assigned military lawyer, Major Kenneth A. Raby.

The Freelancer

Seymour Hersh grew up on the West Side of Chicago, the son of Yiddish-speaking Lithuanian immigrants who ran a dry cleaner. He earned a history degree from the University of Chicago, flunked out of law school, made ends meet for a while working in a drugstore, then started reporting Chicago police stories for the City News Bureau in 1959. He joined United Press International (UPI) a short time later and was posted in South Dakota, before he found more promising work in 1963 with the AP in Chicago and Washington. But when his AP editors refused to publish his exposé of U.S. biological and chemical weapons research, he quit, sold the story to the more adventurous *New Republic*, became a freelance journalist, and then, in 1968, press secretary to antiwar presidential candidate Eugene McCarthy. When that campaign ended, he freelanced as a Vietnam War correspondent.

On October 22, 1969, nearly two months after his old employer, the AP, had sent out its brief and barely acknowledged story of murder, Hersh took a call from a Washington contact, who told him he had "a fantastic story" about "a guy down in Benning who is being held on a charge of murdering 70 to 75 Vietnamese civilians" in a hamlet called My Lai 4 in the Son Tinh District of South Vietnam's south-central coast.

The freelancer went after it and, on November 9, interviewed Calley and wrote a story the very next day. He peddled it to *Life* and *Look*, only to discover that the nation's most popular glossy magazines had no interest in it. Determined to get the story out, Hersh contacted an outlet nobody had ever heard of, Dispatch News Service (DNS), a miniscule start-up bureau that had opened its doors just months earlier in Washington. David Obst, twenty-three-year-old cofounder and general manager of DNS, cold-called newspaper editors across the country. Of the fifty or so he contacted, thirty-five bought the story for $100 each and ran it in their papers on November 12 and 13, 1969.

> ## "I didn't discriminate between individuals in the village, sir. They were all the enemy, they were all to be destroyed, sir."
>
> ✯✯✯
>
> —Second Lieutenant William L. Calley, response to prosecutor at his court martial

Charlie Company

The news broke, but it failed at first to shatter. Some national news organizations did nothing more than briefly note the story after it appeared in those thirty-five papers. Some simply ignored it. Hersh kept at it.

He turned up eyewitnesses, including Paul Meadlo, a twenty-two-year-old farm boy from West Terre Haute, Indiana, who had served in the C Company platoon led by Calley. He told how Charlie Company ("Charlie" is "C" in the army's phonetic alphabet) had been assigned to sweep through the My Lai hamlets, which the troops collectively called "Pinkville" because they were supposed to be harboring Viet Cong. Meadlo told Hersh how he and the other soldiers "began gathering up" villagers. When they had forty to forty-five "standing in one big circle in the middle of the village," Meadlo reported that Calley said, "You know what I want you to do with them." The lieutenant left, returning about ten minutes later. "Get with it," he told Meadlo and the other soldiers with him. "I want them dead."

As Hersh's stories accumulated over the next few days, the floodgates finally opened. Television news programs interviewed Meadlo and others. The *Cleveland Plain Dealer* published horrific photographs of what was now being called the "My Lai Massacre," taken by Ronald L. Haeberle, a combat photographer attached to Charlie Company.

In one of the photographs taken by Ronald L. Haeberle at My Lai, a U.S. Army specialist identified as Capezza sets fire to a village "hooch" (home) on March 16, 1968.

Obscene Pictures

"Guys were about to shoot these people," U.S. Army combat photographer Ronald L. Haeberle later told investigators. "I yelled, 'hold it,' and shot my picture. As I walked away, I heard M16s open up. From the corner of my eye I saw bodies falling, but I didn't turn to look."

Haeberle took two sets of photographs at My Lai, some using his army-issued camera and others using his personal camera. The former material he turned over to the army, which censored the massacre images and published innocuous photographs in *Stars and Stripes*, the official U.S. Army newspaper. The latter he sold in November 1969 to the *Plain Dealer* in his hometown of Cleveland, Ohio, after his honorable discharge. The next month, he sold more photographs to *Life* magazine.

Haeberle was subject to criminal indictment both for the unauthorized release of the photographs and for failing to report the atrocities he witnessed; however, no charges were ever brought against him. He told investigators that he chose not to submit his personal photographs to the army because he believed they would have been destroyed. The images were beyond shocking. One, showing the bodies of women and children lying in the ditch where they had been gunned down, was published internationally as an antiwar poster, overlaid with the text of an exchange between CBS newsman Mike Wallace and Paul Meadlo: "*Q*: And babies? *A*: And babies." This and other Haeberle images put continued attempts at official cover-up out of the question. Secretary of Defense Melvin Laird telephoned Henry Kissinger: "There are so many kids just lying there; these pictures are authentic."

Bloody Icon

So the My Lai Massacre hit the American public—in painful pieces, first from Hersh, then on television, then in newspaper photographs, then in a trial that dragged on for more than four months. The episode itself had been brief, horrific, and—worst of all—a blood-drenched icon of what combat in Vietnam had become.

The soldiers of Captain Ernest Medina's Charlie Company, 1st Battalion, 20th Infantry Regiment, 11th Infantry Brigade, 23rd Infantry Division ("American Division") had recently suffered twenty-eight casualties from landmines and booby traps, five of them fatal. The captain and his men were frustrated and angry when they were sent on a sweep of My Lai 1, 2, 3, and 4, hamlets within Son My village, believed to be harboring the 48th Battalion of the National Liberation Front: Viet Cong. Their regiment had been ordered by its colonel, Oran Henderson, to "close with the enemy and wipe them out for good." Houses were to be burned; livestock killed; food stores destroyed; and wells filled in, closed up, or poisoned. Captain Medina told his men that most civilians would be away at market when the company arrived and that the troops should therefore assume that anyone remaining was VC or a VC sympathizer. One soldier later testified that Medina advised them that "They're all V.C. Now go and get them." According to the soldier's testimony, Medina posed a rhetorical question: "Who is my enemy?" Then Medina answered it. The witness paraphrased the captain: "Anybody that was running from us, hiding from us, or appeared to be the enemy. If a man was running, shoot him, sometimes even if a woman with a rifle was running, shoot her."

Charlie Company landed in the My Lai area on the morning of March 16, 1968, and went into the hamlet shooting. As soon as the first old men, children, and women fell to the indiscriminate fire, the general massacre began, M-16 rifles set to automatic.

Verdict and Punishment

Seymour Hersh's stories lifted the lid from a long cover-up, but it was not until November 17, 1970, that the U.S. Army brought charges against fourteen officers, the highest ranking of whom was Major General Samuel W. Koster, commanding officer of the Americal Division. Most of the charges, including those against Koster, were subsequently dropped. The 11th Brigade commander did stand trial for the cover-up but was acquitted. Tried for murder, platoon commander Calley pleaded not guilty on the grounds that he was following orders from his commanding officer, Captain Ernest Medina. He was nevertheless convicted on March 29, 1971, but his initial sentence, life imprisonment, was later "adjusted" downward as part of a limited presidential pardon, and he served just three-and-a-half years of house arrest at Fort Benning. In a separate trial, Captain Medina testified that he had never ordered a massacre. He was acquitted.

Beyond the single conviction and its attenuated sentence, there *was* punishment for My Lai. Every American soldier who served in Vietnam or returned from service there was punished by the popular perception that he was probably a psychopath, a "baby killer." The morale of the American military, forced to fight a war in which everyone—men, women, children, the elderly—was to be regarded as an enemy, disintegrated. Worst of all, every American citizen was punished as yet another "front" opened in this dark, bloody, borderless, and seemingly endless war. The latest battlefield was the collective American identity, the nation's very soul.

NUMBERS

The Dead of My Lai

No one knows precisely how many Vietnamese civilians were killed in the My Lai Massacre. Figures vary from 347 (official U.S. estimate) to 504 (the Vietnamese government figure). The victims' ages ranged from one year to eighty-four years old.

Lieutenant Calley on Trial

From Paul Meadlo's testimony, November 17, 1970–March 29, 1971

Q [Prosecutor Aubrey Daniels]: What did you do in the village?

A [Paul Meadlo]: We just gathered up the people and led them to a designated area.

Q: How many people did you gather up?

A: Between 30 and 50. Men, women, and children.

Q: What kind of children?

A: They were just children.

Q: Where did you get these people?

A: Some of them was in hooches and some was in rice paddies when we gathered them up.

Q: Why did you gather them up?

A: We suspected them of being Viet Cong. And as far as I'm concerned, they're still Viet Cong. . . .

Q: What did you do when you got there?

A: Just guarded them.

Q: Did you see Lieutenant Calley?

A: Yes.

Q: What did he do?

A: He came up to me and he said, "You know

Women and children huddle at My Lai—shortly before U.S. troops gunned them down on March 16, 1968. This photograph, often reproduced, emerged as one of the ghastly icons of the war. It was originally included in the Report of the Department of the Army Review of the Preliminary Investigations into the My Lai Incident, *released March 14, 1970.*

what to do with them, Meadlo," and I assumed he wanted me to guard them. That's what I did.

Q: What were the people doing?

A: They were just standing there. . . .

A: [Calley returned and] said, "How come they're not dead?" I said, "I didn't know we were supposed to kill them." He said, "I want them dead." He backed off twenty or thirty feet and started shooting into the people—the Viet Cong—shooting automatic. He was beside me. He burned four or five magazines. I burned off a few, about three. I helped shoot 'em.

Q: What were the people doing after you shot them?

A: They were lying down.

Q: Why were they lying down?

A: They was mortally wounded. . . . [Then] Calley said to me, "We've got another job to do, Meadlo."

Q: What happened then?

A: He started shoving [more villagers] off and shooting them in the ravine.

Q: How many times did he shoot?

A: I can't remember.

Q: Did you shoot?

A: Yes. I shot the Viet Cong. He ordered me to help kill people. I started shoving them off and shooting.

THE SOLDIERS' BATTLE

MILITARY HISTORIANS HAVE A PHRASE FOR A BATTLE won not because of the brilliance, commands, or strategy of the top brass but because of the guts, brains, and initiative of the ordinary troops in the field. They call it a "soldiers' battle."

In testimony given at William Calley's court martial, ordinary GIs effectively confessed to having been transformed into mass murderers because they followed the orders of higher command. After My Lai—and other "battles" like it—some ordinary GIs began to question orders from the top. The war, they decided, needed to end, and if the politicians and the generals were unwilling or unable to end it, they would. Much as freelance journalist Seymour Hersh decided to report a story that the mainstream media had passed over, so a growing cadre of individual American soldiers became determined to bypass the Pentagon, Congress, and the White House itself by turning the antiwar movement into a soldiers' battle.

The most dramatic demonstration of opposition to the war within the military was the unprecedented volume of desertions during the Vietnam era: 503,926 between 1960 and 1973—a number roughly equal to the peak strength of the U.S. force in-country during 1968. Although President Nixon's emphasis on Vietnamization and the withdrawal of U.S. ground forces was intended to reduce dissent at home, the drawdown actually had a demoralizing effect on soldiers serving in combat. The more their numbers dwindled, the more it appeared to those who remained that their country had given up on the war in which they were expected to fight and quite possibly die. There were many young men who counted themselves patriots and were willing, if necessary, to die for their country; however, no one wanted to be the last man killed in an abandoned cause. For this reason, operations officially designated "search and destroy missions" were wryly dubbed "search and avoid missions" by troops who no longer aimed at achieving victory but simply at surviving their twelve-month rotation in-country. The grunts taped so-called countdown calendars to barracks walls or their own footlockers. These were crudely photocopied calendar pages with each passing day elaborately colored in and the "DEROS" (Date of Estimated Return from Overseas) starred and otherwise decorated. Many such calendars were adorned with patriotic or sexually explicit images—frequently with some combination of the two.

NUMBERS
Frag Stats

The word *fragging* refers specifically to blowing someone up with a fragmentation (hand) grenade, but, in practice, fragging was often carried out with a rifle. More than 230 cases of U.S. officers killed by their own troops were documented during the Vietnam War, but more than 1,400 additional officers' deaths were never adequately explained, and fratricide was suspected though never officially charged. During 1970–71, the U.S. Army documented 363 cases of "assault with explosive devices" against officers in South Vietnam.

The "non-regulation" decoration of helmets was ubiquitous among Vietnam War soldiers, who inserted good luck charms, military patches, souvenirs, cigarettes, and other items into the standard-issue helmet's chin strap or camouflage net. Cynical sayings abounded. "Murphy was a grunt," a soldier might mutter—"Murphy" referring to "Murphy's Law," the proposition that if anything *can* go wrong, it *will* go wrong, and "grunt" being a synonym for the lowly infantryman. To this, another might respond, "The only thing more accurate than incoming fire is incoming friendly fire" or perhaps quote the motto USAF general Curtis LeMay adopted for the Strategic Air Command, "Peace is our profession," and then conclude, "Mass murder is just our hobby."

Drugs and Violence

Some soldiers went far beyond countdown calendars and good luck charms. Illicit drug use, already high in the U.S. civilian population during the late 1960s and early 1970s, grew to epidemic proportions in Vietnam, where marijuana and such opiates as heroin were widely and readily available. By 1971, nearly 50 percent of U.S. military personnel serving in Vietnam admitted to having "tried" opiate drugs. Of this number, approximately half exhibited hallmarks of addiction, including tolerance and withdrawal symptoms. Marijuana use was far more common. It was regularly smoked by more than two-thirds of soldiers.

Even more disturbing than desertion and drug use and addiction was the increased incidence of what the military bureaucracy officially referred to as "fratricide" and what the soldiers themselves called "fragging." Both were terms for the assassination of fellow soldiers. Victims of fragging were typically company or platoon commanders or senior noncommissioned officers who were perceived as eager to risk the lives of their men—to actually search and *destroy* rather than search and *avoid.*

Despair

Families began sharing letters they received from their sons, brothers, husbands, and fathers serving in Vietnam. Most were grim, many poignant. On the *ABC Evening News* for Monday, May 17, 1971, reporter Harry Reasoner broadcast a story about a letter written by U.S. Army medic Keith Franklin, who had been killed in Cambodia a year earlier, on May 12, 1970. He had slipped the letter into the family Bible in his parents' Salamanca, New York, home. "If you are reading this letter, you will never see me again," Franklin wrote, "the reason being that if you are reading this I have died. The question is whether or not my death has been in vain. The answer is yes. The war that has taken my life and many thousands before me is immoral, unlawful and an atrocity. . . . I had no choice as to my fate. It was predetermined by the war-mongering hypocrites in Washington. As I lie dead, please grant my last request. Help me inform the American people, the silent majority who have not yet voiced their opinions."

By 1970, when this photograph was taken, some surveys showed that at least two-thirds of U.S. ground personnel in Vietnam regularly smoked marijuana, which was available in great abundance. This soldier, stationed at fire support base Aries in the jungle some fifty miles outside of Saigon, uses the barrel of a shotgun as an improvised pipe. Christened "Ralph," the barrel was freely passed among the comrades-in-arms.

The Veterans' Protest

Some supporters of the war criticized demoralized soldiers as malingerers and cowards. It was, however, much harder to attack veterans—those who had already served in Vietnam, often heroically and with the decorations to prove it. Now, having returned home, many were passionate to persuade their fellow Americans that the war had to end.

Vietnam Veterans Against the War (VVAW) was founded by six Vietnam War vets in June 1967 and grew to a peak membership of 25,000 by 1971. The group sponsored such mass demonstrations as Operation RAW (Rapid American Withdrawal) during Labor Day weekend, September 4–7, 1970, marching from Morristown, New Jersey, to Valley Forge State Park in Pennsylvania—two famed sites of the American Revolution—dressed in fatigues and carrying toy weapons to suggest a "search and destroy mission." As the two hundred or so protestors passed through some towns, they staged what they called "guerrilla theater," making a show of mock capture and interrogation. In January of the following year, VVAW sponsored the "Winter Soldier Investigation," assiduously collecting and presenting war crimes testimony from returned troops. In April, "Operation Dewey Canyon III" was billed as "a limited incursion into the country of Congress." More than eleven hundred veterans marched on Washington, ending the procession at the Tomb of the Unknown Soldier in Arlington National Cemetery.

On December 26, 1971, fifteen VVAW members "occupied" the Statue of Liberty, barricading themselves inside the monument for two days. At the same time, other VVAW protestors took over the Betsy Ross house in Philadelphia (for just forty-five minutes) and even occupied part of Travis Air Force Base in California (for twelve hours).

Perhaps the most persuasive, and certainly best remembered, VVAW member was John Kerry, a U.S. Navy veteran who earned three Purple Hearts, a Silver Star, and a Bronze Star in Vietnam.

On April 22, 1971, while still a member of the U.S. Naval Reserve (lieutenant, junior grade), he became the first Vietnam veteran to testify before Congress about the war, appearing, in green fatigues with service ribbons, before a Senate committee hearing on proposals to end the war. The day following his testimony, Kerry appeared with some one thousand other veterans, who publicly tossed their medals and ribbons over a fence that had been raised to block the front steps of the United States Capitol.

After his Senate appearance, which was partially televised, Kerry was interviewed on a variety of popular television programs, including *Meet the Press*, on which he admitted to having committed "atrocities." He cited indiscriminate machine gunning in "free fire zones," participa-

Future U.S. senator and 2004 Democratic presidential candidate John Kerry, a Navy veteran who earned three Purple Hearts, a Silver Star, and a Bronze Star in Vietnam, became on April 22, 1971, the first Vietnam vet to testify to a Senate committee about the war. He was at the time the director of Vietnam Veterans Against the War.

tion in "search and destroy missions, and in the burning of villages." He concluded, "All of this is contrary to the laws of warfare, all of this is contrary to the Geneva Conventions and all of this is ordered as a matter of written established policy by the government of the United States from the top down." Kerry voiced his belief that "the men who designed the free fire zone, the men who ordered us, the men who signed off the air raid strike areas, I think these men, by the letter of the law, the same letter of the law that tried Lieutenant Calley, are war criminals." Kerry went on to a political career as a district attorney, lieutenant governor of Massachusetts, U.S. senator, and, in 2004, Democratic candidate for president of the United States.

> "By every conceivable indicator, our army that now remains in Vietnam is in a state approaching collapse, with individual units avoiding or having refused combat, murdering their officers and noncommissioned officers, drug-ridden, and dispirited where not near-mutinous."

> ★★★

> —Colonel Robert Heinl Jr. USMC (ret.), "The Collapse of the Armed Forces," *Armed Forces Journal*, June 7, 1971

THE PENTAGON PAPERS

DANIEL ELLSBERG SURELY QUALIFIED AS ONE OF THE NATION'S "best and brightest." A summa cum laude graduate of Harvard (he would earn a PhD in economics in 1962) and a United States Marine Corps officer, Ellsberg became a military analyst in the Pentagon under Secretary of Defense Robert McNamara in 1964. After serving two years in a State Department assignment to Vietnam, he returned to a former employer, the RAND Corporation strategic "think tank." In 1967 he joined the staff of the Vietnam Study Task Force, which Secretary McNamara had created that year to write what he described as an "encyclopedic history of the Vietnam War." It was to be encyclopedic—but top secret. In fact, neither President Lyndon Johnson nor Secretary of State Dean Rusk knew about it.

The forty-seven-volume study ran to 3,000 pages of historical analysis plus 4,000 pages of government documents and was completed only after McNamara had stepped down to be replaced by Clark Clifford. The new secretary accepted delivery of *United States–Vietnam Relations, 1945–1967: A Study Prepared by the Department of Defense* on January 15, 1969, five days before Richard M. Nixon was inaugurated. Clifford, himself replaced as defense secretary by Melvin Laird in the new administration, claimed never to have read the study.

In the course of his experience both inside Vietnam and as a RAND analyst, Ellsberg had turned against the war. He was intimately familiar with the study he had helped create, and he knew it was explosive. It chronicled in excruciating detail the deepening involvement of the United States in Vietnam, beginning with the Truman administration and culminating in the Johnson administration. It detailed how, under President Kennedy, a policy of "very limited involvement" was subtly but inexorably transformed into a "broad commitment," which included the CIA-instigated and engineered ouster/coup/assassination of South Vietnamese president Ngo Dinh Diem. It documented the uncertainty and outright fabrication that lay behind the Gulf of Tonkin Incident and the Gulf of Tonkin Resolution. It revealed in great detail how President Johnson ordered the bombing of North Vietnam in 1965 despite the consensus of the U.S. intelligence community that even massive air raids would neither discourage nor prevent North Vietnam from continuing its support of the Viet Cong insurgency in South Vietnam. In short, the study was a long history of delusion and deception put into action as war.

Working with his friend Anthony Russo, Ellsberg, who had ongoing access to the study, laboriously photocopied all forty-seven volumes during October 1969. He informed President Nixon's national security advisor, Henry Kissinger, about its existence, and he also approached the leading antiwar senators, William Fulbright and George McGovern. None were interested in seeing the study or in making it public. Ellsberg understood that the mere possession of a top-secret government document, let alone the leaking of it, exposed him to charges of treason. He wrestled for many months over what to do with it. As he pondered, the Vietnam War ground on.

At last, in February 1971, Ellsberg first approached *New York Times* reporter Neil Sheehan, giving him forty-three volumes in March. The paper began publishing excerpts on June 13. During the storm of publicity that followed, the cumbersomely named document was more dramatically dubbed "The Pentagon Papers."

The revelations included coverage of the Eisenhower years, but by far the most stunning and damaging material emerged from the Democratic administrations of Truman, Kennedy, and Johnson. President Nixon was initially elated, believing that this background of Democratic misdeeds and mistakes would thrust his own war policies into a far more flattering light. On further reflection, however, he decided that, as the nation's chief magistrate, he could hardly allow the leaking of classified documents to go unchallenged. The president ordered Attorney General John Mitchell to threaten the *Times* with criminal charges of espionage. When this intimidation failed, the Department of Justice secured a temporary injunction that forced the suspension of publication of the Pentagon Papers series. The *New York Times* turned to the U.S. Supreme Court, which ruled six to three on June 30, 1971, to overturn the injunction based on the First Amendment's guarantee of freedom of the press. With that, the series continued, and revelation piled on revelation.

Four Facts

The Pentagon Papers made for reading that was at once surreal, enraging, tragic, and exhausting. In the welter of words, four facts loomed uppermost.

First: The United States had purposely expanded the war with secret bombing missions in Laos and Cambodia as well as raids on the coast of North Vietnam.

Second: President Johnson was deliberate and resolute in his expansion of the war even though, during the election campaign of 1964, he assured the world and the American people "we seek no wider war."

Third: Johnson's Defense Department prepared an analysis of rationales for continuing to fight the Vietnam War. The most important reason—quantified as "70 percent" of the motive for continuing the war—was to avoid a "humiliating" U.S. defeat. Just 10 percent of the rationale was to "permit the people [of South Vietnam] to enjoy a better, freer way of life." The remaining 20 percent was to keep

REALITY CHECK

Vietnam: The Necessary War

The idea, as revealed in the Pentagon Papers, that the United States persisted in the Vietnam War mainly to avoid a "humiliating defeat" was shocking to many people in 1971, but it is worth reassessing today. In the Cold War calculus of a "free world" versus a "Communist world," political and military credibility were powerful and precious. In 1999, historian Michael Lind published *Vietnam: The Necessary War*, in which he provocatively argued that preserving American credibility in a bipolar world, in which power was divided between the starkly different ideologies of democracy and totalitarian Communism and in which both sides possessed the means of thermonuclear intimidation and annihilation, was not just a valid and sufficient reason for war but also a compelling reason.

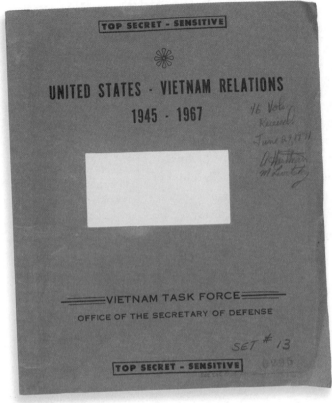

The cover sheet of what the world came to know as "The Pentagon Papers." Note the handwritten inscription at right: "46 vols" (it was actually forty-seven). The massive "Top Secret-Sensitive" document was leaked to the New York Times *by one of its original authors, Daniel Ellsberg, and revealed a long history of American deception, bungling, and forlorn hope in Southeast Asia.*

South Vietnam and its neighbors out of Chinese hands.

Fourth: Every president, from Harry S. Truman through Lyndon Baines Johnson, had lied about the motives for, the commitment to, and the extent of the Vietnam War.

A Second White House Casualty

The Pentagon Papers had a second effect on the course of the Vietnam War and on America's commitment to it. Had President Nixon responded to the revelations positively, by pledging to conduct the war in ways that might redeem rather than repeat the accumulated errors of the past, his stock with the American public might well have risen and, along with it, support for his goal of "peace with honor" might have grown. Instead, he responded by instituting what the news media would later characterize as the "bunker mentality" of the Nixon White House. In the wake of the publication of the Pentagon Papers, the administration launched a series of covert—and usually illegal—operations to stop further leaks and to discredit the principal "leaker," Daniel Ellsberg. President Nixon created a covert operations unit, reporting directly to the White House and dubbed "the Plumbers" because their mission was to find and plug leaks. The first mission of the Plumbers was to burglarize the office of Ellsberg's psychiatrist in the hope of finding embarrassing material concerning his patient. Also discussed was a plan to physically assault Ellsberg in order to intimidate him into silence. Ultimately, of course, the Plumbers were sent to Democratic National Headquarters in Washington's Watergate apartment and office complex, where police apprehended them as they were in the process of bugging and burglarizing the headquarters to gather material that might be useful to ensure President Nixon's reelection in 1972.

TAKEAWAY
From Vietnam War to American Nightmare

As the 1960s rolled into the 1970s, the Vietnam War assumed the character of a national nightmare, not only dividing the United States politically but also eroding it morally and spiritually while simultaneously undermining, from within, the American military. Revelations of the My Lai Massacre, the explosive growth of an antiwar movement within the American military, and publication of the Pentagon Papers delivered blows to continued support for the war and to the Nixon presidency. Neither of these would ever recover.

President Richard M. Nixon presides over a cabinet meeting in December 1971—six months after the release of the Pentagon Papers and six months before the Watergate scandal.

Thus began the chain of events that would culminate in the Watergate scandal and the end of the Nixon presidency. Within a matter of months, the Vietnam War, having already destroyed the presidency and presidential legacy of Lyndon Johnson, would, in essence, claim its second executive casualty.

CHAPTER 14

TRICKY DICK

Nixon's War: The Final Battles

T HE MY LAI MASSACRE, THE DISINTEGRATION OF AMERICAN MILITARY morale, and the publication of the Pentagon Papers all made a cruel mockery of Richard Nixon's goal of achieving "peace with honor." No one realized this more than the president himself, especially as his reelection campaign drew near. A widely publicized poll taken just after Lieutenant Calley was convicted of murder at My Lai reported that 58 percent of Americans believed the United States was "morally wrong" to be fighting in Vietnam; 60 percent favored withdrawal of all U.S. troops—even if this brought about the collapse of South Vietnam. The Nixon White House responded to this major shift in public opinion—albeit, in typical Nixon fashion, covertly. In May 1971, at Paris, using the secret back channel both sides had agreed to establish, President Nixon's negotiator, Henry Kissinger, offered to withdraw all U.S. ground forces from South Vietnam *without* the simultaneous withdrawal of NVA and VC forces from the South.

THE "DECENT INTERVAL" SOLUTION

IN PART A STANDARD NIXONIAN DIPLOMATIC STRATAGEM and in part a secret surrender, the stunning Kissinger concession was first and foremost a belated acknowledgment of reality—one of precious few in a war marked by deception and delusion. The reality to which the White House bowed was this: no matter what military action the United States took, North Vietnamese forces were not going to leave the South. This being the case, Nixon and Kissinger agreed that the best remaining option was to continue the troop withdrawals and push Vietnamization harder by persuading the Thieu government that the survival of South Vietnam depended solely on the ARVN alone. The Nixonian stratagem was this: both Nixon and Kissinger agreed that the success of Vietnamization was a very long shot at best. Indeed, it was unlikely that the ARVN alone would last long against the NVA and VC. In view of this, at the very least, Kissinger planned to use the concession at Paris to buy what he called a "decent interval" between the completed U.S. withdrawal from South Vietnam and what was probably an inevitable Communist takeover. Such an interval would allow the Nixon administration to claim something that at least had the appearance of "peace with honor." After all, if the ARVN was finally defeated months or (better yet) years after the withdrawal, the fault would not lie with the United States. America could salvage at least some degree of international diplomatic and military credibility.

Operation Lam Son 719

The next major ARVN campaign demonstrated that there were good reasons for Nixon and Kissinger to hedge their bets on the effectiveness of the South Vietnamese military. Operation Lam Son 719 was planned as an incursion into Laos for the purpose of disrupting the Ho Chi Minh Trail to preempt future major NVA-VC offensives in South Vietnam. This was the strategic reason for Lam Son. Tactically, the easy victory U.S. and ARVN commanders anticipated in what was no more than a "spoiling attack"—a disruption of a logistical network—would serve to build morale and self-confidence in the ARVN and would prove to both Hanoi and the American people that Vietnamization was working effectively. The Nixon administration was eager to be able to point to such a victory as evidence that South Vietnam could defend itself.

Conducted between February 8 and March 25, 1971, Lam Son 719 had objectives that were both reasonable and valid. Nevertheless, the operation was doomed from its inception. The degree of secrecy ARVN and U.S. commanders enforced during preparation made thorough

---

DETAILS, DETAILS
Choking Off Funds

The revised version of the Cooper-Church Amendment, sponsored by Senators John S. Cooper and Frank Church and attached to the Foreign Military Sales Act, passed on December 22, 1970, ended all funding for U.S. ground troops in Cambodia and Laos after January 5, 1971. It banned air operations in Cambodian (but not Laotian) air space without congressional approval and ended all U.S. ground support of ARVN forces outside of South Vietnam. By law, therefore, U.S. troops could not accompany ARVN into Laos, although air support was still permitted.

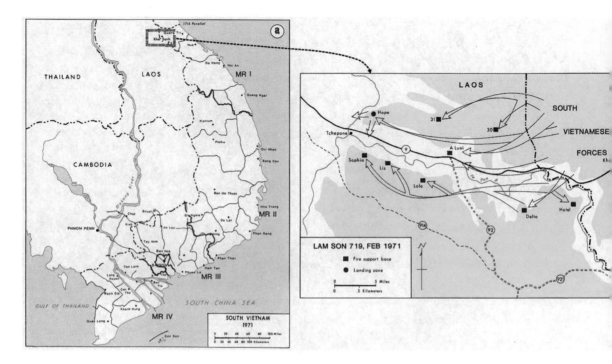

Operation Lam Son 719—a doomed incursion into Laos—was a crushing defeat for the ARVN, which President Nixon nevertheless cited, in a televised speech of April 7, 1971, as proof "that Vietnamization has succeeded."

planning and coordination impossible. Worse, despite these security measures, North Vietnamese intelligence discerned the troop build-up along the Laotian border, anticipated ARVN's intentions, and laid a strong defensive trap within Laos.

Beginning on February 8, 1971, some 20,000 South Vietnamese troops—the best ARVN could field—crossed the border into Laos, where they were outnumbered by 25,000 to 35,000 NVA and VC, who slowly closed the jaws of their trap, alternately harassing and mauling the ARVN for nearly a month, until the South Vietnamese withdrew on March 25. Three of ARVN's best divisions were decimated. Equipment losses were staggering: some two-thirds of the ARVN fleet of armored vehicles were destroyed, along with hundreds of U.S. helicopters and fixed-wing aircraft.

Operation Lam Son 719 was a crushing defeat in terms of direct losses of personnel and equipment. Even more catastrophic was the destruction of the already fragile ARVN morale and credibility. Despite this, Richard Nixon appeared on television on April 7, 1971, to announce the operation as proof "that Vietnamization has succeeded"; the announcement is excerpted here:

First, the South Vietnamese demonstrated that without American advisers they could fight effectively against the very best troops North Vietnam could put in the field.

Second, the South Vietnamese suffered heavy casualties, but by every conservative estimate the casualties suffered by the enemy were far heavier.

Third, and most important, the disruption of enemy supply lines, the consumption of ammunition and arms in the battle has been even more damaging to the capability of the North Vietnamese to sustain major offensives in South Vietnam than were the operations in Cambodia 10 months ago.

Consequently, tonight I can report that Vietnamization has succeeded. Because of the increased strength of the South Vietnamese, because of the success of the Cambodian operation, because of the achievements of the South Vietnamese operation in Laos, I am announcing an increase in the rate of American withdrawals.

Between May 1 and December 1 of this year, 100,000 more American troops will be brought home from South Vietnam. This will bring the total number of American troops withdrawn from South Vietnam to 365,000. Now that is over two-thirds of the number who were there when I came into office.

> **NUMBERS**
> ## Lam Son 719 Losses
> Estimates of ARVN losses vary wildly, from a low of 1,529 killed, 5,483 wounded, and 625 missing, to a high of 8,483 killed, 12,420 wounded, 691 missing, and 1,149 captured. No U.S. ground forces entered Laos; nevertheless, U.S. aircrews and troops operating in South Vietnam to clear Route 9 into Laos suffered casualties that included 215 killed, 1,149 wounded, and 38 missing. NVA-VC losses were reported as 2,163 killed and 6,176 wounded.

President Nguyen Van Thieu followed Nixon's lead by addressing an assembly of ARVN troops lucky enough to have survived the Lam Son debacle. "The biggest victory ever," he called it. In fact, intended to disrupt the Ho Chi Minh Trail, Operation Lam Son 719 actually spurred Hanoi into expanding the trail network westward. Intended to preempt a major North Vietnamese offensive, the failed operation prompted Hanoi to plan a major invasion for early 1972.

The POW Issue

President Nixon's televised speech of April 7 notwithstanding, the outcome of Operation Lam Son 719 did not bode well for Vietnamization. Nevertheless, the president's back-channel concession in Paris did produce the first genuine breakthrough in three long years of negotiations. Hanoi pledged to release all U.S. prisoners of war (POWs) as soon as the last U.S. troops had been withdrawn.

Of all the contentious issues wrought by the Vietnam War, for

REALITY CHECK
A Failure of Air Power

Another casualty of Operation Lam Son 719 was the U.S. military's overweening confidence in the sovereign efficacy of airpower and the airmobile/air cavalry doctrine. One hundred eight helicopters were destroyed and 430 damaged during the campaign. Nineteen U.S. Army aviators were killed, 59 wounded, and 11 went missing. In more than 8,000 defensive sorties, U.S. Air Force tactical aircraft dropped 20,000 tons of bombs and napalm while B-52s dropped 32,000 tons of ordnance in 1,358 offensive sorties. Seven U.S. fixed-wing aircraft were shot down (6 USAF and 1 U.S. Navy), with the loss of 4 Air Force pilots (2 killed in action [KIA], 2 missing in action [MIA]) and 1 naval aviator (KIA). For all the effort and cost, airpower failed to be decisive in the operation.

U.S. POWs Richard Kiern and Kile Berg (left to right, front row), Robert Shumaker and "Smitty" Harris (second row), and Ronald Byrne and Lawrence Guarino (third row), all U.S. Air Force, are paraded through the streets of Hanoi to the taunts of angry citizens.

many Americans the fate of the POWs was the most anguishing. The first American POW in the Vietnam War, Specialist 4th Class George F. Fryett of Long Beach, California, had been captured on December 26, 1961. He was released in June of the following year. The longest held was Captain Floyd James Thompson, Army Special Forces, captured on March 26, 1964, and released on March 16, 1973, after the conclusion of the Paris Peace Accords, ten days short of having spent nine years in captivity. The main prison was dubbed (by captives) the Hanoi Hilton, but camps were located throughout the North. Frequently, the Communists exploited prisoners, filming and broadcasting confessions of war crimes and denunciations of the U.S. role in the war. Such displays were patently the products of torture both psychological and physical.

EYEWITNESS

A POW REMEMBERS

Weapons Officer in an F-4 Phantom, Major Richard Lyman Bates, 433rd Tactical Fighter Squadron, 8th Tactical Fighter Wing, was shot down over North Vietnam on October 5, 1972. He and the aircraft pilot ejected and were captured. This is excerpted from his interview with a Library of Congress researcher:

. . . The shock of the shoot down itself is enough that sort of puts [you] into I would say a little bit of a time warp. . . . I was captured essentially immediately. I was in the southern part of North Vietnam about 350 miles or so, I think, from Hanoi, which is where . . . all of the POWs ended up. So I spent the next two months there on the ground in a bunker or traveling on the way to Hanoi. It didn't take two months of travel, but initially they just kept me right on the ground.

And finally, we started moving north and both by truck and on foot [and]—at that time I was reunited with my pilot; he and I were together. He . . . sustained two broken legs in the ejection. . . . [We] were kept for another week or two without moving and finally were put into a truck and spent all night and half the next day traveling into Hanoi until we reached the prison that everybody calls the Hanoi Hilton. From there it was another thirty days or so of solitary and an initial interrogation. And it was, there was physical, there was physical abuse.

I don't know that . . . I suffered what would be considered torture as some of the guys who were there for a year for every month I was there. The first day I was captured in the southern part of the country, I did get my arms, my elbows roped up and pulled back behind my back until my elbows touched, which dislocated my shoulders. I spent about four hours like that. So you know, and I also suffered some physical abuse when I got to Hanoi that was mostly just beatings and getting struck with rifle butts and that sort of thing.

This aerial reconnaissance photograph from May 31, 1973, shows the main North Vietnamese POW camp, the infamous "Hanoi Hilton."

EYEWITNESS (CONTINUED)

. . . You found out very quickly if you were religious or not. I . . . initially would recite the Lord's Prayer. I eventually very quickly I changed . . . to the Twenty-third Psalm because of the part about the valley of the shadow of death seemed to be very meaningful. You did some mind games. Throughout my captivity . . . I tried to break my day up into periods of physical activity, mental activity, and then rest. I had, I say my arms when they were tied up, my arms were pretty useless when they untied me. So I was initially just trying to get my motion, some strength in my arms. One of the things I started doing for the mental activities were I started thinking back on my life . . . . I [also] tried to memorize all of the states. So I memorized the 50 states and I alphabetized them. And then I tried to recall all of the capitals, so I did those, and I did the capitals in the alphabetical order that I remembered the states. . . . Then I tried to start remembering some times of my youth, and I graduated with a high school class of I think about ninety-six. I was able to pull, I was able to recall all of the names of ninety-four of my high school graduating class. There were two that I never got. And that didn't happen like overnight. That was you either got ten or fifteen immediately. Then you get five or six more. . . .

. . . I lost sixty pounds in six months . . . [N]ot any, no adequate medical treatment of any kind. Food was just barely enough to sustain life. The food that they fed us in the prison in Hanoi was food they wouldn't eat themselves. . . . Many of us had dysentery. . . .

You will see that there weren't a lot of amputees over there. They didn't do that. They tried to set it [a broken limb] or either you recovered or you died. You know, one of my guys over there had, when he ejected he caught his hand on the campy rail and it partially severed his thumb. Their answer to that was just to finish it, but there just wasn't any real medical treatment over there per se. It was some but it was pretty rare.

. . . The Red Cross, International Red Cross before I was a prisoner had been there once or twice. What they were allowed to see was extremely controlled. Extremely controlled. They were not allowed anywhere near where we were. Once again, within the last thirty days before I was released we all did receive Red Cross packages, but that was, you know, the last thirty days.

. . . We had I believe a number, I think a total of seven early releases. Six of those were absolutely dishonorable as far as we were concerned. Our code essentially said I'll accept no treatment that's better than my fellow prisoner. Going home was better treatment. So six of those guys went home pretty much against orders. I realize that may sound very harsh, but that's the way it was.

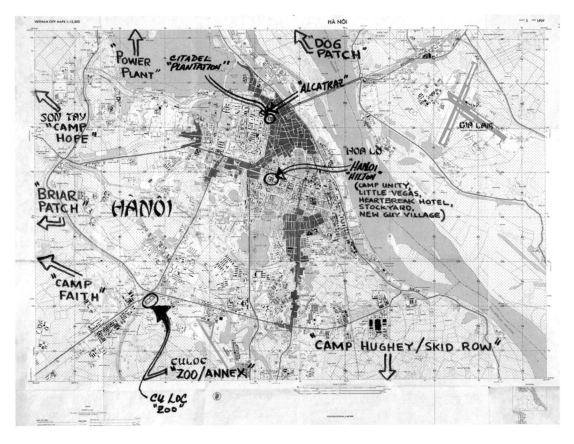

By the best estimates, some 866 Americans were prisoners of war. About this same number were reported as missing in action (MIA) and some 1,200 as killed in action (KIA) but without bodies having been recovered. The reported missing and killed (without a recovered body) created gnawing doubt, leading many to believe that the actual POW count was significantly higher than reported. The fact was that, without reliable intelligence sources inside North Vietnam, the United States military had remarkably little idea of how many prisoners were actually held. For the Nixon administration, the POW issue became distinctly political. Estimated POW numbers were deliberately inflated from approximately 850 to 1,350 or even 1,500 in an effort to build up "return and recovery of POWs" as a compelling rationale for prolonging the war. After the administration agreed in Paris to U.S. withdrawal in exchange for the release of all prisoners, the White House made the POW issue a leading justification for withdrawal.

Former POW Mike McGrath drew a map of Hanoi and its POW camps so that he would not forget where they were. The "Hanoi Hilton" was one of several that received similarly colorful names from inmates.

"PEACE IS AT HAND"

HANOI'S AGREEMENT TO THE REPATRIATION OF POWs was encouraging, but the Paris talks stalled in September 1971 over the issue of the future of the Thieu regime in South Vietnam. Hanoi's chief negotiator, Le Duc Tho, stood firm in his demand that Thieu be removed. President Nixon not only bridled at ignominiously deserting an ally but also feared that agreeing to Thieu's ouster would result in the immediate collapse of South Vietnam, thereby sacrificing Kissinger's credibility-saving "decent interval." At the same time, the president was keenly aware of the ARVN's miserable performance in Operation Lam Son 719 and that, by January 1972, only 133,000 U.S. troops would remain in South Vietnam—a demoralized force that was itself increasingly unreliable with each passing day.

The Easter Offensive

With the Paris peace process stalled and the American ground presence dwindling, Hanoi decided to launch the three-pronged offensive across the 17th parallel it had been planning since Lam Son. The operation would rely not on Viet Cong—whose ranks at the time were sorely depleted—but on the NVA, the regular North Vietnamese Army. That is, it would be a conventional campaign that included a large fleet of just received Soviet-built tanks. The tactical objective of the offensive was to expose, yet again, the weakness and inadequacy of the ARVN. The strategic objective was to pressure President Nixon, facing reelection in November 1972, to back away from his support of Thieu. Hanoi called it the Nguyen Hue Offensive. The United States would refer to it as the Easter Offensive.

It began on March 30, 1972, and, by the time that it ended on October 22, some 200,000 NVA soldiers were involved. Unlike the Tet Offensive of 1968, which had been intended to win the war in a single blow by inciting a popular uprising, the Easter Offensive was meant only to acquire control of territory while also killing as many ARVN troops as possible, thereby putting the North in the strongest possible negotiating position in Paris.

Neither the MACV, the Joint Chiefs of Staff, nor the Nixon administration was surprised that the North launched a major attack. Its breadth and intensity, however, were profoundly shocking, especially since it had been unleashed with simultaneous fury against three widely separated fronts: in the north across the DMZ against Quang Tri (sending a flood of refugees surging southward), against Kon Tum in the Central Highlands (which threatened to split South Vietnam in two), and in the south against An Loc, driving toward Saigon itself. This southernmost attack allowed the Communists to occupy huge tracts along the Cambodian border.

A 122-mm artillery battery of the North Vietnamese Army (NVA) fires salvos on the Kon Tum front during the Easter Offensive.

Just below the DMZ, the NVA overran the ARVN, taking Quang Tri City after a month of combat, then advancing south against the ancient capital of Hue. In the Central Highlands, the NVA destroyed the ARVN frontier defense forces then assaulted the provincial capital of Kon Tum. Had the North Vietnamese army succeeded in capturing Kon Tum, the Communists would have had a clear opening to the sea, and South Vietnam would have been split, perhaps fatally. At the southernmost prong, northeast of Saigon, the Communists overran Loc Ninh and advanced to menace An Loc, capital of Binh Long Province.

Operation Linebacker

President Nixon was quick to appreciate that the Easter Offensive could well bring down the Saigon regime, an eventuality that would not simply weaken but utterly destroy Kissinger's bargaining position in Paris, as well as quite probably cost his own reelection. The president also understood that there was even more at stake. He had just returned from his breakthrough trip to Beijing, which he intended as the first step to restoring full diplomatic relations between China and the United States. He planned next to travel to Moscow to conclude the landmark Strategic Arms Limitation Treaty (SALT I). If Saigon fell, not only would the Paris Peace Talks go against the United States but also the nation's standing in the starkly bipolar world of the Cold War would be badly undermined, imperiling both the strides that had been made in China and the upcoming treaty with the Soviets. The election, the global balance of power, and the Nixon diplomatic legacy all hung in the balance.

A careful and deliberate diplomat on the world stage, Richard Nixon, in the privacy of the Oval Office, exploded in profanity to his

REALITY CHECK

The NVA Fights an American-Style Campaign

The Easter Offensive was shocking in its scope and intensity. U.S. military planners had not believed Hanoi capable of mounting so ambitious an offensive at this stage of the war. In some ways, the even greater shock was the entirely conventional nature of the offensive. For years, since the beginning of U.S. involvement in Vietnam, the American military had been thrashing away in what was mainly a guerrilla-style war. High command had defined its mission as combating an insurgency, not a "regular" army. Now the NVA suddenly proved itself proficient using the same class of modern conventional hardware the U.S. Army possessed: heavy artillery, tanks, and well-equipped infantry. It was a capability no one had expected.

advisers. The exchange was recorded on the hidden taping system Nixon (like Kennedy and Johnson before him) maintained:

> Here's those little cocksuckers [North Vietnam] right in there, here they are. Here's the United States. Here's Western Europe, that *cocky* little place that has caused so much devastation. . . . Here's the Soviet Union, here's the Mid-East. . . . Here's the silly Africans . . . and the not-quite-so-silly Latin Americans. Here *we* are. They're taking on the United States. Now, goddamit, we're gonna *do* it. We're going to *cream* them. This is not anger or anything. This old business that I'm "petulant." That's all bullshit. I should have done it long ago. I just didn't follow my instincts.
>
> I'll see that the United States does not lose. I'm putting it quite bluntly. I'll be quite precise. South Vietnam may lose. But the United States cannot lose. . . . For once, we've got to use the maximum power of this country . . . against this shit-ass little country: to win the war.

The president authorized a new air campaign to take up where Rolling Thunder had left off. He also ordered the mining of Haiphong Harbor and the establishment of a naval blockade of the entire North. The air campaign, called Operation Linebacker, commenced on May 10 with U.S. Air Force and U.S. Navy planes. The North Vietnamese had skillfully timed their offensive to coincide with the end of the monsoon, so that heavy cloud cover would hamper any air operations against them. Without a clear view of the ground, aircraft either had to rely heavily on instruments and LORAN (Long Range Navigation) systems to guide missions or consistently fly below the cloud cover, which exposed them to the North's extensive antiaircraft artillery network. Another problem was a shortage of aircraft and the ground personnel to maintain them. Although the troop reductions had focused on army personnel, Air Force ground personnel had also been drawn down. Planes and ground crews were rushed in from various Asian bases and the United States. To the 76 combat aircraft stationed in South Vietnam were added 114 fighter-bombers out of Thailand, 83 B-52s from Guam and Thailand, and 140 carrier-based navy strike craft. From South Korea and the United States, 176 F-4 Phantoms and a dozen F-105 Thunderchiefs were brought in for the operation, and the Strategic Air Command (SAC) flew 124 bombers into the theater from its U.S. bases. The navy's Seventh Fleet was augmented by the addition of four aircraft carrier groups along with their aircraft. In addition, Operation Linebacker made use of the South Vietnamese Air Force's 119 strike aircraft.

By the end of June, Linebacker had flown more than 18,000 defensive combat sorties in direct aid to ARVN ground forces, and B-52s had flown 2,724 offensive sorties—at first north to the 18th parallel then, in an operation code-named Freedom Train, north of the 20th parallel. Hanoi and Haiphong were targeted between May 1 and June 30. Coinciding with this, beginning on May 8, Operation Pocket Money dropped mines from the air into Haiphong Harbor and other North Vietnamese ports.

Operation Linebacker risked reigniting antiwar protest at home. That was bad enough, but Operation Pocket Money carried the even greater risk of derailing the upcoming SALT I negotiations. An inveterate risk taker, President Nixon gambled that both the Soviets and the Chinese were now so eager to improve relations with the United States that they would withhold any serious negative response to what was quite arguably both an international provocation and a direct violation of their rights to navigate the high seas. In the end, Nixon was right. Moscow and Beijing made very little noise.

At its height a program of round-the-clock bombing, Operation Linebacker inflicted heavy losses on North Vietnam and severely blunted the Easter Offensive. The NVA was prevented from splitting the South in two through the Central Highlands, and the ARVN was able to retake some territory lost earlier. The bottom line was that Linebacker averted the total defeat of the South Vietnamese military. From President Nixon's perspective, one of the most positive outcomes of both Linebacker and Pocket Money was that the majority of the American public interpreted them as justified responses to Communist aggression. While there was a measurable uptick in antiwar protest, it was nothing like what had followed the Cambodian incursion. And far from taking a hit as he approached reelection, the president's approval numbers climbed. This was all gratifying to the White House, but best of all was the refusal of the Soviets and the Chinese to object to any of it. The president dared to hope that "triangular diplomacy" was at long

A camera aboard a U.S. Navy A-7E Corsair II (launched from the carrier Kitty Hawk *and piloted by Michael A. Ruth, call sign "Baby") snapped this picture of its bombing attack on the Hai Duong Bridge in North Vietnam. This sortie, on May 10, 1972, was part of day one of Operation Linebacker I.*

last paying dividends. Could it be that Beijing and Moscow were finally cutting Hanoi loose?

BACK TO THE CONFERENCE TABLE

AS WITH THE TET OFFENSIVE, THE INITIAL IMPACT of the Easter Offensive was staggering, but the NVA proved unable to sustain all that it had gained and suffered very high casualties. Most important, it failed to discredit the ARVN, which had held its own during the onslaught (in large part because it outnumbered the NVA force seven to three). Nevertheless, Hanoi did succeed in gaining control of significant territory in the South, which would serve as bases from which it could launch future offensives. This added significantly to the North's bargaining power in Paris.

The Easter Offensive and the punishing U.S. response to it gave added urgency to the Paris Peace Talks, prompting Le Duc Tho to make a concession as profound as Nixon's agreement to unilateral withdrawal. He no longer demanded the removal of Nguyen Van Thieu and instead called for the establishment of a special council of reconciliation and the participation of the Saigon government alongside the Communist-controlled Provisional Revolutionary Government. With this in place, Kissinger and Le Duc Tho hammered out the details of an agreement governing the withdrawal of U.S. troops and the return of POWs. Although Thieu rejected these peace terms because they permitted Viet Cong forces to remain in place in the South, the Kissinger-Tho breakthrough enabled President Nixon to echo Kissinger's public announcement that "peace is at hand."

"We believe that peace is at hand. What remains to be done can be settled in one more negotiating session with the North Vietnamese negotiators, lasting, I think, no more than three or four days."

∗∗∗

—Henry Kissinger, announcement to the press, Paris, October 26, 1972

"Peace is at hand": Those four words may well have put the seal on Richard Nixon's landslide reelection victory in a race against antiwar Democratic candidate Senator George McGovern, whose campaign had been irretrievably damaged when it was revealed that his original running mate, Senator Thomas Eagleton, had been treated for "manic depression." Shortly after affirming his intention to continue to back Eagleton "1000 percent," McGovern suddenly dropped him from the ticket, replacing him with Sargent Shriver. The McGovern-Shriver ticket carried just one state (plus Washington, D.C.), eking out seventeen electoral votes. In a stunning turn of events, once Nixon was safely returned to office on November 7, he suddenly threw his support behind Thieu and summarily repudiated the peace terms Kissinger had negotiated. *"Tricky"*: Not for nothing was Richard Milhous Nixon, even in 1972, unable to shed the epithet he'd been saddled with back in 1950, when he first earned his reputation as a politician for whom winning an election was an end that justified any means.

Predictably, Le Duc Tho and his delegation accused Kissinger of a double-cross, causing the talks to break down. To bring the North Vietnamese back to the table, President Nixon ordered Operation Linebacker II, eleven consecutive days of bombing North Vietnamese cities in a campaign that spanned the Christmas season, from December 18 to December 29. The raids were so intensive and extensive that the operation was nicknamed the "Eleven-Day War."

The "Eleven-Day War" did bring the North Vietnamese back to the negotiations, and, on January 8, 1973, a draft of the Peace Accords was prepared. President Nixon approved, and the document was signed on January 27, 1973.

Peace without Peace

"Peace with honor," President Nixon finally announced to the nation. In fact, the January 1973 document was virtually identical to the October 1972 version the reelected Nixon repudiated in November. Thieu still objected, of course. This time, however, the American president attempted to mollify him with a promise that the United States would return to Vietnam "in full force" if Hanoi failed to live up to the agreement.

Not that the pieces of paper signed in Paris ended the fighting.

DETAILS, DETAILS
The Draft Ends
On January 27, 1973, Secretary of Defense Melvin Laird announced the creation of an all-volunteer force (AVF) and, in consequence, an end to the military draft. With this, one of the principal motivators of antiwar protest ceased to exist. Two years later, on March 29, 1975, President Gerald R. Ford signed an executive proclamation (Proclamation 4360), which ended the requirement that male citizens, ages eighteen to twenty-five, register with the Selective Service System. President Jimmy Carter, on July 2, 1980, reinstituted registration (Proclamation 4771), but while males between eighteen and twenty-six must now register, the U.S. military remains an all-volunteer force. The relatively low levels of protest against the wars in Iraq (2003–) and Afghanistan (2001–) may well be the result of the AVF.

Secretary of State Henry A. Kissinger and Le Duc Tho (center, directly to the left of Kissinger, with his interpreter) shake hands after initialing the Paris Peace Accord on January 23, 1973. It was essentially identical to the agreement President Nixon had repudiated some two months earlier—just after his reelection.

The U.S. POWs are released pursuant to the Paris Peace Accords. Here, freed U.S. Air Force captain Robert Parsels is greeted at Gia Lam Airport in Hanoi.

The shooting went on, even as the U.S. withdrawal continued until, on March 29, 1973, the last American ground combat troops departed Vietnam, leaving behind some 8,500 U.S. civilian "technicians." A new ceasefire was concluded on June 13, 1973, in an effort to silence the guns. As a matter of routine, both the South and the North violated it.

The American POWs began coming home on February 12, 1973, and continued through March 29. The United States continued to pour military and economic aid into South Vietnam, resumed bombing Cambodia, then menaced North Vietnam with reconnaissance overflights. The nation was relieved, but Richard Nixon was a wounded warrior.

In his zeal to defeat his political enemies (both real and perceived), including the likes of Pentagon Papers leaker Daniel Ellsberg, and in his single-minded determination to stack an already overwhelmingly favorable deck to assure his reelection, Nixon directed his campaign organization, the Committee to Re-elect the President (universally known by the acronym *CREEP*), to sabotage the Democratic Party with a combination of illegal espionage and "dirty tricks" aimed at smearing all challengers. On June 17, 1972, five "burglars" were arrested in the headquarters of the Democratic National Committee at the Watergate office building in Washington, D.C. It was soon revealed that these were no ordinary second-story men but members of the White House covert action team known as the "Plumbers." They served as a kind of palace guard, performing missions outside of the chief executive's constitutional mandate and even outside of the law. The Watergate break-in, which involved bugging Democratic headquarters, was such a mission. Thanks to a combination of the Plumbers' amateurish incompetence, the limits of loyalty among the members of Nixon's inner circle, the dogged journalism of *Washington Post* reporters Bob Woodward and Carl Bernstein, and the hostile exuberance of members of Congress burning to "nail" Tricky Dick Nixon once and for all, the Watergate conspiracy unraveled with increasing velocity during the president's second term. The scandal finally consumed not only the thirty-seventh presidency of the United States but also whatever future there might have been for an independent South Vietnam.

Washington's Watergate Hotel, where the Nixon presidency began to unravel.

TAKEAWAY
Anatomy of Defeat

The collapse of Operation Lam Son 719—an ARVN invasion of Laos— convinced President Nixon that, without a U.S. military presence, South Vietnam would fall. He and Henry Kissinger made concessions at the Paris Peace Talks aimed at creating a "decent interval" between the completion of the U.S. withdrawal and the almost certain downfall of the Saigon government. The object was to end the war in a way that at least looked like "peace with honor" and would preserve some portion of U.S. military and diplomatic credibility. After securing his reelection by promising that peace was "at hand," President Nixon repudiated a first version of a ceasefire, launched the war's most intensive bombing offensive to bring the outraged North Vietnamese negotiators back to the conference table, and then agreed to essentially the same ceasefire he had earlier rejected. Signed on January 27, 1973, the Paris Peace Accords ended the war but hardly brought peace.

CHAPTER 15

DECLINE AND FALL

Nixon Resigns, South Vietnam Surrenders

ICHARD NIXON'S PRESS SECRETARY, RON ZIEGLER, TRIED TO DISMISS Watergate as a "third-rate burglary," but Secretary of State Henry Kissinger was much closer to the mark when he called it and its far-reaching consequences "a Greek tragedy." In sabotaging the Democratic presidential campaign of 1972 and authorizing other illegal acts, many of them aimed against antiwar activists, Richard Nixon, like a protagonist of Sophocles, was "fulfilling his own nature." Kissinger explained, "once it started it could not end otherwise."

> **"I brought myself down. I gave them a sword. And they stuck it in, and they twisted it with relish. And I guess if I had been in their position, I'd have done the same thing."**
>
> ★★★
>
> —Richard M. Nixon, television interview with David Frost, May 4, 1977

"I HAVE NEVER BEEN A QUITTER"

THE WATERGATE "BURGLARS" WERE ARRESTED AT 2:30 IN THE MORNING of June 17, 1972; President Nixon was reelected on November 7 of that year; Nixon's young counsel and confidant John Dean ("We have a cancer within, close to the presidency," he warned

Nixon in March 1973) began cooperating with federal prosecutors on April 6, 1973; and on May 17, the Senate Watergate Committee convened nationally televised hearings.

The hearings riveted the nation. The disclosures exploded, one after the other, like the bombs of Rolling Thunder and Linebacker. After each shock of revelation, it seemed, the president announced the "resignation" of a key member of the White House inner circle, including White House counsel John Ehrlichman and White House chief of staff H. R. Haldeman. Among the crimes the congressional investigation uncovered were the fact that former Nixon attorney general John Mitchell, in his capacity as Nixon's reelection campaign manager, controlled secret monies used to finance the "dirty tricks" intended to sabotage the Democratic party; that major corporations had made millions of dollars in illegal campaign contributions; that the president had promised the Plumbers clemency and even outright bribes in return for their silence; that L. Patrick Gray, Nixon's nominee to replace the recently deceased J. Edgar Hoover as FBI director, had illegally turned over FBI records on Watergate to John Dean; that Mitchell and CREEP (Committee for the Re-election of

Former White House aide and Nixon confidant John Dean III is sworn in before testifying to the Senate Watergate Committee, June 25, 1973. With his back to the camera is committee chairman Senator Sam Ervin (D-NC).

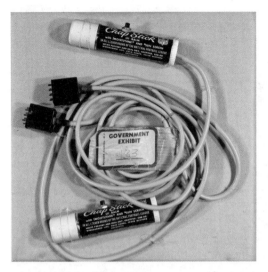

Government Exhibit 133 in the trial of White House "Plumber" E. Howard Hunt, the former CIA officer who organized (quite ineptly, as it turned out) the Watergate break-in and bugging. Convicted of conspiracy, Hunt spent thirty-three months in a low-security federal prison camp. Pictured are Chapstick tubes fitted with miniature microphones, which were among the espionage paraphernalia discovered in Hunt's White House office safe.

the President) finance chairman Maurice Stans took bribes; that the White House possessed illegal wiretap tapes; and that President Nixon obstructed justice by ordering the CIA to instruct the FBI not to investigate Watergate. Added to this was the discovery that, during 1969 and 1970, the chief executive had secretly bombed Cambodia without the knowledge, let alone the approval, of Congress.

United States v. Nixon

Late in the Watergate investigation process, the existence of covert White House tapes was discovered. When Congress subpoenaed them, the president claimed "executive privilege" and refused to turn the tapes over. While his lawyers fought the subpoena in court, President Nixon ordered Attorney General Elliot L. Richardson to fire Watergate special prosecutor Archibald Cox. (Richardson succeeded Richard G. Kleindienst, who had replaced John Mitchell as attorney general when Mitchell had resigned that post to head up CREEP.) Attorney General Richardson refused and resigned in protest; his deputy, William Ruckelshaus, likewise refused and also stepped down. The duty to discharge Cox fell to Nixon's solicitor general, Robert H. Bork, who complied. All of this took place in the space of a single day, October 20, 1973; the press called it the "Saturday Night Massacre." At last, on July 24, 1974, the Supreme Court handed down its unanimous decision in *United States v. Nixon*, holding that, to "read the Article II [constitutional] powers of the President as providing an absolute privilege as against a subpoena essential to enforcement of criminal statutes on no more than a generalized claim of the public interest in confidentiality of nonmilitary and non-diplomatic discussions would upset the constitutional balance of 'a workable government' and gravely impair the role of the courts under Article III."

Faced with this ruling, President Nixon released typed transcripts of some of the tapes. Partial, redacted transcripts were hardly enough to mollify the House Judiciary Committee, which, on July 27–30, recommended that the president be impeached on three charges: obstruction of justice, abuse of presidential powers, and attempting to impede the impeachment process by defying committee subpoenas. This prompted

Nixon to release the remaining tapes on August 5, 1974, including what was widely called the "smoking gun": proof from his own mouth that the president of the United States had taken steps to block the FBI's inquiry into the Watergate burglary.

"We Have Ended America's Longest War"

On the evening of August 8, 1974, three days after releasing the Watergate tapes, Richard Milhous Nixon faced television cameras in the Oval Office. "This is the 37th time I have spoken to you from this office. . . ." It would be his last. He announced that, effective at noon on August 9, he would resign the presidency, to be replaced by Gerald R. Ford. As an appointed vice president, Ford would thus become the only U.S. president not elected to the executive branch.

The president spoke of having begun his second term with "high hopes." He asked that the American people now "begin healing the wounds of this Nation." He apologized for "any injuries" he may have caused, adding, "I would say only that if some of my judgments were wrong, and some were wrong, they were made in what I believed at the time to be the best interest of the Nation."

President Nixon spoke of his administration's accomplishments, including unlocking "the doors that for a quarter of a century stood between the United States and the People's Republic of China" and having begun, with the Soviet Union, "the process of limiting nuclear arms." He spoke, too, of having "ended America's longest war."

President Nixon poses with the edited transcripts of the infamous White House tapes during an April 29, 1974, broadcast to the nation. His release of these records, which he personally redacted, was insufficient to stave off a recommendation of impeachment by the House Judiciary Committee on July 27–30, 1974.

Even Nixon's detractors—and at this moment of history, they were legion—acknowledged his Chinese and Soviet breakthroughs. But *ending* the Vietnam War? The fact was that, even as the president had struggled to beat back the relentless tide of Watergate, he continued to fight the war with what weapons remained to him: airpower against Cambodia, reconnaissance flights over North Vietnam, and money, lots of money, poured into the crumbling, corrupt government of Nguyen Van Thieu. It was precisely because he refused to end the Vietnam War that Congress, in November 1973, had passed the War Powers Resolution. It required the president to inform Congress within forty-eight hours of deployment of U.S. military forces abroad and mandated their withdrawal within sixty days if Congress did not approve the deployment. Although the legislation had been propelled by the Watergate revelations of Nixon's secret bombing of Cambodia, it was aimed even more directly at the legacy of Lyndon Baines Johnson, who had exploited the largely fabricated Tonkin Gulf Incident to seize from Congress the power to make war. Other legislation had targeted the beleaguered thirty-seventh president. In 1974, Congress slashed appropriations for U.S. military and economic aid to South Vietnam from $2.56 billion to $907 million.

President Richard M. Nixon Announces His Resignation

From the televised address of August 8, 1974:

"**G**ood evening.

"This is the 37th time I have spoken to you from this office, where so many decisions have been made that shaped the history of this Nation. Each time I have done so to discuss with you some matter that I believe affected the national interest.

"In all the decisions I have made in my public life, I have always tried to do what was best for the Nation. Throughout the long and difficult period of Watergate, I have felt it was my duty to persevere, to make every possible effort to complete the term of office to which you elected me.

"In the past few days, however, it has become evident to me that I no longer have a strong enough political base in the Congress to justify continuing that effort. As long as there was such a base, I felt strongly that it was necessary to see the constitutional process through to its conclusion, that to do otherwise would be unfaithful to the spirit of that deliberately difficult process and a dangerously destabilizing precedent for the future.

"But with the disappearance of that base, I now believe that the constitutional purpose has been served, and there is no longer a need for the process to be prolonged.

"I would have preferred to carry through to the finish whatever the personal agony it would have involved, and my family unanimously urged me to do so. But the interest of the Nation must always come before any personal considerations.

"From the discussions I have had with Congressional and other leaders, I have concluded that because of the Watergate matter I might not have the support of the Congress that I would consider necessary to back the very difficult decisions and carry out the duties of this office in the way the interests of the Nation would require.

"I have never been a quitter. To leave office before my term is completed is abhorrent to every instinct in my body. But as President, I must put the interest of America first. America needs a full-time President and a full-time Congress, particularly at this time with problems we face at home and abroad.

"To continue to fight through the months ahead for my personal vindication would almost totally absorb the time and attention of both the President and the Congress in a period when our entire focus should be on the great issues of peace abroad and prosperity without inflation at home.

"Therefore, I shall resign the Presidency effective at noon tomorrow. Vice President Ford will be sworn in as President at that hour in this office.

"As I recall the high hopes for America with which we began this second term, I feel a

August 8, 1974—the digital time stamp on this video image reads 9:04 p.m.: the moment at which Richard Milhous Nixon became the first American president to announce his resignation from office.

great sadness that I will not be here in this office working on your behalf to achieve those hopes in the next two and a half years. But in turning over direction of the Government to Vice President Ford, I know, as I told the Nation when I nominated him for that office 10 months ago, that the leadership of America will be in good hands.

"In passing this office to the Vice President, I also do so with the profound sense of the weight of responsibility that will fall on his shoulders tomorrow and, therefore, of the understanding, the patience, the cooperation he will need from all Americans.

"As he assumes that responsibility, he will deserve the help and the support of all of us. As we look to the future, the first essential is to begin healing the wounds of this Nation, to put the bitterness and divisions of the recent past behind us, and to rediscover those shared ideals that lie at the heart of our strength and unity as a great and as a free people.

"By taking this action, I hope that I will have hastened the start of that process of healing which is so desperately needed in America.

"I regret deeply any injuries that may have been done in the course of the events that led to this decision. I would say only that if some of my Judgments were wrong, and some were wrong, they were made in what I believed at the time to be the best interest of the Nation.

"To those who have stood with me during these past difficult months, to my family, my friends,

President Richard M. Nixon Announces His Resignation (continued)

to many others who joined in supporting my cause because they believed it was right, I will be eternally grateful for your support.

"And to those who have not felt able to give me your support, let me say I leave with no bitterness toward those who have opposed me, because all of us, in the final analysis, have been concerned with the good of the country, however our judgments might differ.

"So, let us all now join together in affirming that common commitment and in helping our new President succeed for the benefit of all Americans.

"I shall leave this office with regret at not completing my term, but with gratitude for the privilege of serving as your President for the past five and a half years. These years have been a momentous time in the history of our Nation and the world. They have been a time of achievement in which we can all be proud, achievements that represent the shared efforts of the Administration, the Congress, and the people.

"But the challenges ahead are equally great, and they, too, will require the support and the efforts of the Congress and the people working in cooperation with the new Administration.

"We have ended America's longest war, but in the work of securing a lasting peace in the world, the goals ahead are even more far-reaching and more difficult. We must complete a structure of peace so that it will be said of this generation, our generation of Americans, by the people of all nations, not only that we ended one war but that we prevented future wars.

"We have unlocked the doors that for a quarter of a century stood between the United States and the People's Republic of China.

"We must now ensure that the one-quarter of the world's people who live in the People's Republic of China will be and remain not our enemies but our friends. . . .

"Together with the Soviet Union we have made the crucial breakthroughs that have begun the process of limiting nuclear arms. But we must set as our goal not just limiting but reducing and finally destroying these terrible weapons so that they cannot destroy civilization and so that the threat of nuclear war will no longer hang over the world and the people.

"We have opened the new relation with the Soviet Union. We must continue to develop and expand that new relationship so that the two strongest nations of the world will live together in cooperation rather than confrontation. . . .

"For more than a quarter of a century in public life I have shared in the turbulent history of this era. I have fought for what I believed in. I have tried to the best of my ability to discharge those duties and meet those responsibilities that were entrusted to me.

"Sometimes I have succeeded and sometimes I have failed, but always I have taken heart from what Theodore Roosevelt once said about the man in the arena, 'whose face is marred by dust and sweat and blood, who strives valiantly, who errs and comes short again and again because there is not effort without error and shortcoming, but who does actually strive to do the deed, who knows the great enthusiasms, the great devotions, who spends himself in a worthy cause, who at the best knows in the end the triumphs of high achievements and who at the worst, if he fails, at least fails while daring greatly.'

"I pledge to you tonight that as long as I have a breath of life in my body, I shall continue in that spirit. I shall continue to work for the great causes to which I have been dedicated throughout my years as a Congressman, a Senator, a Vice President, and President, the cause of peace not just for America but among all nations, prosperity, justice, and opportunity for all of our people.

THE WHITE HOUSE
WASHINGTON

August 9, 1974

Dear Mr. Secretary:

I hereby resign the Office of President of the
United States.

Sincerely,

Richard Nixon

11.35 AM

HK

The Honorable Henry A. Kissinger
The Secretary of State
Washington, D.C. 20520

*The Nixons leave the White House. The
former president bids farewell to the former
vice president—now president—Gerald R.
Ford, and Pat Nixon kisses the new first
lady, Betty Ford. The photograph was taken
through the doorway of the U.S. Marine Corps
helicopter that would transport the Nixons to
a waiting airplane at Andrews Air Force Base.*

*The eleven-word sentence in this letter addressed to Secretary of State Henry
Kissinger ended a presidency and, in the process, ensured an end to the Republic
of Vietnam. Note Kissinger's acknowledgment of receipt: "11.35 AM / HK."*

"There is one cause above all to which I have been devoted and to which I shall always be devoted for as long as I live.

"When I first took the oath of office as President 5½ years ago, I made this sacred commitment, to 'consecrate my office, my energies, and all the wisdom I can summon to the cause of peace among nations.'

"I have done my very best in all the days since to be true to that pledge. As a result of these efforts, I am confident that the world is a safer place today, not only for the people of America but for the people of all nations, and that all of our children have a better chance than before of living in peace rather than dying in war.

"This, more than anything, is what I hoped to achieve when I sought the Presidency. This, more than anything, is what I hope will be my legacy to you, to our country, as I leave the Presidency.

"To have served in this office is to have felt a very personal sense of kinship with each and every American. In leaving it, I do so with this prayer: May God's grace be with you in all the days ahead."

THE FALL OF PHUOC LONG

IF ANYONE WAS AFFECTED MORE DIRECTLY BY RICHARD NIXON'S resignation from office than Richard Nixon himself, it was South Vietnam's Nguyen Van Thieu. What hope of survival remained to him and his country depended on continued support from the Nixon administration, and as that administration crumbled, Congress slashed funding to the Thieu regime. For 1975, after the resignation, the $907 million appropriation became just $750 million. When President Ford sought several hundreds of millions dollars in emergency "supplemental aid," Congress handed him a rebuff instead of the cash.

South Vietnam was enduring not only one military defeat after another but also economic implosion. The withdrawal of U.S. troops and most of the American civilian contingent—technicians, State Department employees, and others—revealed just how hollow the South Vietnamese economy was. What prosperity the nation had enjoyed (and its leaders had illegally profited from) was due to the presence of so many Americans. In their absence, Vietnamese hoteliers, restaurateurs, clerks, waiters, taxi drivers, construction workers, and prostitutes all found themselves unemployed and with no hope of regaining an income. The prolonged boom created by the American presence had brought with it gross inflation, which receded much more slowly than the precipitous decline of the consumer economy. Throughout the long years of war, the country had developed no enduring industries, no significant exports, and no viable indigenous economy. As the purchasing power of city dwellers dwindled, so the income of farmers dried up. The peasants, who had suffered under one corrupt and cruel South Vietnamese regime after another, were, by and large, ready to embrace the so-called Liberation: the Communist onslaught from the North.

The Pivotal Campaign Begins

On December 12, 1974, the NVA IV Corps, some 14,500 troops, commenced a campaign against Phuoc Long, a city and surrounding area about sixty miles north of Saigon. NVA high command had three objectives. First, they wanted to provoke the United States. Nixon had warned that violations of the ceasefire would result in America's return to Vietnam. President Nixon was gone. What would America do now? Second, the NVA wanted to test the ARVN's combat capability in the absence of a supporting U.S. military presence. Finally, by capturing Phuoc Long, the NVA wanted to acquire an open route into the region surrounding Saigon. Capture and control this region and the daunting logistical problems of a full-scale final invasion would be solved.

Outnumbered

Over the next twenty-five days at Phuoc Long, the ARVN was indeed defeated, but not for lack of a will to fight. Often demoralized and reluctant to give battle in the past, the South Vietnamese army now fought with a passion, sacrificing itself in large numbers. As was rarely the case during the American phases of the war, the Communists greatly outnumbered the forces arrayed against them. Facing 14,500 NVA soldiers were about 7,800 ARVN troops. Worst of all for Thieu and his government, as these soldiers fought and died and thereby yielded ground, the U.S. Congress repeatedly voted down additional aid to South Vietnam. Objective one of the campaign was therefore quickly realized. Tested, the United States proved it had indeed abandoned its one-time ally and client.

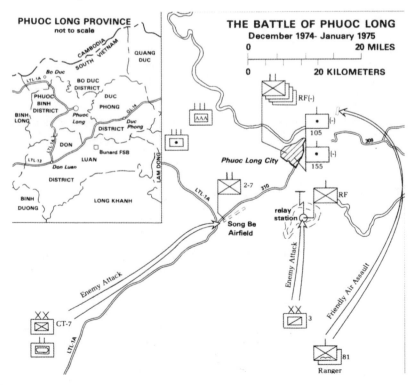

Phuoc Long, December 1974–January 1975: For the Communists in Vietnam, it was the culminating battle of a war that had begun long before many of its combatants had been born.

Surrounded

By the morning of January 4, 1975, the Battle of Phuoc Long had entered its final, desperate phase. ARVN commander Lieutenant General Du Quoc Dong ordered what remained of the South Vietnamese air force to attack advancing NVA columns. When this succeeded in slowing the attack, Dong airlifted the 81st Airborne Ranger Battalion into action, landing them at Dac Song, northeast of Phuoc Long City. No sooner had they landed, however, than they were heavily shelled by NVA artillery, which inflicted severe losses. While the artillery barrage continued, the NVA 16th Regiment attacked Dac Song and gave chase to the survivors of the 81st Airborne landing. With this attempt at reinforcement and relief defeated, the NVA advanced on and captured most of Phuoc Long City.

On the next day, two North Vietnamese regiments doggedly completed their encirclement of Phuoc Long's government centers while simultaneously maintaining an artillery barrage. On January 6, the NVA sent another regiment, equipped with tanks, to reinforce the attacking units and to cut off all routes of escape from Phuoc Long. By eight that evening, the last survivors of the ARVN 81st Airborne Ranger Battalion were captured, and the battle was over.

All of the North's objectives had been achieved in the Phuoc Long victory. The United States was clearly no longer a danger to the Communists in Vietnam; the ARVN—though it fought valiantly—was now too reduced and too poorly supplied to offer meaningful resistance; and, in taking Phuoc Long, the NVA and VC now had a single continuous link between the Ho Chi Minh Trail, the Central Highlands, and the Mekong Delta. All of South Vietnam was open to invasion. The country was ripe for the taking.

THE FALL OF SAIGON

AFTER SO LONG A WAR—a struggle that might be measured in years, decades, centuries, or even millennia, depending on one's perspective—the end came with stunning velocity following the collapse of Phuoc Long. The NVA and VC launched a lightning campaign through the Central Highlands, taking the key city of Ban Me Thuot, capital of Dak Lak Province, during March 3–18, 1975. Making a stand there with a force of 78,300 against 65,141 NVA troops, the ARVN suffered a cataclysmic 75 percent casualty rate—killed, wounded, and missing. The force's stock of U.S.-supplied tanks, artillery, and aircraft was destroyed or captured.

After Ban Me Thuot, the ARVN evacuated all of the Central Highlands, thereby delivering six entire provinces into the hands of the Communists. By the end of March, the rout of the South Vietnamese military was general, having spread to the coast. Hue and Da Nang fell on March 25 and 29, respectively, followed by one major city after another—many of them surrendering without a fight because there was no one left to put up a fight. The CIA, which, at the beginning of the year had predicted that South Vietnam could hold out well into 1976, now declared prospects for a turnaround in the war nil—unless the United States flew in with massive B-52 strikes. Congress would authorize no such thing, and the president was now legally barred from doing so.

> "Today, America can regain the sense of pride that existed before Vietnam. But it cannot be achieved by refighting a war that is finished as far as America is concerned. . . . We, of course, are saddened indeed by the events in Indochina. . . .
>
> We can and we should help others to help themselves. But the fate of responsible men and women everywhere, in the final decision, rests in their own hands. . . ."

***

—President Gerald R. Ford, speech at Tulane University, New Orleans, April 23, 1975

The Ho Chi Minh Campaign

In mid-April, the Hanoi government ordered General Van Tien Dung to advance "to the heart of Saigon" and told him the offensive he commanded was now to be called the "Ho Chi Minh Campaign."

On April 9, Dung's army attacked Xuan Loc, the final line in

President Gerald R. Ford addresses an audience at Tulane University in New Orleans on April 23, 1975, declaring that the Vietnam War "is finished as far as America is concerned."

the defense of Saigon. With the same degree of resolve seen at Phuoc Long, ARVN forces took a stand, holding off the NVA for eleven days before being overrun on April 20. In tears, President Nguyen Van Thieu broadcast the news on television the following day, cursing the United States for having failed to aid its ally.

With the NVA on the doorstep of Saigon—Xuan Loc was just twenty-six miles from the capital's center—Dung sent forces south into the Mekong Delta, which had been stripped of ARVN troops in an effort to defend the capital. This allowed the Communists to encircle Saigon by April 27.

Flight

As the Communists swept through the country during March and the early part of April, most Americans, other Westerners, and many prominent South Vietnamese fled. U.S. nationals could and did secure flights through the Defense Attaché's Office (DAO), but U.S. law forbade the DAO from evacuating Vietnamese. Because many American evacuees demanded that their Vietnamese friends, employees, lovers, common-law spouses, and in some cases children be evacuated with them, DAO officials freely broke the law.

Babylift and New Life

President Ford announced Operation Babylift on April 3, which used giant C-5A Galaxy military transport aircraft to evacuate approximately two thousand Vietnamese orphans. Tragically, one of the aircraft crashed, killing 138 evacuees. Another U.S. operation, dubbed New Life, successfully evacuated some 110,000 Vietnamese.

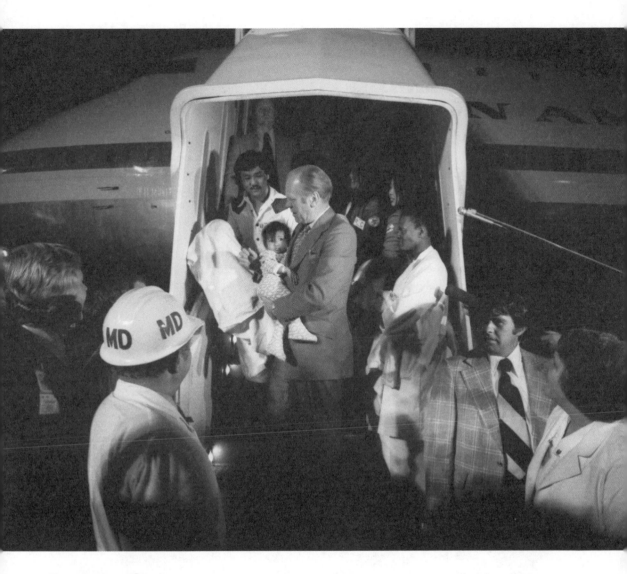

Evacuation Plans

While Operations Babylift and New Life were under way, the Ford administration worked with the U.S. military to ensure the evacuation of all American nationals remaining in Saigon, especially those attached to the embassy. Military brass wanted an immediate, high-speed evacuation, but U.S. ambassador Graham Martin demanded caution. He feared that any display of panic would turn the South Vietnamese against the Americans, transforming an orderly evacuation into a bloodbath. Anxious to save lives and to

President Ford carries a Vietnamese baby from one of the planes that transported approximately 325 South Vietnamese orphans from Saigon to the United States, April 5, 1975.

FORGOTTEN FACES
Graham A. Martin

Graham A. Martin (1912–90) was the last U.S. ambassador to South Vietnam, succeeding Ellsworth Bunker in 1973.

The son of a North Carolina Baptist minister, Martin served during World War II, as a U.S. Army intelligence officer, and then entered the U.S. Foreign Service in 1947, rising to deputy chief of mission in Paris by 1955. Martin served as U.S. representative to the European Office of the United Nations in Geneva from 1960 to 1962, then as ambassador to Thailand from 1963 to 1967. In 1969, he was appointed ambassador to Italy, leaving that post in 1973 to become ambassador to South Vietnam on June 21 of that year.

Martin viewed the desperate situation of South Vietnam with an almost incomprehensible optimism, believing that Saigon and the Mekong Delta would hold out even if the rest of the South fell. As the end neared, his rosy view crossed into delusion. He refused to acknowledge signals intelligence (SIGINT) reports of the overwhelming build-up of NVA forces around Saigon. The ambassador's consequent refusal to allow the embassy-based South Vietnamese intelligence staff to evacuate from the embassy resulted in their capture. As for Martin himself, he reluctantly obeyed a presidential order to evacuate by helicopter on April 30.

President Ford (back to camera) meets with Ambassador Graham A. Martin (third from right), Army chief of staff General Frederick Weyand (in uniform), and Secretary of State Henry Kissinger (right). Brent Scowcroft, deputy assistant to the president for national security affairs, is mostly obscured at the far left. The Oval Office meeting took place on March 25, 1975.

salvage some good from the chaos of downfall, President Ford decided on a compromise. He authorized a large-scale military evacuation of all but 1,250 essential American personnel. The number remaining was large enough to show a presence to the South Vietnamese but small enough to be airlifted by helicopter—when necessary—in a one-day operation. In the meantime, the ambassador took it upon himself, without administration authorization, to issue exit visas to any South Vietnamese who wished to leave by whatever means were available. Nevertheless, a thriving black market in visas exploded.

Incredibly, President Ford persisted in appealing to Congress for emergency aid to the Thieu government, and Ambassador Martin held out hope that negotiation between the South and the North was still possible. All of this ended on April 21, 1975, when Nguyen Van Thieu abruptly stepped down, turning his government over to Vice President Tran Van Huong.

> ## "I will give you large sums for evacuation, but not one nickel for military aid."
>
> ★★★
>
> —Senator Jacob Javits (Rep., NY), response to President Gerald R. Ford's plea for emergency funds to the Thieu government, April 14, 1975

Frequent Wind

If Thieu's departure was intended to signal to the Communists a desire for a negotiated settlement, Hanoi turned a blind eye and a deaf ear. On April 27, Saigon came under heavy rocket attack. Two days later, Tan Son Nhat Airport and Tan Son Nhut Air Base were shelled by artillery and attacked by rockets. Remarkably, the attack itself failed to crater the runways, but a South Vietnamese air force pilot, deciding at the last minute to defect to the North, took off, jettisoning his ordnance as he did so, destroying the still-usable runways. After this incident, General Homer D. Smith, the U.S. defense attaché in Saigon, informed Ambassador Martin that remaining personnel had to resort to helicopter evacuation.

Evacuation from U.S. Embassy, Saigon: Cable Traffic, April 29, 1975 [April 30 in Vietnam]

TO: EMBASSY SAIGON
TO: AMBASSADOR GRAHAM MARTIN
FROM: HENRY A. KISSINGER

1. THE PRESIDENT HAS MET WITH THE NATIONAL SECURITY COUNCIL AND HAD MADE THE FOLLOWING DECISIONS:

A. IF THE AIRPORT IS OPEN FOR FIXED-WING OPERATIONS TODAY, YOU ARE TO CONTINUE THE EVACUATION OF HIGH RISK VIETNAMESE BY FIXED-WING AIRCRAFT. YOU ARE ALSO TO EVACUATE BY THE END OF THE DAY ALL AMERICAN PERSONNEL AT TAN SON NHUT AS WELL AS ALL BUT BARE MINIMUM PERSONNEL FROM THE EMBASSY.

B. WHILE YOU SHOULD NOT SAY SO, THIS WILL BE THE LAST REPEAT LAST DAY OF FIXED-WING EVACUATION FROM TAN SON NHUT.

C. IF THE AIRPORT IS UNUSABLE FOR FIXED-WING AIRCRAFT OR BECOMES SO DURING THE DAY AS A RESULT OF ENEMY FIRE, YOU ARE IMMEDIATELY TO RESORT TO HELICOPTER EVACUATION OF ALL REPEAT ALL AMERICANS, BOTH FROM THE DAO COMPOUND AND FROM THE EMBASSY COMPOUND. FIGHTER CAP AND SUPPRESSIVE FIRE WILL BE USED AS NECESSARY IN THE EVENT OF HELICOPTER EVACUATION.

2. ADMIRAL GAYLER WILL BE RECEIVING IDENTICAL INSTRUCTIONS FROM DEFENSE.

3. WARM REGARDS,

0208 . . .

. . . APR. 29, 75 1605
S E C R E T
523-119-FYI (DI25) FREQUENT WIND (C)

LADY ACE 09 HAS THE AMBASSADOR AND HIS IMMEDIATE STAFF ON BOARD AND THAT THEY ARE MOVING THE GSF TO THE ROOF TOP FOR PICKUP. . . .

APR. 29, 75 1612+
S E C R E T
523-119-FYI (DI25) FREQUENT WIND (C)

REPORTS ARE THAT THERE ARE 200 AMERICANS LEFT TO EVAC. GUNNER SIX TO GSF COMMANDER BRING UP PERSONNEL UP THRU THE BUILDING DO NOT LET THEM (THE SOUTH VIETS) FOLLOW TOO CLOSELY. USE MACE IF NECESSARY BUT DO NOT FIRE ON THEM. . . .

APR. 29, 75 1624
S E C R E T
523-119-FYI (DI25) FREQUENT WIND (C)

LADY ACE 09 REPORTS FEET WEET [WET] AT 2121Z. LADY ACE 13 REPORTS OUTBOUND WITH 16 USA AND LADY ACE 10 GOING IN FOR LNDG. . . .

APR. 29, 75 1637
S E C R E T
523-119-FYI (DI25) FREQUENT WIND (C)

LADY ACE 14 IS GOING INTO THE ROOF TOP. IF HE HITS ANY GAS HE WILL PULL OFF IMMED. . . .

APR. 29, 75 1641
S E C R E T
523-119-FYI (DI25) FREQUENT WIND (C)

LADY ACE 14 IS ON THE ROOF HE REPORTS SMALL ARMS FIRE ON THE NORTH EAST CORNER OF THE BUILDING IN A SMALL CLUMP OF TREES AT GROUND LEVEL. LADY ACE 19 LOADING THIS TIME. . . .

APR. 29, 75 1644
S E C R E T
523-119-FYI (DI25) FREQUENT WIND (C)

SPECTRE REPORTS NUMEROUS FIRE FIGHTS ALL AROUND THE BUILDING. SWIFT 33 INBOUND FEET DRY. LADY ACE 14 REPORTS OFF WITH 21 PAX. . . .

In one of the iconic images of abject military and political defeat in the Vietnam War, on April 29, 1975, a CIA civilian contract Air America helicopter loads Vietnamese evacuees from the top of 22 Gia Long Street, about a half-mile from the U.S. Embassy in Saigon—a city soon to be renamed in honor of Ho Chi Minh.

After braving artillery fire to personally inspect Tan Son Nhut, Ambassador Martin authorized the helicopter evacuation to begin, cabling Secretary of State Kissinger at 10:48 a.m. (Saigon time) to activate Operation Frequent Wind. On Kissinger's command, the local U.S. radio station played Irving Berlin's "White Christmas," the pre-arranged signal for U.S. personnel to proceed to assigned evacuation points.

Immediately, Sikorsky CH-53 Sea Stallion and Boeing CH-46 Chinook helicopters took flight from aircraft carriers stationed in the South China Sea, landing within the DAO Compound at Tan Son Nhut, the principal evacuation point, to which evacuees had been driven in buses. Between noon and evening, 395 Americans and more than 4,000 Vietnamese had been airlifted. A few thousand people, Americans as well as Vietnamese, had not reached the airport, however, and were stranded at the embassy. More Vietnamese climbed over the wall of the embassy compound in a desperate bid to secure refugee status. Helicopters were therefore dispatched to the embassy, plucked evacuees from the rooftop, and flew them to Tan Son Nhut, from which they were flown by other helicopters to aircraft carriers waiting offshore. The images of Americans and

Vietnamese being rescued in this desperate fashion were carried on televisions across the world. They became ignominious icons of the defeat not so much of South Vietnam as of the United States of America.

The helicopters made round trips between the embassy and the airport all night and into the early morning hours. At 3:45 on the morning of April 30 (local Vietnam time), Secretary of State Kissinger ordered a halt to refugee evacuation. From this point on, only the remaining Americans were to be flown out. President Ford personally ordered Ambassador Martin to board the helicopter designated by the call sign "Lady Ace 09," which took off at about five. The U.S. Marines of the embassy guard were evacuated on the last helicopter at 7:53.

"The Enemy's Final Lair"

On April 28, Tran Van Huong, who had assumed the presidency after the resignation of Nguyen Van Thieu, turned over his office to General Duong Van Minh, known as "Big Minh" because, at six feet and nearly two hundred pounds, he was far larger than the average Vietnamese. On April 30, NVA general Van Tien Dung acted on the orders he had received from Hanoi early in the morning of the day before, to "strike with the greatest determination straight into the enemy's final lair."

The 324th Division of the NVA entered the city before midmorning. For his part, President Minh wasted no time. At 10:24, he broadcast a proclamation of surrender, ordering all ARVN forces "to cease hostilities in calm and to stay where they are." He then called on the Provisional Revolutionary Government to initiate "a ceremony of orderly transfer of power so as to avoid any unnecessary bloodshed in the population." Dung was, however, unwilling to concede even that degree of control to the fallen Saigon regime. Without acknowledging Big Minh's broadcast or the invitation to formalize the surrender with a ceremony, he summarily ordered his tanks to smash through the gates of Independence Palace and raise the flag of the National Liberation Front over it. This was done at 11:30 local time. At 4:30 that afternoon, Duong Van Minh made another brief broadcast: "I declare the Saigon government . . . completely dissolved at all levels." The last chief executive of the nation of South Vietnam had been president for three days.

TAKEAWAY
All Fall Down
The downfall of Richard M. Nixon largely coincided with the final defeat of South Vietnam. As the American president became more deeply mired in the Watergate scandal, Congress reduced funding for the war. After Nixon's resignation, Congress effectively disengaged the United States from its erstwhile ally and client. Without U.S. military support and funding, the ARVN was unable to defend against a general invasion by the forces of North Vietnam. The culmination of the Communist victory was the fall of Saigon, which was accompanied by a frenzied evacuation of U.S. nationals and Vietnamese refugees, including a series of last-minute helicopter airlifts from the roof of the U.S. Embassy. Captured by television newsreel broadcasts, this even became an international icon of America's defeat in what was to that time the nation's longest war.

PART FIVE

WAKE

CHAPTER 16

COLLATERAL DAMAGE

Consequences of War: Unintended, Inevitable

"MY FELLOW AMERICANS," GERALD FORD TOLD THE AMERICAN PEOPLE after his swearing-in on August 9, 1974, "our long national nightmare is over." He was referring to Watergate and the Constitutional crisis averted by Richard Nixon's resignation. He might, however, have employed the very same phrase later, on April 30, 1975, when the last American evacuee was airlifted off the Saigon embassy roof. People would have understood it. But President Ford made no such statement. Perhaps he realized that, although Americans could now stop dying in Vietnam, the anguish of the United States was far from finished. Understandably, most American books on the Vietnam War end with a discussion of the legacy of that collective national anguish, the guilt, the humiliation, the self-doubt. And we will talk about that, too; but the lingering American nightmare, bad as it was, is nothing compared to what Vietnam and its neighbors were about to suffer.

"OUR FUTURE IS VERY BRIGHT"

THE COMMUNISTS HAD WON THE WAR, but they had been battered and depleted in doing so. NVA/VC losses totaled perhaps more than a million. Total civilian losses, North and South, ran to at least two million. Neither half of the broken nation had a viable economy. Clearly,

The fall of Saigon was accompanied by violent looting. This photograph, taken on April 29, 1975, the day before the official unconditional surrender, shows a South Vietnamese policeman hopelessly attempting to restore order in front of an American hotel.

years of General William Westmoreland's attrition strategy had failed to win the war, but attrition had made a terrible impact nonetheless. In the South, thanks to a combination of the attrition strategy and the pacification program (mainly Operation Phoenix), the VC and Communist political cadres had been decimated by the time of the NVA's final campaign. Without these elements to hold the population in line, looting and riots broke out in Saigon immediately after the fall. The NVA, under General Van Tien Dung's administrative deputy, General Tran Van Tra, put Saigon (which was immediately renamed Ho Chi Minh City) under martial law. Tran Van Tra quickly cut off communication with the outside, held a victory rally on May 7, then, with other Communist commanders throughout the country, set to work rounding up anyone perceived as having been prominent in South Vietnam, including government officials and cultural and community figures. Some—perhaps as many as 65,000—were summarily executed. Probably more than 200,000 others were sent to "reeducation camps."

PREVIOUS PAGES: *Forgotten, even scorned, by many Americans during the war, Vietnam veterans were later honored with numerous memorials throughout the nation. Here, a U.S. Marine Corps rifle guard awaits the start of a Vietnam Recognition Day ceremony at the Vietnam Veterans Memorial near the entrance to Camp Johnson, North Carolina, on April 30, 2011.*

NUMBERS
The Lost

United States armed forces lost between 58,178 and 58,272 killed in action (KIA); 303,644 wounded in action (WIA); and 1,687 missing in action (MIA). Of 866 POWs, 765 were released, 36 escaped, and 65 died in captivity. A total of 2,594,000 U.S. personnel served in Vietnam. The ARVN lost approximately 266,000 soldiers from 1959 through 1975 KIA; there are no reliable data on ARVN WIA and MIA. Hanoi claims that 1.1 million NVA and VC military personnel were KIA; other estimates put this at 931,000; reliable data on WIA and MIA are unavailable. Civilian deaths in South Vietnam are estimated at two million, including approximately 643,000 killed in the final invasion of the South and in its aftermath. Estimates of civilian deaths in North Vietnam range from 50,000 to several hundred thousand, with 65,000 being the most generally agreed-upon figure. None of the statistics quoted include war-related deaths from disease and privation.

DETAILS, DETAILS

Sentenced to Reeducation

In May 1975, Hanoi ordered large numbers of South Vietnamese in areas controlled by the NVA and VC to register with the Communist regime. The next month, many of these registrants were ordered to report to various places designated as "reeducation camps." Ostensibly set up to rehabilitate counterrevolutionaries, they were in fact concentration camps, where deprivation and outright torture were the favored instruments of "reeducation." Disease and starvation were convenient adjuncts in a program intended to reduce the population of a Saigon bursting at the seams with refugees from the Communist invasion. Presumably in a bid to ward off charges of human rights violation from the international community, the Hanoi government classified all inmates of the camps as "war criminals."

Famine

As in Mao Zedong's China during the Cultural Revolution of 1966–76, city dwellers were forcibly relocated to collectivized farms throughout the Vietnamese countryside. (More precisely, they were given the choice between starvation and "voluntary" relocation.) Untrained and ill-suited to farming, most, not surprisingly, made very poor agricultural laborers. Production was inefficient, a problem compounded by the ravages of war. Farmlands had been bombed out of existence, cratered, and generally ruined; fields had been left untended for months or years; and the Americans' use of herbicides and defoliants had created a general environmental catastrophe.

Because the U.S. military had been ill prepared to fight a guerrilla insurgency, especially in a region that included vast expanses of dense tropical jungle, the U.S. Department of Defense made large purchases of bulk defoliant agents from Monsanto Corporation and Dow Chemical. A mixture of two especially potent herbicide compounds (2,4,5-T and 2,4-D), the most widely used defoliant, known as Agent Orange, was highly effective in denuding foliage from large tracts of land. Between 1962 and 1971, U.S. aircraft sprayed some twenty million gallons of Agent Orange and related herbicides over much of Southern Vietnam as well as eastern Laos and the portions of Cambodia through which the Ho Chi Minh Trail ran. The tactical purpose of this treatment was to deny concealment to insurgent guerrillas. The strategic purpose was to institute so-called forced-draft urbanization. By selectively destroying farmland, rural peasants—who were likely to cooperate with the Viet Cong and Communist political cadres—were forced to migrate to the cities, which were firmly under the control of the United States military and the ARVN.

Contamination

Environmental warfare on so vast a scale was unprecedented. That was bad enough, but the effects of Agent Orange went beyond ecological cataclysm, economic devastation, ruined croplands, and artificially induced famine. After years of applying Agent Orange in Vietnam, it was discovered that it had been contaminated in manufacture with 2,3,7,8-tetrachlorodibenzodioxin (TCDD), a deadly dioxin compound. According to the Vietnam Red Cross, some three million Vietnamese had been exposed to Agent Orange contamination. The Vietnamese

Ministry of Foreign Affairs puts the number at 4.8 million. Red Cross in Vietnam experts blame Agent Orange for some 150,000 birth defects. The Ministry of Foreign Affairs puts the birth defect number at a half-million, with an additional 400,000 Vietnamese having been killed or maimed by direct exposure.

Vietnamese were not the only victims of Agent Orange. As a group, U.S. Vietnam veterans suffered (and continue to suffer) from increased rates of cancer as well as a variety of disorders and diseases affecting the skin and the nervous, digestive, and respiratory systems. Specifically, veterans show higher rates of throat cancer, leukemia, Hodgkin's lymphoma, non-Hodgkin's lymphoma, prostate cancer, lung cancer, soft tissue sarcoma, and liver cancer. Some soldiers—especially those whose assignments included handling Agent Orange and who were suspicious of dangers inherent in exposure to large amounts of herbicide—questioned their superiors. They were assured that the chemicals were perfectly safe. As evidence to the contrary accumulated, veterans began filing disability claims with the Department of Veterans Affairs in 1977. Most of these were routinely denied until passage in 1991 of the Agent Orange Act, which gave the Department of Veterans Affairs authority to declare certain conditions "presumptive" of dioxin exposure. Since then, more of the compensation claims have been paid.

DETAILS, DETAILS
Dioxin Time Bomb

By-products of various industrial processes, dioxins are persistent organic pollutants known to cause developmental disorders, immune system damage, and compromise of hormonal action in human beings. It is believed that the chemical is carcinogenic in that it accelerates tumor growth and probably interferes with bodily mechanisms that normally inhibit the development of tumors; however, dioxin does not cause (in the sense of instigate) cancer. Although Agent Orange has been blamed for an increase in birth defects among populations exposed to it, dioxins are not believed to be in themselves mutagenic (causing genetic mutation).

A UH-1D "Huey" helicopter from the 366th Aviation Company sprays chemical defoliant on agricultural land in the Mekong Delta. The objective of defoliating operations was to deny the Viet Cong both concealment and food sources.

A U.S. settlement with Vietnam was even longer in coming. Vietnam and the United States jointly sponsored a conference on Human Health and Environmental Impacts of Agent Orange in 2002, but discussions on a joint research project on the human health impacts of the substance broke down in 2005. In that year, however, the U.S. Environmental Protection Agency (EPA) began to cooperate with the Vietnamese government on dioxin contamination measurement projects, and in 2006 the two nations agreed to "further joint efforts to address the environmental contamination near former dioxin storage sites." Congress voted appropriations for this work in 2007, 2009, and 2010, and in 2011, U.S. funding financed decontamination of Da Nang and other dioxin hotspots.

Poverty

Traditionally, the United States has been extravagantly generous to its vanquished enemies. Germany and Japan in particular, among other World War II belligerents, benefited from rich aid and relief packages. Few Americans, however, were eager to help the putative victor in the Vietnam War, even though the Communists had suffered catastrophic casualties and property destruction. The 1973 Paris Accords included a U.S. agreement to "contribute to healing the wounds of the war and to postwar reconstruction"; in a secret letter to the Hanoi government, Nixon is said to have pledged $3.25 billion. The language of the Paris Treaty agreement was so tentative as to be—arguably, at least—nonbinding. In any case, the United States Congress chose not to be bound. The government turned a deaf ear to Vietnamese demands for the "promised" compensation.

For its part, the Hanoi regime made a dire situation much worse. Adhering to a rigidly Maoist vision of Communism, the government enforced collectivization of agriculture, which made the already critical food shortages even worse. Hanoi also outlawed all private enterprise. Even in the North, the Vietnamese people had been accustomed to an entrepreneurial culture. Compelled now to labor under a total command economy, they grew resentful and unproductive. In the South, the results of forced collectivization and the total ban on free enterprise produced a massive refugee exodus, typically and precariously via improvised boats held together with little more than a few nails and desperate hopes.

The "Boat People"

From roughly 1975 into the early 1980s, more than two million refugees fled Vietnam (and, to a lesser extent, Cambodia and Laos). When war broke out between Vietnam and the People's Republic of China in 1979, many ethnic Chinese living in Vietnam also fled.

Methods of escape were multifarious and typically began with large bribes made to local officials. Most refugees resorted to escape by sea, either by covertly buying passage in large boats, holding as many as four hundred passengers—and typically overloaded with even more—or by finding

During the "boat people" refugee crisis, thirty-five Vietnamese refugees wait to be loaded aboard the amphibious command ship USS Blue Ridge *(LCC-19) on May 15, 1984, 350 miles northeast of Cam Ranh Bay. The dangerously overloaded fishing boat is just thirty-five feet long, and the passengers have endured eight days at sea.*

or building smaller craft, including makeshift rafts. None but the very largest of these vessels were intended for navigating open seas. Most sought to land in ports in Malaysia, Thailand, the Philippines, or Hong Kong, but many simply sailed into the crowded international shipping lanes some 150 miles out to sea. Here they bobbed and drifted, exposed to vagaries of weather, including storms, waiting to be spotted and rescued by passing freighters. Some authorities estimate that half a million of what the world began calling the "boat people" died at sea—either from drowning or from hunger, thirst, exposure, or the depredations of Thai pirates. (The lower estimates range from 30,000 to 250,000 deaths.)

The volume of boat people became so great that the United Nations recognized a major humanitarian crisis and established refugee camps throughout Southeast Asia, in Malaysia, Thailand, the Philippines, Hong Kong, and Indonesia, to accommodate and "process" the refugees. Although the office of the United Nations High Commissioner for Refugees (UNHCR) received the 1981 Nobel Peace Prize for efforts to aid the boat people, conditions in the refugee camps were almost uniformly poor. Refugees were the victims of abuse, beatings, rape, and robbery (of what little they had). Although the United States—the government, charitable agencies, and private citizens—was generous with monetary aid, much of the funding provided was siphoned off by corrupt officials.

In 1979, the UNHCR instituted the

The "Boat People"(continued)

Orderly Departure program, which worked to permanently resettle refugees in the United States and other Western countries. The program did require refugees to return to Vietnam for assessment before being allowed to emigrate for resettlement. Despite this daunting condition, the program is credited with resettling at least a half-million refugees before it was discontinued in 1994.

During the boat people crisis, the United States took steps to expedite the resettlement of refugees who had worked for the Saigon government or for the United States in South Vietnam. The half-Vietnamese children of U.S. military personnel were also admitted to the expedited program. Instituted with the best of intentions, this latter provision created a lucrative black market by which well-to-do Vietnamese purchased immigration rights from real mothers or foster parents, obtained custody of the half-American children, and then used them to obtain family visas to emigrate to the United States.

One bright spot in the boat people crisis occurred on June 10, 1977, when an Israeli cargo ship encountered a ramshackle craft holding sixty-six Vietnamese refugees. The Israeli captain and crew fed them and invited them on board. They were landed in Israel, where Prime Minister Menachem Begin granted Israeli citizenship on the grounds that their situation was analogous to that of the Jews who fled the Holocaust in search of safe harbor.

By the 1980s, the United States granted refugee status to 823,000 Vietnamese and other Indochinese. Canada accepted 137,000; Australia, also 137,000; France took in 96,000 boat people; Germany, 40,000; the United Kingdom, 19,000; and Japan, 11,000.

DETAILS, DETAILS

Perpetual Target

The United States dropped 2,756,941 tons of ordnance on Cambodia between October 4, 1965, and August 15, 1973. During all of World War II, in all of its theaters, Allied air forces (United States, United Kingdom, and others) dropped a little over two million tons of ordnance. Cambodia, population 7,100,000 in 1970, is roughly 70,000 square miles in area, and almost certainly the most heavily bombed nation in history.

NEIGHBORS

VIETNAM'S NEIGHBORS, CAMBODIA AND LAOS, which had suffered throughout the war, fell victim after it to even crueler, more ideologically uncompromising Communist regimes than those that now held sway in Vietnam. On April 17, 1975, the militant nationalist-Communist Khmer Rouge overran and captured Phnom Penh, Cambodia's capital. President Nixon's quasi-covert war against the Communist insurgency in this country, including the secret bombing revealed during the Watergate scandal, had done nothing to wipe out the Khmer Rouge. When the War Powers Act of August 1973 put an end to U.S. military involvement in Cambodia, the hyper-Maoist zealot Pol Pot rose to power and forced upon his beleaguered nation his own version of Mao Zedong's Cultural Revolution. Everything had to change. Cambodia became Democratic Kampuchea; Pol Pot's government designated the first year of its absolute rule as "Year Zero"; and the inhabitants of Cambodia's cities were forced into the countryside to become collective farmers. Everyone was to be equal—equally low, as it turned out—in an agrarian Communist utopia. Purge of dissent or potential dissent drove an orgy of genocide in which some two million Cambodians, mostly urbanites, ethnic minorities, and members of the educated classes, were murdered en masse in the "killing fields," which were not only the sites of their execution but also the places of their immediate interment.

Laos came under the rule of the nationalist-Communist Pathet Lao in August 1975. Its victory in the Laotian civil war coincided with the end of intense U.S. bombing during the Vietnam War. Although the regime was less extreme than that of Pol Pot, the Pathet Lao set about taking vengeance on the Hmong, a passionately anti-Communist ethnic minority that had, as early as 1961, collaborated with the CIA against them. Of some 200,000 Hmong living in Laos in 1975, half were killed by the regime and half managed to flee. Most of them settled in the United States, which at first only grudgingly allowed immigration. Eventually, Congress passed the more welcoming Refugee Act of 1980.

A company of Hmong fighters stands to receive a final briefing before a mission in the spring of 1961. All of their weapons are U.S. supplied and include M1 Garand rifles, M1 carbines (the shorter rifles), a Browning Automatic Rifle (BAR), and a 57-mm M8A1 recoilless rifle.

The Dominoes

Cambodia and Laos proved to be the only two "dominoes" that fell after the American "loss" of Vietnam. Beyond this, the vaunted domino theory (predicting that the loss of Vietnam to Communism would mean the loss of all Southeast Asia as well as the Philippines and perhaps even Australia), introduced by Dwight Eisenhower in 1954 and taken as gospel by the next three presidents after him, proved unfounded.

October 1, 1989: The last Soviet armored personnel carriers cross the border between Afghanistan and the USSR, completing the withdrawal from the country and the war. Many compared the Soviet Union's ruinous decade in the Afghan War of 1979–89 to America's experience in Vietnam.

Observing the chaos, poverty, violence, and suffering of Vietnam, Cambodia, and Laos, the other nations of Southeast Asia became resolute in their opposition to Communism and stronger in their alignment with the United States.

Some historians (most notably Michael Lind, in his provocative *Vietnam: The Necessary War*) have argued that the United States' loss of political and military credibility in the Vietnam War emboldened the Soviet Union to embark on a resurgent Cold War push, supporting Communist regimes in Central America, Africa, and Afghanistan. Yet it is also true that the Soviet bid to extend its sphere of influence, to become, as it were, an empire (an "evil empire," as President Ronald Reagan characterized it), was both short lived and, ultimately, ruinous for the Soviets. It is not for nothing that the Soviet experience in its Afghan war, which spanned 1979 to 1989, has often been characterized as the "USSR's Vietnam." Unlike the United States, however, the Soviet Union, its economy stretched to the breaking point by its empire building and its thermonuclear arms race with America, could not survive the military, financial, and social strains of its Afghanistan quagmire. The Soviet military withdrawal from that country came just three years before the USSR itself ceased to exist.

The Soviet Union, it turned out, was the final domino to fall. As for "Red China," the breakthrough Richard M. Nixon had made, even as Watergate was just beginning to engulf his presidency and disgrace him, transformed what many American politicians had called "the mad dog of nations" into a quasi-capitalist powerhouse and the United States' most valuable trading partner and most formidable economic competitor.

A World Turned Inside Out

The United States was drawn into the Vietnam War by the dynamics of the Cold War, most specifically by the implications of the "Truman Doctrine," which demanded that the global spread of Communism be combated not by directly confronting the USSR (and, later, the People's Republic of China as well) but by "containing" Communism wherever it threatened to engulf a presumably unwilling people or country. Containment led the United States to support Turkey and Greece. It led to U.S. intervention in the Korean War. And it compelled the United States to pour 58,000 young American lives and 111 billion American dollars ($738 billion in today's dollars, adjusted for inflation) into a small, poor country in Southeast Asia. All of these military, diplomatic, and economic adventures were efforts to ensure that the global balance of power did not tip against the "free world." To Washington, Vietnam never mattered much as a country and a people. It was a domino, a placeholder in global power politics. For that reason, one American president after another invested heavily—even ruinously—in it. Two of those presidents were destroyed by it.

> "All along we argued that we wanted South Vietnamese independence, yet . . . when the South's elected officials objected to the makeup of Johnson's peace talks in Paris, we threw off the mask and said, in effect, that it was our war to dispose of as we would."

***

—Garry Wills, *Nixon Agonistes:*
The Crisis of the Self-Made Man (1969)

In the end, the resounding irony was that global power politics ultimately made the "loss" of Vietnam remarkably inconsequential—at least in geopolitical terms. In the USSR, the Soviet system was defeated by its own inability to compete in the world, not so much militarily but economically. In China, the Chinese found a way to marry Maoism to capitalism, coming in this way to discover far more common cause with the West than reasons to fear and fight it. When the world's great powers thus found they no longer had a need to fight proxy wars, the proxies themselves became largely irrelevant. Vietnam returned to being a small country, which was still poor by U.S. standards, but, thanks to gradual ideological reform and liberalization, no longer desperately so. Today, Vietnam's chief trading partners are China, Japan, Australia, Western Europe, *and* the United States, which sends nearly 440,000 tourists to the country annually.

AMERICA'S VIETNAM GENERATION

THE UNITED STATES DID NOT SUFFER, AS A RESULT OF VIETNAM, the physical ravages of war. That, of course, is the point of a proxy war. It is fought by one major power against another major power at the expense of a smaller third-party nation. Nevertheless, the financial drain was highly damaging, first to the ambitious programs of LBJ's Great Society, which were ultimately starved for funds, and, second, to the general economy, which, during the administrations of Nixon and Ford, descended into a condition economists dubbed "stagflation." It was a particularly cruel combination of recession (a *stag*nation of growth) and in*flation* (a condition that rarely occurs during a recession but did this time).

The combination of the lost opportunities of the Great Society, economic doldrums (with high unemployment), and the sense of having fought—and lost—a very dirty, almost certainly immoral, war had high costs. Jimmy Carter, who defeated Ford in the presidential election of 1976, said that the United States was immersed in a "profound moral crisis" and diagnosed the era as one of collective national "malaise."

The Great Society had been an expression of idealistic national optimism, the fulfillment of the martyred Kennedy's vision of Camelot, a bid to give everyone a share of the "American dream." Now, after a decade of seemingly futile war, California governor Jerry Brown spoke not of a nation of endless possibilities but of an American people having entered an "era of limits."

"War makes men like me, hollow men, men weighed down by memory, out of time and out of place, men who spend their lives trying to recover what has been lost, men haunted by the awful mystery that spared them, that left them alone, walking in the empty spaces."

✱✱✱

—Michael Norman, "The Hollow Man,"
New York Times Magazine, May 26, 1996

Johnny Comes Marching Home

The election to the presidency of Georgia governor Jimmy Carter, a Washington "outsider" who ran on an idealistic platform emphasizing America's global role as a defender of human rights, may be seen as a positive step in a national effort at reform and atonement. Carter pledged transparency in government (anathema to both Johnson and Nixon) and promised to put the self-determination and rights of indigenous populations ahead of any geopolitical agenda (a sharp departure from American foreign policy in the entire post–World War II era). Yet while many Americans were inclined to make amends to the world, they were not so kind to their own nation's soldiers, airmen, sailors, and marines who had returned from Vietnam. Yes, there was relief and jubilation at the repatriation of the POWs, but among the most culturally and emotionally wrenching of the war's effects on American society and culture was a persistent view of the Vietnam vet as a combination victim and psychopathic fiend. Whereas the returning soldiers of World War I were enshrined in the romantic myth of a noble "lost generation," and the veterans of World War II were celebrated (with considerable justification) as the saviors of the world and members of the "greatest generation," the Vietnam vet was too often either pointedly shunned or assumed to be damaged goods—emotionally shattered, psychologically warped, quite possibly a drug addict, and almost certainly no longer fit to make a productive contribution to civilian society.

Twenty-seven-year-old Vietnam War Marine vet Ron Kovic, paralyzed from the waist down as a result of his wounds, speaks during a 1974 press conference following a two-week hunger strike to protest "disgraceful conditions" in Veterans Administration hospitals. Kovic became famous for his 1974 memoir Born on the Fourth of July, *which was powerfully adapted in 1989 as an Oliver Stone film starring Tom Cruise.*

REALITY CHECK
The Criminality Myth

Statistically, there is no evidence to suggest a higher rate of criminal behavior among Vietnam veterans than among the U.S. general male population of comparable age and socioeconomic background.

While it was true that drug use among soldiers in Vietnam was widespread, it was also widespread among the U.S. civilian population during the late 1960s and 1970s. As for full-blown addiction, the rate was actually no greater among returning veterans than among the general American population. The neuropsychiatric effects of prolonged exposure to combat and other stresses of war, post-traumatic stress disorder (PTSD), are better understood today than they were in the 1960s and 1970s, and it is undeniable that a significant number of returning veterans had difficulty adjusting to civilian life, especially those who returned in the 1970s, when the employment outlook was increasingly bleak. Nevertheless, movies, television, and popular fiction greatly exaggerated and stereotyped the condition of the burned-out vet, no longer fit to live in civilized society, a danger to himself and others, a man whose only professions were criminality and killing.

In the next unpopular American war, the Iraq War that began in 2003 (and that was winding down by 2011), popular outrage was directed at political leaders, especially President George W. Bush and his circle, but not against soldiers. Troops were, in fact, routinely honored and thanked "for their service"—not only on public occasions but also by ordinary folks who happened to encounter a camo-clad soldier "in transit" in an airport or a bus station. During the Vietnam War, in contrast, protestors frequently referred to GIs as "baby killers." This stigma remained firmly embedded for years, even after 1975.

Emerging from the Shadow

President Jimmy Carter, who served a single term from 1977 to 1981, has been praised for his efforts to refocus U.S. foreign policy on human rights, but he also has been criticized for effectively bowing out of the Cold War, retreating into what some have called "minimal realism" or "neoisolationism," a policy aimed at preventing (as a popular phrase put

President George W. Bush, in flight suit, deplanes from an S-3B Viking, which has just landed on the flight deck of USS Abraham Lincoln *(CVN-72) on May 1, 2003. A short time later, after changing into a business suit, the president would return to a podium on the flight deck to announce an "end to major combat operations" in Iraq: "In the Battle of Iraq, the United States and our allies have prevailed," he proclaimed. Behind him, hung from the carrier's superstructure, a giant banner trumpeted, "Mission Accomplished." The war would not officially end until December 18, 2011. As of early 2013, so-called sectarian violence continues.*

it) "any more Vietnams." During the Carter years, Moscow renewed its overtures and interventions in the Third World, especially in Africa and Central America. In 1979, Marxist revolutionaries toppled the U.S.-backed government of Nicaragua. That same year, Islamic militants (not Communists) overran the U.S. Embassy in Tehran, Iran, and took its personnel hostage, holding them from November 4, 1979, to January 20, 1981. The Carter administration refused to intervene in Nicaragua and was, for 444 days, ineffectual in freeing the hostages in Iran.

President Carter was opposed in his bid for reelection in 1980 by Republican candidate Ronald Reagan. The former governor of California—who, before that, was a film and television actor—campaigned on a platform of restoring America to its former willingness and capability to intervene militarily against Communist regimes or other aggression in the world. Reagan compared the Carter foreign policy to "the sorry tapping of Neville Chamberlain's umbrella on the cobblestones of Munich." He portrayed the incumbent president as having steered the nation on a path of disengagement in the long shadow of what he repeatedly called the "Vietnam syndrome." In

President Ronald Reagan gestures toward Attorney General Edwin Meese during a White House press briefing on the Iran-Contra Affair, November 25, 1986.

contrast to Carter, candidate Reagan proposed to reengage the United States with the world, oppose the Soviets and the Chinese where necessary, and generally reclaim what the nation had lost—or felt it had lost—as a result of the course President Carter had pursued in the wake of the Vietnam War. The Reagan message resounded, and he was carried to a landslide victory. He received 489 electoral votes against Carter's 49 (representing just six states, plus the District of Columbia).

The appeal by candidate, then president, Reagan to shake off the "Vietnam syndrome" and reassert U.S. influence and power internationally had its critics. Many Americans intoned warnings of "remember Vietnam" whenever the prospect of military or quasi-military intervention was raised; however, it was Ronald Reagan who the majority elected, and it was Ronald Reagan who dared to include, in an August 19 campaign speech, the assertion that "ours was, in truth, a noble cause" in Vietnam.

The new president soon showed his willingness to engage in new proxy wars with the Soviets. In November 1981, the administration authorized funding for a CIA program to train the so-called Contras in their effort to overthrow the Marxist Sandinista regime in Nicaragua.

This aid to the right-wing guerrillas President Reagan called "freedom fighters" was publicly known and approved by Congress. But, it turned out, there was also a channel of secret, illegal, and unconstitutional support, nefarious enough to have been worthy of Richard Nixon himself.

In November 1986, during his second term, President Reagan was forced to confirm emerging reports that the United States had secretly sold arms to Iran (the very nation that had held the U.S. Embassy staff hostage for 444 days during the Carter administration). At first, the president denied rumors that the arms sale had been intended to gain the release of U.S. hostages held by terrorists in Lebanon, but he later admitted the existence of an arms-for-hostages swap. Shortly after this admission, Attorney General Edwin Meese revealed that a portion of the profits from those sales had been secretly diverted to finance the Contra rebels—even though Congress, concerned about repeating in Central America the "mistakes" of Vietnam, specifically barred such aid. Clearly, President Reagan had violated the constitutional separation of powers by acting not only without congressional approval but also in outright defiance of the expressed will of Congress. Not for nothing did the media dub the Iran-Contra Affair "Iran-gate" in deliberate echo of "Watergate."

NUMBERS
The Reagan Reelection

President Reagan had been reelected in 1984 with 59 percent of the popular vote over Democratic challenger Walter Mondale's 41 percent; however, the Democrats retained a large majority in the House and, in 1986, took the Senate as well.

"Let us beware that while they [Soviet rulers] preach the supremacy of the state, declare its omnipotence over individual man, and predict its eventual domination over all the peoples of the earth, they are the focus of evil in the modern world. . . . I urge you to beware the temptation . . . to simply call the arms race a giant misunderstanding and thereby remove yourself from the struggle between right and wrong, good and evil."

★★★

—Ronald Reagan, speech to the
National Association of Evangelicals,
March 8, 1983

There was a congressional inquiry, and many predicted that Ronald Wilson Reagan was about to go the way of Richard Milhous Nixon—into early retirement. That Reagan suffered no such fate is testament both to his personal charisma and popularity and, even more significantly, to the mood of a nation more than ready to emerge from the shadow of Vietnam.

A NEW WORLD ORDER

THE U.S. ELECTORATE DID NOT RETREAT from the Reagan foreign policy in the presidential election of 1988. Vice President George H. W. Bush handily defeated Democrat Michael Dukakis, winning 53.4 percent of the popular vote to 45.7 percent for Dukakis. In August 1990, President Bush took the nation into war against Iraq, which had invaded and annexed America's oil-rich ally Kuwait and posed a threat to Saudi Arabia, an even more important oil-rich ally. There was fear of "another Vietnam." Yet there was also overwhelming congressional support for the war and little popular protest. The main phase of the "Gulf War"—which began with an air campaign on January 17, 1991—was over approximately one hundred hours after the ground campaign kicked off on February 24. It resulted in the decimation of the Iraqi army, its weapons, and vehicles. That seemed ample vindication not only of faith in the restored competence of the all-volunteer American military but also of the Reagan-Bush interventionist foreign policy.

The American victory in the Gulf War coincided with the high drama of the imminent collapse of the Soviet Union, which would formally dissolve on December 26, 1991. More than a year before this event, on September 11, 1990, President George H. W. Bush addressed a joint session of Congress regarding the Gulf War. "We stand today," he declared, "at a unique and extraordinary moment. The crisis in the Persian Gulf, as grave as it is, also offers a rare opportunity to move toward an historic period of cooperation. Out of these troubled times . . . a new world order . . . can emerge: a new era—freer from the threat of terror, stronger in the pursuit of justice, and more secure in the quest for peace. An era in which the nations of the world, East and West, North and South, can prosper and live in harmony." With the Soviet Union crumbling and an American triumph in the Middle East seemingly certain, there was reason, this president claimed, to

see the United States as the leader, sole and unopposed, of a "new world order." The swift and total tactical victory against Iraq would, in the eyes of many Americans, redeem the American military from the stain of Vietnam. The nation's commanding position in the new world order also seemed to render the entire experience of the Vietnam War, in a word, obsolete.

President George H. W. Bush is accompanied by General H. Norman "Stormin' Norman" Schwarzkopf in a Humvee during a visit to U.S. troops stationed in Saudi Arabia as part of Operation Desert Shield in the run-up to Operation Desert Storm, a.k.a. the (first) Gulf War. The photograph was taken on November 22, 1990.

CHAPTER 17

LESSONS LEARNED,
LESSONS UNLEARNED

An American Political and Military Legacy

YEARS BEFORE IT ENDED, people were already talking about "the lessons of Vietnam." There was a broad spectrum of opinion, but three main lines of argument repeatedly emerged. Americans furthest to the left blamed the war on what they identified as essential flaws in the national character: a collective selfishness and sense of global entitlement that reached back to a nineteenth-century belief in America's "manifest destiny" and that first reached international expression in the imperialist aims of such turn-of-the-century military adventures as the Spanish-American War (1898) and the U.S. response to the Boxer Rebellion (1899–1901) in China. The sense that America was destined to dominate global affairs, the leftists argued, led the United States to make reckless alliances with inept and brutal partners in Vietnam and then prompted one president after another to double down after each inept and brutal regime failure.

Somewhat to the right of this group, liberals and centrists interpreted America's involvement in Vietnam as the product of a political-cultural myopia that could not see past Cold War motives of containing

Communism by stopping the Vietnamese "domino" from falling. This deficiency of vision prevented policymakers from seeing the realities of Vietnamese history and society. As a result, the United States supported a series of despotic and corrupt South Vietnamese leaders who neither had nor deserved the support of the Vietnamese people.

American conservatives—a bloc that grew larger after the war and during the economic crises that followed it—rejected both the "radical" and the "liberal" notions that the Vietnam War was the misbegotten spawn of flaws in the American character or perception. There was, they argued, nothing wrong with basic American values. The failure in Vietnam was a failure to wage war wholeheartedly. General of the Army Douglas MacArthur had said it back in 1951, after President Truman fired him as commander in Korea: *there is no substitute for victory*. In Vietnam, as in Korea, timid political leaders (the conservatives argued) had unconscionably sent the military in search of something less than victory. They tied the warriors' hands behind their backs. They "limited" the war. They set stunted objectives. To the degree that the top military brass accepted such misguided marching orders, the military was also to blame. And to the degree that "hippies," the antiwar movement, and the media (controlled, the conservatives argued, by liberals) protested and otherwise impeded the war effort, they, too, were to blame for the war's tragic outcome.

Out of this spectrum of opinion on lessons learned, one feeling predominated: *Let there be no more Vietnams.*

REAGANISM AND ITS DISCONTENTS

IF THE ELECTION OF RONALD REAGAN IN 1980 signaled a national readiness to emerge from the shadow of Vietnam—the "Vietnam syndrome," as Reagan called it—that election also stirred the old anxieties. These surfaced urgently on October 23, 1983, when suicide bombers drove a pair of trucks, loaded with the total equivalent of 12,000 pounds of TNT, one into the U.S. Marine barracks at Beirut International Airport and the other into the French barracks in West Beirut. Both barracks housed members of the Multinational Force (MNF) tasked by the United Nations with peacekeeping operations in perpetually troubled Beirut, Lebanon. Two hundred ninety-nine lives were lost in the attacks, most of them U.S. Marines. The month before, in September, Democratic Speaker of the House

The concrete slabs and rubble in this photograph are all that remain of the USMC barracks at Beirut International Airport after the terrorist bombing of October 23, 1983, which killed 241 marines.

Thomas "Tip" O'Neill had dispatched a congressional delegation to Lebanon to report on conditions there. Representative John Murtha of Pennsylvania issued a report on behalf of the delegation, warning of the dangerous vulnerability of the U.S. Marine detachment in Beirut. He recommended the dispersal of the marines over a wider area rather than their concentration at a location vulnerable to terrorist attack. Coming shortly after the issue of the report, the suicide bombing unleashed a storm of criticism against Reagan, including dire warnings of swaggering American global adventurism leading to the kind of recklessness that brought the nation into the "quagmire" of Vietnam.

Reagan Inoculates against the Vietnam Syndrome

President Reagan was not about to let the voices of criticism revive the "Vietnam syndrome." He would, in fact, withdraw the marines from Lebanon in February of 1984. But long before he did that—actually, on the very day after the Beirut bombing—the president briefed House and Senate leaders on his intention to invade Grenada, a tiny island nation (total population 110,000 as of 2012) in the West Indies. His objective, he explained to the legislators and would soon explain to the American people, was to rescue some one thousand U.S. nationals— mostly students at a local medical school—apparently imperiled by Grenada's Cuban-backed Marxist regime. House majority leader Jim Wright, who attended the briefing, recalled in his 1996 memoir, *Balance of Power: Presidents and Congress from the Era of McCarthy to the Age of Gingrich*, that President Reagan added, "The people there don't want to be taken over by Cuba," and went on to speculate about how wonderful it would be (in Wright's paraphrase of Reagan) "to see the local citizens once again standing on the sidewalks, waving little American flags as our liberating troops marched into the city."

Operation Urgent Fury

At the behest of Grenada's anti-American Marxist regime, Cuban troops had been sent to the island to bolster the regime of Maurice Bishop, whose Marxist-Leninist "New Jewel" movement had overthrown the existing government in a 1979 coup d'état.

Particularly alarming to President Reagan's military advisers was surveillance revealing that the Marxist-Leninist pro-Cuban regime was building a 9,800-foot airstrip, far longer than what was warranted by local commercial or tourist services and almost certainly intended to accommodate high-performance military aircraft. It was also discovered that the airstrip was being built with the aid of Cuban military personnel.

In October 1983, a new coup resulted in the deaths of Bishop and others and put Deputy Prime Minister Bernard Coard and General Hudson Austin at the head of the government. Sir Paul Scoon, Grenada's governor general (Grenada was legally part of the British Commonwealth of Nations), communicated secretly with the Organization of Eastern Caribbean States (OECS), appealing for aid to restore order. In turn, OECS requested U.S. military intervention, to which the Reagan administration responded enthusiastically.

The invasion of Grenada was code-named Operation Urgent Fury and included a naval battle group centered on the aircraft carrier USS *Independence*, as well as the helicopter carrier *Guam*, two U.S. Marine amphibious units, two Army Ranger battalions, a brigade of the 82nd Airborne Division, and various special operations units. These forces landed on Grenada on October 25, 1983. Opposing them were 500 to 600 Grenadian regulars, 2,000 to 2,500 ill-equipped Grenadian militiamen, and about 800 Cuban military construction personnel. The invasion force seized the airport and destroyed Radio Free Grenada, the government's principal broadcast facility. The U.S. nationals were evacuated without casualty among them; however, 18 U.S. personnel were killed in the assault on Grenada, and 116 were wounded. Grenadian forces lost 45 dead and 358 wounded, while Cuban casualties were 25 dead and 59 wounded. Grenada was under U.S. military control and declared secure by November 2.

Spinning Grenada

Congress did not object to the invasion, but there was a feeling—chiefly among Democrats (and, later, among many in the public, regardless of party affiliation)—that the Grenada operation was blatantly intended to quickly refocus public attention away from the tragedy in Beirut by providing the opportunity for an easy U.S. win against a soft target.

Again, President Reagan masterfully seized control of the post-Vietnam message. On October 27, 1983, he delivered a

A flight deck crewman aboard the amphibious assault ship USS Guam *(LPH 9) guides a CH-46 Sea Knight helicopter to a landing during Operation Urgent Fury— the U.S. "liberation" of Grenada.*

President Ronald Reagan, seen through the Oval Office window, drafts his televised speech on Lebanon and Grenada, October 27, 1983.

televised address on Beirut and Grenada, framing the invasion of Grenada as a necessary stand against international terrorism. He did this not by talking about Grenada but by citing "the brutal massacre of 269 men, women, and children, more than 60 of them Americans, in the shooting down of a Korean airliner" on August 31, 1983, linking this incident to *both* Beirut and Grenada by simply declaring that "in these past several days, violence has erupted again, in Lebanon and Grenada."

Strictly speaking, the airliner tragedy to which the president referred, the downing of Korean Air Lines Flight 007, was not a terrorist act. The aircraft had violated Soviet airspace—almost certainly by accident—and, presumably mistaken for a military aircraft, was shot down by overly zealous Soviet air defense personnel. At the time of the incident, President Reagan called it the "Korean airline massacre," a "crime against humanity," and an "act of barbarism . . . [and] inhuman brutality." Two months later, in his television address, he identified it as the first in a series of terrorist acts. The attack on the marines in Beirut was the second, but a third—in Grenada—had been prevented by the timely intervention of the armed forces of the United States. The association of the three episodes was neither accurate geopolitical analysis nor good history. After all, three totally different actors were involved: the Soviet Air Defense Ministry, Muslim extremists, and Cuban-supported Communists. Moreover, of the three incidents, only the Beirut bombing was unambiguously a terrorist act. Nevertheless, the collocation of the three events *was* brilliant political and emotional spin. The "Great Communicator" (as President Reagan was so often called) communicated to the American public that the invasion of Grenada had been a preemptive strike against terrorism, in effect, a necessary act of American intervention in defense of the free world against Cuban-inspired Marxist extremists.

The "Great Communicator" Stumbles

The Reagan administration took great pains to ensure that the American people would see the Grenada invasion as a stand against terrorism. To block what he feared was the liberal bias of the media (which some in the Reagan administration blamed for the failure of the Vietnam War), reporters were barred from landing with the troops, so that no reporter covered the actual landings or initial operations. No live reporting issued from Grenada until some sixty hours after the operation had been launched.

This heavy-handed information management, uncharacteristic from so media-savvy a president, alienated the press, provoking reporters to emphasize not the mission's overall success but its significant failures. The chief failure was inadequate intelligence. The invasion force was poorly informed on the whereabouts of the American medical students, who were not centrally located but were dispersed over three locations. Somewhat less critical, but highly embarrassing, were failures of military communications. Incredibly, the invading forces were not equipped with an integrated, interoperable radio system. Because they had failed to coordinate radio frequencies in advance, marines and Army Rangers were unable to talk to one another. Newspeople reported with some glee that one frustrated member of the invasion force had to place a commercial long-distance telephone call to Fort Bragg, North Carolina, in order to secure AC-130 gunship support for his unit when it came under fire.

Indeed, instead of promoting Urgent Fury as a triumphant mission to foil terrorism, the media blackout created a backlash, which reported the operation as a somewhat ineptly executed cakewalk against a pushover target.

Enter the "Weinberger Doctrine"

Surprisingly, the most significant discordant voice countering the president's triumphalist spin on the first U.S. combat deployment since the Vietnam War came from high up in the Reagan administration itself, when Secretary of Defense Caspar Weinberger delivered a speech titled "The Uses of Military Power" to the National Press Club on November 28, 1984. As if to suggest that Urgent Fury had been reckless, Weinberger sternly enumerated six conditions that, from now on, would have to be met before the United States deployed its armed forces:

1. A danger to the vital interests of the United States or its allies had to clearly exist.

2. If commitment was to be made to the use of military force, it had to be made wholeheartedly and with the unambiguous intention of winning.

3. There had to be clearly defined political and military objectives, and it must be known in advance precisely how the forces committed can accomplish them.

4. The relationship between the forces committed (composition, size, and so on) as well as the objectives had to be continually reassessed and adjusted if necessary.

5. There had to be in place "reasonable assurance we will have the support of the American people and their representatives in Congress" before combat forces could be committed abroad.

6. The use of armed force should always be regarded as the last resort.

Secretary of Defense Caspar Weinberger speaks in the Memorial Amphitheater of Arlington National Cemetery at a state funeral for "Unknown Servicemen of the Vietnam Era," May 28, 1984.

This so-called Weinberger Doctrine was clearly the product of the Beirut tragedy, the Grenada invasion, and, above all else, the Vietnam War. In the hindsight of history, the six conditions—lessons learned from Vietnam, Beirut, and Grenada—seem both eminently rational and even self-evident; yet no less a figure than Secretary of State George Shultz took issue with the Weinberger Doctrine. He protested that it created a danger of the United States becoming the "Hamlet of nations, worrying endlessly over whether and how to respond" to events and provocations in the world. Nevertheless, the Weinberger Doctrine generally prevailed until the beginning of the twenty-first century, as evidenced by the fact that when President Reagan wanted to intervene aggressively against the Marxist Sandinistas in Nicaragua, he felt he had no choice but to hide the operation from Congress. Indeed, every other military intervention through the rest of the twentieth century was eyed warily, critically, and with suspicion, including the U.S. invasion of Panama in 1989–90; the first Gulf War of 1990–91; the intervention in the war in

Bosnia and Herzegovina in 1992–95; the Somali civil war during 1992–95; and U.S. intervention in the Kosovo Crisis during 1999.

> **"One of the big lessons [of the Vietnam War] is, if you are going to be in a war, you better be in it to win, and not tie your hands the way we did."**
>
> ✳✳✳
>
> —President Reagan's secretary of state
> George P. Shultz, *New York Times Magazine*,
> January 2, 1983

THE PENTAGON PERSPECTIVE

AFTER EVERY OPERATION, LARGE OR SMALL, the U.S. military inevitably compiles a document with the phrase "Lessons Learned" in the title. The Vietnam War was no exception. Although many soldiers, sailors, marines, and airmen of every rank and grade expressed feelings of betrayal in Vietnam—betrayal by the U.S. civilian government (which ordered them to somehow prevail but not necessarily to win) and betrayal by the American people (who allowed them to go to war on their behalf only to ignore, revile, pity, or shun them when they returned)—the military did not simply grouse and brood. They pondered, and they drew up their lists of lessons learned.

Chief among these lessons was the necessity of adapting tactics to suit—precisely—whatever geopolitical strategy the United States operated from in a given situation and whatever sociopolitical context the United States operated within during a given span of time. The major tactical error of the Vietnam War was clear enough: the military tried to fight what was (at least through 1968) a guerrilla insurgency with a force equipped and trained primarily to fight a thermonuclear war against the Soviets and, secondarily, equipped and trained to fight large-scale conventional (non-nuclear) conflicts. The U.S. military was almost completely unequipped and untrained to fight against unconventional, small-unit (insurgent, guerrilla) military forma-tions. Even the "flexible response" doctrine President John F. Kennedy and his secretary of defense, Robert McNamara, advocated was never

Elite special forces at their very finest: U.S. Navy SEALs emerge from the water during a tactical warfare training exercise in 1986.

flexible enough to prevail militarily in Vietnam during the early and most critical years of the U.S. involvement in the war.

The most advanced post-Vietnam military thinkers concluded that what the United States most needed in the "new world order"—a world dominated by only one thermonuclear superpower, a world without an arms race—was a small, highly trained, thoroughly motivated professional military capable of conducting low-intensity combat missions (mainly in guerrilla conflicts and insurgency situations) anywhere in the world.

There is no doubt that, since Vietnam, the United States military has in fact developed its elite small-unit forces more extensively, including army Special Forces, marine combat units, and the Navy SEALs. Yet three factors have consistently tended to oppose and retard the evolution of a truly flexible response capability.

First, there is the culture of the American military. One of the motivations for the American Revolution was the British insistence on maintaining a large, obtrusive, and costly standing army in the American colonies. It was an imposition and an economic burden profoundly resented. Ever since then, Americans have distrusted and shunned the concept of large "regular" armies, preferring instead to raise forces only when the outbreak of war required it. As a result, the U.S. military, especially the army, has been for most of its history a small and underfunded institution. Massive armies were frenetically raised to fight the Civil War, World War I, and World War II, only to be disbanded after each conflict. With the rise of the Soviet Union as a presumably permanent threat during the Cold War, the American military became a large and politically powerful institution. Having become big, potent, and rich, there developed a natural organizational inertia dedicated not just to holding onto the gains in size, power, and budget but also to making them even bigger. The small units of the flexible response doctrine would contribute to none of this.

Second is the continued influence of the "military-industrial complex" against which President Dwight D. Eisenhower warned in his farewell address of January 17, 1961. A big military benefits big business and, thus benefited, big business supports both a big military and the elected civilian leaders who make a big military possible. The small units of the flexible response doctrine would contribute to none of this.

Third is the fact of the first Gulf War of 1990–91. Brief though its main combat phase was, that war was hardly a "low-intensity" conflict. On the contrary, it pitted the half-million-man Iraqi army—at the time the fifth-largest conventional force in the world—against the United States at the head of an international coalition of forces that included large infantry and armor (tank) formations, naval fleets, and vast numbers of aircraft ranging from helicopters, to jet fighters, to ground-attack aircraft, to heavy bombers (including the B-52 that had

Two F-16 Fighting Falcons (the aircraft in the foreground and background) and three F-15 Tomcats (the aircraft between the F-16s) fly in Operation Desert Storm, 1991.

been ubiquitous in Vietnam). The Gulf War seemed to offer conclusive proof of the ongoing need for a large conventional force. Also, the total triumph of that force (which inflicted more than 100,000 Iraq army casualties, killed and wounded, for a cost of just 1,168 coalition killed and wounded) seemed overwhelming vindication of the effectiveness of a large conventional force.

FROM NO MORE VIETNAMS TO TWO MORE VIETNAMS?

THERE WAS MUCH CELEBRATION in the immediate aftermath of the first Gulf War. President George H. W. Bush's approval rating (according to the Gallup poll) rose from a lackluster prewar 50+ percent to a high of 89 percent immediately after the liberation of Kuwait. (This did not last. Amid a deepening economic crisis, it drifted to a low of 32 percent in the summer of 1992, and Bush was defeated by Democratic upstart Bill Clinton.) The triumph against Iraq seemed so lopsided, so thorough, so unambiguous—and had come so fast—that the specter of defeat in Vietnam simply evaporated. Moreover, the nature of the war—fought with unprecedented global cooperation, with overwhelming force and availability of resources, and with a clear objective (the liberation of Kuwait and the protection of Saudi Arabia)—seemed a thorough vindication of the efficacy of the Weinberger Doctrine. Those six principles had not transformed the United States into the "Hamlet of nations"; quite the contrary, the United States performed with decisive might. The Weinberger Doctrine did, however, seem to effectively limit U.S. involvement in the war. The American military came, it saw, it conquered—then it got the hell out.

Vietnam? We *had* learned our lessons, and, contrary to the fears of some, those lessons had not paralyzed us.

Asymmetric Warfare—Lesson 1: Lowest Intensity, Highest Impact

Not everyone saw it this way. There were those who believed the first Gulf War had been left unfinished because anti-American dictator Saddam Hussein was still in power. They believed that, having won so great a military victory, the coalition or—if need be—the United States alone should have continued the war until Saddam had been toppled and a friendly regime installed. George H. W. Bush had contemplated

President George H. W. Bush meets with Secretary of Defense Dick Cheney, Chairman of the Joint Chiefs of Staff General Colin Powell, National Security Advisor Brent Scowcroft, White House Chief of Staff John Sununu, and Deputy National Security Advisor Robert Gates in the Oval Office on December 17, 1990, during the first Gulf War. As defense secretary, Cheney agreed with the president's decision to withdraw from Iraq with Saddam Hussein still in power. A dozen years later, as vice president in the George W. Bush administration, Cheney, now a confirmed "neocon," pushed for a full-on invasion to overthrow the dictator.

precisely this but rejected it because he believed that attempting to effect *and* maintain a regime change would draw the United States into a quagmire, thereby transforming Iraq into "another Vietnam." Many U.S. political leaders and many Americans accepted Bush's decision to limit the war, and they moved on; however, a group of ideologically motivated conservatives—some called them the "neocons" (*new* conservatives: *neo*conservatives)—could not let it go.

"I would guess if we had gone in there, I would still have forces in Baghdad today. We'd be running the country. We would not have been able to get everybody out and bring everybody home. . . . And the question in my mind is how many additional American casualties is Saddam [Hussein] worth? And the answer is not that damned many. So, I think we got it right."

★★★

—Secretary of Defense Dick Cheney
(under George H. W. Bush), 1992

Through the 1990s—and the two-term administration of Democrat Bill Clinton, who defeated George H. W. Bush's bid for a second term in 1992—the neocon position continued to crystallize around the issue of the "unfinished" Gulf War. The neocons believed that the United States had a duty to sow democracy throughout the world. It was both a sacred calling—God wanted all men to be free—and a pragmatic one: democratic nations do not fight one another.

In 2000, neither the Democratic presidential candidate, Vice President Al Gore, nor the Republican candidate, George H. W. Bush's son George W. Bush, provided the neocons any traction. Candidate Bush, in fact, voiced his opposition to what he called "nation building" and generally advocated a foreign policy so restrained as to verge on isolationism.

Sent to the White House after a bitterly contested election, President George W. Bush radically altered his foreign policy views after the September 11, 2001, terrorist attacks on the World Trade Center in New York City and the Pentagon in Washington, D.C., as well as the disrupted attack that had been aimed at either the White House or the U.S. Capitol and which resulted in a plane crash near Shanksville, Pennsylvania. These terrorist acts were an extreme form of asymmetric warfare—warfare in which a small, weak power attacks a much larger, much stronger power. In this case, the smaller power was not a state but was nineteen men operating under the aegis of a small but influential group of Islamist extremists calling themselves al-Qaeda (Arabic, "the Base"). For the attacker, the advantage of such asymmetry is that it left the targeted nation, big and powerful as it was, with no state against which to retaliate. President Bush pronounced the attacks the beginning of "the first war of the twenty-first century." But just who was the enemy?

The first choice was the extreme Islamist government of Afghanistan, the Taliban, which was known to shelter and support al-Qaeda and its leader, Osama bin Laden. After securing on September 18 a joint resolution from Congress authorizing the use of military force, President Bush, two days later, defined in a speech to a joint session of Congress what he called a "war on terror." On October 7, he ordered an air strike against the Taliban and al-Qaeda in Afghanistan. He then followed this on October 20 with ground raids conducted by a very small group of U.S. Special Forces working in concert with an indigenous anti-Taliban confederation of tribes dubbed the Northern Alliance. At this point, the war in Afghanistan was being fought as a low-intensity conflict in which small American units cooperated with local "assets." It was precisely the kind of warfare advanced military thinkers had contemplated in the post-Vietnam world.

Asymmetric Warfare—Lesson 2: Assess the Threat Realistically

Early progress against the Taliban was impressive, and, although bin Laden and other al-Qaeda leaders remained at large, by December 2001, the last major Taliban stronghold, Kandahar, had fallen and a new U.S.-supported government with a new U.S.-supported prime minister, Hamid Karzai, was installed. At this point, the war in Afghanistan seemed to be all but won.

This is when the clamor of neocon voices from within the Bush administration—including that of the vice president, Dick Cheney (who, as the first President Bush's secretary of defense, had vigorously opposed regime change in Iraq)—rose in volume. An improbable case was cobbled together in an attempt to frame Saddam Hussein and his regime as the ultimate perpetrators of the 9/11 attacks in that they supported anti-American terrorism. While this proved unconvincing, many Americans were nevertheless convinced. After all, Saddam had a history of ruthless tyranny, including having waged chemical warfare (with the nerve agents sarin, tabun, and VX plus mustard gas and possibly hydrogen cyanide) against Kurds in Halabja, Iraqi Kurdistan, in March 1988. At least fifteen thousand were killed or injured in those genocidal attacks. In any case, even though Saddam Hussein had *not* actually masterminded the 9/11 attacks, the Bush administration put forth evidence that he was manufacturing and stockpiling "weapons of mass destruction" (WMDs), including nuclear materials, biological agents,

U.S. Marines at their base in Kandahar prepare for a patrol in Afghanistan, December 28, 2001. They are mounted on a light armored vehicle (LAV), and an AH1W Super Cobra helicopter flies overhead.

DETAILS, DETAILS
Framing a Tyrant

In a poll taken immediately after 9/11, which asked Americans an open-ended question about who they thought was behind the attacks, 3 percent said "Iraq" or "Saddam Hussein." By January 2003, a Knight Ridder poll reported that 44 percent of Americans believed that "most" or "some" of the 9/11 terrorists were Iraqis. (None were.) A *New York Times*/CBS poll in March 2003 revealed that 45 percent of Americans believed Saddam Hussein was "personally involved" in 9/11. (He was not.)

After marines secure this area of Baghdad, an Iraqi civilian enthusiastically defaces an outdoor painting of Saddam Hussein, April 8, 2003.

and the same kinds of chemical agents he had used at Halabja. His intentions, the administration declared, were unmistakable.

Many outside of the Bush administration remained unconvinced by the evidence, until the president's secretary of state, Colin Powell, who had earned national hero status as chairman of the Joint Chiefs of Staff during the first Gulf War, presented the evidence before an internationally televised plenary session of the United Nations Security Council on February 5, 2003. In itself, the evidence was hardly conclusive, yet Saddam had proven himself to be a terrible man, bloodthirsty and vicious, and Colin Powell, well known to be opposed to the neocon element in the Bush administration, was highly respected and thoroughly trusted. Many in the international community remained unconvinced, but a majority of Americans were prepared to allow George W. Bush to go to war against Iraq.

The story, from this point on, is all too familiar. The United Nations dispatched weapons inspectors to search for the WMDs. No weapons and no evidence of weapons were found. On March 16, 2003, having previously demanded that Saddam Hussein reveal and remove the WMDs, President Bush now appeared on television with a new ultimatum to Saddam, a demand that he and his inner circle permanently leave Iraq within forty-eight hours. When the deadline passed, on March 19, the president authorized a "decapitation" attack on the Iraqi leadership, an aerial bombardment of a Baghdad bunker believed to shelter Saddam. The attack failed to kill the dictator, and a series of air strikes commenced. On March 20, ground operations began with the capture of key oil fields. U.S. and British forces (the British contributed the only sizable number of combat troops to what was otherwise overwhelmingly a U.S. effort) advanced against major Iraqi cities, one after the next falling to them.

On April 3, U.S. Special Forces troops seized the Tharthar presidential palace, just northwest of Baghdad, while other American units attacked Baghdad's Saddam International Airport, which was captured on April 4 and immediately renamed Baghdad International Airport. From the airport, the American military made its assault on Baghdad proper, which was occupied by April 9. Television pictures were beamed to the world showing massive statues of Saddam Hussein being pulled down all over the capital and elsewhere. On April 14, the Pentagon announced that the major combat phase of "Operation Iraqi Freedom" had ended, and on May 1, 2003, President Bush, arrayed in full fighter pilot gear, landed on the deck of the aircraft carrier USS *Abraham Lincoln* riding at anchor off the coast of San Diego, California. After changing into a suit and tie, he assumed a position at a lectern above and behind which, slung from the aircraft carrier's superstructure, loomed a large and colorful banner proclaiming *Mission Accomplished*. "In the Battle of Iraq," President Bush announced, "the United States and our allies have prevailed."

As we now know, of course, the "Battle of Iraq" had scarcely begun. In many respects, the war began to echo Vietnam. From the Oval Office, the administration had seen Iraq as a geopolitical objective. Close up, however, the Iraq War actually was compounded of insurgency, civil war, tribal war, religious war, and a cross-border war involving Iran. Like Vietnam, Iraq turned out to be much more than an ideological target to be hit with the golden arrow of democracy. Like Vietnam, it turned out to be a real country with real people who had real conflicts among themselves that had nothing to do with geopolitics, U.S. politics, or a desire for democracy. And none of it, of course, actually had anything at all to do with what happened in the United States on September 11, 2001.

By the time President Barack Obama announced on October 28, 2011, that most U.S. troops would be withdrawn from Iraq by the end of the year, the nearly nine-year war had cost 4,409 American lives and at least one trillion American dollars. As costly as this was, the military mission in Iraq, a nation that had had nothing to do with 9/11, had even further ramifications in that it drained resources from the war in Afghanistan, a country directly linked to the terrorist attacks that had precipitated both wars. As a result, many of the gains made early in the

NUMBERS
Iraq War Casualties

The U.S. armed forces lost 4,409 killed in action (KIA) and 31,922 wounded in action (WIA) in the Iraq War. Other coalition deaths totaled 318 KIA. U.S.-aligned Iraqi security forces lost 16,623 KIA. The number of Iraqi civilian, military, and insurgent battle deaths are disputed, but certainly number in excess of 100,000.

After landing on the flight deck of the USS Abraham Lincoln off the coast of San Diego, President George W. Bush announces an "end to major combat operations" in Iraq on May 1, 2003. The words "Mission Accomplished" emblazoned on the banner behind him would haunt the remainder of the Bush presidency with their unintended bitter irony. They would not, however, prevent his reelection in 2004.

NUMBERS

Afghanistan War Casualties

U.S. military deaths in Afghanistan as of September 6, 2012, stood at 2,114 KIA. Total NATO coalition deaths, including U.S. deaths, were 3,171 KIA. Afghani military deaths numbered 10,086 KIA; civilian deaths, more than 10,000.

Afghanistan war were lost. The Taliban and other Islamic extremist contenders have become resurgent, relatively little of the country is under the direct control of the Karzai government, and, as of fall 2012, the war continues—although President Obama has announced a plan to withdraw the last American troops in 2014.

The war in Iraq did result in the overthrow and, ultimately, the execution of Saddam Hussein. In 1992, Dick Cheney—former secretary of defense under George H. W. Bush, and future vice president under

George W. Bush—had posed the rhetorical question, "[H]ow many additional American casualties is Saddam [Hussein] worth?" His answer (back then): "not that damned many." Suicide bombings, the explosion of mines (improvised explosive devices, or IEDs), and shootings continue routinely. The fate of Iraq's government and people after the December 2011 American military withdrawal continues to be difficult to predict. How that fate will affect the United States is even more difficult to speculate about. The same might be said of Afghanistan, except that the current condition of that country is far more chaotic than that of Iraq. Its fate after the projected 2014 U.S. pullout may therefore be more easily predicted in just two words, *continued violence*, though how the United States will respond is also beyond speculation.

Funeral for a Navy SEAL, Arlington National Cemetery, October 4, 2010. Lieutenant Brendan Looney was one of nine service members killed in a helicopter crash in Zabul Province, Afghanistan, on September 21, 2010.

TAKEAWAY

The Weinberger Doctrine Rises— and Falls

The Vietnam War yielded very useful, prudent, and carefully articulated lessons intended to prevent "more Vietnams," to ensure that future wars would be both necessary and winnable, and to create military tactics for fighting likely future wars more effectively than the U.S. military waged war in Vietnam. As codified in the Weinberger Doctrine of 1984, these lessons guided the use of military force through the rest of the twentieth century. In response to the September 11, 2001, terrorist attacks against the United States, the Weinberger Doctrine, together with all other lessons of the Vietnam War, was set aside in an ideologically driven rush to war, first in Afghanistan and then in Iraq. As with the Vietnam War, both of these conflicts were born of a failure to assess threats accurately and resulted in human and economic costs far beyond any conceivable benefit.

It would be difficult to find anyone in American political life who is satisfied with the current status or outcome of the wars in Iraq and Afghanistan; however, very few politicians or political pundits have compared these wars to Vietnam. Perhaps that is best. For they are, in fact, very different. Yet, for all their differences, there is one overriding lesson from Vietnam that applies to all three wars and should apply to any future provocations. Call it Lesson 2 in the nature of asymmetric warfare: *assess the threat realistically.*

In Southeast Asia, one American presidential administration after another assessed the threat posed by Vietnam as that of a "domino" whose fall would inevitably trigger a hemispherical Communist revolution. It was not a realistic assessment, and it therefore led to a

disproportionate expenditure of blood and treasure to achieve an unrealistic outcome that nevertheless resulted in all-too-real agony and loss.

On September 11, 2001, nineteen religious zealots hijacked four commercial airliners to commit acts of unspeakably murderous criminality. Ideological zealots highly placed in the American presidential administration assessed these acts as threats to the very existence of the United States, and a terrified nation (for the objective of terrorism is of course the creation of terror) allowed itself to be persuaded of the accuracy of this assessment. As in Southeast Asia in the 1950s, 1960s, and 1970s, the threat was incorrectly assessed and the response, accordingly, disproportionate. In Afghanistan and Iraq, as in Vietnam, far more was sacrificed than won in war.

Thousands gather before the Vietnam Veterans Memorial to commemorate Veterans Day, November 11, 2006. Designed by American architect Maya Lin for placement on the National Mall in Washington, "The Wall," etched with names of all U.S. service personnel who were killed in the Vietnam War, draws some four million visitors annually.

VIETNAM WAR TIMELINE

1944

DECEMBER 22: The Vietnam People's Army, known during the Vietnam War as the North Vietnamese Army (NVA) or People's Army of Vietnam (PAVN), is created in response to French colonization.

1945

SEPTEMBER 26: OSS operative A. Peter Dewey is shot by Viet Minh, becoming the first American fatality in French Indochina.

1950

AUGUST: President Harry S. Truman sends the U.S. Military Assistance Advisory Group (MAAG) to South Vietnam to assist the French in the First Indochina War (1946–54).

1954

MAY 7: Communist forces defeat the French at Dien Bien Phu, effectively ending the French Indochina War (1946–54).

OCTOBER 24: President Eisenhower pledges support to the State of Vietnam (South Vietnam) government of Ngo Dinh Diem.

1955

OCTOBER 23: Diem holds a referendum to approve the creation of a Vietnamese republic with himself as its president.

OCTOBER 26: Based on the (rigged) results of the referendum, Diem proclaims himself president of the new Republic of Vietnam (South Vietnam).

1956

APRIL: France withdraws all troops from Vietnam.

JUNE 8: Technical Sergeant Richard B. Fitzgibbon Jr. becomes the first American serviceman officially classified as KIA in Vietnam.

1959

MAY 19: The NVA creates Group 559, responsible for infiltrating troops and supplies from North Vietnam into South Vietnam via the Ho Chi Minh Trail, which the group develops in neighboring Cambodia.

1961

AUGUST 10: The aerial spraying of herbicides (Agent Orange, etc.) is first tested in Vietnam.

DECEMBER 11: As part of President John F. Kennedy's increase in the size of MAAG in Vietnam, U.S. helicopters arrive in South Vietnam, to be flown and maintained by U.S. personnel (who join some 3,000 MAAG "advisers" already in-country).

25 U.S. service members killed from 1956–61.

1962

JANUARY: Operation Ranch Hand begins—the massive aerial spraying of defoliant herbicides; it will continue into 1971.

JANUARY 12: In Operation Chopper, U.S. Army helicopter pilots fly Army of the Republic of Vietnam (ARVN) troops into combat near Saigon. This is the first U.S. combat mission of the Vietnam War.

52 U.S. service members killed in 1962.

1963

JANUARY 2: In the Battle of Ap Bac, the Viet Cong (VC) defeat an ARVN unit and kill three U.S. Army "advisers."

NOVEMBER 2: South Vietnamese president Ngo Dinh Diem is overthrown and assassinated in a CIA-supported coup d'état; he and his government are replaced in the short term by a series of provisional leaders and governments fitfully propped up by the United States.

NOVEMBER 22: President John F. Kennedy is assassinated; Vice President Lyndon Baines Johnson is sworn in.

118 U.S. service members killed in 1963.

1964

APRIL–JUNE: President Johnson authorizes a massive buildup of U.S. air power in South Vietnam.

JUNE: William Westmoreland assumes overall command of U.S. military operations in South Vietnam.

AUGUST 2 AND 4: The Gulf of Tonkin Incident is reported.

AUGUST 7: Congress passes the Gulf of Tonkin Resolution.

NOVEMBER 1: VC shell the USAF Bien Hoa Air Base, inflicting four U.S. deaths, wounding seventy-six, and destroying or damaging several USAF aircraft.

DECEMBER 24: VC agents bomb the Brinks Hotel, used as bachelors' quarters by U.S. military officers.

206 U.S. service members killed in 1964.

DECEMBER 28: VC overrun Binh Gia, South Vietnam, killing some two hundred ARVN troops and five U.S. advisers.

1965

FEBRUARY 7: President Johnson orders U.S. Navy air attacks inside North Vietnam as retaliation for an attack on a U.S. helicopter base in the Central Highlands.

FEBRUARY 10: A VC bomb explodes in a Qui Nhon hotel frequented by GIs, killing twenty-three U.S. soldiers.

FEBRUARY 13: Johnson authorizes Operation Rolling Thunder, which commences on March 2.

MARCH 8–9: The first American combat ground forces (not advisers) arrive in Vietnam.

APRIL 3: A combined U.S. Navy and Air Force air campaign targets North Vietnam's transport network.

APRIL 7: President Johnson offers North Vietnam civil and educational aid in exchange for peace. The offer is spurned.

APRIL 17: Protestors stage the first major antiwar rally in Washington, D.C.

MAY 11: The VC attack Song Be, capital of Phuoc Long Province.

JUNE 9–13: U.S. Marines and NVA troops fight the largest battle to date near the DMZ at Dong Xoai. After overrunning the ARVN district headquarters and U.S. special forces camp there, the Viet Cong withdraw under heavy U.S. air attack.

JUNE 28: General Westmoreland launches the first combined U.S.-ARVN offensive operation into VC territory northwest of Saigon.

AUGUST 18-24: Operation Starlite is a major U.S. victory at Chu Lai.

OCTOBER 23–NOVEMBER 20: Operation Silver Bayonet—After the NVA attacks the USMC base at Plei Mei, the U.S. 1st Cavalry Division (Airmobile) responds, initiating the four-day Battle of Ia Drang (November 14–18), in which the Communists are forced to withdraw into Cambodia.

NOVEMBER 17: An NVA regiment on the march near Plei Mei ambushes a U.S. battalion, exacting a 60 percent casualty rate; one third of the U.S. force is KIA.

U.S. personnel in Vietnam: 189,000

1,863 U.S. service members killed in 1965.

1966

JANUARY 8: Operation Crimp is launched to interdict ("crimp") Communist lines of infiltration, including the Cu Chi tunnels.

MARCH 5: At the Battle of Lo Ke, U.S. air assaults force VC attackers to retreat.

APRIL 24–MAY 17: Operation Birmingham kills 119 VC; survivors retreat into Cambodia.

JULY 15–AUGUST 3: In Operation Hastings, U.S.-ARVN forces push the NVA north across the DMZ.

SEPTEMBER 14–NOVEMBER 24: U.S.-ARVN forces conduct a major search-and-destroy sweep northwest of Dau Tieng, killing more than two thousand NVA and VC and capturing or destroying a large amount of weapons and supplies.

U.S. personnel in Vietnam: 385,000

6,143 U.S. service members killed in 1966.

1967

JANUARY 8–26: In Operation Cedar Falls, U.S.-ARVN forces conduct a search-and-destroy sweep of the "Iron Triangle," a Communist stronghold near Saigon; the results are mixed: while militarily successful in the short term, the accompanying pacification program failed both morally and strategically.

JANUARY–MAY: North Vietnamese forces bombard U.S. bases near the DMZ.

FEBRUARY 22–MAY 14: In Operation Junction City, U.S.-ARVN forces conduct the largest airborne operation since World War II. The operation fails to make a strategic impact, but does kill (according to the U.S. commanders) 2,728 VC.

APRIL 24: U.S. air assaults against North Vietnamese air bases degrade the Communists' ability to engage U.S. aircraft with their Soviet-built MiGs.

MAY 1967: U.S. pilots shoot down twenty-six North Vietnamese MiGs over Haiphong and Hanoi. Also during this period, U.S. forces intercept NVA units in the Central Highlands, inflicting heavy casualties.

OCTOBER 21–23: Between 50,000 and 100,000 demonstrate against the war in Washington, D.C.

U.S. personnel in Vietnam: 486,000

11,153 U.S. service members killed in 1967.

1968

JANUARY 21: The Battle of Khe Sanh and its six-month siege begins near the DMZ.

JANUARY 30: The Tet Offensive begins. Phase 1 continues to March 28; Phase 2, from May 5 to June 15; Phase 3, from August 17 to August 30. A joint U.S.-ARVN tactical triumph, the Tet Offensive

is nevertheless a major strategic psychological victory for the Communists, effectively undercutting U.S. popular and political support for continuing the war.

MARCH 16: The My Lai massacre occurs; it is not revealed until November 1969.

MARCH 31: President Johnson announces his decision not to seek reelection.

APRIL 8: The seventy-seven-day Battle of Khe Sanh ends with the withdrawal of Communist forces; however, General Westmoreland orders the abandonment of Khe Sanh.

MAY 13: The Paris Peace Talks begin.

NOVEMBER 1: Operation Rolling Thunder ends.

NOVEMBER 5: Richard M. Nixon is elected president—in part on a platform that promises "peace with honor" in Vietnam.

U.S. personnel in Vietnam: 542,000

16,592 U.S. service members killed in 1968.

1969

FEBRUARY 23: A major Communist offensive throughout much of South Vietnam kills 1,140 U.S. troops.

MARCH 18, 1969–MAY 28, 1970: Authorized by President Nixon, Operation Menu is the massive but secret (unknown to Congress and the American public) bombing of North Vietnamese troop and supply bases in Cambodia and Laos.

JUNE 8: After meeting with South Vietnam's President Nguyen Van Thieu, Nixon announces the withdrawal of 25,000 U.S. troops in a program to "Vietnamize" the war.

NOVEMBER 15: 250,000–500,000 people demonstrate against the war in Washington, D.C.

U.S. personnel in Vietnam: 475,200

11,616 U.S. service members killed in 1969.

1970

APRIL 29–JULY 22: U.S. and South Vietnamese forces invade Cambodia, inflicting many casualties and capturing large amounts of supplies and equipment, but failing to interdict the flow of supplies and personnel into South Vietnam via the Ho Chi Minh Trail.

MAY 4: Ohio National Guardsmen kill four students and wound nine in shootings at Kent State University during protests that are part of demonstrations on many U.S. campuses sparked by the Cambodian invasion.

U.S. personnel in Vietnam: 336,000

6,081 U.S. service members killed in 1970.

1971

FEBRUARY 8–MARCH 25: South Vietnamese and U.S. forces invade Laos in Operation Lam Son 719, which is yet another attempt to interdict the Ho Chi Minh Trail; the operation not only fails but also becomes a costly U.S.-ARVN defeat.

U.S. personnel in Vietnam: 133,200

2,357 U.S. service members killed in 1971.

1972

MARCH 30: "Easter Offensive"—With the U.S. ground combat presence in South Vietnam reduced by two-thirds from its 1968 high of 542,000, the NVA launches heavy conventional attacks across the DMZ, using artillery and armor. On this date, some 20,000 NVA cross the DMZ into South Vietnam, sending ARVN units into panicked retreat.

APRIL 1–9: "Easter Offensive"—In the Battle of Hue, NVA units assault the city, but are forced into retreat.

APRIL 13: "Easter Offensive"—Renewing the attack on Hue, the NVA seizes part of the old capital before being forced to withdraw by a combination of ARVN ground defense and U.S. B-52 bombardment.

APRIL 29: "Easter Offensive"—Dong Ha falls to the NVA.

MAY 1: "Easter Offensive"—Quang Tri City falls to the NVA.

JULY 19–SEPTEMBER 15: "Easter Offensive"— Supported by U.S. air power, ARVN units counterattack in Binh Dinh Province in an effort to retake Quang Tri City and Dong Ha. The NVA partially withdraws.

OCTOBER 22: The so-called Easter Offensive ends.

OCTOBER 26: U.S. negotiator Henry Kissinger and North Vietnam's Le Duc Tho reach a ceasefire agreement in Paris; Kissinger announces that "peace is at hand."

NOVEMBER 7: Largely on the promise that "peace is at hand," Richard M. Nixon is reelected; he repudiates the Kissinger–Le Duc Tho ceasefire agreement almost immediately.

DECEMBER 13: The Paris Peace Talks break down.

DECEMBER 18: In a bid to force the North Vietnamese back to the conference table in Paris, President Nixon authorizes Operation Linebacker II, a massive eleven-day bombing of North Vietnamese targets, with concentration at Haiphong and Hanoi. Haiphong Harbor is also mined from the air during this period.

U.S. personnel in Vietnam: 45,600

641 U.S. service members killed in 1972.

1973

JANUARY 8: The Paris Peace Talks resume.

JANUARY 27: The Paris Peace Accords are signed; Secretary of Defense Melvin R. Laird suspends the U.S. military draft.

MARCH 29: The last U.S. ground combat troops leave Vietnam.

168 U.S. service members killed in 1973.

1974

AUGUST 9: Finally succumbing to the Watergate Affair, Richard M. Nixon resigns as president and is replaced by Vice President Gerald Ford. Congress repeatedly slashes funding for the Vietnam War.

SEPTEMBER 16: President Gerald Ford offers clemency to draft evaders and military deserters.

DECEMBER 26: Dong Xoai falls to the NVA.

178 U.S. service members killed in 1974.

1975

JANUARY 6: Phuoc Long falls to the NVA.

JANUARY 8: North Vietnamese politburo orders offensive to "Liberate" South Vietnam by NVA cross-border invasion.

MARCH 1: A massive NVA offensive begins in the Central Highlands; throughout the month, all major South Vietnamese cities begin to fall or do fall to the Communists.

MARCH 25: Hue falls to the NVA.

APRIL 21: South Vietnamese President Thieu resigns; Tran Van Huong becomes president.

APRIL 28: Tran Van Huong resigns; Duong Van Minh becomes president.

APRIL 29–30: U.S. Air Force fixed-wing aircraft and U.S. Navy and Marine helicopters evacuate American personnel and South Vietnamese refugees.

APRIL 30: Saigon falls. After serving for three days, South Vietnamese President Duong Van Minh surrenders, and Vietnam is reunified under a Communist regime.

161 U.S. service members killed in 1975.

839 U.S. service members killed from 1976.

LIVE AND IN PERSON

In Vietnam

Vietnam has a lively tourist industry, and the government maintains a number of historic war sites that may be visited.

CU CHI TUNNELS

This remarkable network of tunnels, some of which are open to visitors, was typical of Viet Cong infiltration of South Vietnam. Located fifty-five miles northwest of Ho Chi Minh City (formerly Saigon), Cu Chi is popular with tourists.

HOA LO PRISON ("HANOI HILTON")

The infamous "Hanoi Hilton" housed U.S. POWs, including senator and 2008 presidential candidate John McCain (a U.S. Navy aviator). It was originally built by the French during 1886–1901. Most of the original prison was demolished in the mid-1990s to make way for two modern high-rise buildings. Part of the prison was preserved, however, and is maintained as a significantly "sanitized" museum; for example, the infamous "blue room"—site of prisoner interrogation—now appears to be a rather comfortable barracks-like quarters. The museum

may be visited daily for a very modest entrance fee (the equivalent of about 50 U.S. cents).

HUE

This extraordinary city was the feudal and imperial capital of Vietnam (and has many sites dating from its ancient past) as well as the object of several major battles during the Vietnam War. Its architectural treasures, which fortunately survived the war, are on the UNESCO list of World Heritage Sites. The city is midway between Hanoi (335 miles to the north) and Ho Chi Minh City (formerly Saigon, 400 miles south).

NHA TRANG

A beach resort during the Vietnam War (when it was frequented by GIs on R&R) as well as today, Nha Trang was also home to the Cam Ranh USAF Air Base (today serving as the city's airport). With traffic and narrow roads, Nha Trang is an eleven-hour bus ride from Ho Chi Minh City (formerly Saigon).

REUNIFICATION PALACE

Formerly known as Independence Palace, this was the combination South Vietnamese "Capitol" and (during the administration of President Thieu) "White House." It was also where the Vietnam War ended with the reunification of the nation under a Communist government on April 30, 1975. Reunification Palace is open to visitors daily;

admission is the equivalent of about 75 cents. English-speaking tour guides are available free of charge.

WAR REMNANTS MUSEUM

Until 1993 known as the Museum of American War Crimes, the War Remnants Museum is located at 28 Vo Tan Tan, District 3, Ho Chi Minh City. Three floors house many artifacts from the war, most of them U.S. weapons, ammunition, aircraft wrecks, and vehicles. The museum is open daily, and admission is the equivalent of 75 U.S. cents.

In the United States

AIR FORCE HISTORICAL RESEARCH AGENCY

The main repository for all historical documents (including photo and film archives) relating to the USAF, the center houses extensive Vietnam-era materials.

Online access: http://www.afhra.af.mil/

AFHRA
600 Chennault Circle
Maxwell AFB, AL 36112-6424
Telephone: 334-953-2395
Operating hours: 8:30 a.m.–4:00 p.m., Monday through Friday

NATIONAL ARCHIVES

The National Archives maintains an extensive collection of military records from the Vietnam War and Vietnam War era.

Online access: http://www.archives.gov/research/military/vietnam-war/

National Archives in Washington, D.C.
700 Pennsylvania Avenue NW
Washington, DC 20409
1-866-272-6272
Operating hours: 9:00 a.m.–5:00 p.m., Monday, Tuesday, Saturday
Operating hours: 9:00 a.m.–9:00 p.m., Wednesday, Thursday, Friday

NAVAL HISTORY & HERITAGE COMMAND (NHHC)

Of particular interest are the resources devoted to river warfare in Vietnam and naval aviation, both of which were central to the war. The headquarters of the NHHC is located at the Washington Navy Yard in Washington, D.C.

Online access: http://www.history.navy.mil/

For information on regional U.S. Navy museums, consult http://www.history.navy.mil/museums/index.html.

National Museum of the United States Navy

Located at the Washington Navy Yard in southwest Washington, D.C. Its hours of operation are 9 a.m. to 5 p.m., Monday through Friday, and 10 a.m. to 5 p.m. on Saturday and Sunday. Telephone 202-433-4882.

National Naval Aviation Museum

An outstanding collection of U.S. Navy aircraft, including all those used in the Vietnam era. It is located at Pensacola Naval Air Station, Pensacola, Florida, 32508, and is open daily from 9 a.m. to 5 p.m. Admission is free. Telephone 850-452-3604.

Navy Department Library

The central location for historical documents and photographs. Located at the Navy Yard in Washington, the library can be contacted at 202-433-4132. It is open from 9 a.m. to 4 p.m. Monday through Friday (with reference assistance unavailable on Wednesdays).

U.S. ARMY CENTER OF MILITARY HISTORY

The Center's Vietnam collections are rich and include documents, photographs, and films (many now available in digital format). This is a good place to research individual unit histories. Also see http://www.history.army.mil/museum.html, which is a detailed directory of the Army Museum System and a good way to find local and regional museums that have Vietnam War collections.

Online access: www.history.army.mil

U.S. Army Center of Military History
Collins Hall
103 Third Avenue
Fort Lesley J. McNair, DC 20319-5058
Telephone: 202-685-4042

Visitor hours are from 9:00 a.m. to 4:00 p.m., Monday through Friday

U.S. MARINES HISTORY DIVISION

As the service branch specializing in small-unit, anti-insurgency operations, the U.S. Marines played a central role throughout the Vietnam War. In addition to an extensive document and photograph collection, the History Division maintains a superb oral history collection, with many recordings and transcriptions from Vietnam veterans.

Online access: http://www.tecom.usmc.mil/HD/Home_Page.htm

Marine Corps University
Marine Corps History Division
3078 Upshur Avenue
Quantico, Virginia 22134
Telephone: 703-784-2606

THE VIETNAM CENTER AND ARCHIVE

An extensive collection of documentary materials on the Vietnam War, with an emphasis on personal histories and oral histories.

Online access: www.vietnam.ttu.edu

The Vietnam Center
PO Box 41045
Math Building, Room 4
Texas Tech University Campus
Lubbock, Texas 79409-1045

The Vietnam Archive

PO Box 41041
Southwest Collection/Special Collections
  Library
Room 108
2805 15th Street
Texas Tech University Campus
Lubbock, Texas 79409-1041

Telephone: 806-742-3742 (Center),
806-742-9010 (Archive)

VIETNAM VETERANS MEMORIAL

Located in Constitution Gardens adjacent to the National Mall in Washington, D.C., the Vietnam Veterans Memorial honors members of the U.S. armed forces who fought in the Vietnam War. Its central feature is the Memorial Wall, designed by American architect Maya Lin, on which the names of 587,175 U.S. service members killed in the war are engraved. The memorial also includes *The Three Soldiers*, a bronze statue by Frederick Hart depicting three Vietnam-era servicemen (one white, one African American, one Hispanic); the Vietnam Women's Memorial, designed by Glenna Goodacre to honor American women who served in the Vietnam War (mainly as nurses); and the "In Memory" memorial plaque, which honors soldiers who died after the war as a result of injuries suffered during the conflict. The Vietnam Veterans Memorial is open 24 hours, seven days a week, with National Park Service rangers on duty from 9:30 a.m. to 11:30 p.m. daily. Admission is free of charge.

READ MORE, SEE MORE

Sources for This Book

NONFICTION

These works of nonfiction narrative and reference are highly recommended.

Allen, Joe. *Vietnam: The (Last) War the U.S. Lost.* Chicago: Haymarket Books, 2008.

Amter, Joseph A. *Vietnam Verdict: A Citizen's History.* New York: Continuum, 1982.

Anderson, David L. *The Columbia History of the Vietnam War.* New York: Columbia University Press, 2010.

————. *The Vietnam War.* New York: Palgrave Macmillan, 2005.

Baritz, Loren. *Backfire: A History of How American Culture Led Us into Vietnam and Made Us Fight the Way We Did.* New York: Morrow, 1985.

Bernstein, Carl, and Bob Woodward. *All the President's Men: 20th Anniversary Edition.* New York: Simon & Schuster, 2007.

Borer, Douglas A. *Superpowers Defeated: Vietnam and Afghanistan Compared.* London: Frank Cass, 1999.

Bradley, Mark Philip. *Vietnam at War.* New York: Oxford University Press, 2009.

Buttinger, Joseph. *Vietnam: A Dragon Embattled.* New York: Praeger, 1967.

————. *Vietnam: The Unforgettable Tragedy.* New York: Horizon Books, 1977.

Carter, James M. *Inventing Vietnam: The United States and State Building, 1954–1968.* New York: Cambridge University Press, 2008.

Colby, William, with James McCargar. *Lost Victory.* Chicago: Contemporary Books, 1989.

Corfield, Justin. *The History of Vietnam.* Westport, CT: Greenwood, 2008.

Daugherty, Leo J., and Gregory Louis Mattson. *Nam: A Photographic History.* New York: Barnes & Noble, 2004.

Davidson, Gen. Phillip B. *Vietnam at War: The History 1946–1975.* Novato, CA: Presidio, 1988.

DeGroot, Gerald J. *A Noble Cause? America and the Vietnam War.* London: Longman, 1999.

Dommen, Arthur J. *The Indochinese Experience of the French and the Americans: Nationalism and Communism in Cambodia, Laos, and Vietnam.* Bloomington, IN: Indiana University Press, 2001.

Duiker, William J. *Sacred War: Nationalism and Revolution in a Divided Vietnam.* New York: McGraw-Hill, 1995.

Dunnigan, James F., and Albert A. Nofi. *Dirty Little Secrets of the Vietnam War.* New York: Thomas Dunne Books (St. Martin's Press), 1999.

Edmonds, Anthony O. *The War in Vietnam.* Westport, CT: Greenwood, 1998.

Elliott, David. *The Vietnamese War: Revolution and Social Change in the Mekong Delta, 1930–1975.* Armonk, NY: M.E. Sharpe, 2003.

Ellsberg, Daniel. *Secrets: A Memoir of Vietnam and the Pentagon Papers.* New York: Viking, 2002.

Esper, George, and the Associated Press. *The Eyewitness History of the Vietnam War, 1961–1975.* New York: Ballantine, 1983.

Fitzgerald, Frances. *Fire in the Lake: The Vietnamese and the Americans in Vietnam.* New York: Random House, 1972.

Gilbert, Marc Jason, ed. *Why the North Won the Vietnam War.* New York: Palgrave Macmillan, 2002.

Guan, Ang Cheng. *The Vietnam War from the Other Side: The Vietnamese Communists' Perspective.* London and New York: RoutledgeCurzon, 2002.

————. *Ending the Vietnam War: The Vietnamese Communists' Perspective.* London and New York: RoutledgeCurzon, 2004.

Halberstam, David. *The Best and the Brightest.* New York: Modern Library, 2002.

Haycraft, William Russell. *Unraveling Vietnam: How American Arms and Diplomacy Failed in Southeast Asia.* Jefferson, NC: McFarland, 2006.

Hearden, Patrick J. *The Tragedy of Vietnam.* Third edition. New York: Longman, 2008.

Herring, George C. *America's Longest War: The United States and Vietnam, 1950–1975.* Fourth edition. New York: McGraw-Hill, 2002.

Hunt, David. *Vietnam's Southern Revolution: From Peasant Insurrection to Total War.* Amherst: University of Massachusetts Press, 2008.

Kahin, George M. *Intervention: How America Became Involved in Vietnam.* New York: Knopf, 1986.

Karnow, Stanley. *Vietnam: A History.* Second revised and updated edition. New York: Penguin, 1997.

Kolko, Gabriel. *Anatomy of a War: Vietnam, the United States, and the Modern Historical Experience.* New York: Pantheon, 1985.

Krepinevich, Andrew F., Jr. *The Army in Vietnam.* Baltimore, MD: Johns Hopkins University Press, 1986.

Lawrence, Mark Atwood. *The Vietnam War: A Concise International History.* New York: Oxford University Press, 2008.

Lederer, William J., and Eugene Burdick. *The Ugly American.* 1958; reprint edition. New York: W. W. Norton & Co., 1999.

Lind, Michael. *Vietnam, the Necessary War: A Reinterpretation of America's Most Disastrous Military Conflict.* New York: The Free Press, 1999.

MacPherson, Myra. *Long Time Passing: Vietnam and the Haunted Generation.* New edition. Bloomington: Indiana University Press, 2002.

Mann, Robert. *A Grand Delusion: America's Descent into Vietnam.* New York: Basic Books, 2001.

Military History Institute of Vietnam. *Victory in Vietnam: The Official History of the People's Army of Vietnam, 1954–1975.* Lawrence: University Press of Kansas, 2002.

Phillips, Rufus. *Why Vietnam Matters: An Eyewitness Account of Lessons Not Learned.* Annapolis, MD: Naval Institute Press, 2008.

Podhoretz, Norman. *Why We Were in Vietnam.* New York: Simon & Schuster, 1982.

Pollard, Robert, ed., *Some Lessons and Non-Lessons of Vietnam: Ten Years after the Paris Accords.* Washington, DC: Woodrow Wilson International Center for Scholars, 1983.

Prados, John. *Vietnam: The History of an Unwinnable War, 1945–1975.* Lawrence: University Press of Kansas, 2009.

Schandler, Herbert Y. *America in Vietnam: The War That Couldn't Be Won.* Lanham, Md.: Rowman & Littlefield, 2009.

Sheehan, Neil. *A Bright Shining Lie: John Paul Vann and America in Vietnam.* New York: Random House, 1988.

Sorley, Lewis. *A Better War: The Unexamined Victories and Final Tragedy of America's Last Years in Vietnam.* New York: Harcourt, 1999.

Summers, Col. Harry. *On Strategy: The Vietnam War in Context.* Novato, CA: Presidio, 1982.

U.S. Department of Defense. *The Pentagon Papers.* N.p.: Grotto Pulp Fiction (Kindle edition), 2010.

Wright, Jim. *Balance of Power: Presidents and Congress from the Era of McCarthy to the Age of Gingrich.* Atlanta: Turner Publishing, 1996.

FICTION

Some of the most popular novels of the Vietnam War.

Coonts, Stephen. *Flight of the Intruder: 20th Anniversary Edition.* Annapolis, MD: U.S. Naval Institute Press, 2006.

Greene, Graham. *The Quiet American.* London: William Heinemann, 1955.

Hasford, Gustav. *The Short Timers.* New York: Harper & Row, 1979.

Marlantes, Karl. *Matterhorn: A Novel of the Vietnam War.* New York: Atlantic Monthly Press, 2010.

Morrell, David. *First Blood.* New York: Morrow, 1972.

O'Brien, Tim. *Going After Cacciato.* Garden City, NY: Doubleday, 1978.

————. *In the Lake of the Woods.* New York: McClelland & Stewart, 1995.

Sherman, David. *A Nghu Night Falls.* New York: Ballantine, 1988.

————. *Charlie Don't Live Here Anymore.* New York: Ballantine, 1989.

Soli, Tatjana. *The Lotus Eaters.* New York: St. Martin's Press, 2010.

Webb, James. *Fields of Fire.* New York: Bantam, 1979.

Wright, Stephen. *Meditations in Green.* New York: Vintage, 2003.

Films

Apocalypse Now. Francis Ford Coppola, 1979.

Born on the Fourth of July. Oliver Stone, 1989.

The Boys in Company C. Sidney J. Furie, 1978.

Casualties of War. Brian De Palma, 1989.

Coming Home. Hal Ashby, 1978.

The Deer Hunter. Michael Cimino, 1978.

The Fog of War. Errol Morris, 2003.

Full Metal Jacket. Stanley Kubrick, 1987.

Gardens of Stone. Francis Ford Coppola, 1987.

Good Morning, Vietnam. Barry Levinson, 1987.

The Green Berets. Ray Kellogg, John Wayne, Mervyn LeRoy, 1968.

Hamburger Hill. John Irvin, 1987.

The Hanoi Hilton. Lionel Chetwynd, 1987.

The Killing Fields. Roland Joffe, 1984.

Path to War. John Frankenheimer, 2002 (TV).

Platoon. Oliver Stone, 1986.

Rescue Dawn. Werner Herzog, 2006.

We Were Soldiers. Randall Wallace, 2002.

Websites

The starting place for any search of websites related to the Vietnam War is Vietnam War Resources at www.cc.gatech.edu/~tpilsch/Vietnam.html. Some of the best websites are:

American Experience: Vietnam Online
http://www.pbs.org/wgbh/amex/vietnam/

National Security Archive: The Pentagon Papers
http://www.gwu.edu/~nsarchiv/NSAEBB /NSAEBB48/

Veterans History Project (American Folklife Center, Library of Congress)
http://lcweb2.loc.gov/diglib/vhp/html/search /search.html
Click on "Vietnam War, 1961–1975" for all of the Project's Vietnam War oral history interviews; the site allows filtering for specific subjects; some interviews are audio recordings only, but others include full text transcriptions.

Vietnam Center, Texas Tech University
http://www.ttu.edu/~vietnam

Vietnam War Declassification Project
http://www.ford.utexas.edu/library/exhibits /vietnam/vietnam.htm

Vietnam: Yesterday and Today
http://servercc.oakton.edu/~wittman/

Wars for Vietnam: 1945–1975
http://vietnam.vassar.edu/index.html

INDEX

PICTURE CREDITS